(ts

Often, while gazing at Constantinople from the bridge of the Sultan
Valideh, I would be confronted by the question, "What is to become
of this city in one or two centuries...?" Alas! there is but little doubt that
the great holocaust of beauty at the hands of civilization will have been
already accomplished. I can see that Constantinople of the future,
that Oriental London, rearing itself in mournful and forbidding majesty
upon the ruins of the most radiant city of the world. Her hills will
be levelled, her woods and groves cut down, her many-colored houses
razed to the ground; the horizon will be shut in on all sides by long rows
of palatial dwellings, factories, and workshops, broken here and there
by huge business-houses and pointed spires; long, straight streets will
divide Stambul into ten thousand square blocks like a checker-board;
telegraph-wires will interlace like some monster spider-web above
the roofs of the noisy city; across the bridge of the Sultan Validéh
will pour a black torrent of stiff hats and caps; the mysterious retreats
of the Seraglio will become a zoological garden, the Castle of the Seven
Towers a penitentiary, the Hebdomon Palace a museum of natural history;
everything will be solid, geometrical, useful, gray, hideous...

Edmondo De Amicis, *Constantinople*, [1874]

To the memory of Hüsnü Ciner and Ziya İnankur...

Constantinople and the Orientalists

Semra Germaner

Zeynep İnankur

Publishing No: 572
Art series: 79
OTMN 11207901
ISBN 975-458-326-9
İstanbul 2002

ENGLISH TRANSLATION
JOYCE MATTHEWS

BOOK DESIGN
ERSU PEKİN

PICTURE CREDITS

ACR ARCHIVES, PARIS 101

ANTİK A.Ş.

ARTI MEZAT 64

ERDAL AKSOY 1, 2, 3, 4, 8, 9, 10, 11, 12, 13, 14, 15, 16, 18, 19, 20, 21, 22, 23, 24, 25, 26, 27, 28, 29, 30, 31, 33, 34, 41, 43, 44, 45, 46, 47, 50, 52, 53, 57, 58, 59, 60, 62, 63, 67, 68, 72, 73, 80, 81, 82, 83, 84, 85, 86, 87, 88, 89, 90, 91, 95, 96, 97, 99, 102, 104, 105, 106, 107, 108, 110, 111, 112, 113, 116, 118, 119, 120, 123, 127, 128, 129, 130, 131, 132, 133, 134, 135, 136, 138, 139, 140, 141, 142, 150, 154, 155, 157, 158, 161, 167, 169, 170, 173, 174, 175, 182, 185, 187, 188, 192, 193, 195, 196, 197, 199, 200, 205, 207, 208, 212, 214, 215, 217, 219, 220, 221, 222, 223, 227, 228, 231, 232, 234, 236, 239, 240, 242, 245, 251, 252, 253, 257, 261, 262, 266, 268, 270, 272, 274, 275, 278, 280

BRIDGMAN ART LIBRARY, LONDON 156

HADİYE CANGÖKÇE 5, 6, 7, 36, 37, 38, 39, 42, 48, 56, 61, 65, 67, 75, 76, 98, 100, 103, 109, 114, 115, 121, 122, 144, 148, 152, 159, 165, 166, 168, 169, 171, 172, 177, 178, 179, 180, 181, 183, 184, 186, 189, 190, 191, 194, 198, 201, 202, 203, 204, 206, 209, 210, 211, 213, 217, 218, 224, 225, 226, 229, 230, 235, 241, 243, 246, 250, 254, 255, 256, 264, 265, 267, 276, 277, 279

CHRISTIE'S IMAGES, LONDON Front cover, 117, 153, 162, 163, 164

COLLECTION BERKO-KNOKKE-LE- ZOUTE - PARIS - BRUXELLES 151

COMUNE DI MASI, PADOVA 66

DOLMABAHÇE PALACE MUSEUM 71, 92, 93, 94, 137

PIERRE DE GIGORD COLLECTION, PARIS 32, 35

IRCICA 269, 270, 271, 273

MUSÉE D'ART ET D'HISTOIRE, VILLE DE GENÈVE 145

MUSÉE DES AUGUSTINS , TOULOUSE, PHOTO DANIEL MARTIN 149

MUSÉE BERTRAND, CHATEAUROUX 79

MUSÉE DU LOUVRE, PARIS 17, 146

P ART CULTURE ANTIQUES 69, 70

PORTAKAL ART AND CULTURE HOUSE ORGANISATION 40

RÉUNION DES MUSÉES NATIONAUX-R. G. OJEDA, P. NERI, PARIS 17, 146

STIFTUNG SCHLÖSSER UND GÄRTEN POTSDAM-SANSOUCİ 51

BAHADIR TAŞKIN 15, 16, 41, 107, 108

TOPKAPI PALACE MUSEUM 49, 54, 55, 77, 78, 124, 125, 126, 147, 238, 258

V& A PICTURE LIBRARY, LONDON 258

COLOR SEPARATION, PRINTING AND BINDING

MAS MATBAACILIK A.Ş.

FRONT COVER: Martinus Rørbye, "Petition Writer in Front of Kılıç Ali Paşa Mosque in Tophane, detail.

Acknowledgements

The authors extend their thanks to the following individuals and institutions who have contributed to the realization of this book.

Güner and Haydar Akın; Nur Akın; Erdal Aksoy; Inci and Erol Aksoy; Hüsamettin Aksu; Hayrünissa Alan; The Ankara Museum of Painting and Sculpture; Antik A.Ş., Nurcan and Turgay Artan; Artı Mezat; Hilal Aslan; Nurhan Atasoy; The Atatürk Library: the İstanbul Collection and the Periodicals Division; Cana Atınç; Aris Bahtiyaroğlu; Axa Oyak Sigorta; Yüksel Pekiş Behlil; Ahmet Benli; The Bosphorus University Library: the Near East Collection; Rossana Bossaglia; Ersin Börteçen; Cengiz Can; Hadiye Cangökçe; Christie's, London; Collection Berko, Knokke-Le-Zoute-Paris-Bruxelles; Mustafa Cezar; Filiz Çağman; Emin Çeşmebaşı; Aysel Çötenoğlu; Muhibbe Darga; Ayşegül and Ömer Dinçkök; The Directorate of the National Palaces of Turkey; Feride Donat; Oya and Bülent Eczacıbaşı; Cenap Pekiş Egeli; Edward Elphick; Serfiraz Ergun; Şebnem Erverdi; Eskici Mezat Evi; Rudolfo Falchi; Isabelle La Bruyère Farisi; Pierre de Gigord; Sevgi and Doğan Gönül; Elif Gökçiğdem; Çelik Gülersoy; The Çelik Gülersoy Foundation and the İstanbul Library; Elmon Hançer; IRCICA; The Italian Embassy, Ankara; Pervin and Metin Kaşo; Danielle and Hasan Kınay; Suna and Inan Kıraç; Sibel Kibaroğlu; Mustafa Küçük; Koç Holding, İstanbul; Philip Mansel; The Marine Museum, İstanbul; The Military Museum, İstanbul; The Mimar Sinan University Library; Museum of Painting and Sculpture, Mimar Sinan University, İstanbul; Nejad Nazır; Charles Newton; Prenses Neslişah Abdülmünim Osmanoğlu; Müge Önal; Engin Özendes; Safiye Özkan; Ersu Pekin; Mine and Güven Kemal Persentili; Raffi Portakal; Portakal Art and Culture House Organisation; Emine Renda; Sarah Searight; Gülsen Sevinç; The Swedish Consulate, İstanbul; Duran Tamtekin; Jale Tamtekin; Baha Tanman; Bahadır Taşkın; Azize Taylan; Hülya Tezcan; Lynne Thornton; Topkapı Palace Museum; Taha Toros; Cesare Mario Trevigne; Celal Üster; Didier Vacher; Neslihan Yalav; Gülenbilge Ersan Zanardi.

Contents

Preface

Since the publication of our earlier study, *Orientalism and Turkey* (1989), we have been exploring the ramifications of Orientalism in the Ottoman capital of İstanbul itself, or as it was generally known in the nineteenth and early twentieth century: Constantinople. The present study, documented by both visual and written records, including memoirs, reveals not only the ways in which İstanbul was perceived and portrayed by European artists in the nineteenth century, but it also tries to represent the contemporary city as it truly lived and breathed. Ordinarily approached by Westerners as but a theme in the study of art history, the subject of Orientalism is here treated in the light of the ongoing societal changes that took place in İstanbul during the Late Ottoman period.

The longstanding attraction exerted on the West by İstanbul's exotic beauty and wealth of historical resources might be attributed as the principal cause of the influx of a vast number of Orientalist artists in the nineteenth century. But another chief factor that must be considered in accounting for the magnitude of its appeal to Western artists at this time was the attitude of the Court, which fostered Westernization in the Ottoman Empire. Crowning the nineteenth-century westward shift in the sphere of art in the empire was the positive initiative assumed by the Ottoman sovereigns in their concurrent inauguration of the Imperial Reforms (*Tanzimat*). Their appointments of Western artists to positions at the Court and the formation of a collection of their artworks rendered İstanbul even more inviting to Western artists. In acknowledgment of the impact of their active role, a significant proportion of the work in hand has naturally been devoted to the Ottoman Court.

In the present work, the reader will discover the identity of Western artists whose works pictorially limned the Ottoman capital, their favorite subjects—the harem, the bath, the coffeehouse, and the slave market—and the nature of their interpretation of these subjects. Emphasis in our selection of the visual material has been placed on depictions of the city of İstanbul itself and of its social life.[1] Our second emphasis in selecting visual records was to rely as much as possible on sources deriving from collections located today in Turkey.

Interest within Turkey in the subject of Orientalism has flourished since the publication of our earlier book. On the one hand, the number of sales of paintings with Orientalist content has significantly increased at the art auctions held in İstanbul by such firms and organizations as Antik A. Ş., Artı Mezat, Maçka Mezat, Portakal Art and Culture House Organisation, "D" Müzayede Merkezi, Küsav /Foundation for the Preservation of Cultural and Artistic Resources, and, in Ankara, Koleksiyon, and, on the other hand, a series of special Turkish auctions have been organized by leading auction houses abroad, such as Sotheby's and Christie's. Stimulated by auctions like "The Turkish Sale" at Sotheby's in 1996 and 1997 and "Ottoman and Orientalists" at Christie's in 2000 and 2001, the circulation of Orientalist paintings from abroad has become perceptible in Turkey. Though principally produced for Western patrons on Ottoman soil in the nineteenth century, Orientalist paintings have since the 1970s been purchased by Middle Eastern collectors, and, starting in the late 1980s, this group of buyers has been joined by Turkish citizens.

Turkey's burgeoning interest in Orientalism has also become evident through the exhibitions mounted on the subject. The year 1985 witnessed the show titled *Foreign Artists at the Ottoman Court* held in the Art Gallery of Dolmabahçe Palace Museum, with a sequel in 1986, and, in the same year, the show titled *The Orientalists* was arranged by Portakal Art Gallery. These events were succeeded in 1996 by the exhibitions titled *Views of the East*, organized by the Italian Cultural Center and held in the Quarters of the Harem Slaves of Dolmabahçe Palace; *The Turkish Journey of Jules Laurens*, sponsored by Yapı Kredi Bank in 1998, and *Seas, Cities and Dreams*, by Türkiye İşbank in 2000, which centered on the works of Ivan Aivazovsky. While the number of such exhibitions has been limited, the number of Orientalist paintings now within the country discloses an increase of noteworthy proportions.

Among the reasons that may be cited for the current interest in Turkey in Orientalism—works on which theme have retained their value for years on the art markets of Europe and the United States—and for the demand by Turkish collectors for paintings with Orientalist subject matter are the economic lib-

[1] The extensive number of institutions, official and social titles have led us to include in the text their Turkish names together with their English translations.

eralization of Turkey in the 1980s and the removal of restrictions on imports. Furthermore, a concurrent rise has occurred in the general level of curiosity in Turkey about the culture and life of its Ottoman past. As a successor state, the Republic of Turkey had, to a significant degree, severed its ties to Ottoman culture and, furthermore, common knowledge concerning the Ottomans had declined because of the ongoing defense of the principles of modernization by the republic and, over time, fell into desuetude. In postmodernist debates, concepts of modernism and of republic have been subjected to re-evaluation in Turkey since the second half of the 1980s, and, in particular, the position that connections existing between the cultural policies advanced during the nineteenth-century era of Ottoman reforms and the republican period has made gains in credibility. Significant changes now occurring in perspectives on the Ottoman world are the result of new research conducted in this area and the advancing of new interpretations. Over the past fifteen years, numerous studies and personal accounts have been published on Ottoman İstanbul and, in consequence, Turkish citizens are just beginning to rediscover their Ottoman heritage.

The newly enhanced value of localism and of the Ottoman has been a factor in shaping and stimulating the interest of Turkish art collectors in Ottoman art products and paintings delineating the era. In addition, modifications in the profile of Turkish art collectors have become evident. For the most part, this group is composed of a second-generation business elite who has consolidated its social standing and who has become acquainted with the international art market through its close contact with the West. In the expression of the artistic preference of this group for representations of Ottoman life, which at one time greatly intrigued the West, may be detected both nostalgia and a kind of stamp of identity. While the first criterion for selection by European and American Orientalist art collectors tends to be that the artists share their own national origins, that of the Turkish collector is that the subject matter be related to the Ottoman Empire and the Turks; and the most sought after quality is realism and accuracy. One incidental consequence noteworthy in this regard is that, through the acquisition of Orientalist paintings, specimens of Western art have now entered Turkish collections. These paintings primarily constitute vistas of İstanbul. One powerful factor urging Turkish collectors to concentrate on İstanbul landscapes is the dramatic changes inflicted on the local urban fabric and topography over the past half century: today, a yearning exists for the İstanbul of yesterday, for the İstanbul once portrayed in these paintings.

Orientalism was the product of both painters and of the memoirs of Western travelers. Our aim in preparing this book was not only presenting the Orientalist point of view reflected in the paintings depicting İstanbul and in the -for the most part partial or exaggerated- travel accounts informing these paintings. Our aim was also one of exposing historical facts outlining cultural, institutional and urban realities of nineteenth century İstanbul. Just as these Orientalist artists transferred to their canvases the exotic Oriental city of their imagination (regardless of the actual accomplishments of the modernization effort), our study is offered to the reader in the hope that it may restore to life the Constantinople of the nineteenth century—now forgotten and largely destroyed.

Semra Germaner and Zeynep Inankur
May 2001

1 Early depictions of the Ottoman capital

The impact of the conquest of Constantinople in 1453 by an Islamic society unfamiliar to the West and its takeover of the wealthy Byzantine Empire—once a central concern of all European polities—had major repercussions on both the history and culture of Europe. With this transfer of power to the Ottomans, the East moved closer to the West, and the Ottoman Empire now acted as the gateway to the Orient for the West. The role of middleman between the Ottoman Empire and the West was first assumed by Venice, and Venetians presented the first authentic images of the Islamic World to the West. In his study on Venice and the East, Julian Raby states that the Venetians' graphic knowledge of the Ottomans originated with the Ottoman merchants and officials in Venice or Gentile Bellini. Though Venetian artists modelled the individual Oriental types on the Ottoman subjects who chanced to find themselves in Venice, they were unable to furnish a realistic setting. As for Bellini, invited to İstanbul by Sultan Mehmed II to depict the private world of the Court, he apparently executed no paintings of the city or local scenes of daily life. Europe had to wait until the mid-sixteenth century for its first views of the city of İstanbul and the Ottoman world.[1]

For the greater part of the fifteenth and sixteenth centuries, the Ottoman Empire constituted a major threat to Europe. As an outcome, the Western world adjudged the Ottomans in a prejudicial fashion, remote from the truth, and their ignorance in regard to the Ottomans gave rise to fantastic representations in the art of painting. Paintings by certain artists who sojourned in the Ottoman Empire during this period, however, worked to ameliorate this biased attitude.

The earliest of the works on the Ottoman world based on first-hand knowledge was the fifteenth-century book of travels by the Bishop of Mainz, Bernhard von Breydenbach, titled *Sanctae Peregrinationes* (1486), which described his pilgrimage to the Holy Land in 1483. Illustrating this work are woodcuts by the Dutch painter, Erhard

[1] Julian Raby, *Venice, Dürer and the Oriental Mode* (London: Islamic Art, 1982), 21–2, 81.

[2] The earliest bird's–eye view of İstanbul following the conquest appeared in *Liber Chronicum* (1493) by Hartmann Schedel; this, however, was a product of his imagination. Additional examples of this type are the fanciful panoramas by Wilhelm Dilich, Matthæus Merian, Giovanni Temini and Johann Friedrich Probst.

[3] This map may have been based on a drawing of 1479 by Gentile Bellini or on a map of İstanbul commissioned by Mehmed II from Georgias Amirutzes, of which no copy has survived. Cf. Wolfgang Müller-Wiener, *Bildlexikon zur Topographie İstanbuls* (Tübingen: Ernst Wasmunt), 33; and İlhan Tekeli, "Haritalar," *Dünden Bugüne İstanbul Ansiklopedisi* (1994).

[4] Doğan Kuban, *İstanbul Yazıları* (İstanbul: Yapı Endüstri Merkezi, 1998), 45–6.

Reuwich, who accompanied Breydenbach on his journey. These depictions constitute models of simple and objective observation.

The first depiction of İstanbul following its capture by the Ottomans was executed by one of the foremost cartographic masters of Venice, Giovanni Andrea Vavassore (1495– after 1572). Incorporated in his woodcut of the city plan titled *Byzantivm sive Constantinepopolis*, the artist, taking Üsküdar as his vantage point, are those portions of the city located on the Historical Peninsula, along the Golden Horn, and in the district of Galata.[2] The presence of the mosque of Sultan Mehmed II (1470) and the absence of the mosque of Sultan Bayezid II (1505) suggests that this work should be dated 1470–1505.[3] Despite its fanciful appearance, this actually quite realistic bird's-eye depiction of Topkapı Palace served as the source for a number of maps of İstanbul subsequently produced in Europe, such as *Cosmographia Generalis* (1544) by Sebastien Münster (1489–1552) and *Civitates Orbis Terrarum* (1572–1617) by Georg Braun (1541-1622) and Frans Hogenberg (1535-90). As noted by Doğan Kuban, "in essence, these panoramas inform the viewer less about its structural forms than about the basic shape of the city, its edifices, and their relative spatial relationship."[4] Other panoramas of İstanbul dated to this century include those by Salomon Schweiger (1578), Michael Heberer von Bretten (1586) and Giuseppe Rosaccio (1598).

ill. 1

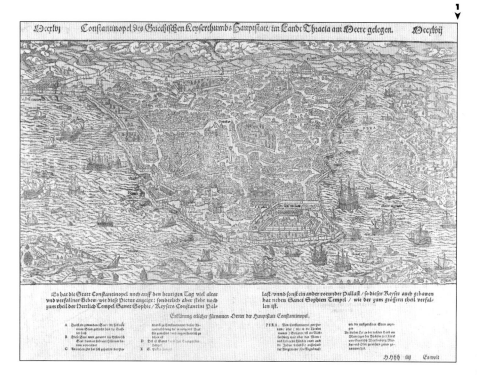

Sent in 1533 by Van der Moyen Brussels Carpet Manufacturers to study carpet weaving in the Ottoman Empire, the Flemish painter and master engraver, Pieter Coecke van Aelst (1502–50), resided one year in İstanbul. The artist, the father-in-law of Pieter Brueghel, produced a woodcut frieze four and a half meters long based on observations conducted on his journey to the Balkans, the Maritza River Valley, Edirne and İstanbul. The frieze is composed of seven panels, separated by caryatides and atlantes attired in Ottoman costume. The most interesting of these is the seventh panel, which depicts the procession of Sultan Süleyman I (1520-66) through the Atmeydanı (Hippodrome) on his way to Friday prayers in the mosque of Mehmed II. In contrast to the pictures by earlier travelers that were concentrated on costume, the artist in *Les moeurs et fachons de faire de Turcz avecq les regions y appartenents* conveys the Ottoman way of life and culture and "employs the principles of composition applied in Renaissance paintings to religious, mythological and historico-political subjects."[5] This work was published in Antwerp by the artist's wife three years after his death, in 1553.

Two years after the appearance of Van Aelst's work, Melchior Lorichs of Flensburg (1527–83), architect, engraver, cartographer, and poet, arrived in İstanbul as a member of the retinue of Augier Ghiselin de Busbecq, envoy of the Holy Roman Empire, and took up a four-year residence (1555–9) in the Elçi Caravansary opposite the Burnt Column.[6] His panorama of İstanbul, measuring eleven meters in length and dated 1559, is centered on the newly completed Süleymaniye Mosque Complex. While in İstanbul, Lorichs completed an album of twenty-eight plates—published posthumously at Hamburg in 1626—whose subjects include Süleyman I, his wives, imperial officials, city residents, mosques, architectural structures, ceremonials, and funerary customs. Titled *Wolgerissen und Geschnittenen Figuren zu Roß und Fuß sampt schönen Türkischen Gebäwden und allerhand was in Türckey zu sehen*, this work, in response to the great demand it generated, was re-issued again the same year and in 1646 and constituted for many years an exemplar for artists who had never been to the Ottoman Empire.

I Costumi et la Vitâ de' Turchi di Gio. Antonio Menavino Genovese de Vultri, written by Giovanni Antonio Menavino (1501–14) on his

5 *Europa und der Orient (1800–1900)*, exhibition catalog (Berlin: Martin–Gropius–Bau, 1989), 24.

6 Semavi Eyice, "Bir Ressamın Gözü ile Kanuni Sultan Süleyman," *Kanuni Armağanı* (Ankara: Türk Tarih Kurumu, 1970), 135.

1 Sebastien Münster. *View of Constantinople.* Woodcut. *Cosmographia Generalis* (1544).

return to his homeland in 1514 after having made an escape from the Ottoman Palace, where he had been trained in the Palace School during the reign of Sultan Bayezid II (1481–1512), and *Les quatre premiers livres des navigations et pérégrinations orientales de Nicolas de Nicolay* (1517-83) by Nicolas de Nicolay, a chamberlain and geographer of the French Court (1517–83), served as the chief contemporary sources of introduction to Ottoman costume and life for Europeans.[7] Coming originally to İstanbul in 1551 in the train of the French ambassador, Gabriel d'Aramon, Nicolay clearly stated his aim in submitting his work for publication: to alter biased views of the Ottoman Empire and to create an objective impression. For "[i]t is a man's duty to travel," he writes, "because by means of such journeys to faraway lands and through the intercommunication

[7] The drawings by Nicolay were subsequently reproduced as engravings by Louis Danet.

[8] Clarence Dana Rouillard, *The Turk in French History, Thought and Literature (1520–1660)* (Paris, Boivin, 1938), 291.

[9] Jean Thévenot, *1655–1656'da Türkiye* (İstanbul: Tercüman, 1978), 143.

that is established a closeness is created among all the different nations of the world and familiarizes them with each other."[8]

Though the Ottomans expanded their frontiers in Europe in the seventeenth century, internal disorders led to a decline in Ottoman power, which somewhat abated the fear of the "Turk" in Europe, and the signing of the Treaty of Carlowicz of 1699 was an additional factor in enabling the West to establish easier relations with the East. Despite the prevalence of stereotypical subject matter in travel books, works issued mid-century from the pens of travelers less prone to exaggeration, like that of Jean de Thévenot (1633–67), brought a new perspective to bear on this tradition. In his work titled *Voyage du Levant*, Thévenot states that a number of people in Christian lands believe that the Ottomans

2 Pieter Coecke Van Aelst. *Procession of Sultan Süleyman I through the Atmeydanı (Hippodrome). Woodcut. Les moeurs et fachons de faire de Turcz avecq les regions y appartenents, (1553).*

are demons, barbaric, unbelievers, and lacking in religious faith, but that those who become acquainted with them and talk with them gain a much different idea, for the Ottomans are good people, and in support of which claim he devotes extensive discussion to their virtues.[9]

One of the most precious vistas of seventeenth-century İstanbul is that by the traveler-artist, Guilliaume Joseph Grelot (1630–?)—a folding panorama contained in his *Relation nouvelle d'un voyage à Constantinople* (1680), which was dedicated to Louis XIV. Here, Grelot spreads out before the viewer's eyes what is visible to anyone coming to the city by sea and asserts that "nothing can be beheld, nor conceiv'd more charming to the sight, than this approach to Constantinople."[10] Grelot, as noted by John Sweetman, provides an excellent idea of which aspects of Ottoman life might please or displease an open-minded European observer. Thus, he liked Ottoman food, but on the subject of politics and religion his attitude was negative; or, he regretted that these "barbaric" people were deficient in their appreciation of painting and sculpture, but, on the other hand, he readily offers fulsome praise of their public works, mosques, covered bazaars, and baths.[11] A close contemporary, the Dutchman, Cornelis de Bruyn (1652–1726), arrived in İstanbul in 1678, where he remained for one and a half years. Appearing in *Voyage au Levant* (1698), his panorama of İstanbul with Seraglio Point, Galata, and the suburb of Üsküdar, as viewed from the ridge above the districts of Galata and Pera, represents a priceless documentary record of the city at this time. "The panoramas of this century are no longer merely a type of geographical source disclosing the remarkable topography of the city, but rather they have been transformed into scenes delineating İstanbul and its people, ceremonials, and customs in their natural setting."[12] Finally, periodicals newly issued in the seventeenth century, like the weekly *La Muse Historique*, which informed the West about current affairs in the Ottoman Empire, and the Ottoman envoys sent to the French Court in 1618 and 1669 also played active roles in altering negative attitudes.

[10] Michèle Longino, *Imagining the Turk in Seventeenth–Century France: Grelot's Version* (2000). http://www.duke.edu/~michelel/projects (1 May 2001).

[11] John Sweetman, *The Oriental Obsession: Islamic Inspiration in British and American Art and Architecture, 1500–1920* (Cambridge: CUP, 1991), 48.

[12] Günsel Renda, "Resimlerde İstanbul," *Yüzyıllar Boyunca Venedik ve İstanbul Görünümleri/Vedute di ed İstanbul attraverso i Secoli*, exhibition catalog (İstanbul: Topkapı Sarayı Müzesi, 1995), 13.

II Ambassadors and "Les peintres de Turcs"

One of the principal spheres of interest in the West in the eighteenth century was Eastern exoticism. As one consequence of technological and scientific progress, the appearance in Europe of elements peculiar to foreign lands introduced by merchants, diplomats, travelers and artists was met by approval in select circles: Western decor now had at its disposal the alternative of an Oriental decor, which found expression in two fashionable trends known, respectively, as Chinoiserie and Turquerie. In the evolution of the vogue for Turquerie—a broad-ranging influence touching everything from fine arts to objets d'art, from music to literature, and from costume to theater—a significant role may be assigned to the ever-expanding commercial relations between Europe and the East. In this era, the "Far East" was associated with China, whereas the "Orient" made direct reference to the Ottoman Empire, which foreigners customarily called "Turkey" and its subjects "Turks." The rage for Turquerie first emerged in France under Louis XIV in response to the arrival in France of Müteferrika Süleyman Agha, sent as a corresponding envoy in 1669. Stimulated by the presence of Süleyman Agha, this vogue "exhibited a significant development at the Court, that is to say at that point in the privileged circles in direct contact with the center of power, and the Court circles, avid in their search for novelty, kept constant surveillance over every action or move of the envoy."[1]

Diplomatic relations greatly contributed to transforming the abstract concept of the Orient in Europe to one specific to the Ottoman Turk. At the tail end of the seventeenth century, the Ottoman Empire underwent defeat at the hands of the Holy Alliance, composed of the Austro-Hungarian Monarchy, Poland, Venice, and the Russian Empire, and which was sealed by the Treaty of Carlowicz in 1699. By the terms of this treaty, the Ottoman realm experienced its first loss of territory and, for the first time, its foothold in Europe began to dwindle. To counter the agreements made between the Russian and Austro-Hungarian empires in the hope of driving the Ottomans out of Europe and dividing up its territories, the Ottomans turned to the European state that was an even match for their power—France. The extraordinary plenipotentiary to Paris designated by the Ottoman Court in the year 1720–1 was Yirmisekiz Çelebi Mehmed Efendi. The primary objective was for him "to inspect fortresses and factories, and to make a thorough study of their instruments of civilization and education, and report on those suitable for application in the Ottoman Empire."[2] The information contained in the relevant report submitted to the sultan and the grand vizier by Yirmisekiz Çelebi Mehmed Efendi on his return to İstanbul, served as a means of implementing a number of innovations in İstanbul, including the founding of a printing press: Grand Vizier Nevşehirli İbrahim Pasha "found the report a source of great inspiration, both in regard to public works of the city and its beautification and to a reordering of spiritual and intellectual life."[3] On the other side, Yirmisekiz Çelebi Mehmed Efendi's visit had served to further intensify the mode of Turquerie in France. The polite correctness of the envoy, his knowledge, and his receptiveness to new ideas had impressed everyone—all of which served as a counterweight in modifying the prevailing negative suppositions. Well-known artists like Charles Parrocel (1688–1752), Pierre-Denis Martin (1673–1742), and Pierre d'Ulin (1669–1748) filled canvases in honor of the ambassador's visit to Paris, and wall tapestries were woven and engravings were executed utilizing the same subject matter. In addition, it is known that Mehmed Efendi granted permission to the artist Justinat to paint his portrait, that one of his portraits was rendered in pastels by François Lemoyne, that another portrait by Pierre Gobert was commissioned by the king, and, finally, that the envoy paid a visit to the atelier of Charles Coypel and posed for a painting commemorating his audience with the king. On account of Mehmed Efendi's visit, interest in the Ottoman Empire received a tremendous boost

[1] Hélène Desmet–Grégoire, *Büyülü Divan: XVIII.Yüzyıl Fransasında Türkler ve Türk Dünyası*. (İstanbul: Eren Yayıncılık, 1991),13.

[2] Fatma Müge Göçek, *East Encounters West: The Ottoman Empire in the Eighteenth Century* (Oxford and New York: OUP, 1987), 4.

[3] Faik Reşit Unat, *Osmanlı Sefirleri ve Sefaretnameleri* (Ankara: Türk Tarih Kurumu, 1992), 56.

and "books began to appear in bookshops on the subject of history, politics, and life in the Orient."[4] The subject of the Ottomans was also treated in French novels.

In 1742, twenty-one years after Mehmed Efendi's visit, which had served to disseminate the popularity of Turquerie in France, his son, Said Effendi, was dispatched to Paris as envoy, thus providing another opportunity to Court circles and Paris under Louis XV of seeing the spectacular pomp of the Ottoman empire. Jacques-André Aved (1702–66), a member of the Academy and one of the foremost painters of the period, painted a full-length portrait of the envoy. Concerning this now-lost portrait of Said Efendi, Maurice-Quentin de La Tour (1704–88) stated in *Mercure de France* (June 1742) that in the course of the sitting the ambassador had "displayed great pleasure and was extremely patient and polite." A great many visitors came to the ambassador's quarters to view the portrait and some even wrote poems about the painting. Thus, the ambassadorship of Said Efendi revived the fashion of Turquerie. For instance, King Louis XV commissioned a large Turquerie-style painting from Coypel, the composition of which was centered on the sultan, surrounded by his favorite concubines, drinking coffee; and a painting was made of Madame de Pompadour, the favorite of Louis XV, by Carle Van Loo (1705–65) and of her replacement, Madam du Barry, by Amédée Van Loo (1705–65), both in the guise of the sultana.

Like the Van Loos in that they had never been to the Ottoman Empire, a number of renowned French painters, such as Jean Antoine Watteau (1684–1721), Nicolas Lancret (1690–1743), Jean-Marc Nattier (1685–1766), Étienne Jeurat (1697–1789), François Boucher (1703–70), Nicolas Cochin (1715–90), Jean-Honoré Fragonard (1732–1806), and Jean-Baptiste Leprince (1734–81), executed paintings with Ottoman figures—the sultan, pashas, the sultan's wives and favorites—as central compositional elements. According to Maria Elisabeth Pape, "Turquerie was conceived as a free and decorative replica of the human figure in Turkish costume."[5] By contrast, paintings like those by Carle Van Loo, such as *The Pasha Who Had a Concert Given for His Favorite* or *The Pasha Having A Portrait Painted of His Favorite*, more accurately reflect the milieu and life of the French Court. French diplomat, Auguste Boppe, the author of *Les peintres du Bosphore au dix-huitième*

ill. 3

[4] Auguste Boppe, *Les peintres du Bosphore au XVIIIe siècle* (Paris: ACR, 1989), 130.

[5] Maria Elisabeth Pape, "*Turquerie* im 18.Jahrhundert und der 'Recueil Ferriol'," *Europa und der Orient (1800–1900)*, exhibition catalog (Berlin: Martin–Gropius–Bau, 1989), 306.

[6] Pape, 307.

[7] Desmet–Grégoire, 256.

siècle—one of the main sources on the subject of Turquerie—employs the term *Les Peintres de Turcs* to refer to such French artists. The primary concern of these painters who had never been in the Ottoman Empire is said to have been "decorative rather than ethnographic."[6] Literary works and theatrical plays treating the Orient in a fantastic and far from realistic manner constituted sources of inspiration for such painters. Fragonard, for example, executed a painting titled *At the Court*, based on a play by Charles-Simon Favart called *Les trois sultanes*. In the performance of this work, the playwright had Madame Favart, who assumed the role of Hürrem Sultan (Roxelane), the wife of Süleyman I, garbed in an authentic Ottoman costume specially ordered from İstanbul.

Hélène Desmet-Grégoire in her study on Ottoman influence on France in the eighteenth century claims that the sources of inspiration for those things produced in France in imitation of Ottoman style were poor and bore little originality. In her opinion, this was a fashion that continually repeated itself, a constant reworking of the selfsame elements: "The sultan, or *Le Grand Turc*, life in the harem (as it is imagined), the coffee-service ceremony, and costumes... a series of counterfeit and superficial imitations that achieved a tremendous success."[7]

The mode of Turquerie, which rapidly spread from France to other European countries, influenced a number of painters, including William Hogarth (1697–1764) in England, and Antonio Guardi (1698–1760) and Francesco Guardi (1712–93) in Italy. This fashion made a significant impression on Europe in the spheres of music, minor handicrafts, architectural ornamentation, and costume. One of the most typical and most beautiful archetypes of the Turquerie fashion is represented by porcelain objets d'art. Porcelain first began to be produced in Europe in the year 1709 in Meissen, and the first porcelain statuettes manufactured in the Turquerie style were produced in the Meissen Porcelain Factory in the 1740s. Factory designers, J. J. Kændler and P. Reinicke, copied the figural types contained in the German edition of the album of one hundred engravings by Jean-Baptiste Van Mour (1671–1737) called *Recueil des cent estampes réprésentant differentes nations du Levant tirées sur les tableaux peints d'après nature en 1707 et 1708*, created at the command of Comte de Ferriol, the French ambassador to İstanbul. The only differ-

ill

3 Etienne Jeurat. *Favorite Imperial Concubine*. Oil on canvas. 51.5 x 76.5 cm. Collection of Sevgi and Doğan Gönül, İstanbul.

4 *Two Ottomans*. Porcelain figures. Meissen. 16 x 6 x 5 cm. Collection of Suna and İnan Kıraç, İstanbul.

ence between the Van Mour figures and the Meissen statuettes produced in twelve different versions is the lively theatrical gestures and postures of the latter. From time to time, inspiration for the Meissen Factory figurines in the Turquerie style was drawn from other pictorial sources. As for the figurines of Ottomans manufactured in the Höchst Porcelain Factory, also in Germany, the influence of the original album was limited to the choice of subject while the finished products were transformed into a variety of imaginary creations. Such, for instance, is the series of figurines called the "Turkish Musicians," produced in 1778 by Johann Peter Melchior (1742–1825), a designer for this factory. Though in name modelled on the Ottoman military band,[8] the musicians are represented by children of European type playing European musical instruments, such as the flute, the trumpet and the French horn. Another artist expert in the production of figurines with Turquerie content was Jacob Petit (1796–1865). The owner of two porcelain factories in France (at Belleville and Fontainbleau), Petit manufactured an Ottoman couple garbed in dress peculiar to the eighteenth century, but it is apparent, just as in the paintings, that a decorative approach was adopted and that emphasis was placed on the

ill. 5

ill. 9
ill. 10

[8] Ateş Acarsoy, "Höchst Porselen Biblolar," *Antik & Dekor Dergisi 2* (1989): 46–50.

5 ➤

5 *Turkish Musicians*. Porcelain figures. Höchst. 18 x 8 x 9 cm. Collection of Danielle and Hasan Kınay, İstanbul.

6 *An Oriental at a Reading Stand*. Fan. 40 x 23 cm. Collection of Danielle and Hasan Kınay, İstanbul.

7 *Harem Scene*. Fan. 40 x 23 cm. Collection of Danielle and Hasan Kınay, İstanbul.

8 *Fountain at Sweet Waters of Asia*. Fan. 24.5 x 18.5 cm. Collection of Sevgi and Doğan Gönül, İstanbul.

exotic effect of the unfamiliar costumes. To this group of minor objects, which constituted a large factor in the dissemination of the Turquerie fashion, may be added fans, whether of wood or of papier mâché. The surface of these elegant fans, designed to protect the face from the effects of the heat emanating from a hearth when seated before it, frequently served as the ground for pictures of a Turquerie character.

Turquerie was a mode whose origins lay in İstanbul and the Ottoman Court. One pillar of this fashion in the branch of painting was located in Paris and the Versailles, where the principal motivating force for the *Peintres de Turcs* who had never stepped foot in Ottoman territories, was embodied by the ambassadorial suites sent by the Ottoman Palace to France. The other pillar of Turquerie was represented by what Boppe termed *Peintres du Bosphore*—European artists who, in contrast to the other group, had at one time or another actually found themselves in the Ottoman Empire and who had for the most part worked in the Pera district in the Ottoman capital.

By the eighteenth century, sightseeing in ancient and picturesque cities like Rome, Venice, and İstanbul were de rigeur for the intellectual European nobility of the period. That is why the studies executed by these artists were done for the touring nobility and members of ambassadorial trains. The artists who filled the commissions and responded to the requests of these eighteenth century-travelers, principally British and French, produced "souvenir compositions" of the cities visited. On their return from Venice, the European gateway to the East, or from İstanbul, these elite tourists displayed with pride the drawings, engravings, and paintings they had brought with them to those who had never been to these cities, and the works served to radiate the light, colors and warmth of the Orient to the cold, northern world. But for the Ottoman Empire, the situation was somewhat different. Despite the fact that it was possible to reach İstanbul by sea, the number of travelers who arrived in the city was very small by comparison with those who visited places like Venice and Rome. Accommodations available in the city afforded until the mid-nineteenth century little comfort. Furthermore, regardless of how curious European travelers might have been to see and discover the world, they found themselves unprepared to embark on an adventure in an environment wholly alien to them. For this reason, the Europeans who came to İstanbul in the eighteenth century were either those appointed to the

9 *Female figurine.* Porcelain. 23 x 11 x 11.5 cm. Collection of Suna and Inan Kıraç, İstanbul.

10 *Male figurine.* Porcelain. 23 x 15.5 x 12 cm. Collection of Suna and Inan Kıraç, İstanbul.

▲
9

▲
10

embassies being opened one after the other in the district of Galata and environs or their relatives who had come to visit them. Starting in the eighteenth century, Western countries with permanent representatives in İstanbul undertook the mission of making known the way of life in the capital of the empire and the Ottoman perspective on the world. The embassies located in Pera, most notably that of the French, were intent on gathering information on the Ottoman Empire and on İstanbul, the imperial capital; artists and draftsmen were therefore employed by the embassies, with the aim of making this information graphic. European envoys coming to İstanbul wished to see on canvas the symbols of their official duties and private lives in the Eastern world and to obtain a pictorial memento of their presentation to the Ottoman sultan and the grand vizier. A great many depictions of ambassadorial ceremonials were composed in this period. Moreover, the envoys' wives had their portraits painted while attired in Oriental costume, which they not only found chic, but also practical and comfortable, and they introduced this mode of dressing to Europe. Europeans serving in these embassies wanted to display the distinctive signs of their having resided in an exotic land. The envoys commissioned from Western artists costume designs charting the local social hierarchy, views of the city, centered primarily on Topkapı Palace and the harbor, and depictions of daily life in the exotic Orient. Artists who executed topographical and panoramic vistas devised compositions frequently as seen from Pera and the gardens of the embassies and occasionally from the Galata tower. These painters used Perotes as their models in figure paintings. Their depictions of interiors with females clearly allows us to infer that the artists selected the homes of Greeks and Armenians by reason of their greater ease of access.

Such artists possessed a variety of European origins and typically held an official position in an embassy, with residence and studios established in the district of Pera or environs. One of the most well known of these artists is Jean-Baptiste Van Mour. Van Mour arrived in İstanbul in 1699 in the retinue of the French ambassador, Comte de Ferriol. Ferriol commissioned the artist to produce more than one hundred depictions of the various costumes in the Ottoman Empire. The ambassador subsequently had Le Hay make reproductions of these paintings by gravure technique, which

were completed in 1707–8, and the resulting publication in Paris in 1712–3 of *Recueil de cent estampes représentant différentes nations du Levant tirées sur les tableaux peints d'après nature en 1707 et 1708 par l'ordre de M. de Ferriol Ambassadeur du Roi à la Porte* (hereafter, *Recueil Ferriol*) caused a great sensation among the French nobility and Court circles. This album was soon reprinted and translated into German, English, Spanish, and Italian, and it comprised a graphic source for their works containing Turquerie subject matter in the case of artists, like Watteau and Guardi, who had never been to the Ottoman Empire.

Van Mour, after Comte de Ferriol's return to Paris, continued to serve the French envoys who succeeded him, such as Comte des Alleurs, Marquis de Bonac, Vicomte d'Andrezel, and Marquis de Villeneuve, for whom he depicted the ceremonials surrounding their audiences in Topkapı Palace. The *bailo*, or Venetian resident at the Porte, also commissioned similar works from Van Mour. Cornelis Calkoen, who assumed his appointment as the ambassador of Holland at the Sublime Porte (*Bâb-ı Âli*) in 1727, and the Swedish envoy Gustaf Celsing, who arrived in İstanbul in the autumn of 1736, also were included among the artist's patrons. A record attesting that Van Mour was among the retinue of Calkoen at his audience on 14 September 1727 is contained in the Hague Royal Archives. In this record it is reported that the ambassador also sent for an artist for the purpose of obtaining a work to commemorate the occasion.[9]

9 *Jean Baptiste Van Mour'un Tablolar/Les Peintures "turques" de Jean–Baptiste Van Mour 1671–1737*, exhibition catalog (Ankara and Amsterdam, 1978), 22, nn. 5, 6.

11 Jean-Baptiste Van Mour. *Repast Given in Honor of an Ambassador in the Public Council Hall.* Oil on canvas. 106 x 131 cm. Koç Holding Collection, İstanbul.

12 *Public Council Hall.* Topkapı Palace, İstanbul.

In Van Mour's painting titled *Repast Given in*
ill. 11 *Honor of an Ambassador in the Public Council Hall* (*Divanhane*), the envoy can be seen beneath the dome of the hall (*Kubbealtı*), one of the most sumptuous constituents of the Topkapı Palace complex. It was the custom for the grand vizier to invite an ambassador for a meal prior to his being presented to the sultan. Seated in the center of this composition are the grand vizier and the envoy, whose back is turned to the viewer, and standing beside them are the dragomans. High-ranking imperial servants, like the chief chancellor (*Nişancı*), and the minister of finance (*Defterdar*), the embassy's secretaries, and select members of the ambassador's retinue, are dining at five separate low dining tables laden with large trays of silver. The lieutenant of the gatekeepers (*Kapıcılar Kethüdası*) is shown holding a rod with silver inlay directing the food service provided by the Palace servants, who are carrying vessels of food. On the wall is delineated the
ill. 12 Pavilion of Justice (*Kasr-ı Âdil*), positioned within an arch, where the sultan could attend to the course of the discussion in a private chamber without his presence being detected.[10]

ill. 13 *Procession of an Ambassador,* another work by Van Mour, illustrates the procession of an ambassador on his return from Topkapı Palace. Forming the backdrop is the Golden Horn—a massed pack of sailing vessels—Süleymaniye Mosque, and the Valens Aqueduct. The ambassador is shown mounted in the foreground wearing an imperial robe of honor, lined with fur, and is followed by mounted and uniformed attendants, and the horses are decked out in trappings of full-length covers with needlework in gold."[11] The guard regiment of janissaries leads the way while on the left, lining the walls, are delineated the onlookers viewing the procession.

In a short time, the artist, whose studio became a meeting place of the high society in Pera, was finding himself hard pressed to keep up with the demand for his work, and, in recognition of his work, he was awarded in 1725 the title *Peintre ordinaire du Roi en Levant* by the French king. Van Mour executed not only an album of costumes and paintings of the ambassador's imperial audience, but he also produced numerous works treating a variety of subjects, such as the rebellion of Patrona Halil which led to the abdication of the throne by Ahmed III (1703–30), wedding festivities, Mevlevi whirling dervishes, and pastoral

[10] İsmail Hakkı Uzunçarşılı, *Osmanlı Devletinin Merkez ve Bahriye Teşkilatı* (Ankara: Türk Tarih Kurumu, 1988), 294, 303.
[11] Uzunçarşılı, 306.

13 Jean-Baptiste Van Mour. *Procession of an Ambassador.* Oil on canvas. 88.5 x 120.5 cm. Collection of Suna and Inan Kıraç, İstanbul.

13
▼

entertainments. The painter also depicted Western visitors to İstanbul in Ottoman dress. One of these was a woman whose letters played a prominent role in acquainting Europe with Ottoman life ways and who served as a source of inspiration for numerous artists: Lady Mary Wortley Montagu.

A knight of Malta named Antoine de Favray (1706–98), who came to İstanbul in 1762, coincident with the reign of Mustafa III (1757–74), and who was resident during the terms of ambassadors Comte de Vergennes and Comte de Saint-Priest, executed a great number of İstanbul landscapes. Besides painting the portraits of De Vergennes and his wife in Ottoman costume, Favray became famed for his paintings rendering envoys at their audiences with the sultan, scenes portraying the life of the local non-Muslims and Levantines, and Oriental costumes.[12]

Arriving in İstanbul in 1784, French ambassador Comte de Choiseul-Gouffier, initiated, with the sultan's permission, restoration work on the French Palace and its decoration, in connection

14 Jean-Baptiste Hilair. *General View of Constantinople from the French Palace.* Engraving. *Voyage pittoresque de la Gréce,* (1822).

[12] Boppe, 96–123.

14

with which project a number of architects, painters and designers were invited to İstanbul. Among the painters arriving on the scene in this connection, the most well known were Jean-Baptiste Hilair (1753–after 1822), Antoine Laurent Castellan (1772-1838), Antoine-Ignace Melling (1763-1831), Armand Charles Caraffe (1762-1822), Louis-François Fauvel (1753–1838), Michel-François Préaulx, and Louis-François Cassas (1756–1827). Hilair, resident in İstanbul during the reigns of Abdülhamid I (1774–89) and Selim III (1789–1807) and under whom European artists worked at ease in the city, executed a portrait of Abdülhamid I in gouache and produced paintings of Ottoman life and traditional costumes as well as panoramic vistas of the city, such as his *A General View of Constantinople from the French Palace.* Hilair had earlier accompanied Choiseul-Gouffier on his tour of the Orient in 1776 and created illustrations for the latter's book titled *Voyage pittoresque de la Grèce*—one of the deciding factors in Choiseul-Gouffier's subsequent appointment as ambassador to İstanbul.[13] Paintings by Hilair are also contained in the multi volume work by Mouradgea D'Ohsson titled *Tableau général de l'Empire othoman* (1791).

Louis-François Cassas, another of the artists who accompanied Choiseul-Gouffier to İstanbul, traveled through the Archipelago, Egypt and Syria between 1784 and 1797 after having resided in İstanbul for a few weeks. At the conclusion of his travels, the artist had in hand approximately three hundred drawings, of which a portion were published in *Le voyage de Syrie* and another portion in the above-mentioned work by Choiseul-Gouffier. His İstanbul landscapes were exhibited in the Paris Salon Exhibitions of 1804 and 1814. The subjects chosen for his artworks include Oriental costumes, customs, and monuments, along with various landscapes of Eastern lands and ceremonials observed on his tour.[14] In his painting called *View of Constantinople* , the central field is occupied by the Sultan Ahmed Mosque, with the city walls and Seraglio Point composing the secondary elements. The most striking configurations, however, are the Sultan Ahmed Mosque and the boats with wind-filled sails in the harbor. It should be noted, however, that the pastoral scene with trees in the foreground with Oriental figures is an unfaithful reflection of the natural environment of İstanbul. Taken as a whole, the painting with the sky and clouds and hills in the background, the combination of

ill. 14

ill. 15

ill. 16

15 16

[13] Boppe, 194.
[14] Boppe, 210–28.

15-16 Louis François Cassas. *View of Constantinople.* Watercolor and pen and India ink. 66 x 102 cm. Collection of Suna and Inan Kıraç, İstanbul.

the mosque and the harbor in the middle ground, and the pastoral scene in the foreground exudes a spirit of a caprice. The artist has transformed the harbor scene into an ode to the picturesque.

Contemporary with Choiseul-Gouffier's term of duty, Michel-François Préaulx, who came to İstanbul in 1796 as an architect in conjunction with a group of artists and workers employed by the Ottoman government to organize the workshops of the navy and the land forces, also interested himself in Ottoman pictorial subjects. Préaulx is known to have still been resident in the city in 1827 although those who had accompanied him to take service under the sultan had already returned home. Numerous engravings duplicating his designs appeared in works published in the first half of the nineteenth century. The most prominent of these were *Constantinople et le Bosphore de Thrace pendant les années 1812,1813,1814 et pendant l'année 1826* by General Andreossy, issued in Paris in 1828 and *Atlas des promenades pittoresques dans Constantinople et sur les rives du Bosphore* by Charles Pertusier.[15]

Armand-Charles Caraffe resided in Egypt and in Turkey in 1788–89. The artist, in addition to painting a portrait of Selim III, also executed compositions relating to Oriental life, with subjects such as the Imperial Harem, the public baths, circumcision festivities, and greased wrestling.[16] Antoine-Laurent Castellan, who saw duty as part of the work unit under an engineer named Ferrégeaux, resided in İstanbul for a few months in 1797 and drew sketches containing Oriental subjects. The work published in 1820 under the title *Lettres sur la Morée, l'Hellespont et Constantinople* gathered together his paintings relating to his travels; these included delineations of monuments, such as Sultan Ahmed Mosque, Yeni Mosque, and the fountain of Ahmed III, and certain familiar districts of the city. In addition, a six-volume work based on his notes from his journeys in the East titled *Moeurs, usages, costumes des Othomans et abrégé de leur histoire* (1812) also contains seventy-two renderings of traditional dress.[17]

Choiseul-Gouffier was not the only foreign ambassador in İstanbul who surrounded himself with artists. A number of Choiseul-Gouffier's colleagues took an interest in the monuments of the historical environment in which they resided while others had in any case been awarded with their appointments because of their knowledge in these

fields or their zeal in amassing collections. Two such men were the Celsing brothers, Gustaf and Ulric, who served as representatives of the Swedish crown in İstanbul for a total of thirty-five years. To the defeat of the Swedish king, Charles XII, by the Russians at Poltava in 1709 and his subsequent application for asylum at Bender (Moldavia), a frontier citadel of the Ottoman realm, and his continued residence in the empire until 1714 may be attributed "[t]he origin of a permanent Swedish mission at İstanbul."[18] Gustaf Celsing, who served as the secretary at the Swedish legation during this time, was succeeded by his son who bore the same name. His son became the resident envoy in 1747 and representative of the Swedish Crown in 1750. On his departure in 1773, his brother Ulric assumed the identical duties and acted as Swedish minister until 1780.

It was at this time that, "at Ulric's suggestion," Ignatius Mouradgea D'Ohsson, employed by the embassy, "directed his attention to the subjects that would present the whole of the Ottoman Empire and that would serve as the future framework for his great work."[19] This work was published in three volumes (1787–1820), with illustrations by Hilair and Le Barbier as *Tableau général de l'Empire othoman, divisé en deux parties, dont l'une comprend la législation mohamétane, l'autre, l'histoire de l'Empire othoman*. D'Ohsson, whose real name was Muradjan Tosunian, was an Ottoman Armenian of İstanbul. He served as dragoman in the Swedish legation in 1763, was promoted to first dragoman in 1768, and became the private secretary of the Swedish legation in 1775, at which date he was granted a title of nobility by the Swedish king. Living in Europe from 1784 to 1792, D'Ohsson then returned to İstanbul and later assumed the post of minister plenipotentiary and head of the Swedish legation. Constituting a work of high value on the social history of the Ottoman Empire, D'Ohsson's exposition contains a very interesting personal incident concerning the prohibition of images. During the reign of Mustafa III, a prominent servant of the Ottoman Court requested that D'Ohsson invite to İstanbul a European artist to paint the most beautiful vistas of İstanbul and commissioned the artist to produce four paintings of the city. This Court official, who kept these works hidden in a special place, also commissioned the artist to paint his own portrait on condition that this act remain confidential; however, he subsequently regretted

[15] Boppe, 288–9.

[16] Boppe, 278.

[17] Boppe, 279.

[18] Sture Theolin, *The Swedish Palace in İstanbul/İstanbul'-da Bir İsveç Sarayı* (İstanbul: Yapı Kredi Kültür Sanat Yayınları, 2000), 33.

[19] *Biographiskt Lexikon öfver Mamkunnige Svenska Män* (Upsala, 1844, X), 206, cited in Kemal Beydilli, "İgnatius Mouradgea D'Ohsson," *Tarih Dergisi: Prof. Dr. M. C. Şehabeddin Tekindağ Hatıra Sayısı* (1984): 253.

his action and fearful of discovery presented the work to D'Ohsson as a gift. D'Ohsson states that, despite the later misgivings of this imperial servant, his action had represented a bold enterprise.[20]

After the Swedish king, Charles XII, had taken refuge at Bender, he sent Major Cornelius Loos (1686–1735) to survey various regions within the Ottoman Empire. As part of his inspection and fact-gathering tour, Loos, who arrived at İstanbul in 1710, executed watercolor sketches of certain prominent monuments, like Süleyimaniye Mosque, Binbirdirek Cistern, Yeni Mosque, the Hippodrome, St. Sophia Mosque and the Arsenal Palace, in addition to a panorama of İstanbul from the heights of Galata and Pera.[21] Much affected by Loos' sketches, Charles XII commanded that the new palace church at Stockholm should be modeled on St. Sophia and, among other things, banned all statues and pictures, and, furthermore, in imitation of the Topkapı Palace compound, as depicted by Loos in his view from the window of the Swedish Palace in Pera, ordered the Brunkeberg Ridge in Stockholm to be planted with pine trees.[22]

Brigadier General Philipp Ferdinand von Gudenus (1710–83), a clerk in the Austro-Hungarian embassy legation in İstanbul, rendered likenesses of the Palace, Ottoman figural types, and monuments in 1740. Gudenus, a good draftsmen, published these pictures under the title *Collection des prospects et habillements en Turquie*. Contained in this collection comprising thirty plates is a panorama of İstanbul as viewed from Galata Tower, in addition to other views of the city, its architectural monuments, and certain Palace servants in their respective dresses. One aspect of interest in his İstanbul panorama is the inclusion of specimens of traditional, wooden domestic architecture. In 1719, Joseph Ernest Schmidt and Johann Semler (1693/94–1748) are known to have worked with Hugo von Virmoundt, the Austro-Hungarian ambassador to İstanbul. Dragoman of the Neapolitan legation, Comidas de Carbognano (Kömürciyan) sketched several vistas of İstanbul for *Descrizione topografica dello stato presenti di Constantinopoli arrichita di figura*, published in 1794.

Military attaché and, at the same time, an agent of the Venetian secret service, Giovanni Francesco Rossini (1688–1764) was in the train of the Venetian ambassador to İstanbul, Francesco

Gritti, between the years 1723 and 1727. Visiting İstanbul once again in 1739, Rossini executed three vistas of İstanbul, which he dedicated to then Venetian bailo, Andrea Erizzo. One of these drawings shows the northern section of İstanbul while the other two consist in views of the city from the garden of the Palazzio Venezia in Pera. All three of these are important topographical records of the city because of their full and complete captions and extremely detailed and true-to-life depictions.[23]

Entering into competition with the French embassy in the final quarter of the eighteenth century, Sir Robert Ainslie the British ambassador commissioned a series of watercolor landscapes of Ottoman territories in Europe and Asia (including Egypt and Palestine) from the illustrator and copyist Luigi Mayer (1755–1803), who was of German origin. The artist, arriving at İstanbul in the company of Ainslie in 1776, made his residence in the city, where he remained—if we discount his various journeys in Ottoman territories—until 1793, when he returned to London at

[20] M.de M. D'Ohsson, *Tableau Général de l'Empire Othoman* (Paris, L'Impremerie de Monsieur, 1891) 2:446-7.

[21] See on this subject Semavi Eyice, "18.Yüzyılda İstanbul'-da İsveçli Cornelius Loos ve İstanbul Resimleri (1710'da İstanbul)," *18.Yüzyılda Osmanlı Kültür Ortamı* (İstanbul: Sanat Tarih Derneği, 1998), 91–130.

[22] Theolin, 47–8.

[23] Giovanni Curatola, "Drawings by Giovanni Francesco Rossini, Military Attaché of the Venetian Embassy in Constantinople," *Art turc: actes de 10ième congrès international d'art turc* (Genève: Fondation Max van Berchem, 1999), 226.

II Ambassadors and "Les peintres des Turcs"

the termination of Ainslie's appointment. His pictures were published as aquatints between the years 1801 and 1810. In his book, *Views in Turkey in Europe and Turkey in Asia* a concentration is noticeable on figural compositions delineating Ottoman life in panoramic views of the city, the Bosphorus, and the harbor in. In this connection, we may note that the writings of Lady Mary Wortley Montagu had previously demonstrated that cultured and modern people of taste could sojourn and live among Ottomans and Muslims, and a great number of nobility included the Ottoman Empire in their tour itinerary. One of these was the Swiss painter, Jean Etienne Liotard (1702–89), who accompanied Sir William Ponsonby; another was Francis Smith brought by Lord Baltimore.

Liotard, the son of a Genevan merchant, dwelled in İstanbul for four years, and, thanks to the British merchant, Mr. Levett, he became known in Pera society and received numerous commissions. He delineated the portraits of a great number of Europeans, like Ponsonby, **ill. 17** Levett, and Richard Pococke and diplomats in Ottoman costume as well as wealthy merchants, musicians, certain residents of Phanar district, local Greeks, and Levantines, and, eventually, he came to the attention of leading Ottoman dignitaries, with the grand vizier of the day even posing for him. The finest works by this artist are, however, those of European or İstanbul women in Ottoman dress depicted seated on a divan, drinking coffee, playing the tambourine, spinning yarn, reading books, greeting guests, dancing or going to the public bath.

Francis Smith, who came to the Orient in the year 1763, returned from his travels with a variety of paintings, of which one titled *A Panoramic View of Constantinople and Environs* was exhibited in the Royal Academy in London in 1770. His work titled *Eastern Costume*, comprised of twenty-six plates and, influenced by Van Mour's *Recueil Ferriol*, includes individuals of Ottoman

17 Jean-Etienne Liotard. *Portrait of M.Levett and Mlle Glavani Seated on a Sofa.* Oil on cardboard. 24.7x36.4 cm. Musée du Louvre, Paris.

18 Antoine-Ignace Melling. *View of Constantinople from Galata Tower*, 1787. Watercolor and pencil on paper. 56 x 80 cm. Collection of Sevgi and Doğan Gönül, İstanbul.

19 Antoine-Ignace Melling. *View of Constantinople from Galata Tower*. Watercolor and pencil on paper. 57 x 76.8 cm. Collection of Sevgi and Doğan Gönül, İstanbul.

24 See Jacques Perot, Frederic Hitzel, and Robert Anhegger, *Hatice Sultan ile Melling Kalfa* (İstanbul: Tarih Vakfı Yurt Yayınları, 2001) 15-6.

type. The artist also executed two other paintings, one depicting the reception by the sultan of the British ambassador, and the other a special occasion held by the grand vizier in honor of the British ambassador.

Gaetani Mercati, who worked under Sir Robert Liston, an ambassador to İstanbul from 1793 to 96, made sketches of Ottoman costumes and local images. In possession of an appointment to the British embassy, James Dallaway, chaplain and physician of the British embassy, drew on Mercati's sketches in his book, *Constantinople Ancient and Modern*. Lord Elgin, sent to İstanbul in 1799 as ambassador, is known to have employed a painter named Luciari. Accompanying Russian ambassador, Kutusov, to İstanbul, Andrei Alexeievitch Serguiew (1771–1837) contributed illustrations to *Reise der russich Kaiserlichen ausserordentlichen Gesandtschaft an die Ottomanische Pforte in Jahr 1793*, published in 1804.

In the employ of the French foreign ministry, Antoine-Ignace Melling was sent to İstanbul by Napoleon Bonaparte, where he arrived with the Russian ambassador, Bulgakov, in 1785. Remaining in the city for eighteen years, the artist rapidly gained recognition, and he gave lessons in painting and drawing. Melling, who served as architect to Selim III and his sister, Princess Hatice, was able on account of their patronage to examine his surroundings at will and to work without hindrance. The artist, who designed the palace and gardens of Princess Hatice at Defterdarburnu in the Bosphorus suburb of Ortaköy, first designed a garden in the form of a labyrinth and then erected a seaside mansion in the neoclassical style. Much pleased by the appearance of this seaside villa, Selim III charged him with the task of enlarging the Beşiktaş Palace. In addition to these works, Melling performed a wide variety of tasks for the Court—decorating the interior of Princess Hatice's palace, including the purchase of fabrics, working diamonds for her comb case, arranging bed canopies, designing dresses, and selecting gifts for the sultan.[24] Melling is also admired for his maps of İstanbul and panoramic vistas of the city. His *View of Constantinople from Galata Tower* of 1787 renders the residential fabric of Galata in the foreground, which is dense, multistoried, and largely of masonry, and two sailing craft in addition to a multitude of caiques in the harbor and, in the background, Topkapı Palace, seaside pavilions,

ill.

18 ➤

19 ➤

II Ambassadors and "Les peintres des Turcs"

and the mosques of St. Sophia and Sultan Ahmed; further distant, the Princes' Islands can be detected beyond the Seraglio Point while the shores of Yalova on the Marmara Sea are shown in silhouette. Another of his works *View of Constantinople from Galata Tower*, looking to the west, presents a dense settlement fabric enlivened by cypress trees, sailing ships in the port at Tophane and the Tower of Leander and Üsküdar, on the opposite side of the Bosphorus. These views of İstanbul by Melling, who was trained in drawing and architecture, are finely detailed, and each of which through its realistic rendering constitutes an invaluable visual and architectural record.

Intending to return to France after falling out of favor at the end of 1800 and suffering dismissal by Princess Hatice, Melling chanced to embark on a new project through the assistance and support of the Orientalist Pierre Ruffin, the chargé d'affaires at the French embassy. This project was a picture collection, to be utilized as an instrument of propaganda for Napoleon Bonaparte's leadership and which was to be carried out under the auspices of the French government. For İstanbul as a whole, the aim was "to produce drawings of all the landscapes, both general and specific, and to execute

25 *MAE, Turquie,* Cor.pol.c.c. 203, f.127, cited in Perot, 64.
26 Perot, 71.

sketches of the plans of mosques, fountains, and the mansions of certain Ottoman officials, and to embellish these sketches with renderings of local costumes and ceremonials."[25] Completing his drawings during the final year of his stay in İstanbul, Melling came to an agreement with the engraver François-Denis Née on his return to Paris and later signed a contract with the publisher Treuttel and Würtz on 7 December 1803. According to the terms of this contract, Melling was to submit fifty-two drawings in pairs, both hand-colored and black and white: the colored drawings were to be executed for sale while the black and white were to be utilized in the engraving process. The engravings were made by the chief engravers of Paris under the direction of Née. As indicated by Jacques Perot, this work, published in 1819 under the title *Voyage pittoresque de Constantinople et des rives de Bosphore* met with limited commercial success, but nevertheless gained great public approval, and through its presentation as a diplomatic gift its merits became known throughout Europe.[26] This album is an important record from the standpoint of recording the daily scene in İstanbul and on the Bosphorus in the late eighteenth and early

ill. 20

20 Antoine-Ignace Melling. *A Turkish Wedding Ceremony.* Engraving. *Voyage pittoresque de Constantinople et des rives de Bosphore* (1819).

21 Artist unknown. *Constantinople and Seraglio Point from Pera*. Oil on canvas. Topkapı Palace Museum, İstanbul.

II Ambassadors and "Les peintres des Turcs"

nineteenth centuries. One unsigned oil painting in the Topkapı Palace Museum collection titled *Constantinople and Seraglio Point from Pera* represents a copy of an engraving by the same name in the work noted above. In the left foreground of this painting, executed from the garden of the French embassy, appear the garden walls of the embassy and a number of multistory structures at the foot of Galata Tower. Behind the harbor crowded with sailing vessels can be seen Topkapı Palace and the mosques of St. Sophia and Sultan Ahmed. After the publication of Melling's album, many British and French natives who had the opportunity to see the panoramic views of İstanbul by Henry Aston Barker (1774–1856) and Pierre Prevost (1764–1823), were stimulated to come to İstanbul for the purpose of becoming better acquainted with the city.

The eighteenth and nineteenth centuries constituted the most brilliant era for engravers. Engravings of the day, most of which were based on the drawings of well-known artists, were developed from sketches executed on the spot by amateurs and by lesser-known artists. These engravings, which boosted the vogue of exoticism, excited a passion for costumes à la Turque and for the fascinating Oriental architecture. Because of the high level of interest in outsized, ornate albums introducing the lands of the East, a new professional class of artists emerged in England to satisfy the demand of this market. Among the most well known of this group were William Bartlett (1809–54) and Thomas Allom (1804–72), who came to İstanbul during the reign of Mahmud II. Allom, who at the outset worked with architect Francis Goodwin and later became one of the founders of the Institute of British Architects, was the most renowned topographical artist of the period. His landscapes were employed to illustrate a number of books on Syria, Asia Minor, and China, of which the most famous is *Constantinople and the Scenery of the Seven Churches of Asia Minor*. Among the most prolific of the topographical landscape masters was William Bartlett, who died in the course of returning from his fifth Near Eastern journey in 1854 and left behind more than one thousand drawings, of which many have been published in book format. One of these is *The Beauties of the Bosphorus* by Miss Julia Pardoe. Engravings of works by Bartlett and Allom on İstanbul formed the model for a great number of artists in the sec-

ond half of the nineteenth century and were reproduced in oils. The engravings and drawings by these artists, whom we may term the "Early Orientalists," made a tremendous contribution in acquainting the West with İstanbul.

The mode of exoticism of the eighteenth century was replaced by that of Orientalism in the nineteenth century. To paraphrase Boppe, neither the diversity of the costumes of Easterners nor imaginary adventures at Court could no longer satisfy Europeans: now, they wanted to see the real Orient for themselves, to investigate the sensations that moved it, and to become acquainted with the world in which it existed. According to Boppe, painters of Turks and Turqueries were vanishing: henceforth, there would only be painters of Turkey.[27]

[27] Boppe, 168.

III Orientalism and orientalist art

İstanbul represented one of the most active centers for nineteenth-century Orientalists. Artists flocked to the city for the purpose of producing paintings, and their output of Orientalist artwork in this period was vast. Orientalism was not a specific style in the art of painting, but it became a favorite theme among the nineteenth century painters of heterogeneous movements. Inspiration for these artists derived from the sense of mystery and the atmosphere of luxury and enchantment associated with the Orient. Various historical events, such as the Egyptian campaign of Napoleon (1798–9), the Greek War of Independence (1821–8), the occupation of Algeria by the French (1830), the Crimean War (1854–5), the opening of the Suez Canal, and Western colonialist designs on the Ottoman Empire, served further to fuel the flames of this vogue.

The artistic geography of Orientalism is characterized by broad diversity and generally comprehends the Islamic countries. Despite the widely varying ethnic composition on the shores of the Mediterranean, Muslim North Africa—Tunisia, Algeria, and Morocco—may be said to form a homogenous whole. Egypt represents a completely unique region. Libya, even at the close of the nineteenth century, was a land largely unknown and closed to travelers. Palestine and Syria, which had no relation whatsoever with the lands of North Africa, and Asia Minor all constitute regions only rarely delineated by artists. These lands made up the Ottoman East and were distinct from the Arab East and more convenient of access. Mainland Greece and the Archipelago were considered a part of Europe and served as a jumping-off stage in introducing travelers to the visual richness of the Eastern world. The desire to capture in graphic format the unfamiliar customs and novel scenery of these areas became transformed into a passion among nineteenth-century artists. The principal reason for the existence of Orientalist art was to portray that which was alien to the artist. Ary Renan states that the best Orientalist artists were

[1] Ary Renan, "La peinture Orientaliste," *Gazette des Beaux Arts* 11 (1894): 43–4.

[2] Rana Kabbani, *Europe's Myths of the Orient* (London: Pandora, 1986), 82.

those whose canvases did not overemphasize exoticism.[1] But, according to Rana Kabbani,

> [v] ery few Orientalist painters were able to offer a narrative-free depiction of the scenes they were witness to. They narrated the East while painting it; they transformed it into metaphor and myth. They offered what Europe wished to see. In fact, the ambitious and serious landscape painters never gained the popularity instantly accorded the more fantastic Orientalists.[2]

Orientalist art is neither a school nor a style. The relation between paintings classified as Orientalist but exhibiting differing styles lies in the subject matter selected by the artist. The odalisques by Ingres, Delacroix or Matisse are all classified as Orientalist paintings, but the styles of these works remain wholly distinct from each other. In any case, the same artists who created works of Orientalist art also produced paintings of other subjects. The styles of the various artists grew apart over time, so that while some were influenced by realism or romanticism, others turned to contemporary currents, such as impressionism.

Victor Hugo in his famous work *Les Orientales* says that the Islamic world is a kind general obsession both for the intellect and the imagination. In the nineteenth century, although an East observed first-hand replaced the image of the East fantasized, the artists persisted in depicting an imaginary world embroidered by their own memories. Artists who, like many other intellectuals, had been nourished on countless descriptions of the East in the popular literary works of the nineteenth century were primarily seeking adventure and exoticism. Such artists, searching for the values of the past beyond the boundaries of their native countries, and in an utterly different culture, chose to become travelers. In this way, artists exchanged their native living environment for a milieu unlike their own: for the first time, they found themselves in the position of creating works that employed alien historical, religious, and cultural references. The essence of the appeal of Orientalist paintings resides in the fact that the East is perceived as mysterious, introvert and irrational and continued to be an object of attraction both for those who produced these pictures and those who purchased them.

No longer satisfied merely by what they felt and imagined, Western artists transformed themselves into travelers and undertook scientific, military, diplomatic, or commercial duties so as to go to the East in search of inspiration. In this connection, they traveled through the lands of the Middle East and North Africa, gathered information, and examined the cultures of these regions. The collection of information brought them to places like Algiers, Cairo, or İstanbul. İstanbul lay on the route of every itinerant artist who came to the Orient, with the city forming either the point of departure or a stop on the way.

As part of the colonialist, commercial, and diplomatic activities of countries like France and England in the late eighteenth and early nineteenth centuries, a number of artists traveled to the East. The Eastern tour of Louis-François Cassas presents an interesting example in this respect. Appointed ambassador to the Ottoman Empire by Louis XVI in 1783, Choiseul-Gouffier brought along Louis-François Cassas, a highly qualified draftsman, when he came to İstanbul in August 1784. After having resided in the city for two months during the reign of Abdülhamid I, Cassas, a member of the group of scientists and scholars working under Choiseul-Gouffier, departed on a comprehensive tour of the East that encompassed a great many of the provinces of the empire. Embarking for Syria and Egypt on 24 October 1784 on the frigate *La Poulette* furnished by the ambassador, Cassas was charged with sketching the designs of the local monuments and costumes in the respective towns and purchasing medals, coins, and statuary to enrich the ambassador's collection. Choiseul Gouffier underwrote all the expenses of the journey.

The hardships and dangers of travel in this era gave rise to the kind of tour suitable for adventurers alone, but the adverse conditions served merely to heighten the curiosity of the artists. The case of Eugène Flandin (1803–76), sent to serve in Iran, is interesting in this regard. Resigning from his diplomatic post, Flandin traveled in Iran for four years, executing drawings and maps, and managed to establish relations with leading officials; nevertheless, he was forced to flee on the death of the shah because he was unable to secure his personal safety. Situations like this make it clear that both an adventurous spirit and a constitution able to bear up under the living conditions encountered in Eastern lands were prerequisites to travel. The roads to the East originating in the Balkans were not very secure in the early nineteenth century, and sea voyages were accompanied by adverse climatic conditions. As a result, no definite schedule could be set for the tours, and the time frame frequently failed to accord with that envisioned at the outset.

The difficult traveling conditions in the Ottoman Empire were a reality known to all who journeyed here in the eighteenth century. In consequence, itinerant artists relied on information passed on by travelers who had previously toured in this region and which led to the establishment of an unvarying itinerary. Cassas' tour of the Orient which began at Alexandretta around mid-December 1784, was interrupted by a layover at Izmir on account of a storm, and after sailing along the coast with stop-offs at Aleppo, Antioch, Cyprus, Syria, Lebanon, Phoenicia, and Palestine, it was completed at Alexandria on 9 December 1785. Planned to cover eleven months, the tour was delayed due to unforeseen circumstances, such as storms, accidents at sea, the eruption of a rebellion at Cairo, and an outbreak of the plague in Syria and Egypt in 1785. The artist, continuing his journey overland through Phoenicia, pursued a route that greatly differed from the one proposed by Choiseul-Gouffier, in order to visit Palmyra and Baalbek, which had not been included in the plan. To reach Palmyra and Aleppo, he followed the caravan routes, but for Phoenicia and Palestine, he traced an itinerary along the seacoast. Anchored at times for extended periods in the Eastern Mediterranean ports of Tripoli, Sidon, and Acre, Cassas dwelled with desert nomads, spent long periods at archeological sites, and gained an opportunity of becoming acquainted with Ottoman towns and the daily life of the people.

On his tour of the Near East in 1869, the American artist, Sandford Robinson Gifford (1823–80), followed the now traditional route taken by British artists. Sailing from Italy to Alexandria, the artist went to Cairo, and, after sailing by steamship down the Nile, he went from

Port Said to Jaffa. A. Jaffa, where a caravan was assembled, Gifford, with the assistance of an interpreter, visited Jerusalem, Damascus, and Baalbek, and then, after reaching Beirut, he made his way to Greece and finally İstanbul. The numerous paintings rendered by the artist of İstanbul were based on drawings he had executed here.[3]

In response to the at times dangerous traveling conditions, some foreign scholars and artists conducting research in the Orient kept their European identity a secret. One of these was Cassas. Cassas let his beard grow like other Eastern males and appeared in public, as the occasion required, in the apparel of a Bedouin, an Arab, a Turk, or an Egyptian. Despite the fact that he concealed his Christian identity and donned Muslim dress, Cassas' surviving drawings reveal that he failed to sketch any mosque interior and that, even in large, densely populated cities like Cairo, he was constrained to be satisfied with simple, rapidly executed sketches. While passing through the Syrian Desert and during his stay at Palmyra, he overcame certain obstacles through the assistance of a local Christian, who acted as an interpreter for Arabic, Hebrew, and Bedouin dialects.

After the 1840s, traveling conditions became relatively easier, and, although very few people were attracted, regular sightseeing tours originating in European countries began to be organized.

Sources of inspiration

The precise distinction between Orientalism and a tour of the Orient and between the Orientalist artist and the tourist is difficult to pinpoint. Nevertheless, a number of prominent Orientalists like Jean-Auguste-Dominique Ingres (1780–1867) and Antoine-Jean Gros (1771–1835), never set foot in the Orient. They drew inspiration from the memoirs of others who had journeyed to the East and relied on the artifacts, engravings, and photographs collected by such travelers.

For some itinerant artists, it was sufficient to journey to the East on but a single occasion to obtain sufficient inspiration for their artistic productions. For instance, Delacroix made one trip to Algeria and Morocco with the Comte de Mornay, whom Louis-Philippe had sent on a special mission to the Sultan of Morocco, Moulay Abd-el-Rahman. Returning with seven notebooks full of pencil and watercolor sketches, the artist managed to profit from their contents for many years.

[3] Gerald M. Ackerman, Les Orientalistes de l'école américaine (Paris: ACR, 1994), 88.

[4] Félix Ziem, Journal (1854–1898) (Arles: Actes Sud, 1994: 82.

Similarly, Gabriel Decamps (1803–60) and Théodore Chassériau (1819–56)—both leading representatives of Orientalism—made only a single journey. Decamps traveled to Greece and to Asia Minor in 1827, and Chassériau, on the invitation of Caliph Ali Ben Ahmed, went first to Constantine and later to Algiers in 1846.

Covering the years 1854–98, the travel diary of Felix Ziem (1821–1911), who made a name for himself as a painter of İstanbul and Venice, is significant for its explication of what meaning the Eastern tour could bear for an artist and of how artistic production was perceived to benefit thereby. The artist, whose first visit to İstanbul took place in July 1856, entered in his diary on 7 March 1855 the following observations:

> Now, a project of journeying to Constantinople-why? Because I believe talent grows and develops by means of the excitement of the inspiration and that every new perspective acquired through travel replenishes our well of inspiration. I feel overwhelmed by a force constantly urging me to move to a new place, and I believe that the new horizons will in an instant open wide the doors to the mystery that is sought and that a sheaf of rays of this Eastern light shining on the life of the artist will be reflected in his future works… Though I cannot remain in İstanbul for an extended period, it will make me a thousand times more productive, and I hope to be able to execute powerful, luminous paintings in thick paint.[4]

Nineteenth-century artists, ever extending their tour itineraries, eventually came to embark on genuine expeditions of long duration. Certain cities, like Cairo and İstanbul, had become more convenient places for itinerant artists to live during this period. To take advantage of sea communications, tours were organized to depart from port cities, like Algiers, Tripoli, Beirut, Alexandria, Izmir, and İstanbul. Having executed drawings and watercolor sketches in the course of their travels, the artists would, on their return to their homeland, base their oil paintings on these preliminary studies. Utilizing the latest technology, certain realist artists like Jean-Léon Gérôme (1824–1904) and Horace Vernet (1789–1863) relied on photography in place of the traditional sketch. To add an authentic touch to their works and to develop the quality of their studio productions, they collected native costumes and artifacts and employed them for their paintings, in conjunction with European models.

Certain problems were confronted in the early twentieth century in working in the Orient on the subject for a painting. While it was an easy matter for the artist to delineate a landscape, drawing a figural composition represented a greater challenge. It was next to impossible to enter a mosque and execute a study. Since Islam prohibited the depiction of human figures, objections were commonly raised in regard to rendering a likeness of a Muslim without obtaining permission. For this reason, artists typically drew their sketches in a furtive manner. A great many artists, like Delacroix, drew on the abundant supply of Jewish models in North Africa. Included among the itinerant artists are those who, like Gustave Guillaumet (1840–87), settled in the East and shared their lives with the impoverished denizens of the desert, so as to be able to convey in their art scenes of life in a truer fashion, and those who, like Jacques Majorelle (1886–1962) and Étienne Dinet (1861–1929), converted to Islam.

A variety of subjects were handled by the makers of Orientalist paintings: demonstrations of valor in military combat and the chase; conventional desert landscapes, oases, and Eastern cities; scenes from the harem with lethargic and sensuous women; and activities of everyday life. Features emphasized include costume, architectural detail, objects of daily use and the habitat. In the majority of the scenes of the slave market, the harem and the bath, which delineate the subject of violence and eroticism, a stance vis-à-vis the Orient that is exaggerated, disparaging, and biased is detectable. Today such a perspective is seen as an identifying characteristic of Orientalist art, and stress is placed on the fact that the East does not only signify a geographical location, but also carries a political significance. In this sense, a parallel is exhibited with the West's perspective on the "Eastern Question" and a notable contrast is revealed between the depiction of the world of the Oriental, who is portrayed as cruel, lustful, and slothful, and that of the specimens of sublime natural beauty and works representing Islamic art and architecture. It is obvious that the artistic milieu was affected by the dominant role played by England and France in the evolution of contemporary policies toward the Near East and North Africa. The Orientalist perspective also displays

5 Kathy McLauchlan, "Nineteenth Century Views of the Near East," *Eastern Art Report* (May 1990): 15.

variation depending on the artist and the country. British Orientalists generally adopted an approach that tends to emphasize factors of a more objective nature, like anthropological and topographical data while French artists, particularly Delacroix and Gérôme, executed works receptive to the production of ideological interpretation. As Kathy McLauchlan has observed, "French artists were more inclined to portray subjects which accorded with their dreams and preconceptions."[5] These artists employed the Near East as a source for their violent and erotic subjects.

It should not be assumed, however, that all Western artists who resided and worked in the East shared this same perspective. In addition to works laden with ideological content, examples exist that heighten the picturesque of the Orient and highlight ethnographic and architectural elements and the characteristics of ornamentation in Islamic art and calligraphy. On the other hand, artists whose late nineteenth and early twentieth century lineage stretches from impressionism to fauvism and expressionism were drawn to the East on account of the strong light and the intense colors. Consequently, one may speak not of a single Orientalism, but rather of an Orientalism in the plural that exploited the East from a variety of standpoints.

Pictorial properties of orientalist paintings

Generally speaking, Orientalist paintings, despite the mutuality of subject matter, displayed variation according to the artist's interpretation based on personal sensitivities. Developments in painting techniques were displayed throughout the nineteenth century, both due to experiments by the individual artist and the emergence of new movements. Significantly, these paintings are imbued with a near-documentary quality that makes their expression credible. This power to convince transports viewers to mystical lands by stimulating their imaginative powers. It is for this reason that we may attribute the fact that the artists frequently resorted to photography, the invention of the day. On the evolution of the modern art movements at the beginning of the twentieth century and the focus by the artist on plastic concerns, like color, light, form, and motif, the characteristics related to the East which had stimulated the viewer's imagination and which had constituted the essence of Orientalism, became greatly diminished.

The powers of observation possessed by the Orientalist artist had become highly developed. This skill was requisite in order to be able to transfer to the canvas the full richness of the milieu. The observation of nature and the notes taken and the studies executed in the open air in the Orient urged the Western artist to exploit both the exotic life of the East and the brilliant light and vibrant colors. Living in the East opened the way for Orientalist artists to perceive light and color anew and enabled them to go beyond the formulae of the Western art academies. The ways in which they were influenced by the light in the open air and the ways in which they dealt with this problem in their works are reflected in their own memoirs. Called by their contemporaries "neo-colorists,"[6] these artists exerted an influence on the impressionist movement

This acquaintance by the itinerant artists with the East endowed them with a unique experience. Their encounter with a non-European culture led to alterations in the artists' aesthetic views, which for a significant proportion of Western artists had constituted an admiration of the antique. European artists perceived the importance borne by both light and color and by ornamentation in a work of art in the East and discovered the existence of an abstract language and a mystical and spiritual expression arising from the strong affinities among religion, art, music, and daily life in Islamic culture.[7]

The end of Orientalism

In the nineteenth century, Orientalist paintings were exhibited at the Salons in Paris and at the Royal Academy in London. Due to the efforts of gallery owners, like Adolphe Goupil in Paris and Ernest Gambart in London and the international exhibitions and the dissemination of published albums, these works began to be sought throughout Europe and the United States and even in countries of the Near East. In the 1880s, Orientalist artists sent their paintings to exhibitions organized in cities outside of London and Paris, in the United States and Europe. At first, French Orientalists exhibited their paintings in the Salon National des Beaux-Arts, established in 1890, but a new outlet for their works was created with the founding in 1893 of Société des Peintres Orientalistes Français. One indicator of the wide interest generated is the opening of a Salon

[6] Jean Soustiel and Lynn Thornton, *Mahmal et Attatichs: peintres et voyageurs en Turquie, en Egypte et en Afrique du nord*, exhibition catalog, (Paris: Galerie Soustiel, 1975), 6.

[7] Semra Germaner, "XIX. yüzyıl Sanatından İki Etkileşim Örneği: Oryantalizm ve Türk Resminde Batılılaşma," *Hacettepe Üniversitesi, Edebiyat Fakültesi, Sanat Tarih Bölümü: Uluslararası Sanatta Etkileşim Sempozyumu Bildirileri* (Ankara: Türkiye İş Bankası, 2000), 118.

Exhibition in İstanbul in 1901 in which the majority of the works were Orientalist. The popularity of Orientalism attracted many second rate artists to this theme. These artists were frequently among the itinerant artists who came to the Ottoman Empire.

The frequency of Orientalist subject matter in works of art had gradually diminished by the early twentieth century. With the growth of tourism and the spread of photography, the East lost to a great extent its former significance for Europeans. The West had discovered the true East. The phases in this discovery were largely experienced in the Ottoman Empire in the process of change that had commenced with the reforms of Mahmud II; the Cairo of Mehmed Ali Pasha of Kavàlla was witness to a similar westernization movement. Westerners were not in favor of these modernization efforts, claiming that they resulted in the destruction of the picturesque life in these countries. Complaints regarding the effects of the reforms undertaken in the Ottoman Empire are a common refrain in the memoirs of Western travelers, and the progress of these changes in İstanbul can be traced in their works of art from time to time.

The extinguishing of the sovereignty of the House of Osman—that is, the end of Ottoman İstanbul—and the adoption by the Republic of Turkey, a successor state of the Ottoman Empire, of the modern Western world as a model at the close of the First World War may be attributed as the chief factors in the disappearance of Orientalism.

IV Western Orientalism and Ottoman westernization

The emergence of Orientalism coincided with Napoleon's Egyptian campaign in 1798; and its continued vitality became evident in the light of the "Eastern Question." Only with the breaking up at the close of World War One of the field of attraction—that is to say, the Ottoman Empire—did Orientalism come to an end. What is interesting is the fact that coincident with the onset of Orientalism, a countercurrent of Westernization began to flow into the Ottoman Empire.

On the failure of the Second Siege of Vienna in 1683 and the signing of the Carlowicz Treaty in 1699, the superiority of the Ottoman polity vis-à-vis Europe had finally come to an end, and the Ottomans were forced to recognize that, at least in the military sphere, Europe was more advanced. This recognition led to Ottoman receptiveness to the West; in other words, "Westernization was seen as an option by the Ottomans not because it was in awe of the West, but rather because it was viewed as a necessary step."[1] Early attempts at change had been initiated in the Tulip Period, such as the appointing of extraordinary ambassadors to Vienna (1719) and Paris (1721); the founding of the first Ottoman printing press and manufactories of tile, paper and cloth; the establishment of a board of interpreters; and the inauguration of certain innovations in the military sphere. These early contacts with Europe exerted an impact on domestic cultural and social life, and progress in the direction of Westernization was registered in both social and intellectual life. The dispatch of Yirmisekiz Çelebi Mehmed Efendi to France in 1721 injected new life into the fashion of Turquerie, and, in a short time, its effects became evident throughout Europe; and, simultaneously, interest was aroused in İstanbul—particularly among Court circles—in Western art and architecture. Despite their different cultural structures, Court life in both Europe and the Ottoman Empire displayed similarities in the eighteenth century. In the Western world, ruled over by the aristocracy, art received the greater proportion of

[1] İlber Ortaylı, *İmparatorluğun En Uzun Yüzyılı* (İstanbul: İletişim Yayınları, 1995), 24.

its resources and power from the monarch and his circle and reflected the style of life and tastes of this circle, most notably in the case of France. The areas deemed most appropriate for the expression of sovereignty were the periphery of the Palace compound and the ceremonial grounds. The diplomatic rapprochement between the French and Ottoman Court in the eighteenth century and the significant outcomes in artistic life to which this gave rise in both realms allowed for a nearly parallel development in the cultural sphere. In truth, the eighteenth century was an era when for the first time worldly pleasures and happiness were portrayed in Ottoman art and when secular rather than religious art became dominant. As in the West, this was a time in the Ottoman world when nature reigned supreme. Refined taste and the exuberance of life was seen everywhere, in garden design and flower arranging, in still life reliefs on fountain façades, in fabric patterns and architecture, in the ceremonials accompanied by artificial trees made of wire and wax (*nahıl*), and fireworks.

Following the Tulip Period, military reforms took priority during the reign of Mahmud I (1730–54), and these reform initiatives continued under Mustafa III (1757–74) and Abdülhamid I (1774–89). Inspired by the French Revolution to undertake the most important military reform, Selim III (1789–1807) organized, in addition to the already existing janissary regiments, a military corps under a new system known as Nizam-î Cedid (1793). Officers from France, England, and Germany were brought in to train this new corps. The Imperial School for Artillery Officers (*Mühendishane-i Berri-i Hümayun*) (1795) was founded, and the first permanent Ottoman mission in Europe was established (1793).

The curriculum of the Imperial School for Artillery Officers boasted for the first time a technical art class. The first illustrated book, in which was contained a picture of the Imperial School for Artillery Officers building, was published in 1798.

This book, written by Mahmud Raif Efendi and titled *Tableaux des nouveaux réglements de l'Empire ottoman*, was prepared for the purpose of acquainting the West with the reforms undertaken by Selim III.[2] Another first was the commission granted by Princess Hatice to a foreign architect, Antoine-Ignace Melling, for the erection of a seaside mansion at her Defterdarburnu Palace.

Alteration of the traditional silhouette of İstanbul became apparent in the eighteenth-century due to the construction of palaces, seaside villas, and mansions along the shores of the Golden Horn, the Asian suburb of Üsküdar, and the Bosphorus, and, at the same time, the city limits were expanded on account of the Western-style military barracks and schools built in conjunction with the military reforms. Apart from the military structures constructed in the neoclassical style, baroque and rococo styles became prevalent in eighteenth-century İstanbul. The most important graphic records of the period were those executed by a group of European artists who came to the Ottoman Empire. Grouped under the name of the "Painters of the Bosphorus," these artists bequeathed works delineating Ottoman architecture and its way of life and costume that are of critical importance for urban history. Despite the evidence for Western influence in this era, the memoirs of the travelers who passed through the city reveal that this caused them little disturbance. No doubt, the chief reason for this is that the Ottoman applications to architecture of the baroque and rococo styles adopted from the West were not exact imitations but unique interpretations of these styles. In the eyes of Westerners, the Orient, rather than suffering change as a result of these innovations, had become further enriched.

After Selim III was removed from the throne by reactionaries opposed to his reforms, Mustafa IV (1807–8) bowed to their wishes and eliminated the *Nizam–î Cedid* corps; however, Mahmud II (1808–39), who succeeded him, completely eliminated the janissary corps and set up a modern military body (*Asakiri Mansure-i Muhammediye*), to train which instructors were imported from Europe. Hence, Ottoman reform movements of the nineteenth century, like those of the eighteenth century, started by reorganizing the armed forces. Mahmud II also took Europe as a model in government administration, awarded importance to education, and founded both civilian and mili-

[2] Mustafa Cezar, *Sanatta Batıya Açılış ve Osman Hamdi* (İstanbul: Erol Kerim Aksoy Vakfı, 1995), 42.

[3] Gustave Flaubert, *Lettres de Grèce* (Paris: Péplos, 1948), 20.

tary schools. Students began to be sent to Europe for education, the first newspaper *Takvim-i Vekayi* was founded (1831), and the Office of Interpreters of the Sublime Porte was established (1833). Moreover, economic reforms were also inaugurated, domestic production was promoted, and the Anglo-Ottoman Trade Agreement, which opened up the Ottoman Empire to foreign capital, was signed in 1838. Abdülmecid (1839-61), who acceded to throne on the death of his father, Mahmud II, also continued to pursue reform initiatives. Minister of Foreign Affairs Mustafa Reşid Pasha, who prepared for the sultan the "Beneficial Imperial Reforms" (*Tanzimat-ı Hayriye*), read out the rescript (1839) in the Palace garden of Gülhane, where were gathered the sultan, top government officials, representatives of religious organizations, foreign envoys, and a large crowd of Ottoman subjects.

This rescript granted to all Ottoman subjects security of life and property, instituted taxation based on one's means, regularized military service recruitment, granted due process of law, the right to own movable and real property and to bequeath it to one's own children, and prohibition of the customary collection of graft and tax farming. The Tanzimat rescript spelled out for the first time the relations between the sultan and his subjects, and the sultan who, prior to this writ had embodied the highest power in the land, now swore to abide by the principles contained in the edict and those laws based on them—thus, acknowledging that the power of the law was greater than himself. This movement put into operation reforms in the military, judiciary, and administration that persisted until the First Constitutional Monarchy and was responsible for attention to the principle of equality among Ottoman subjects and the changes experienced in life ways and dress. One eyewitness of these changes, Gustave Flaubert, stated in this connection that "in Constantinople, the great majority of the males had adopted European-style dress and operas were performed" and that "there were tailors who kept up with Paris fashions and clubs where newspapers and books published in Europe were read. By the end of the century," he predicted, "the harems will vanish due to influence of European ladies and soon both the veil, which with every passing day is becoming more and more sheer, and Islam will disappear."[3]

In an article headed "Eastern Fantasies" appearing in *Journal de Constantinople* (1 November 1845), the writer under the pseudonym "L'hermite de Pera" offered the following commentary on the İstanbul of his day:

> The struggle in Turkey is between two different civilizations, and the interesting image formed by their constant effort to influence one another is much clearer than in any other region. In particular, the struggle over the last several years between the European mentality and the Asian mentality has become quite heated. In view of its geographic position, Turkey represents a special area wherein the problem of the fusion of the two different worlds will be resolved.[4]

Due to the favorable climate created by the 1838 Anglo-Ottoman Trade Agreement, the attraction of the Ottoman Empire as a foreign market rose sharply, and the number of foreigners resident in İstanbul registered an increase. A similar increase occurred during the Crimean War, in which the Ottoman Empire was allied with England and France against the Russian Empire, when numerous foreigners—including illustrator-journalists posted by periodicals, like *L'Illustration*, *The Times*, and *The Illustrated London News*—poured into the city. By the second half of the nineteenth century, fifteen per cent of the city's population was composed of foreigners. All these developments altered the Eastern life-style of the Ottoman capital, and these changes were reflected in the physical environment. The number of books and newspapers increased, presentations of theatrical productions, which previously had been staged at foreign embassies for foreigners by private invitation, were soon being attended by Ottoman intellectuals.[5] At the end of the Crimean War and prior to the Paris Congress of 1856, an edict of Imperial Reforms—in essence, a reiteration of the earlier Tanzimat reforms decree—was issued in 1856 that granted Christian and Jewish subjects new rights and privileges.

On the premature death of Abdülmecid in 1861, Abdülaziz (1861-76) mounted the throne and later became the first Ottoman sultan to pay a formal visit to Europe, including France, England, Prussia, and Austro-Hungary. When the reforms were not put into force in their entirety despite the reform edicts, certain intellectuals closely familiar with Europe, that is to say, the Young

[4] "Fantaisies Orientales," *Journal de Constantinople* (1 Nov.1845).

[5] Doğan Kuban, *İstanbul: Bir Kent Tarihi* (İstanbul: Tarih Vakfı Yurt Yayınları, 2000), 348.

[6] Ortaylı, 89.

[7] Bernard Lewis, *The Emergence of Modern Turkey* (London: Oxford UP. 1968), 1779.

[8] Tarık Zafer Tunaya, *Batılılaşma Hareketleri, I* (İstanbul: Cumhuriyet, 1999), 118.

Ottomans, concurred that these innovations were inadequate to rescue the country and that the only remedy was a constitutional monarchy. As part of the cure, Abdülaziz was dethroned and Murad V (1876) was installed; but shortly thereafter the deterioration in his mental health led to his removal from the throne, his succession by Abdülhamid II (1876–1909), and the proclamation of the First Constitutional Monarchy (1876). Paradoxically, the reins of government passed once again from the hands of the Westernizing "bureaucrats of the Sublime Porte" into the hands of an idiosyncratic sultan[6]. Bernard Lewis is of the opinion that the goals of the Tanzimat movement—legal, administrative, and educational reforms—had attained their peak during the early years of Abdülhamid II's reign.[7] Already existing schools were enlarged and a number of new higher institutions and vocational schools were opened; railways were constructed, and, despite the existence of a strong censorship, journalism and the press thrived. But the increasing absolutism of Abdülhamid II's rule provoked a strong reaction, and the Union and Progress Society under the leadership of the Young Ottomans compelled Abdülhamid II to bow to the Second Constitutional Monarchy in 1908. This organization, subsequently taking the name Union and Progress Party, was nourished on the ideas of the Young Ottomans and occupied, directly or indirectly, the seat of power during the years 1908–12; and transformed the government into a dictatorship that put its stamp on Ottoman political and social life between 1913 and the end of the First World War. The Second Constitutional Monarchy became a "political laboratory"[8] where the idea that the citizens were a constructive element of the state was promoted and where the cadres who would found the future Turkish Republic gained experience.

Efforts to modernize the government and social system of the Ottoman Empire altered the physical fabric and lifestyle of the capital city: İstanbul, where secular architecture registered important gains, was transformed into a more European, a more cosmopolitan city. Abdülmecid, the sultan who proclaimed the Tanzimat edict, was also the sovereign who abandoned Topkapı Palace. In the opinion of Michael Levey,

> [w]hen the sultans quitted Topkapı, they virtually signaled surrender of their native culture,

without substituting anything individual or profound to replace it. Topkapı, with residual exoticness and beauty still overwhelming today, became a symbol of the out-of-date and the primitive....Along with the railway, corsets and female sovereigns, Western artifacts had taken on an awful allure merely by being different, distant or novel.[9]

Thus, the baroque, rococo and Empire styles, which had been interpreted and adopted in wholly unique manner in the context of Ottoman architecture in the early nineteenth century, were replaced in the second half of the century by eclectic styles applied as a direct import from Europe, and the number of foreign architects working in İstanbul swelled. The trend of Western imitation also left its mark on everyday life. The Court furnished the model: the furnishings of Dolmabahçe Palace came from Paris, purchased from Séchan, the decorator of the Paris Opera House, and from London, purchased from William Gibbs Rogers, the furniture maker for the British Royal family. Prior to the visit by Empress Eugenie, the sultan's maitre d'hotel Marco was sent to Paris to hire chefs and waiters and to order a dinner service;[10] and the orchestra of the sultan played in an adjacent chamber while wine was being imbibed at the banquets given in the Yıldız Palace.[11] Beneath their half open street coats (*ferace*), the daughters of pashas, who spoke French and English in the large shops in Pera, wore fashionable Paris clothes and high-heeled shoes.[12] John Murray states in his *Handbook for Travelers in Turkey* published in 1878 "[t]he Great Changes which have taken place in Turkey within the last few years has rendered necessary a new edition of the *Handbook*."[13]

From this point onward, Westerners revised their attitude in regard to the Ottoman Empire and constantly voiced complaints, especially in written sources, to the effect that Westernization had brought about negative changes in İstanbul life. One of these was Lamartine, who stated in *Voyage en Orient* that

> Turks had deserted their Eastern garb—turbans, fur-lined outer robes, loose-fitting trousers, belts, and caftans with gold needlework— in exchange for a miserable, badly fitting European costume, which they carry in an absurd manner, and that this had transformed

the solemn and magnificent appearance of these people to a pitiful caricature of a European.[14]

Vicomte René Vigier related his impressions of Dolmabahçe Palace as follows:

> How much I long for Arab and Persian art! Turkey is making a bad bargain with civilization: she has borrowed the defects [of the West, who in return] hands over the no longer wanted qualities she herself has banished. In the Dolmabahçe Palace bad taste and opulence is everywhere. The ultimate in ugliness is a fireplace faced with modern Sévres revetment tiles. In one gallery, the bare branches of dead trees boast birds stuffed with straw. The entire, three-room bath is made of alabaster. The only truly beautiful thing is the view of the Bosphorus.[15]

Orientalist artists expressed a similar attitude. In his article titled "The Sublime State," Christopher Ferrard expresses the opinion that in the 1830s, when romanticism was in full bloom, Europeans viewed the Ottomans as a medieval society on the brink of modernization that was worth recording before it disappeared completely in the modern world.[16] This explains why they tried to document the picturesque spots of İstanbul and the traditional way of life that was quickly vanishing and why they ignored the evidence of modernization in the city. Linda Nochlin has founded this longing for the picturesque in the Europe of the nineteenth-century on the "fact of destruction." According to Nochlin, the customs, religious rituals, and costumes of a society that is passive in the cultural sense are viewed as picturesque only on the brink of destruction, in the course of incipient modification and cultural dilution. An "important function... of the picturesque-Orientalizing in this case-is to certify that the people encapsulated by it, defined by its presence, are irredeemably different from, more backward than, and culturally inferior to those who construct and consume the picturesque product. They are irrevocably 'Other'."[17]

[9] Michael Levey, *The World of Ottoman Art* (London: Thames and Hudson, 1975), 129.

[10] Philip Mansel, *Constantinople: City of the World's Desire, 1453–1924* (London: Penguin, 1997), 274.

[11] Samuel S.Cox, *Diversions of a Diplomat in Turkey* (New York: Charles L. Webster, 1887), 56.

[12] Anna Bowman Dodd, *In the Palaces of the Sultan* (New York: Mead, 1903), 393.

[13] John Murray, "Introduction," *Handbook for Travellers in Turkey* (1878) cited in Andrew Wheatcroft, *The Ottomans: Dissolving Images* (London: Penguin, 1995), 155–6.

[14] Alphonse de Lamartine, *Voyage en Orient* (Paris: Hachette, 1874), 2: 147.

[15] René Vigier, *Un parisien à Constantinople* (Paris: G.Rougier, 1886), 206.

[16] Christopher Ferrard, "The Sublime State," *Visions of the. Ottoman Empire*, exhibition catalog (Edinburgh: Scottish National Portrait Gallery, 1994), 13.

[17] Linda Nochlin, *The Politics of Vision* (London: Thames and Hudson, 1991), 50–1.

V A new fashion in the West

By the 1840s, the level of Western interest in the Orient appears to have become substantial. One measure is the fact that contemporary memoirs by those formerly resident in the East disclose that souvenirs of their visit composed not simply a subject of interest but an element of prestige. Those individuals in possession of such a distinction joined, forming clubs that organized special evening occasions.

An article on the subject in *L'Illustration* (2 September 1843) discloses that the costumes from the lands visited by the itinerant artists were carefully stored and that these were not merely keepsakes, but that they also represented irrefutable evidence that they had actually been to those places. Consequently, the article reports

> A traveler formerly in the Orient would show to friends an evzone dress purchased on Samos or Chios, a fez from İstanbul, a dervish's headgear, or a Turkish sword. Further, these people enjoyed making an appearance themselves dressed in the costumes they had once donned in the East, sprinkling their conversation with a few words from the languages of these distant lands, and adding further zest by a mimicking of the appropriate body gestures.

Another sign of the interest in the East noted in the same article was a gathering attended by artists and travelers in the house of an architect in Paris one beautiful, summer night in the month of August 1843. For the occasion, an elegant tent decorated with floral arrangements served as the setting, but which contained no other furnishings than a sofa, and all the guests present were garbed in Eastern costume. At the party, described as a Tower of Babel due to the multitude of Eastern languages being spoken, some of the guests appeared as Arab sheikhs of Yemen, attired in long garments of silk, bound by sashes of cashmere, and wearing sandals, and conversed with Assyrian mountain dwellers while sitting cross-legged on a carpet; or another in a picturesque dress falling to tatters, armed with large, crude weapons, had struck up an acquaintance with an agha allied with France; or a Greek irregular soldier dressed in an outfit with brightly colored embroidery was engaged in conversation with an Albanian who spoke in a corrupt variant of the Homeric tongue; or while someone else dressed in an Egyptian peasant garment attempted to imitate the monotonous sound of the muezzin, another sang an Arab folksong expressing intense longing; and some smoked Indian tobacco, some Persian water pipes, and others Ottoman clay pipes with long reed stems. Present on this occasion, it is stat-

22 Karl Girardet. "A Night in the Orient Club in Paris," *L'Illustration* (2 Sept, 1843).

ed, were representatives of all the Oriental peoples—Tatars, Persians, Indians, Japanese, Turks, Egyptians, and Nubians.[1] The draftsman, Karl Girardet, himself an Eastern traveler, appeared among the invited guests, and one of his drawings executed that evening accompanied the article.

Oriental Nights like these also included theatrical presentations. An announcement inserted in the 4 May 1844 issue of the same periodical reports that a one-act vaudeville sketch with a set by Séchan *L'Ours et le Pacha* by a certain Scribe was to be presented at "An Oriental Night in Paris" in the Académie Française.[2] But such plays might also be met with disapproval by the Court in İstanbul. During the reign of Abdülhamid II, the contents of a communiqué from Karaca Pasha, the Ottoman ambassador to The Hague, dated 17 July 1894, indicate that the play and dances scheduled to be performed in an Eastern coffeehouse and whose set was a harem interior was canceled by the Dutch government in response to a request by the Ottoman government.[3]

[1] *L'Illustration* (2 September 1843): 5.

[2] *L'Illustration* (4 Mai 1844): 156.

[3] BOA, Yıldız Tasnifi Mütenevvi Maruzat, no. 26.

[4] *L'Illustration* (4 Avril 1846): 80.

Clubs were also established by Europeans—but which were open to Easterners as well—with the aim of keeping alive interest in the East. As reported by *L'Illustration* (4 April 1846), on the initiative of one Orientalist who had served for many years as a minister plenipotentiary in the East a club called Cercle Oriental was founded in Paris in 1846. The article states that previously no meeting place had existed where the travelers could come together to keep their memories alive. Stressing the importance of an organization to answer this need, it indicated that anyone who had made a trip to the Orient or was anticipating making one would appreciate the opportunity to renew the contacts established in foreign countries and to restore the intimate and personal friendships that had been, of necessity, abandoned since their return. The club opened on Rue de Richelieu, under the auspices of a prince of the royal family. Its interior decoration by Bassetti possessed an Oriental atmosphere reminiscent of the Alhambra. A description of the interior informs us that the staircases were covered with carpeting, that it was decorated with flowers and lighted with elegant lamps, that it had spacious halls suitable for various purposes, that the holdings of its library were such as to satisfy a linguist, and that in the dining room Eastern dishes would also be served in addition to those of French cuisine.

The special occasions held in the ballroom of

Cercle Oriental were, reportedly, attended by the French, who enjoyed watching the Eastern exotic dancers, along with members of the Egyptian and Ottoman diplomatic corps, chests gleaming with diamond-studded medals of honor—who joined in by dancing the waltz and the polka—and the elite of various nations. Finally, the same piece relays the information that preparations were being made for a reception to be held in the near future at which a certain İbrahim Pasha would appear as a guest.[4]

Another aspect of this rage for things Oriental was the numerous illustrated anecdotes and cartoons related to the East in the newspapers and journals of the day.

23 "The Opening of the Orient Club in Paris," *L'Illustration* (4 Avr, 1846).

Aventures de M. Verdreau, par Stop. — (Suite et fin. — Voir les Nos 359, 360, 361 et 362.)

Misérable!

Une lettre attendait M. Verdreau à son domicile.....

.....Elle était ainsi conçue:

..... La rue n'était pas indiquée!

Arrivé au bord de son puits, M. Verdreau recule d'horreur..... Nick établi dans un des seaux le regardait avec d'horribles yeux!

Alors éperdu, fou de désespoir, et décidé à en finir.....

..... M. Verdreau fait ses malles, achète une paire de moustaches.....

..... monte dans la diligence de Constantinople..

..... et renonçant à jamais à Cupidon, à ses pompes et à ses œuvres, va se faire recevoir premier chanteur de Sa Majesté le grand Turc.

SÉRAIL.

MORALITÉ

MORALITÉ.

Ceci doit vous apprendre, amis lecteurs et aimables lectrices, que les grandes passions font faire beaucoup de *malles*, sans beaucoup d'*effets*. Il faut les fuir avec une grande *diligence* et se renfermer dans son *intérieur*; car, une fois lâché, vous voilà en *train de faire*....... des bêtises. Dieu vous en garde! et moi aussi!

[5] *Ceride-i Havadis* 21 Cemaziyelevvel 1267.

24 "Adventures of Verdreau," *L'Illustration* (9 Fev, 1850).

[5] *Ceride–i Havadis* (21 Cemaziyelevvel 1267).

The Ottomans at international expositions

National and international expositions in the nineteenth century on agriculture, manufacturing, handicrafts, and the fine arts organized by Western countries exerted a broad-ranging influence on the cultural structure of the period. The earliest, in 1798, was on a national level and organized by France on manufacturing, but which was regularly held throughout the nineteenth century and attended by millions of Europeans. Reaching for the first time vast numbers of the public, these exhibitions made widely known a variety of goods. Besides agricultural products and manufactured goods, a sizeable proportion of the manufacturing fairs was composed of objects produced by the handicrafts and in the fine arts of every participant country: by this means, Western visitors to the exhibitions became aware of the existence of other cultures and the way was opened for the adoption of new tastes in Western society. In the early phase, the Western observer gained the opportunity of viewing cultural and ethnographic artifacts from the Eastern world. On the other side, the Ottoman Empire first participated in an international exhibition in 1851 as part of its effort after the proclamation of Tanzimat to find solutions to its economic problems and to demonstrate to European states the progress being made in the areas of agriculture and manufacturing. Ottoman participation in these exhibits bore both an economic and cultural import.

The first international exhibition in which the Ottoman Empire participated was the London Exhibition of 1851. It was opened in the Crystal Palace at Hyde Park in London. Prior to being loading on the ship in İstanbul, the Ottoman goods to be sent to London were briefly exhibited, so that the chief imperial officials, envoys, merchants, and tradesmen could view them.[5] Though this exhibition was of short duration and not open to the public, it may be regarded as the first of this kind of exhibition in the Ottoman Empire. The frigate *Feyz-i Bahri* set out for England after being boarded by high-ranking dignitaries, such as Musurus Bey, Mustafa Pasha, and Cemaleddin Pasha and loaded with two hundred chests filled with agricultural and handicraft goods. Due to adverse sailing conditions, the ship managed to dock in Southhampton only in April, with the consequence that the Ottoman goods were put on display after the opening of the Crystal Palace, and the arrangement of their display had to be rushed due to the delay. The Ottoman pavilion in the exhibition hall in Hyde Park was organized under the direction of Zohrab and Major. Though the space assigned for the Ottoman goods was cramped, the agricultural products, minerals, fabrics, needlework work, and costly shawls generated a good deal of interest, and the Empire was rewarded with medals and honorable mentions for their successful exhibit.[6] Among the goods awarded prizes were gilt-thread needlework from Tunisia, fezzes and light shawls, silk tissues, and cloth of cotton and linen, long pipe-stems of amber worked by Uzunçarşılı Hacı Naim Agha and of jasmine wood by Uzunçarşılı Said Agha, goods produced by the Beykoz Imperial Factory, combs and spoons, saddle-cloths, purses and scarves with needlework, perfumes from İstanbul, silk fabrics from Bursa, and rose- and flower-water bottles from Egypt.[7]

The 1855 Universal Exhibition of Paris was the second international exhibition in which the Ottoman Empire participated. The fact that the Ottomans were allies with England and France was a factor in their participation in the exhibition. Displayed in the Champs-Elysées Palace of Industry, the Ottoman exhibit, with Master of Ceremonies Kâmil Bey representing the Sublime Porte contained an array of some two thousand different items of nineteenth-century Ottoman handicrafts, including carpets and prayer rugs from Uşak, Gördes, Demirci, Afyonkarahisar, Sivas, and Hereke; products of the Tophane Imperial Factory; guns from Damascus; and silver gilt revolvers from Ioannina; braziers of copper and bronze; copper dishes and trays; musical instruments peculiar to the East, like large drums, double-reed wind instruments, and small violins; articles made of wood, decorated with inlay and relief like small chests of drawers, cupboards and bath clogs; needlework in gold and silver; porcelain and glass from the İncirköy Imperial Factory; Çanakkale ceramics; glazed tiles of Kütahya; fired clay pipe-bowls and objets d'art.

The Paris Exhibition of 1855 demonstrated that France occupied a position of some weight in the second half of the nineteenth century in both political and artistic terms. Of the more than five thousand paintings on display in the Palace of Fine Arts, those attracting the greatest amount of attention were by French artists, among who were Delacroix, Corot (1796–1875), Millet (1814–75), Daubigny (1817–78), and Gérôme. Charles

Baudelaire served as the critic for the exhibition. The Orientalist painting by Ingres—*The Valpinçon Bather*—and his numerous preliminary studies for this work were also part of the exhibition.[8] It is clear that the Ottoman carpets, fabrics, tiles and other handicraft items on display in the exhibition served as documentary material for the artists actively involved in the contemporary mode of portraying Orientalist subjects.

Seven years after the Paris Exhibition of 1855, the Ottomans participated in the Second International Exhibition of London held in 1862. The area set aside for Ottoman goods at this exhibition was at least twice as large as that of the 1851 exhibition. Among the twenty-five different groups of Ottoman items on display, both traditional agricultural products and specimens of handicrafts once more occupied a major place. The exhibition pavilions contained cases of ornamented swords, regarded as gems by aficionados; guns with gold and silver inlay in unique designs; carpets of Uşak, Manisa, Thessalonica, Damascus, Adana, and Philippopillus; furnishings, like sofas and pillows; boxes with inlaid mother-of-pearl and pearls; small tables and stools; and a brass brazier with a design *à la franque*, in addition to specimens of jewelry; bracelets of baked ceramic with specially perfumed clay; pipe stems of jasmine wood and amber; lace and knitted goods; silks and velvets from the Hereke Imperial Factory competing with fabrics from Lyon and Milan; objects of carved wood from Edirne; musical instruments; coffee cup holders; cigarette boxes; objects formed of woven gold or silver wire; and small objets d'art made of carved ivory, tortoise shell, mother-of-pearl, coral, and coconut shell. Nazım Bey, the son of Grand Vizier Fuat Pasha, served as exhibition commissioner.[9]

Without a doubt, the most important of the international exhibitions in which the Ottoman Empire participated is that of Paris in 1867. From the Ottoman perspective, this exhibition stood out on account of Sultan Abdülaziz's visit. By comparison with previous exhibitions, the 1867 Paris Salon exhibition was much more spectacular: in attendance were European heads of state, like the Russian czar, the ruler of the Austro-Hungarian monarchy, the kings of Belgium, Portugal, Sweden, and Prussia, and the Prince of Wales. The Paris exhibition, which attracted eleven million visitors, overflowed to the park around the exhibition palace and to the banks of the Seine

[6] Salaheddin Bey, *La Turquie à l'exposition universelle de 1867* (Paris, 1867), 12–3.

[7] Rifat Önsoy, "Osmanlı İmparatorluğunun katıldığı İlk Uluslararası Sergiler ve Sergi-i Umumi-i Osmani (1863 İstanbul Sergisi)," *Belleten* (1984): 196–9.

[8] John Rewald, *Histoire de l'Impressionnisme, I (1855–1873)* (Paris: Albin Michel, 1965), 15–21.

[9] Salâheddin Bey, 14–23, Önsoy, 204–6.

River. At this exhibition with fifty-two thousand two hundred exhibitors, the pavilion of the Ottoman Empire with 4,946 exhibitors was in third place after France and England.[10]

The book by Salâheddin Bey, the commissioner of the Ottoman exhibition, published in Paris in 1867 and titled *La Turquie à l'exposition universelle de 1867* forms our main source on the Paris Salon exhibition. In the exhibition area within the park, each country constructed a stand conforming to its own architectural style. The Ottoman pavilions were comprised of a mosque, a Bosphorus mansion, and a bath. The mosque was modeled on the Yeşil Mosque of Bursa, reduced in scale but faithful in every detail. The structure, with its decorated interior dome, and the prayer niche, five meters tall and faced with glazed tile, was well received. In addition, a pavilion was situated on the left- and right-hand sides of the mosque façade; that on the right boasted a monumental fountain while the other bore clockfaces indicating the times of the daily prayer services. The Ottoman mansion represented a reconstruction of one of the—even at that time—few surviving specimens from the Asian side of the Bosphorus. Decorated with stained glass, the main hall of the mansion was graced by a pool in the center of the room, whose margins were edged on all sides by a divan. Every aspect of the interior decoration of this structure, whose detailing received high approbation, constituted a model of Ottoman art; in particular, the stained glass technique employing plaster of Paris, which differs from that of European stained glass, produced a notably delicate effect. The bath, domed and comprising three interconnecting spatial units, was situated opposite the mansion and constituted a miniature copy of the traditional Ottoman bath. The prayer niche of the mosque, the bath door, and the facade of the Ottoman gallery were faced with glazed revetment tiles of Kütahya in a replica of the ancient tiles utilized in Bursa mosques. Léon Parvillée, who had worked on the erection of the Ottoman Exhibition Hall in 1863, executed the Ottoman pavilions, whose construction commenced quite late.

At the exhibition of 1867, the Ottoman Empire displayed products and goods in sixty-four separate categories of agriculture, manufacturing, handicrafts, and fine arts. For the first time, a special section was reserved for architectural plans, projects, oil paintings, photography, and sculp-

[10] H.Lamirault et al, *La grande encyclopédie inventaire raisonné des sciences, des lettres et des arts*, 16: 974.

25 "A Turkish Neighborhood, 1867 Paris Exhibition," *L'Illustration* (2 Mars 1867).

ture; also included here for the first time by the Ottomans were scientific studies, natural history collections, and archeology.

Among the works on display in the section devoted to the fine arts of the empire were three paintings by Osman Hamdi (1842–1910)—*Gypsies Stopping by the Wayside*, *Zeybek in an Ambush*, and *The Death of a Zeybek*. Amadeo Preziosi (1816–82) was represented by a watercolor sketch depicting the *Procession of the Sultan's Bodyguards* and Charles Labbé (1820-85) by the oil paintings *Women in a Garden* and *Picking Oranges*. Since both Labbé of France and Preziosi of Malta had been long-time residents of İstanbul, they were awarded the right to exhibit their paintings with Ottoman artists. Other works that may be mentioned were *Circassian Slave Girl Serving Coffee*, an oil painting by Virginia Serviçen, *Portrait of Sultan Abdülaziz* by Marie Adelaide Walker, *View of Ok Meydanı* by Rıza Efendi, scenes of daily life and seascapes by Pierre Montani, a number of paintings by Serabyan, and *Portrait of a Young Girl* by Iphigénie Zipcy of Izmir. A portrait in charcoal of Sultan Abdülaziz by Şeker Ahmed Pasha (1841–1907) was also exhibited.[11] Photography was also included in the 1867 Paris Salon exhibition, such as a series of portraits by the Abdullah Frères, including one of Sultan Abdülaziz and four panoramic vistas of İstanbul.

Carpets and covering fabrics, occupying a prominent position in the Ottoman Exhibition, captured the attention of many visitors. A velvet-like fabric patterned in a gilt, floral motif on a lavender ground, manufactured in İstanbul and employed as a wall covering, represented just one selection in the textile division. The majority of the white or cherry-colored silk rugs and the deep crimson broadcloth were also manufactured in İstanbul. Cloths beautified by gold and silver needlework were used as covers on copper coffee trays or low stands. Durable, napped cloths with a dark red, matte finish were spread over the divans in the pavilion erected on Champs-de-Mars. All specimens of this cloth, manufactured in Philippopillus, were purchased by Princess Mathilde. As for the felts and thick felts, employed as a floor covering or door curtain, those ornamented with needlework were from Bursa and those plain in color were manufactured in Trabzon and Konya.

At the exhibition of 1867, the Ottoman Empire displayed two hundred and seventeen different weapons made in İstanbul or the provinces.

[11] Salâheddin Bey, 139–43.
[12] Salâheddin Bey, 155–9.

These included muskets, revolvers, carbines with inlay of silver, coral, and ivory, daggers, swords, poniards, heavy, curved knives with sheaths of solid silver, studded with emeralds and rubies, niello-decorated hunting knives, Arab javelins, shields made of rhinoceros hide, and carved and painted bows and arrows.[12]

The great proportion of the furnishings in the Ottoman exhibit were worked, just as with the boxes, in mother-of-pearl inlay, and at times further enriched by ebony, outlined in silver, and inlaid tortoise shell—the wood itself was lost beneath this ornate overlay. Over these items of furniture of cypress wood with mother-of-pearl inlay was spread yellow and red silk coverings.

After the 1867 exhibition, the Ottoman Empire next participated in the Vienna Exhibition of 1873, organized by the Austro-Hungarian monarchy. The exhibition, which took shape under the chairmanship of Archduke Regnier, was opened in the renowned Prater Park on 1 May 1873. The commissioner of the Ottoman section was Osman Hamdi, while Montani was in charge of the architectural works. A replica the fountain erected by Ahmed III was situated between the east entrance of the exhibition hall and the fine arts pavilion. In the spacious area allotted to the Ottomans in the exhibition palace, Master Builder Yorgi Papazoğlu

26 " Fine Arts Pavilion and the Fountain of Ahmed III, 1873 International Vienna Exhibition," *L'Illustration* (21 Juin 1873).

erected an Ottoman house in replication of a typical İstanbul mansion, with ornamented ceilings and porches. The Ottoman pavilion also contained a traditional bath with marble paving and basins, a coffeehouse, and a kiln to demonstrate the manufacturing process of ancient-type porcelain ware. The chairman of the Ottoman exhibition commission, Minister of Public Works İbrahim Edhem Pasha, had two albums in separate French and Ottoman editions specially prepared for the exhibition—one on domestic dress titled *Les Costumes Populaires de la Turquie* (*Elbise-i Osmaniye)* and the other on Ottoman architectural and ornamental art, *L'architecture ottomane* (*Usul-u Mimari-i Osmanî*). At the 1873 Vienna Exhibition, the Ottomans besides exhibiting their traditional handicrafts, represented a more scientific approach by publishing an album on Ottoman architecture and were awarded six medals for the paintings by Osman Hamdi.[13]

One other important exhibition in which the Ottoman Empire participated in an official capacity was the Chicago Exhibition of 1893. Participating by formal invitation at this exhibition commemorating the four hundredth anniversary of the discovery of the Americas by Christopher Columbus, the Ottoman Empire was represented by a special delegation sent by Sultan Abdülhamid II. Hakkı Pasha, who served as commissioner, and his deputy, Fahri Bey, set up a model of an Ottoman village for the exhibition, a mosque was built, and various handicrafts, like carpets, cloth, glazed tiles, furnishings, and weapons were on display, along with reconstruction models of buildings and ships.[14] Occupying a place in the model of the Ottoman village were a mosque in characteristic Ottoman architecture, a covered market reminiscent of the Spice Bazaar with forty to fifty shops, a two-story restaurant, and ten to fifteen houses used as offices, and kiosks on the street corners selling miscellaneous items and candies.

In celebration of the dawn of a new century, the 1900 Paris Salon exhibition, at which were introduced artworks, manufacturing and agricultural products, and the newest scientific discoveries, was one of the last great exhibitions. Along the Quai d'Orsay, which was reserved for foreigners, the Ottoman pavilion on the Avenue des Nations was represented by a mosque with a magnificent dome, a hallmark of the traditional East.

The architectural form of the Ottoman pavilions at the international exhibitions of the nineteenth century and the ethnographic goods and samples of handicrafts—besides stimulating the interest of European visitors and earning their approval—ultimately, reinforced the vogue for the Oriental in the Western world, in areas such as contemporary architecture, painting, photography and fashion design.

Illustrations of İstanbul in the European press

As a result of Western curiosity about the East, İstanbul, as the capital of the Ottoman Empire, was constantly in the news reports appearing in foreign newspapers and journals, and, as a natural outcome, the city acquired importance as an atelier for illustrators. Western draftsmen for the current affairs section in these publications sketched important events, traditional holidays, celebrations and ceremonials and balls in the capital.

The Crimean War, led by Sultan Abdülmecid and joined by the powerful European allies of England and France, brought to İstanbul a number of illustrators and artists assisting the war correspondents. Besides news on the war and politics, those who came to the city or those who were passing through began to discover interesting aspects of the local milieu. The fascination with the East already existent in the nineteenth century was thereby further intensified and the Ottoman Court once more formed the focus of interest. Departures from the Palace by the sultan, ceremonials, processions, and the places visited by the sultan constituted not only an event of interest to the local residents, but they also represented a not-to-be-missed show for foreigners in the city. These occasions, which were rich sources of material for both written works and graphic treatments, appear to have attracted the attention particularly of the draftsmen artists of European newspapers and journals. Those who worked on Orientalist subjects, like François-Claude Hayette (1838-?), Montani, Henri Pierre Léon Pharmond Blanchard (1805-73), Fabius Brest (1823-1900), Giovanni Brindesi, Louis Ernest, Alberto Pasini (1826-99), Preziosi, Alexandre Bida (1823-95), and Stanislaw Chlebowski (1835-84), were in the majority. These artists, who executed their early studies on the spot, would send their sketches by the first available means to draftsmen in Paris and London, where they would be readied for publication. This meant that both the news

[13] Cezar, *Sanatta*, 496.
[14] Haydar Kazgan, "Osmanlı Sanayiinin Dışa Açılması: 1893 Şikago Sergisinde Osmanlı Pavyonu," *Ekonomide Diyalog* (Şubat 1984): 63–5.

pieces and the related drawings would be published with a delay of a week or ten days. Clearly, these artists, who earned their livelihood while in İstanbul both by producing paintings on Orientalist subjects and delineating the leading events in the city, also fostered the fashion of Orientalism in Europe by their pictures published in the popular press of the day, such as *L'Illustration*, *Le Tour du Monde*, *Le Monde Illustré*, and *The Illustrated London News*. Some of the illustrator-artists who temporarily settled in İstanbul and were availed of the opportunity of becoming acquainted with the local atmosphere and life of the city transferred the visual wealth and experience garnered here to the Paris Salon.

Illustrating the news pertaining to the Ottoman sultan was one of the most legitimate subjects for newspapers and journals and, consequently, for graphic artists as well. Apart from the sultan's going to Eyüp on the occasion of girding of the sword of Osman or attendance at the Friday procession to the mosque, it is known that he also visited the Sublime Porte from time to time. In an article appearing in the 5 July 1852 edition of *L'Illustration*, the reporter and draftsmen Henri Blanchard indicates that despite his having arrived in İstanbul only a short time previous he had seen Abdülmecid three times on the streets and had attempted to sketch a drawing of him. This statement bears importance in regard to the manner in which the pictures of ceremonials were delineated. The writer states that the sultan went to the Sublime Porte by sea from the Old Çırağan Palace. The presence of several Palace guards and Palace servants at the side of richly caparisoned horses at the landing stage always utilized by the imperial caique was sufficient to inform the public that the sultan had arrived in the city center. He reports that

> [t]he hushed crowd awaited the ruler in
> an attitude of profound respect. When they
> recognized that I was a foreigner, with great
> courtesy, they attempted to open a space for
> me in the front row. Thus, on the approach
> of the sultan I was able to come up to the rear
> of the small squad of Palace guards who had
> formed a cordon to keep the way open.
> In a few minutes, Abdülmecid appeared, riding
ill. 27   > on the finest of the horses, reining in his
> mount—which refused to stand still for his
> noble rider—forcefully but with ease. The

sultan, despite his possession of a patient and gentle physiognomy, made his authority palpable. He was attired in a plain, short military coat with a gold embroidered collar, complemented by a light sword. There was no need to resort to the ostentatious display exploited by his ancestors in order to underscore the fact that he was the sovereign of a great empire, the respect that his presence aroused was sufficient to demonstrate this.[15]

[15] P.Blanchard "Les Fêtes du Ramazan à Constantinople", *L'Illustration* (24 Juillet 1852): 53.

In this era, information of all kinds regarding the Ottoman sultan was greeted with interest in the West, including the relevant visual material. Montani illustrated news reports on the funeral of Abdülmecid and the accession of Sultan Abdülaziz appearing in the 3 August 1861 issue of *L'Illustration*. The news article of 10 July 1861 concerning two momentous ceremonials that took place in İstanbul reports that an effort was made to execute accurate depictions. The first drawing is a rendering of the funerary procession of the deceased sultan, Abdülmecid, as it exited the Topkapı Palace. The sultan's coffin, very plain and simply wrapped in velvet, is being carried by ill the halberdiers to its final resting place. A mount-

▲
27

27 "Abdülmecid on the Way to the Sublime Porte on 23 June 1852." Engraving by Best, based on a drawing by Blanchard. *L'Illustration* (24 Juillet 1852).

28 Montani. "Sultan Abdülmecid's Funeral
Procession," L'Illustration (3 Aout 1861).

ed imperial servant riding behind the coffin is scattering coins among the crowd standing in an attitude of respect, and two halberdiers are advancing on either side of the coffin holding a tray on which a censer is burning. The Palace guards preceding the coffin are opening the way amidst the crowd, followed by Arabs from Mecca in white garb, who are offering prayers. Mounted on horses, two high religious dignitaries and the grand vizier are among the mourners present.[16]

The second illustration appearing in the same issue of *L'Illustration* delineates the sultan Abdülaziz making his entrance into İstanbul by the city gate of Topkapı, on his return from the ceremonial of girding the dynastic sword. Because sultans returning from Eyüp after this ceremonial, traditionally, entered İstanbul by the same gate as had Sultan Mehmed II on his conquest of the city, Abdülaziz is also conforming to custom by riding along Edirnekapı Avenue toward the tomb of Mehmed II. In the picture, the crowd of curious bystanders seems eager to obtain a close-up

ill. 29

[16] P.Paget, "Obsèques d'Abdul-Medjid", *L'Illustration* (3 Aout 1861): 67.

▲
29

29 "Accession of Abdülaziz and His Entrance into the City," *L'Illustration* (3 Aout 1861).

glimpse of the new sultan, who is advancing toward them on horseback.

The festivities held in honor of the anniversary of the sultan's accession to the throne or for weddings also occupied a special place among the events of interest to everyone and that lent color and liveliness to the city scene. The eighth anniversary of Abdülaziz's accession on 28 June 1869 was celebrated by public attendance at the festive illumination of the night, as is shown in the engraving executed from a drawing by Hayette, which was printed in the 17 July 1869 edition of *L'Illustration*. M.Alexis who wrote an article on the subject, states that the grateful public expressed its very warm and lively appreciation and gratitude to the sultan for his efforts to rejuvenate the empire. The writer in this connection notes that, because the illumination was a sight worth seeing, a formal ceremonial had been arranged in the Palace in the morning and that in the evening Grand Vizier Ali Pasha had given a large banquet in his seaside mansion and that a number of buildings, particularly the mansions lining the shores of the Bosphorus from its entrance up to the suburb of Tarabya, had been illuminated, and that throughout the night fireworks were set off, endowing the Bosphorus with an appearance of rare beauty. Shown in the picture are numerous boats floating on the sea, so as permit their occupants a view of the festivities, illuminated buildings, and exploding fireworks.

ill

Retaining their customary way of life in the capital of the empire, Levantines and Europeans typically arranged for the holding of ballroom dances in the embassies situated in the districts of Galata and Pera or in the foreign merchant ships anchored in the harbor. The 7 February 1856 edition of *L'Illustration* informed its readers of a most unusual ball held in the French embassy on the fourth of February in the year 1856—Sultan Abdülmecid had been in attendance. By six in the evening, the article reports, Grand Rue de Pera had become filled to overflowing with crowds clustered to view the sultan's procession; further, all the houses of the French residents were specially illuminated while the route over which the sultan was to pass was cordoned up to avenue on which the embassy was located; the garden of the French embassy was embellished with lighted balloons, and the embassy façade shone with oil lamps spotlighting the architectural lines of the structure, where armed soldiers were lined up on the risers of the staircase, the full extent of the ramp leading to the entrance, and the perimeters of the flower beds. At this event in which both French and Ottoman troops participated jointly, the Sultan's private guards stood to the right of the entrance in blue trousers and gold-embroidered jackets, and on the left, under the command of Poteau, the firemen formed one file; while on the upper slope the formation of the eighty-fourth Ottoman regiment was under the command of Jouannier. In the entryway of the embassy, the crew of the ambassador's steamship *Ajaccio* and in the corridors and waiting rooms detachments of every rank was in evidence. Two zouave soldiers in green turbans, two soldiers from the African hunting battalion and two infantrymen were guarding the entrance to the large ballroom.

At a quarter past seven when the illumination of the palace was completed, the sound of horse

30 François- Claude Hayette. "Night Festivities on the Bosphorus on the Anniversary of the Sultan's Accession," *L'Illustration* (17 Juillet 1869).

30
▼

hooves was heard and the glow of torches could be seen on the slopes of Tophane. The sultan on horseback, accompanied by imperial dignitaries, aides-de-camp, the Palace chamberlain and secretaries, arrived at the embassy with some one hundred cavalry. Abdülmecid, adorned with the Légion d'Honneur medal with diamonds presented personally to him by Napoleon III, was welcomed at the entrance by the French ambassador, Edouard Thouvenel, and embassy staff and after being saluted by music played by a military band he was taken to the Throne Room. Ali Pasha, Mehmed Pasha of Cyprus, Ali Galip Pasha, Mehmed Rüştü Pasha, Muhtar Pasha, Mehmed Ali Pasha, and others arrived afterwards, and at eight o'clock the halls were filled with elegant uniforms from every country and sparkling gowns worn by the guests. The writer goes on to state that while taking his ease in the red hall, that is, the Throne Room, the sultan examined with interest a full-length portrait of Emperor Napoleon III, executed by Winterhalter.[17] At one point, Abdülmecid met with the ambassador and presented him with the

medal of the Order of Mecidiye and promised to give him a portrait of himself.[18] At eight-thirty, the doors of the large ballroom were opened, and Court Chamberlain Kamil Bey announced the honor of the presence of the sultan. As Sultan Abdülmecid entered the ballroom, musicians located in the gallery played the "Sultan Mahmud March" composed by chief Court Musician Donizetti Pasha. Abdülmecid sat in the ballroom in an armchair placed on an elevated platform covered by a costly Persian rug, and, after observing for a time dances like the quadrille, the polka, and the mazurka, he once again withdrew to the red hall. Throughout the evening, a number of women of the diplomatic corps were presented to the sultan. At a quarter to eleven, Abdülmecid departed from the embassy and was seen off by a display of fireworks at Tophane.[19]

[17] Arthur Baligot de Beyne, "Le bal donné à l'ambassade de France," *L'Illustration* (1 Mars 1856):147–8.

[18] Necdet Sakaoğlu, *Bu Mülkün Sultanları* (İstanbul: Oğlak Yayınevi, 1999), 495.

[19] Beyne, 148.

31 Louis Emile Pinel de Grandchamp. "Ball Held in French Embassy at Constantinople," *L'Illustration* (7 Fevrier 1856).

VI Istanbul: early encounters

One of the factors influencing the art of literature and painting in nineteenth-century Europe were the tours engaged in by artists. The increase in the number of railroads and steamships and the improvement in travel conditions allowed tourists to travel outside Europe and led to encounters, particularly by the intelligentsia, with the wealth of material culture in these lands. In this era, when Thomas Cook was arranging tours to the Holy Land and Egypt and the *Orient Express* was carrying wealthy passengers from Paris to İstanbul, the Orient no longer represented a fantasy for Western writers and artists.

The creation of a secure environment through the enactment of the Imperial Reforms edict and the improvement in lodging facilities for Westerners in İstanbul encouraged greater numbers of foreigners to visit the city. For numerous Western travelers, the Ottoman Empire constituted a stepping-off point. The 1854 edition of Murray's *Guide to Turkey* offered detailed information on the various routes that travelers to İstanbul might choose. Under the tutelage of the guidebooks in their hands, tourists were enabled to sightsee on their own and explore the environs of the Ottoman Palace, the chief monuments of Byzantine and Ottoman architecture, the Bosphorus, the sacred precinct of Eyüp on the Golden Horn, and the Princes' Islands. Much evidence survives, in the form of memoirs, letters, and travel diaries as well as drawings and oil paintings, to indicate that, besides those who traveled in connection with official duties or for purposes of trade, itinerant writers and artists who responded to the East with a sense of wonder were among those who visited the city in those years.

Nineteenth-century tourists came to İstanbul either by sea on a ship or overland by train. The founding of steamship lines in this era played an important role in increasing the numbers of passengers arriving in the East. Besides British, French, and Austro-Hungarian steamships, it was possible to see in the port of İstanbul sailing ships flying Ottoman and Greek flags and some Russian, Austro-Hungarian and Italian vessels. In the eighteenth and nineteenth centuries, İstanbul was a port where commercial ships frequently anchored, and, because travel by these ships was more economical, some Western travelers, including artists, preferred such ships.

Among the most prominent of the partners in the overseas trade conducted in the port of İstanbul were the French and the Austro-Hungarians. In nineteenth-century İstanbul, ship companies had a number of agents and trading factories in İstanbul. The first British steamship entered the port of İstanbul in 1827 and through to the end of the century ships underwent modifications and advances. Steamships, because of their scheduled regularity, soon became preferred over sailing ships by both merchants and travelers. In 1829, the British began to operate the Danube steamship company whose route originated at Galati on the Danube, crossed the Black Sea to Trabzon and thence to İstanbul, and from there to Izmir and Thessalonica.[1] In 1845, service to the Levant was commenced by the British P & O (Peninsular & Oriental) Company, with scheduled trips between Liverpool and İstanbul. The names of ships making regular scheduled trips to İstanbul, such as *Tagus, Iberia, Pottinger, Sultan, Erin, Euxine, Queen, Nautilus* and *Haddington*, appeared in the newspapers *Journal de Constantinople* and *La Turquie* from 1843 onwards.

France whose economic life was interrupted for a time by the Napoleonic wars began to reinvigorate its commercial connections in the Levant after 1815 from the port of Marseilles. Starting in 1837, the French firm Compagnie des Messageries Maritimes undertook regular postal service between Marseilles and İstanbul. In the 1850s, the weekly ferryboat service between Marseilles and İstanbul made stops in Genoa, Livorno, Civitavecchia, Naples, Messina, Piraeus, Izmir,

[1] Wolfgang Müller-Wiener, *Bizans'tan Osmanlı'ya İstanbul Limanı* (İstanbul: Tarih Vakfı Yurt Yayınları, 1998), 95.

ill. 32

PARIS·LYON·MÉDITERRANÉE
MESSAGERIES MARITIMES

PARIS en ORIENT
(Vià Marseille) Trains rapides et Express, Billets directs à prix réduits, simples, aller et retour et circulaires.

and İstanbul, a trip of roughly twelve days. A great number of French artists came to İstanbul by ship from Marseilles. With a document drawn up in his name by the French foreign ministry on 17 October 1855, the artist, Fabius Brest, left Marseilles for İstanbul on 25 October 1855 and on 26 July 1858 received permission from the French embassy at İstanbul to go to Trabzon.

Austro-Hungary began regular postal and passenger service between Trieste and İstanbul in 1837 with the Austria Lloyd Ship Agency. Trieste represented an important transit point for travelers to and from the Orient. Here, one could transfer from the train to an Austria Lloyd steamship. It made weekly stops at Venice, Ancôna, Corfu, Patras, Piraeus, Syros, Izmir, and İstanbul. In 1854, this firm published an album *Souvenirs de Constantinople* in French, German and English, especially for its international clientele; twenty plates from this album composed of twenty-eight engravings, without text, were based on photographs by James Robertson.[2]

In the years 1860–1, eight maritime companies operated scheduled trips to İstanbul. An Egyptian maritime firm established in the 1860s by the name of Aziziye-Mısriye, which later became Compagnie Egyptienne Khédivié, provided service to İstanbul from Alexandria.[3] After 1852, ferryboat service to İstanbul, both long and short distance, increased in frequency, and accidents in the harbor, dense with caiques and sailboats, sometimes occurred. The subject of a news-piece in *L'Illustration* of the same year was a collision at Seraglio Point between the French steamship *Le Cygne* with side wheels and the *Imperatrice*, a ship of the same type belonging to the Austria Lloyd Company.[4]

İstanbul was first and foremost a maritime city and the port established at the mouth of the Golden Horn constituted one of the most distinctive aspects of this Eastern city. Procedures in the İstanbul port were largely regularized. Each ship that entered had first to pass through quarantine. Foreign war vessels and ships carrying official visitors among their passengers would fire a salute as they passed before Topkapı Palace and the Ottoman batteries located at Tophane and in the Yalı Kiosk at Seraglio Point would answer the salute. The ships were permitted to anchor at certain specified places according to the type of ship and its size and cargo. Long-distance vessels would anchor along the shore in front of Galata

[2] B. A. Henisch and H. K. Henisch, "James Robertson," *Visions of the Ottoman Empire*, exhibition catalog (Edinburgh: Scottish National Portrait Gallery, 1994), 82.

[3] Müller-Wiener, *Bizans'tan*, 98–9.

[4] Müller-Wiener, *Bizans'tan*, 110.

32 Poster executed for Messageries Maritimes in Paris, 1909. Collection of Pierre de Gigord, Paris.

33 Jean-Baptiste Hilair. *General View of the Port and the city of Constantinople.* Engraving. *Voyage pittoresque de la Gréce,* (1822).

34 Passport belonging to Fabius Brest, 17 October 1855, Paris. Didier Vacher Collection, Les Oliviers La Celle.

[5] Müller-Wiener, *Bizans'tan,* 107, 143.

or before the Arsenal in the Golden Horn. But this situation was changed in 1836 by the erection of the first bridge between Azapkapı and Unkapanı. To reduce the burden on the main port area, ships remaining but a short time in İstanbul would anchor across the Bosphorus at Üsküdar, either next to the Tower of Leander or at the Harem landing stage.[5]

A panoramic view of all these many ships would reveal a particular concentration at the mouth of the harbor where sailboats, barges, and rafts, interspersed by long narrow caiques with slender prows, were busy providing mass transportation. Passenger and cargo ships from Northern Europe, the United States, the Far East, and all the ports of the Mediterranean and Black seas regularly moored in İstanbul harbor, producing a constant scene of animated and colorful activity. The port of İstanbul was perennially found attractive by Westerner travelers and artists on account of its commercial liveliness, its ethnic diversity, and striking life pattern. The natural beauty of the site of the city and the harbor added to its attractiveness.

Travelers arriving in İstanbul by seaway would first be made aware of their approach to the city while still at a distance on perceiving a silhouette

ill. 33

of minaret spires and lead-covered domes. Those coming from the direction of the Dardanelles Strait would enter the port after a glimpse of the suburbs of Kadıköy, the Princes' Islands, Moda Point, the lighthouse at Ahırkapı, Üsküdar and the Tower of Leander at the entrance to the Bosphorus, the mosques of Sultan Ahmed and St. Sophia, and Topkapı Palace. Those arriving from the Black Sea would skirt the beauties of the Bosphorus and the seaside mansions prior to anchoring before the district of Galata. The panorama of the city presented a breathtaking array of picturesque beauties.

Miss Pardoe, who came to the city by ship on 30 December 1835, describes her first encounter with İstanbul, which she had dreamed of for so long:

> The 'Queen of Cities' was before me, throned
> on her peopled hills, with the silver Bosphorus,
> garlanded with palaces flowing at her feet…
> as we swept along, the whole glory of her
> princely port burst upon our view! The gilded
> palace of Mahmoud [II]; with its glittering gate
> and overtopping cypresses, among which may
> be distinguished the buildings of the Seraî,
> were soon passed; behind us, in the distance,
> was Scutari, looking down in beauty on the
> channel, whose waves reflected the graceful
> outline of its tapering minarets, and shrouded
> themselves for an instant in the dark shadows
> of its funereal grove. Galata was beside us, with
> its mouldering walls and warlike memories;
> and the vessel trembled as the chain fell heavily
> into the water, and we anchored in the midst
> of the crowd of shipping that already thronged
> the harbour. On the opposite shore clustered
> the painted dwellings of Constantinople,
> the party-coloured garment of the "seven
> hills"… Every instant a graceful caique,
> with its long sharp prow and gilded ornaments,
> shot by the ship: now freighted with a bearded
> and turbaned Turk; squatting upon his carpet
> at the bottom of the boat, pipe in hand,
> and muffled closely in his furred pelisse,
> the very personification of luxurious idleness…
> Thus far, I could compare the port
> of Constantinople to nothing less delightful
> than poetry put into action. The novel
> character of the scenery—the ever-shifting,
> picturesque, and graceful groups—the constant
> flitting past of the fairy-like caiques—
> the strange tongues—the dark, wild eyes—

6 Miss [Julia] Pardoe, *The City of the Sultans; and Domestic Manners of the Turks, in 1836* (London: Henry Colburn, 1837), 1:1-5,8
7 Marcelle Tinayre, *Notes d'une voyageuse en Turquie* (Paris: Calmann Levy, n. d.), 5.
8 Behzat Üsdiken, "Beyoğlu'-nun Eski ve Ünlü Otelleri, I," *Tarih ve Toplum* (Eylül 1991): 36–7.

all conspired to rivet me to the deck, despite the bitterness of the weather…[6]

Ship and railroad companies to İstanbul would expressly coordinate their arrival times with the time of the sunset in order to insure that their passengers could enjoy this beautiful vista.[7] To the eyes of a Western artist, this first impression of the city was quite dramatic, and a number of travelers attempted to recapture this pictorial memory in writing, but only painters possessed the capacity to make their visual experience concrete.

The Orient Express, the Sirkeci train station, and the hotels

Despite the availability of sea transport, overland travel to İstanbul became the first preference on the invention at the end of the century of trains powered by steam and the expansion of railroads. The appearance of the *Orient Express* became the travel mode of choice by wealthy members of European society.

The first Orient Express departed Paris for İstanbul on 5 June 1883, but for the first few years this train did not go directly to İstanbul. Leaving from Paris, the train passed through Vienna, Budapest, Bucharest and, finally, Giurgiu, a small port city on the Danube River in Rumania. Here the passengers transferred to another train in Russe, at the opposite bank of the river and after a seven-hour journey to Varna, they proceeded to İstanbul by passenger ship and arrived at the destination in fifteen hours. The first Orient Express traveling directly to İstanbul left Paris on 1 June 1889. In 1894, the Orient Express came to İstanbul once a week via Bucharest-Varna and twice a week via Belgrade-Sofia. Starting in 1895, the Paris-Belgrade-Sofia-İstanbul line began to make the trip four times a week. The Orient Express furnished accommodations comparable to those of a luxury-class hotel.[8]

Unlike those coming by ship, those arriving in the city by train had no opportunity to glimpse the beauties of the city. Passengers abruptly found themselves in the city as soon as they had passed through the old Byzantine city walls at Yedikule, the first station within the city limits. Sirkeci Station, the last stop on the Orient Express was, simultaneously, the beginning of the Hejaz line and the last gate to the East from the West. Completed in 1889, Sirkeci Station, a work by the

German architect, Jachmund, possesses an Orientalist atmosphere, with a dominant Eastern eclectic style. The axial order and symmetry of the structure, which is peculiar to nineteenth-century eclecticism, also brings to the fore the shapes of Islamic architecture of the Mamlukes and of North Africa. Though this work occupied a symbolic status as the last stop of the Orient Express, it should also be noted that it sought a connection to the urban image of Muslim, Ottoman İstanbul.

As the numbers of travelers increased in nineteenth-century İstanbul, the growing number of hotels offered the possibility of lodging and certain amenities. The main district where Europeans coming to the city could obtain accommodations and hotels to meet their requirements was Pera. But, from the traveler's perspective, the most interesting places to lodge were on the Historical Peninsula where were concentrated the monuments of the city. It seems that by the second half of the century visitors also wanted to stay here. As a result of the growing interest in İstanbul, touristic guides were prepared and began to be issued for those who wanted to visit the old monuments of the city. The oldest among these are F. Lacroix's *Guide de voyageur à Constantinople et dans ses environs*, printed in Paris in 1839, and *Petit guide du voyageur dans l'interieur de Constantinople* by Alexandre Timoni, published in 1841.[9] Another of the guidebooks of the period and one in the series, *Guide–Joanne*, is *Itinéraire descriptif, historique et archéologique*, written by Adolphe and Emile Isambert and appearing in 1861, in which are listed the good quality hotels in Pera but which additionally notes that for those who might wish to lodge in the environs of the Hippodrome one could spend the night in a Ottoman home, where an avariciousness was exhibited not unlike that found in Damascus and among the Europeans in Pera.[10]

Hotels at which foreigners could stay were clustered in the districts of Galata and Pera. Foreigners, who had formerly lodged in rooming houses now, after the 1840s, found it possible to stay in facilities offering comfort at a level comparable to that in Europe. One of the first of such hotels was the Hôtel des Quatre Nations, located near the church of St. Georges in Galata. Hôtel d'Angleterre, established in 1841 in Pera by M. Missirie, a Levantine, was the first hotel to possess comfort and order in the Western sense. A select, local crowd from Pera seems to have met here for

the concerts and balls held in its halls. For their foreign guests, the hotels prepared illustrated albums about the city. From a news report appearing in *Journal de Constantinople* (19 June 1852), we learn that Missirie, known as a generous benefactor of art, had had lithographs prepared at his own expense by Sabatier in Paris from drawings of the Bosphorus panorama by Guiseppe Schranz (1803–after 1853). Bound as an album titled *Panorama du Bosphore*, these prints were presented by M.Missirie to Sultan Abdülmecid. The sultan complimented him and as a sign of his pleasure, through the mediation of the British ambassador, sent him a cigarette box studded with brilliants.

A notice that Schranz' panorama could be purchased at both Hôtel d'Angleterre and at Christich, opposite the theater, also appeared in the same newspaper.[11] Apparently serving many years as one of the most modern and comfortable accommodations in the city, the Hôtel d'Angleterre relocated in 1854 to the former Prussian Palace on Dörtyol Street, whose view included the harbor at the entrance to the Bosphorus.[12] Hôtel de Byzance, opening in 1849, became one of the first well-known hotels of Pera. Located in Petit-Champs des Morts, it became preferred because of its amenities, its view and, particularly, its masonry construction, which furnished security in case of fire.[13] Edmondo De Amicis, who visited İstanbul in 1874, notes that he stayed at this hotel.[14] Hôtel de Byzance moved in 1875 to Grand Rue de Pera, opposite the Dutch embassy.[15]

The hotels in Pera assisted their guests by their provision of guides. Théophile Gautier, who came to İstanbul during the reign of Sultan Abdülmecid and stayed at Hôtel de Byzance, states that the hotel interpreters helped foreign travelers about the Court ceremonials.[16] Henri Blanc, in İstanbul during the spring and summer months of 1854, indicates in his journal that Hôtel Europe in Pera secured a rescript granting permission to visit the principal monuments of the city. With this document in hand, a group composed of nearly twenty British and Spanish military officers and several French travelers accompanied by an interpreter and a guard was enabled to visit Topkapı Palace.[17] Based on the notices appearing in daily newspapers published in French in İstanbul, like *Journal de Constantinople*, *La Turquie*, and *Le Moniteur Oriental*, it

[9] Semavi Eyice, "İstanbul'un İlk Turistik Rehberlerinden Timoni'nin Rehberi," *Tarih ve Toplum* (Temmuz 1989): 13.

[10] Willy Sperco, *Istanbul paysage littéraire* (Paris: La nef de Paris, 1955), 36ff; Adolphe and Emile Isambert, *Itineraire Descriptif, Historique et Archeologique ee L'orient* (Paris: L. Hachette, 1861).

[11] *Journal De Constantinople* (19 Juin 1852).

[12] Nur Akın, *19. Yüzyılın İkinci Yarısında Galata ve Pera* (İstanbul: Literatür, 1998), 247.

[13] Akın, 246–8.

[14] Edmondo De Amicis, *Constantinople* (Philadelphia : Henry T.Coates, 1896) 1:286.

[15] Üsdiken, "Beyoğlu'nun Eski ve Ünlü Otelleri, V," *Tarih ve Toplum* (Mart 1992): 29.

[16] Théophile Gautier, *Constantinople en 1852* (Istanbul: İsis, 1990), 176.

[17] Henri Blanc, *Journal de mon voyage* (Marseille: Marius Olive, 1880), 55.

seems that the number of hotels offering comfort and luxury had increased in number by the second half of the nineteenth century. These hotels promoted tourism by providing Europeans not only with familiar amenities, such as fully equipped kitchens, but also by supplying guides who knew European languages and arranging masked balls and concerts.

The most widely recognized hotel in Pera, both in terms of its architectural features and its furnishings, was Pera Palace, which opened in 1895. Pera Palace, part of the Compagnie Internationale des Grands Hôtels, was projected to lodge travelers coming to İstanbul with tours organized by Wagons-Lits on the *Orient Express*; and, in fact, the great majority of the participants in these tours stayed at Pera Palace. Designed by Alexandre Vallauri, a leading architect of the period, and Henri Duray, an architect with the firm of Compagnie Internationale des Grands Hôtels, Pera Palace was opened on Kabristan Street on 1 February 1895.[18] The interior decoration conforming to the taste of the era and the expectations of the guests, was in Orientalist style. The office of Thomas Cook, famed for its Eastern tours and travelers service, was located opposite the hotel on the corner, next to the Sheikh apartment building.[19] During this same period, Tarabya Summer Palace Hotel on the Bosphorus, which belonged to the same firm, represented one of the most exclusive summering spots in İstanbul.

ill. 35

[18] Akın, 252–4.

[19] Üsdiken, "Beyoğlu'nun Eski ve Ünlü Otelleri, II: Pera Palas," *Tarih ve Toplum* (Kasım 1991): 27.

35 Baggage label, Pera Palace Hotel, ca. 1902. Collection of Pierre de Gigord, Paris.

VII Western artists and their ateliers in Istanbul

Western artists in İstanbul in the nineteenth century can be divided into three groups. Comprising the first group are those artists who were invited by the Court or whose existence was made known to the Court through an ambassador. The second group was composed of itinerant artists who made their way to İstanbul on their own. Residing in İstanbul for an extended period, these itinerant Europeans set up ateliers and typically sold painted scenes of İstanbul, although some were privileged to paint the portraits of Ottoman elite. Nonetheless, the principal objective of the members of this second group was entry into the exhibitions in Paris and London and the European art market. Making up the third group were the leading artists of Europe who sojourned but briefly in İstanbul and then returned to their native countries.

Producing paintings for the art markets of the West, these artists tended to conceive their compositions with an eye toward the tastes and preferences of their future customers—European bourgeoisie, industrialists, and bankers and ship owners who were enjoying at the time an ever-increasing level of prosperity. Paintings of Orientalist subjects in scenes of exoticism, eroticism, and violence were created for these new customers, the majority of whom preferred contemporary art, which provided an exciting avenue of release from their own society that was bound to a tradition whose highest values were work and duty. Hence, after the 1850s, an Orientalist period can generally be encountered at some point in the evolution of the career path of even the most renowned artists. But the fact that Orientalist paintings were so popular and that the Orientalist art market was active to this degree, in a sense, served to bring about its end: the turning to this subject by a great many second-rate artists led to a decline in the quality of Orientalist art, which aroused a negative reaction on the part of the buyers. Orientalist paintings became plain and unin-

[1] Pierre Paget, "Le Salon de 1889," *L'Illustration* (27 Avril 1889).

spiring. For instance, Pierre Paget states in his review of the 1889 Paris Salon exhibition that

> [f]ormerly, it was the fashion to devote a special article in every Salon exhibition review to the Eastern painters; though their numbers have not diminished, nonetheless, no longer are we blessed with the likes of a Delacroix or a Decamps. Benjamin Constant is unable to fill their shoes; not because he lacks a genuine talent—for he is especially capable of employing his professional capacities—but this is precisely what stands in the way of our full admiration: simple mastery has gained precedence in his work, and its studio quality is all too perceptible.[1]

The very popularity of Orientalism rendered nineteenth-century İstanbul very attractive to the West as its gateway to the East. İstanbul served as the point of embarkation of the Eastern tour joined by a great many Western artists, and a great many artists first encountered the mysterious atmosphere of the East on their entrance into the İstanbul harbor. In the second half of the nineteenth century, numerous Western travelers who came to İstanbul, like Baronne de Fontmagne, Gerard de Nerval, and Edmondo De Amicis, mention frequently in their memoirs the names of European artists present in İstanbul in the same period.

Most of the Western artists, who came to İstanbul in the nineteenth century resided in Pera, the most Europeanized district, and some of them set up housekeeping and their studios in districts, like Teşvikiye or Şişli, which began to modernize during the reign of Abdülaziz. Those residing in Pera in connection with their duties and associations were, as in the eighteenth century, guests at the embassies, while the others stayed in rooming houses or in houses that they rented on their own. Western artists, despite their having established residence in the modern districts, chose their subjects from the traditional neighborhoods of İstanbul, which conformed to the Orientalist style of their drawings and paintings.

In the eighteenth century, the artists and draftsmen under the protection of the embassies by whom they had been invited generally resided in embassy quarters in Pera; moreover, their studios in which they executed paintings of costumes, portraits, and landscapes were also either in these buildings or in their proximity.

For those artists who wished only to draw sketches and have them subsequently reproduced in Paris or London, a room reserved for them in the embassy was perhaps sufficient. But for artists who worked in oils, like Jean-Baptiste Van Mour, a separate workspace was clearly a requisite. Van Mour, known for his Ottoman paintings and who was awarded by Louis XIV on 27 November 1725 the title of the "Painter in Ordinary to the King in the East," delineated in his atelier scenes of ambassadors being received by the sultan; land- and seascapes of the Bosphorus and İstanbul; historical events of the Tulip Period, such as the rebellion of Patrona Halil; and scenes of daily life in the city; in addition to portraits of the İstanbul diplomatic corps.

Van Mour established relations with high-ranking Ottomans, participated in Ottoman life, and was present at the imperial reception ceremonies with officials, like Nevşehirli Damad İbrahim Pasha. Van Mour's studio in İstanbul, acquiring ever-increasing renown, became a favorite haunt for Court intimates, ambassadors, embassy staff, and foreign travelers. Most of these visitors came to see him at work in his studio, some bought a souvenir painting, some commissioned paintings, or, as with Lady Mary Montagu and the Dutch ambassador, Calkoen, had themselves portrayed in Ottoman costume.[2]

In later periods, paintings by Van Mour—broad in perspective and didactic in tone—of ceremonials, of audiences with the sultan, or of historical content were taken as models by his colleagues, both in regard to the subject and the composition. Furthermore, the artist's renderings of scenes set in Topkapı Palace and of costumes, the Imperial Harem, an excursion spot, or whirling dervish rituals, came to constitute prototypes.

The dimensions (roughly 90 x 120 cm) of his paintings of audience ceremonials and the number of paintings he executed strongly suggest the existence of a well-equipped studio. The artist

died on January 1737 in the district of Galata. Since it is known that following the death of the artist, his benefactors, Cornelis Calkoen and Gustaf Celsing, divided among themselves certain studies found in his atelier and purchased them, we may infer that Van Mour possessed a studio of his own outside the compound of the French Embassy. Van Luttervelt, who has examined the Van Mour painting collection in the Amsterdam Rijksmuseum, is of the opinion that local artists were employed in the artist's studio under his direction and that the posthumous works, which bear a close resemblance to his works, were executed in this atelier.[3] In the study titled *The 'Turkish' Paintings by Van Mour and His School*, Van Luttervelt asserts that a synthesis occurred of the earlier works by the artist and those he later produced in İstanbul, and that, after his death, local Greeks and Armenians founded an anonymous school in terms of subject and technique. Van Mour's works served as exemplars for artists in the eighteenth century, not only in İstanbul but also in Izmir, and in Venice, Sweden, Germany, England, and Holland.[4]

Three paintings in the Palazzio Venezia Collection of the Italian General Consulate in İstanbul—*The Sultan's Reception of an Ambassador* (1757), *Reception of a European Ambassador: Repast Offered by the Grand Vizier in the Public Council Hall*, and *The Ambassador Watching the Exit of Troops from the Palace after an Audience with the Sultan* —may be attributed to artists of the Van Mour studio (thought to have been the earliest artist's studio in Pera), who continued to work in his style after the artist's death in 1737.

The Swiss artist, Jean-Etienne Liotard, who accompanied Sir William Ponsonby, to İstanbul, is one of the rare painters who happened to depict the room in which he lodged in the city. Though it is unknown in which district he resided, considering the conditions of the period, he probably lived in the vicinity of Pera and Galata districts.[5] Liotard, who arrived in the East—that is, the Greek Archipelago and Izmir—in 1737, arrived in İstanbul in 1738 and left for Vienna in 1743. The drawings and paintings rendered by him during this first trip to the East, resulted in his receiving the appellation of *Peintre Turc*. Living in İstanbul for five years, the artist executed numerous engravings from drawings with Eastern subjects. The greater proportion of his paintings depict Ottoman women, daily life and costume, one of his works

---

[2] Boppe, 31.

[3] *Jean Baptiste*, 10.

[4] R. van Luttervelt, *De "Turkse" Schilderijen van J. B. Van Mour en zijn school* (Istanbul, 1958), 45.

[5] Liotard executed a charcoal sketch of his room in Istanbul. The room is bare except for a divan before the window with iron grating. The drawing is preserved in a cabinet of drawings in the Museum of Art and History in Geneva.

36 School of Van Mour. *The Sultan's Reception of an Ambassador*, 1757. Oil on canvas. 104 x 128 cm. Collection of Palazzio Venezia, İstanbul.

37 School of Van Mour. *Reception of a European Ambassador: Repast Offered by Grand Vizier in the Public Council Hall*, 1757. Oil on canvas. 104 x 128 cm. Collection of Palazzio Venezia, İstanbul.

38 School of Van Mour. *The Ambassador Watching the Exit of the Troops from the Palace, after his Audience with the Sultan,* 1757. Oil on canvas. 108 ×130 cm. Collection of Palazzio Venezia, İstanbul.

is a portrait of Comte de Bonneval (Humbaracı Ahmed Pasha). His compositions stand as witnesses to the fact that a European artist could easily enter the homes of Ottomans of high rank and paint portraits of them and their family. Residing for a time in Izmir, the artist let his beard grow and appeared in public dressed in Ottoman costume.

During the reign of Abdülhamid I, Louis-François Cassas, a renowned itinerant painter and draftsman of the era and who accompanied the French ambassador, Comte de Choiseul-Gouffier, to İstanbul in 1784, too, was provided accommodations in the French Embassy, Palais de France. After dwelling in the city two months, the artist embarked on a journey, rich and full of discovery, through parts of the empire, and returned to İstanbul on 9 January 1786 with approximately two hundred and fifty drawings in hand. He quickly became the focus of interest by the French and other foreigners interested in these subjects. Sojourning in İstanbul from January 1786 to early February 1787—during which time, as documented by his letters and diary, the artist, by special permission of the sultan, visited the mosques of St. Sophia, Süleymaniye, and Sultan Ahmed in İstanbul—Cassas received an invitation to dinner in the Imperial Kavak Palace, and in March, 1786 was received with Choiseul-Gouffier in Topkapı Palace by Grand Vizier Yusuf Pasha. During this same interval, he attended, among other things, a picnic at Fener Bahçe, dinners, balls, and concerts at various embassies in Pera.[6]

Coming to İstanbul in 1784, Antoine-Ignace Melling took up residence in Pera. One drawing, now in a private collection, that Melling executed of a view of the Bosphorus in pencil and pen and ink is inscribed the words: "A view from my window in Pera."[7] To earn a living, the artist, once he had settled in the city, gave art lessons to members of European families and the children of diplomats, and he began to receive commissions for paintings from diplomatic circles. Among those to whom Melling gave lessons were the children of the Dutch ambassador Van Dedem van de Gelder.[8]

Throughout the nineteenth century, the majority of the European artists coming to İstanbul lived in Pera, painted in their studios here, and gave art lessons. In 1837, Bartlett's atelier in Pera became a gathering place for foreign and local artists.[9] It may be noted that well-known artists visiting the city at this time were welcomed at the embassies. Horace Vernet, who arrived in İstanbul in February 1840

from Damascus via Izmir, was a guest in the French embassy. Prevented by the cold, wet winter conditions from moving about the city, the artist accounted İstanbul insufficiently picturesque when compared with Damascus and states openly in his letters that he preferred Arabs to Turks. Vernet returned to France via Malta. The artist, whose paintings delineated life in large, Arab tents, neglected to make any study of İstanbul.

Amadeo Preziosi of Malta, who came to İstanbul in late 1842 and whose days were ended in the same city in 1882, is mentioned in the memoirs of Paul Eudel as having a studio located in Pera. The writer notes that, on his way back to his hotel —the Hôtel de Byzance on Pera Avenue—after observing an Easter celebration that took place in Elmadağ valley, he paid a visit to Preziosi's atelier. Paul Eudel, in whose opinion Preziosi was one of the most masterly artists in the empire, states that the artist had prepared a fascinating album in water color depicting porters, Imperial Harem eunuchs, confectioners, harem interiors, and coffeehouses, along with vivid market scenes, and all the diverse types of Ottoman figures. The writer further informs us that Preziosi, whose studio contained carpets with needlework, small tables ornamented with inlaid mother-of-pearl, illuminated *Korans*, and a very rich collection of janissary weapons and firearms, was a man of taste and that princes who passed through İstanbul employed him as a guide in making their purchases and placing custom orders.[10] Preziosi's atelier was located at 28 Yeni Çarşı Street in Pera from 1868 to 1881.[11]

During the reign of Abdülaziz, Pierre Désiré Guillemet (1827–78), French by birth but who became a long-term resident of İstanbul, opened in 1874 a school called the Academy of Drawing and Painting in Pera on the most picturesque and busy avenue of Kalyoncu Kulluğu. It is known that Guillemet and his wife had another studio at 60 Hammalbaşı Street. The studio was open every day except Sunday, from eight in the morning to five in the evening, with Tuesday and Saturday reserved for females only, and, according to the notices and articles in the newspapers, information on requirements and registration was available every day from noon to three in the afternoon.[12] This first art school of İstanbul was opened with the support of Sultan Abdülaziz. Armenians and several Levantines eagerly made their registrations. Among its first students were Sarkis Direnyan, who had lived for many years in

6 M. Bohusz, R. Chevallier, A. Gilet, and P. Pinon, *Louis–François Cassas 1756–1827: Im Banne der Sphinx* (Mainz am Rhein: Philipp von Zabern, 1994), 114.

7 Boppe, 246.

8 Perot, 8.

9 Esin Atıl, "The Ottoman World in the Nineteenth Century," *Voyages and Visions: Nineteenth Century European Images of the Middle East from the Victoria and Albert Museum* (Washington: Smithsonian Institution, 1996), 38.

10 Paul Eudel, *Constantinople, Smyrne et Athènes: journal de voyage* (Paris: Dentu, 1885), 162–3.

11 *Annuaire almanach du commerce* (1868–1881).

12 *L'Orient Illustré* (16 Mai 1874): 125.

Paris, Bedan, an Armenian doctor's son; Nişanciyan; Civanyan, a well-known tenor of Pera and his brother, the junior Civanyan, Schultz of the Alsace, Coppens of Belgium, and Zolos, a Greek. At the end of the first year, three Muslim Turks were registered in the school, which specialized in still lives and landscapes. The Guillemets' students entered their work in the large painting exhibition mounted by Şeker Ahmed Pasha, which was held in the Municipal Theater in Petit-Champs in 1877. Among the Orientalists participating in this exhibition were Preziosi, Palmieri, and Luigi Acquarone (1800-96); yet, among the two hundred and fifty canvases in the exhibition only thirty were Orientalist in subject.[13]

Another atelier was established at 8 Linardi Street (now Eski Çiçekçi Street) by the artist Moretti, who rendered a Bosphorus landscape for Sultan Abdülaziz. Here, he tutored in drawing and oil painting[14] and welcomed visits by art lovers.[15] On 12 August 1887, an announcement appeared in the newspaper La Turquie stating that Moretti had completed five landscapes and seascapes and that those wishing to view and purchase them should apply to the newspaper office.[16]

It is, nevertheless, clear that opportunities were limited for Western artists in residence to earn a living through the sale of their pictures in the newly emerging artistic milieu of nineteenth-century İstanbul. These artists, continuing a practice current since the eighteenth century, executed paintings for the members of the embassy of European countries and their relatives and friends, and hoped to receive a commission from the Ottoman Court and, thereby, be granted a generous reward from the sultan; in point of fact, some of them actually managed to render the portraits of progressive, reform-minded pashas. Rudolf Ernst (1854–1932), renowned both for his Orientalist works and his fine portraits, received quite a few portrait commissions after coming to İstanbul. One of these came in 1891 from the Treasurer of the Sultan's Privy Purse (*Hazine-i Hassa Nazırı*), Agop Pasha.[17]

To secure an income, some artists gave private art lessons or, after the founding of the Imperial School of Fine Arts (*Sanayi-i Nefise Mektebi*) in 1883, obtained an appointment as an instructor. Executing religious paintings for churches in İstanbul also constituted a remunerative avenue for artists. Gérard de Nerval in his book titled *The Women of Cairo* mentions that "At Pera I had

rediscovered one of my oldest friends. He was a French painter, and for three years he had lived in a magnificent style on the proceeds of his portraits and paintings—a proof that Constantinople is not at variance with the Muses as people would seem to believe."[18] Some time later when Nerval went to pay a visit to this friend, they told him that he had moved to the house of an Armenian family in Kuruçeşme who had commissioned a painting from him. Nerval states that this family possessed a considerable standing among the Armenians of the city and that, on reaching the house of this family acting as a benefactor of French art, he found his friend in a magnificent hall furnished in an Oriental style resembling that of the Turkish coffeehouse in Boulevard du Temple in Paris. Among those present in the hall examining the designs for a fresco proposed by the artist were several attachés of the French embassy, a Belgian prince, and the vaivode of Transylvania. Afterwards, they entered a chapel where the major portion of the decoration was on display. The entire wall behind the high altar was covered by a great fresco representing *The Adoration of the Magi*. The compositions to flank either side had been sketched in. The family who had commissioned this work, having several winter and summer residences, had vacated the house, leaving the servants and horses also at the artist's disposal.[19]

ill. 39

---

[13] Adolphe Thalasso, "Les origines de la peinture Turque," *L'art et les artistes* (Octobre, 1907): 366–7.

[14] *La Turquie* (22 Novembre 1873).

[15] *La Turquie* (8 Janvier 1874).

[16] *La Turquie* (12 Août 1874).

[17] *Thieme–Becker, 1999* ed.

[18] Gérard de Nerval, *The Women of Cairo* (London: Routledge,1929), 2: 161.

[19] Nerval, *The Women*, 2: 231.

[20] *Annuaire almanach du commerce et de l'industrie* (Constantinople: Bureaux de l'administration, 1880), 202.

[21] *Annuaire almanach du commerce et de l'industrie, de l'administration et de la magistrature* (Constantinople: Bureaux de l'administration, 1881), 351.

[22] *Annuaire oriental (ancien indicateur oriental) du commerce* (Constantinople: Bureaux de l'administration, 1893–4), 589.

[23] Cezar, *Sanatta*, 153.

Galata and Pera were districts of İstanbul where the workshops of artists, draftsmen, and theater set designers, and artisans could all be found. According to *Annuaire almanach du commerce* and *Annuaire oriental du commerce*, published between the years 1868 and 1913, Muslim artists like Hamdi Kenan Bey, Şevket Bey, Adil Bey, Fahri Bey, and Ahmed Ziya Bey also had studios here. In Pera, European artists worked together with both the non-Muslim artists of Pera, like Civanyan, Assadour, Antranik, Nişanyan, Onnik Pulcuyan, and Kalfayan, and the Muslim artists.

Luigi Acquarone, arriving in İstanbul in 1841 and designated Court Artist (1881–96) by Abdülhamid II, possessed a studio at 39 Tepebaşı Street in Pera in 1880,[20] in Maison Meunier on Linardi Street in 1881,[21] and at 31 Ağa Hamam Street in 1894. At this same time, the miniature painter, Joseph Manas, worked in a studio at 34 Yağhane Street,[22] and Therenzio Consoli, about whom we learn that he had presented an oil painting to Abdülaziz portraying a battle in the Veneto-Ottoman War of 1659, had an atelier at 63 Kabristan Street in Pera in 1880.[23] The studio of Italian artist, Leonardo de Mango (1843-1930), was located on Minare Street in 1894 and moved to 11 Galata Saray Arcade in 1912.[24] In the early twentieth century, Pietro Bello (1837–1909) had a studio in the suburb of Yeşilköy. In 1881, Giovanni Brindesi was active at 6 Yeni Çarşı Street, and Preziosi was on the same street at number 28. Preziosi lived at 37 İstanbul Avenue in Yeşilköy, which also boasted an atelier. Around this time, Pierre Guès, employed as a draftsman in the technical office of the Sixth District, set up an atelier at 12 Sümbül Street.[25]

Fausto Zonaro (1854-1929), who came to know and love İstanbul through the book titled *Constantinopoli*, written by Edmondo De Amicis and illustrated by Cesare Biseo (1843–1909), and his wife, Elisa, left Venice for İstanbul in early 1891, and at first settled in a wooden house located in the vicinity of Taksim. Zonaro, believing that before one could transfer the atmosphere of İstanbul to canvas one had to enter into the spirit of the Ottoman Empire, chose to live in this small wooden house, which he also used as an atelier. The paintings executed by Zonaro during this period, when he would set up his easel in the central districts of the city, represent the most interesting examples of his artistic output. İstanbul became the place where his artistic talent

39
▼

39 Moerman. *An Artist*, 1870. Oil on canvas. 38.5 x 29 cm. Private Collection, İstanbul.

[24] *Annuaire oriental: commerce, industrie, administration, magistrature de l'Empire ottoman* (Constantinople: The Annuaire Oriental Ltd.,1912) 983.

[25] *Annuaire almanach de commerce de l'industrie, de l'administration et de la magistrature* (Constantinople: Bureaux de l'administration, 1881), 351.

40 G. Zanaro. *Pierre Loti in an Artist's Studio
in Pera*, late 19th c. Oil on canvas.
65 x 81 cm. Private Collection, İstanbul.

blossomed and flourished and the place where his art was acclaimed.

In order to earn a living, the artist began by painting male heads covered by a red fez or a green turban, veiled women, and scenes of İstanbul with views of the Galata Bridge and the Golden Horn and displaying them for sale in the window of a shop in Pera. In keeping with the spirit of the period, the artist, having made the acquaintance of certain French artists when living in Paris, executed the scenes in the open air. One day, however, when he had set up his easel in a square of İstanbul and started to work, he was apprehended by a policeman and warned that it was prohibited to make paintings: he was set free on condition that he not repeat this action. Zonaro, who now became closely watched, resorted to taking notes and making sketches while walking, with officers and soldiery trailing him. Small paintings executed from nature by the artist in this period were warmly received, and his name became known among both non-Muslim families in Pera and certain Muslim circles eager to adopt a European life style. Zonaro, supported and protected by foreign embassies, offered art lessons in the Russian embassy and was much sought after even though his fees were high.[26] An article by Kevork Pamukciyan indicates that the young daughters of two Ottoman pashas connected with Yıldız Palace worked in his atelier. These young ladies Celile, the daughter of the Pole, Enver Pasha, an aide-de-camp to Sultan Abdülhamid II, and Mihri (Müşfik), the daughter of the minister of health, Doctor Mehmed Rasim Pasha, were to become the first female Ottoman painters.[27]

Zonaro, receiving in 1896 the title of "Artist to the Sultan," was allocated a house in Akaretler in the district of Beşiktaş in 1898. At the command of Abdülhamid II, the artist's home was furnished and a painting studio was established, completely equipped with whatever supplies might be desired by the artist.[28] It became known that Zonaro worked in his studio in the mornings, reserving the afternoons for personal visitors, and that whoever knocked on his door would be greeted by a pleasant smile. In his house in Akaretler, one great hall was given over to paintings of executed in Naples and Venice. In a small hall on the right were located sketches, water colors and small-scale works of Eastern themes while that on the left was devoted to portraits—those of his own family as well as those commissioned. At the rear

in a large hall were housed landscapes inspired by Yıldız Park and paintings of various Eastern characters; like Georgians, Circassians, and Gypsies. Covering the four walls of one large and spacious chamber of the house were preliminary studies for a painting titled *The Assault*. On the story above was a very large, glassed-in studio. The studio, extending the whole of the top floor and was constructed by the order of Abdülhamid II, contained a random arrangement of easels and sculpture stands amidst draped fabrics, costumes, chests, mannequins, and incomplete canvases. Here, Zonaro would work until dawn, producing such works as *There's a Fire*, *The Bath*, and *The "Howling" Rifaî Dervishes*. Ambassadors, archbishops, members of European royal families, Ottoman ministers of state, pashas, and any and all personages of note passing through İstanbul were guests and clients of this atelier.[29] Situated at the foot of Akaretler Hill, Zonaro's home and studio in the large three-story building served as the space for his first individual show in 1898. Based on an article by Rafayel Şişmanyan in the Armenian weekly art magazine *Luys* (12 April 1908), published in İstanbul by Pamukciyan, the entrance hall of Zonaro's house was furnished in Eastern fashion. The five halls and side chambers on the upper story, all receiving natural light and—holding some two hundred paintings, both small and large-scale, in oils, water colors, and pastels—gave the impression of a perfect art museum. Şişmanyan reveals that the artist, who had produced more than a thousand works devoted to Ottoman life, often drank coffee and smoked a narghile with the sitters while executing their likenesses and studying them carefully.[30]

Newly developed neighborhoods of the city, like Beşiktaş, witnessed the settlement of European artists, such as Zonaro in Akaretler, or *Akaret-i Seniyye*, in the late nineteenth and early twentieth centuries. Salvatore Valeri (1856–1946), arriving in the city in the early 1880s, was appointed instructor in the oil painting studio of the Imperial School of Fine Arts, founded by Osman Hamdi Bey, where he served from March 1883 to August 1915. Coming to İstanbul in the early twentieth century, the Italian writer, Angiolo Mori, states that the artist possessed a studio in the district of Şişli. The 1893–4 edition of *Annuaire oriental du commerce* indicates that Valeri's atelier was on Büyükdere Avenue in Şişli. Mori reports that Valeri was at work on a painting

[26] Caroline Juler, *Les Orientalistes de l'école italienne* (Paris: ACR, 1987), 280.

[27] Kevork Pamukciyan, "Fausto Zonaro'nun Bilinmeyen Bazı Tabloları," *Tarih ve Toplum* (Ağustos 1987): 24–5.

[28] Adolphe Thalasso, "Fausto Zonaro peintre de S.M.I. le Sultan," *Figaro Illustré* (1907): 29

[29] Thalasso, "Fausto, " 29–30.

[30] Pamukciyan, "Fausto," 24–30.

in vivid but light colors whose subject was a caravan in the desert[31] and that the studio contained a great many studies of female figures and animal heads.[32] The artist, Naciye Neyyal (1875-1960), recalls in her memoirs that Valeri, her painting teacher, was a very talented artist and that his house in Şişli, especially his studio had been designed by himself. The walls of his studio, reportedly on the top floor, were lined with valuable paintings, side by side or stacked one on top of the other. Among these works and capturing Naciye Neyyal's attention was one very large painting representing a caravan in the desert. Valeri started this work in Egypt and completed it in İstanbul. As Naciye Neyyal reports the shadow of the halter on the neck of the lead camel has fallen across the sand as the train wends its way through the desert, and the effect was so realistic that she felt she was an actual observer. The writer also states that Valeri wanted to employ as models the Gypsies who at that time were numerous in the district.[33]

One other artist enjoying a studio was Théophile Console, a portrait artist. Console, whose studio, open to visitors, was located in the district of Tekke, painted a portrait of a dervish lodge sheikh named Kudretullah, which, we learn from a newspaper notice, was much admired.[34] The Pole, Josef Warnia Zarzecki (1850–?), an oil painting instructor at the Imperial School of Fine Arts, also had a studio in Tekke.[35]

Another news piece from 1893 informs us that the artist, Meyer Elbing, was then in İstanbul with a studio, that he rendered portraits and figural compositions, and that he had executed a painting of "a young Romanian girl, wearing a robe, about to enter the bath and whose shoulders are partly exposed," and that this painting along with others was on display in the store Maison Leduc.[36] In the last quarter of the nineteenth century, art exhibitions were opened in a number of places in Pera— hotels, shops, and photography studios—such as the Pera Palace Hotel, the studio of the Abdullah Frères, Maison Leduc, Maison Rosenthal, and Maison Baker. Like many others of his Western colleagues, the French artist, François Prieur-Bardin (1870–1939), who came to İstanbul as a tourist and stayed until 1901, exhibited paintings in the shops of Pera. The artist opened individual shows in stores named Gülmez Brothers, Maison Baker, Viskonti, and Stefano Nouveau Bazaar and participated in a joint exhibition in Hacopulo Arcade.

[31] A painting by Valeri with this title (*La Carovana nel deserto*) is in the collection of Museo Africano in Rome.

[32] Angielo Mori, *Gli İtaliani a Constantinopoli* (Modena: Soliani, 1906), 241–2.

[33] Fatma Rezan Hürmen, ed., *Ressam Naciye Neyyal'ın Mutlakiyet Meşrutiyet ve Cumhuriyet Hatıraları* (İstanbul: Pınar, 2000), 506.

[34] *La Turquie* (7 Fev. 1872). The area whose name is given as "Tekke" was a neighborhood in the vicinity of the Galata Mevlevi Tekkesi.

[35] *Annuaire oriental (ancien indicateur oriental) du commerce* (Constantinople: Bureaux de l'administration, 1893–4), 58.

[36] *Le Moniteur Oriental* (9 Oct. 1893 and 21 Oct. 1893).

During this period, a number of Orientalist artists relied on photographs for their oil paintings. Most of the studios where these photographs were taken were in Pera—one of which was Atelier Phebus , which also executed oil paintings. The first studio established by Bogos Tarkulyan—also known as Febüs Efendi—was located at the site of the Mısır apartment building on Pera Avenue. When this burnt in a fire, he moved to number 82 on the same avenue. As a personality, Bogos Tarkulyan attracted notice both within the Court circles and the art world.[37]

In the photograph studio opened by the Swede, Guillaume Berggren, in the early 1870s on the corner of Piremeci Street at number 414, vistas of İstanbul, street scenes, and a variety of human figures were documented. The most well known photographic studio of the period was that of the Abdullah Frères, whose photography shop occupied several locations on Pera Avenue between 1860 and 1899. Their last location was on the same avenue, near the Russian embassy.[38] In the studio opened in 1857 by Pascal Sébah, contemporary polyethnic Ottomans were photographed in their native costumes. The studio took the name Sébah Joailler in 1888, with the addition of Policarpe Joaillier, and work was continued at 346 Pera Avenue. An article appearing in *L'Orient Illustré* on 13 February 1875 notes that Sébah Joailler possessed a very fine collection of artworks, shown in the halls of their photography studio, and, in particular, that this studio was successful in the making of hand colored, glossy portraits in relief and had become popular place with gentle folk. The Sébah Joailler studio, whose pictures were employed by Osman Hamdi Bey for his paintings, took over in 1899 the location formerly belonging to Abdullah Frères.[39]

In the late nineteenth and early twentieth centuries, İstanbul possessed an art scene more active than has been presumed. The press showed an interest in art and the foreign Orientalist painters who stayed in the city permanently or for short periods kept the ties alive with the Western world of art. Pera, on account of its exhibitions and a variety of artistic activities appealing to Westerners, became in the 1870s and later a lively center, and it provided an artistic milieu for the Muslim Ottoman artists who were just beginning to emerge. The Levantines who were settled in Pera, the non-Muslims, and the European Orientalist artists in transit—all, in a sense, relied on the Ottoman Court as a benefactor while they carried out their artistic activities. As a matter of fact, some of these artists had submitted works to the Court or had worked for the Court. The viability of Pera as a focal point of art in this era may be regarded as having been dependent on the lively commercial activities, the closeness to European culture felt by the Levantines, the enterprise of the foreign embassies, and the support of the Ottoman Court, which was a protagonist of Westernization.

[37] Münevver Eminoğlu, ed., *1870 Beyoğlu 2000: Bir Efsanenin Monografisi* (İstanbul: Yapı Kredi, 2000), 142.

[38] Eminoğlu, 104.

[39] Eminoğlu, 104.

VIII The imperial court

Between the sixteenth century and the dissolution of the Ottoman Empire in the twentieth century, the city universally known as Constantinople and the Court were prime factors in attracting numbers of European artists to the East. By virtue of its glorious past and special geographical position within the city, Topkapı Palace, which had for centuries occupied a privileged niche among Eastern palaces, embellished the imaginary world of Westerners. Théophile Gautier, who came to İstanbul in 1852, expressed his thoughts on the Ottoman Court as follows:

> Swayed by the influence of Arab fairy tales, exaggerated fancies concerning the glorious East were fashioned in the lands of the North: even the most sober thinkers were unable to restrain themselves from creating in their imaginations a fabulous architecture—columns of lapis lazuli, capitals of gold with leaves of emerald and ruby, and crystal fountains with jets of silver. Dreaming of Alhambras, they confused the wholly unrelated Ottoman style with the Arab style. For in reality, the mansions here are airy and the decor of the chambers is very plain.[1]

[1] Gautier, *Constantinople*, 252.

Topkapı Palace, esteemed as a symbol of the Ottoman Empire until the mid-nineteenth century, now was compelled to share this special status with other palaces along the shores of the Bosphorus, like Dolmabahçe, Çırağan and Beylerbeyi. These structures, as representatives of the Ottoman dynasty and an integral part of the Bosphorus landscape, constituted invariable elements of engraved and painted depictions of İstanbul. Nonetheless, although Yıldız Palace formed the center of government during the Late Ottoman period under Abdülhamid II, it never became identified with the Oriental image and never served as a subject for Western artists. This was, undoubtedly, in part the consequence of its comparatively remote site, far from the eyes of the city dweller and reminiscent more of a miniature Italian quarter, and its being devoid of the splendor of an Eastern palace; it was also a conse-

41 Louis-François Cassas. *Panorama of Seraglio Point.* Watercolor, pencil, and India ink on paper. 74 x 237 cm. Collection of Suna and Inan Kıraç, Istanbul.

41

quence of the fact that no permission to paint it was ever granted to a foreigner. Paintings of Yıldız Palace are limited to works executed by a group of artists known in Ottoman art as the "Primitives," who based their depictions on photographs taken from the Palace gardens.

ill. 271

Topkapı Palace, the focus of interest of Orientalist painters, was an ideal setting for fantasies. Eighteenth- and nineteenth-century landscapes of İstanbul employed the Palace and the Historic Peninsula as symbols of the city. Eighteenth-century artists awarded appointments in the embassies always placed Topkapı Palace at the center of their topographical panoramas, executed while looking from the heights of Pera, the terrace of the French or the Dutch embassy, and from the hillside above Galata and Tophane. Louis-François Cassas, who was in İstanbul during the reign of Abdülhamid I, sketched close to a total of thirty panoramic views of the Ottoman capital and close-up drawings of certain structures. Among his panoramas, the most typical vista is that of Seraglio Point, delineated as seen from the vicinity of Galata—very likely, the terrace of the Palais de France or the garden of the Swedish Palace. The composition depicts the bustling life on the sea from a panoramic angle: seaside mansions and structures built atop the city walls, Topkapı Palace, the church of St. Irene, the mosques of St. Sophia and Sultan Ahmed, sailing vessels floating past the Seraglio Point towards the entrance of the Golden Horn, commercial boats, and caiques with a marquee on the afterdeck. The technique of pen and ink with watercolor employed by Cassas is peculiar to those artists in the second half of the eighteenth century with professional training, according to which the primary method utilized to represent topographical scenes was tinted drawing.

ill. 41

Though a good many of the paintings of Topkapı Palace delineate the exterior as viewed either from the land or the sea—the majority is from the sea—those depicting its courtyards and interiors are limited in number. One solution was to rely on photographs, as in the case of Jean-Léon Gérôme. His delineations of certain interior features of Topkapı Palace, such as the Marble Terrace and its pool with water jets, the baldachin (*Iftariye Kasrı*), and the glazed revetment tiles of the Golden Path, were all based on photographs by the Abdullah Frères. Those artists who managed to view the Palace from within are limited to

ill. 101

a select few: Jean-Baptiste Van Mour, who executed imperial audience scenes for eighteenth-century European ambassadors, Melling and Preáulx during the reign of Selim III, and Allom and Bartlett in the early nineteenth century. Life in the Imperial Harem of Topkapı Palace, a subject fraught with curiosity in every period and which, generally, could only be pictured from the exterior, remained a fantasy for Western artists.

The painting called *Palace Interior* by Carlo Bossoli (1815–84), dated 1845, is of interest for its depiction of the interior of Gülhane Pavilion (*Gülhane Kasrı*), attached to the Topkapı Palace. Bossoli, who attracted notice among nineteenth-century Italian Orientalists due to his success in rendering detail and sensitivity of line, came first to İstanbul in 1843 and several times thereafter in the same decade. The artist, whose subjects were the İstanbul harbor and Abdülmecid's imperial caique in *An Eastern Harbor* and *The Turkish Sultan's Caique*, respectively, also executed a portrait study in charcoal of Sultan Abdülmecid.[2]

ill.

Sedat Hakkı Eldem's hypothetical reconstruction of the now-vanished Gülhane Pavilion was based on the visual information contained in three paintings—one of which is by Carlo Bossoli. In Eldem's judgment,

> [t]he painting [of Gülhane Pavilion] was done from memory, assisted by his [i.e., Bossoli's] notes jotted down on the site, and, for this reason, it contains quite a few errors, such as the projections on the corners of the hall reminiscent of theater loggias and the discontinuous cushion arrangement. Apart from these aspects, the expression of the atmosphere and style of the main hall is admirable. Its' architecture is in the Empire style which became increasingly heavy in the final years of the reign of Mahmud II and tended more and more to the baroque. Notably, the upper row of windows is absent. In the main hall, enclosed on three sides, the festoon of tasseled garlands beneath the vaults, the cornice with modillions, the heavy ornamentation, and, finally, the animated drapery arrangement—all exude a character of excess. The Gülhane Pavilion, like the other pavilions here, was torn down in 1865 on account of the high cost of upkeep.[3]

After Abdülmecid left Topkapı Palace, the palace continued to attract the notice of travelers.

[2] Juler, 56–61.
[3] Sedat Hakkı Eldem, *Köşkler ve Kasırlar, II*, (İstanbul: Devlet Güzel Sanatlar Akademisi, 1974), 399–401.

42 Carlo Bossoli. *Palace Interior*, 1845.
Distemper on paper. 4.5 x 58 cm.
Collection of Oya and Bülent Eczacıbaşı,
İstanbul.

43 Hercule Catenacci. "Interior of a Seaside Mansion," *Tour du Monde* (4ième année, 1863).

44-45 Artist unknown. *Main Hall in Seaside Mansion of Köprülü Hüseyin Paşa.* Watercolor on paper. 37 x 52 cm. Collection of Azize Taylan, İstanbul.

[4] Blanc, 56.

[5] Hercule Catenacci was a painter and illustrator of the nineteenth–century French school. Born in Ferrara, he later became a French citizen. He dwelled for a time on Corfu and also stayed in Greece and elsewhere in the East. He participated the 1869 and 1870 Paris Salon Exhibitions. He illustrated numerous books. *Bénézit,* 1999 ed.

[6] Eldem, *Köşkler,* 137.

43 ➤

44 ➤

Foreigners obtaining special permission were allowed to view the interiors about which they had expressed curiosity. Henri Blanc, who toured the palace in May 1854, noted in his diary that he visited a number of the large reception halls with heavily ornamented gilded ceilings, graceful cornices. The walls of these halls were decorated with landscapes in oils framed by wooden gilt reliefs, where no living creature was represented because it was forbidden by Islam, and the rendering of the pictures was mediocre. The floors of the palace were, Blanc indicates, covered with fine reed mats and almost no furniture other than a few in the style of Louis XV were in evidence on account of the remove to Dolmabahçe Palace.[4]

In addition to palace structures, the architectural characteristics and interior decoration of the mansions and seaside villas in which the elite resided in İstanbul were of interest to draftsmen. One of the oldest surviving structures on the Bosphorus today is the seaside mansion of Amcazade Köprülü Hüseyin Pasha (1699), a sketch of whose large main hall by Hercule Catenacci (1816–84)[5] was published in 1883 in a book-length work on the Ottoman art of ornamentation by E. Collinot and Adalbert de Beaumont, the latter of whom had interested himself in the mansions and palaces of İstanbul on his visit in 1848.[6] This same engraving became well known on account of its being reprinted in various periodicals, like *L'Illustration*. In the unsigned water color (slightly altered) reproduction of this picture, as in many other similar works, the setting on the Bosphorus furnishes a view in three different directions—a panorama as seen from the interior, made possible by the opening of the shutters of the windows. The interior of the domed hall is completely faced with wood ornamented by painted designs. On the walls are stylized floral motifs and in the center of the room is a marble pool with water spraying from jets. On the raised divan on the right-hand side, two women are seated, one of whom is smoking a long pipe, and a girl is presenting them a single tulip.

Dolmabahçe Palace is the second largest among the imperial palace structures and, after Topkapı Palace, the second in importance. Even while under construction, the vast size and unusual style of this edifice of the Tanzimat period drew the attention of foreign visitors to İstanbul. Théophile Gautier wrote in 1852 that it was neither Greek nor Renaissance nor Gothic nor North

46-47 Luigi Querena. *Dolmabahçe Palace*,
1875. Oil on canvas. 69 x 104 cm.
Collection of Azize Taylan, İstanbul.

48 Ernst Karl Eugen Koerner. *Dolmabahçe Palace on the Bosphorus*, 1923. Oil on canvas. 81 x 120.5 cm. Collection of Güner and Haydar Akın, İstanbul.

[7] Gautier, *Constantinople*, 259.

[8] Blanc, 51.

[9] *Thieme–Becker*.

African nor Arab nor Ottoman, but rather that it was more Spanish in its fascination with frenzied detail and the attempt to create a luxuriate complexity, reminiscent of the Plateresque style, in which the surface of the monuments display a faceted, gem-like ornamentation.[7] Henri Blanc, viewing Dolmabahçe Palace in 1854 prior to its completion, noted that the entrance resembled an arch of triumph and that the ornamentation of the structure was extremely dense.[8]

The Venetian artist, Luigi Querena (1820/24-90), painted the Dolmabahçe Palace in 1875, nineteen years after its completion. The area in front of the Treasury Gate of the palace is pictured as a **ill. 46** square enlivened by the passage of coupés, mounted riders, women in colorful street coats, and men in long robes and turbans side by side **ill. 47** with soldiers strolling in blue uniforms with red fezzes. As the left-hand side of the painting reveals, the trees lining the avenue between the districts of Dolmabahçe and Beşiktaş are yet but saplings, and the clock tower erected during the reign of Abdülhamid II in 1891 is absent.

In the painting by Ernst Karl Eugen Koerner of Prussia (1846–1927) called *Dolmabahçe Palace on* **ill. 48** *the Bosphorus*, Dolmabahçe Mosque and the palaces Dolmabahçe and Çırağan and, in the distance, Küçük Mecidiye Mosque are delineated within a perspective that deepens in the direction of the Bosphorus. Koerner, a painter of land- and seascapes, made an exploratory tour in Egypt, Palestine, Asia Minor, Athens, and İstanbul in the year 1873–4, and it is known that he returned to his homeland with a number of watercolor studies.[9] This picture, executed in 1923, must have been based on these sketches. The two seaside palaces appearing in all their loveliness in this painting—whose vantage point is the ridge above Kabataş—and erected by the reform sultans, Abdülmecid and Abdülaziz, assume their place as symbols of Westernization on the shores of the Bosphorus.

IX Sultans, artists, and the role of the embassies

Recognized as the era of Westernization in the Ottoman Empire, the nineteenth century witnessed the advance guard of the changes introduced in representational art and their diffusion—a phenomenon closely related to the interest shown in the art of painting by the sultans of that time. During this century, the rules of Western-style art and the depiction of the real world replaced those of the traditional Ottoman miniature painting. Members of the House of Osman, from Mahmud II to Prince Abdülmecid, the caliph, and high-ranking bureaucrats became the initiators and patrons of the Westernization movement in the arts.

In this era, none of the sultans rejected the Western style art of painting. In consequence, the support that originated in the highest office of the society and exhibited continuity played an important role in the fundamental cultural change. This decision by the nineteenth-century Ottoman Court brought with it the demand for artists who could execute paintings conforming to this new understanding. While one reason European artists came to İstanbul in this period was the interest displayed by the Western world in exoticism and the Orient, another reason was the new requirements created in the sphere of art due to Westernization in the imperial capital. In the framework of its reforms, the Ottoman Court sent students to Europe for training and opened the door to European artists by awarding them appointments. As a result, an increase occurred in the numbers of those European artists who came to İstanbul in the hope of acquiring commissions from the Court or who applied to the Ottoman embassies in Western capitals. The application by the Rumanian artist, Thèodore Aman, to the Ottoman embassy in Paris in 1854 with the aim of presenting to the sultan a painting he had executed depicting the battle of Oltenita is an interesting example in this regard. Correspondence related to this matter discloses that permission was granted for a lithograph

[1] BOA, İrade Hariciye, no. 5517

[2] Wall paintings which became fashionable in the eighteenth century, increased in frequency in the nineteenth century due to the requisites of the increasing number of eclectic structures in the city.

copy of the painting to be sent to İstanbul to give an idea of its quality.[1] In the relations between the Ottoman Court and Western artists, the embassies played a leading role as intermediaries, both in the identification of the artists and their presentation to the Court.

Another reason why European artists arrived in the city was to execute mural paintings for the newly built palaces of Dolmabahçe or Beylerbeyi.[2] There was a great demand for artists who could apply western art and this demand ranged from portrait paintings of the sultan and his family to the interior decoration of the new palaces and mosques. Western artists' perception of the Ottoman Court and of the Imperial Harem was one of excessive imagination as well as of bias. In their eyes, the Ottoman sultan was both a powerful administrator and a despot without mercy and a cruel and ruthless warrior and, at the same time, as the Islamic caliph and the focus of Eastern culture and its way of life, he was the possessor of a representative identity laden with complex and contradictory meanings. To be able to execute a portrait of the Ottoman sultan who nearly gathered in him the mystery, the dissolution, and the eroticism of Orientalism and who was in an inaccessible position was an extremely attractive subject. This identity, which was first handled in a general manner as a sultan of the east and was increasingly transformed to the Ottoman sultan, had been depicted in different senses and styles from the Middle Ages to the nineteenth century in Western art.

But in the nineteenth century, conditions at the Ottoman Court were undergoing change and while putting their Western stamp on the military and political life of the empire, the sultans and the Court circle, acting as the leaders of their own reforms, applied the principles of Westernization to their own lives. This change was not rapid and its adaptation by the age-old institutions of the empire was slow; and the city including the Court and its way of life continued to a certain extent to retain its established state until the end of the First World War.

Regardless of the fact that the Ottoman sultans of the reform period resided in a palace of eclectic European style rather than in Topkapı Palace and that their attire, their attitudes, and their tastes were increasingly westernized, in the eyes of Western artists they remained as figures of attraction. For this reason, the portrait of the caliph-sultan, beyond its bearing documentary value in terms of Ottoman history, preserved an Orientalist meaning in Western eyes.

In response to the regularizing of the traveling and lodging conditions in this era, a significant increase occurred in the numbers of Western artists coming to İstanbul. Undoubtedly, the production of works with Orientalist content was not the only aim of all the artists. Some came with the objective of marketing their paintings here in order to present paintings to the reforming sultans who had begun to express interest in Western-style art. Some of these artists were invited expressly for an appointment at the Court, and some were rewarded for the works they presented with imperial medals.

The support by the nineteenth-century sultans of the aesthetics of Western-style art was initiated by their having foreign artists execute their own portraits. In this era when the cultural identity of the Ottoman empire had begun to change, the Orientalist artists were as willing to paint the sultan's portrait as the sultan was desirous of having his portrait painted—although for different reasons. The sultan's portrait in the nineteenth century signified both the efforts by the reformist Ottoman sultans to adapt to the Western diplomatic rules and standard of living and the desire by the Westerners for the status quo, so that they could continue to pursue their Eastern fantasies.

Prior to the nineteenth century, the Ottoman sultans had had European artists execute their portraits. It is known, for instance, that the French artist, Simone Vouet (1590–1649), who came to İstanbul on December 1611, wished to paint the portrait of Sultan Ahmed I. Vouet, who had achieved renown as for his historical canvases and portraits, came to İstanbul in the train of French ambassador, Baron de Sancy et de la Mole, and remained for one year.[3]

The first sultan to sit for Ottoman and foreign artists to paint his portrait and which were print-

ed for distribution was Selim III. The 1793 engraving of the sultan by an Ottoman Greek, Court Artist Kostantin Kapıdağlı, who was active 1780–1810, constituted a model in this respect.[4] As a requirement of diplomacy, Selim III sent his portrait to Napoleon with Ottoman ambassador to France, Muhib Efendi, serving as intermediary. After Mahmud II ascended the throne, the series on the House of Osman printed by John Young in London were presented to the Ottoman Court in 1815 and similar albums were subsequently executed and reproduced for sale in Europe.[5] Writing the names of the sultans included in the albums in English or French orthography promoted its appeal on the market and is an expression of the popularity of the "image of the Sultan of the East."

Mahmud II, adopted Selim III's ideas for reform in the military and social arena and carried them out. During his reign the traditional Ottoman image underwent a perceptible change. The memoirs of travelers who came to İstanbul at this time stress this change with a hint of disappointment. The modernization of the Ottoman armed forces which had for centuries occupied a place in the European consciousness because of their terrifying implications and their rich array of splendid costumes led to the elimination of the turban and caftan by a uniform of trousers, jacket, cape and fez, by which the image of the Oriental incurred a certain amount of damage. To secure a permanency for the reforms Sultan Mahmud II who had achieved this change at great cost, personally adopted the new Ottoman image and served as a role model. He ordered his portraits to be hung in government offices in order to institutionalize his reforms. The esteem shown toward the portrait was equivalent to that shown to the sultan in person. The fact that he commissioned François Dubois (1790-1871) to depict the new army corps, *Asakir-i Mansure-i Muhammediye* (Victorious Mohammedan Soldiers) is another evidence that he wanted his reforms to be permanently sealed.

Leading representatives of Orientalism came to İstanbul during the reign of Mahmud II—the Frenchman Alexandre-Gabriel Decamps in 1826 and the Belgian Jacob Jacobs (1812–79) for four months in 1838. On his return to his own country, the romantic Russian portrait artist, Karl-Pavlovich Bryullov (1799–1852), executed scenes from the harem based on the drawings he had executed while in İstanbul in 1835. The British

[3] Pape, 306 and *Bénézit*, 627.

[4] For further information on Konstantin Kapıdağlı see Günsel Renda, "Selim III's Portraits and the European Connection," *Art turc: actes de 10ième congrès international d'art turc* (Genève: Fondation Max van Berchem, 1999).

[5] Günsel Renda, "Portrenin Son Yüzyılı," *Padişahın Portresi: Tesavir–i Âl–i Osman* (Istanbul: Türkiye İş Bankası Kültür, 2000), 443–4.

artist, William Allan (1782–1850), was in İstanbul in 1830 and William Purser (1790–1852) arrived in İstanbul after the 1820s. Henry Aston Barker was another Briton who came to İstanbul during the reign of Mahmud II. But no information is available in regard to whether these artists had any relation contact with the Ottoman Court.

Starting in the early years of the reign of Mahmud II, it appears that European artists were commissioned by the sultans to execute their portraits. The sultan's portrait was executed by such artists as the French portrait artist, Achille Devéria (1800–57), Blasius Hoefel (1792-1863) and Henri-Guillaume Schlesinger (1814–93), and it appears he sat for Devéria, Hoefel, and Schlesinger. In addition, Pavlo Verona and Thomas Allom painted depictions of Mahmud II.[6] After the reforms of Mahmud II, the Imperial Depiction (*Tasvir-i Humayun*), in which he is attired in a cape, a uniform and a red fez with tassel—a reflection of the decisiveness of his efforts at reform—was placed in military and administrative offices and presented to eminent personages. One anonymous painting, in which Mahmud II appears seated in an armchair, shows the sultan pointing ahead with his right hand and the firman held in his left hand is extended toward the viewer.

The presentation of the sultan's portrait to the imperial offices was performed in conjunction with a special ceremonial. Mehmed Memduh believes that the ceremonial veneration of the Imperial Depiction was important from the perspective of the representative power of the sultan's portrait in the reign of Mahmud II.

> By the grace of God, it has been planned that the servants and units to be present at the ceremonial in formation for the submission of the sultan's portrait to the Sublime Porte are as follows: to proceed in front of the phaeton which will carry the portrait, brigade commanders, adjutant majors, captains, lieutenants and sergeants selected from the infantry and cavalry regiments at İstanbul, and, to close the rear, two companies of troops from the New corps and thirty to forty guards; in addition, starting from the home of the Doorkeeper of the Imperial Apartments, Ali Beyefendi, opposite the Soğukçeşme gate, until they reach the mounting stone at the Sublime Porte, two brigades from the battalion under Major General Hayrettin Pasha and, from the

ill. 49

mosque of Firuz Ağa adjacent to the square of Sultan Ahmed up to the place called the Intersection, or Dört Yol Ağzı, at the mosque of St. Sophia, one battalion of the New corps under Abdi Bey, lieutenant colonel in charge of provisions for the annual religious fast, will, in unison, call out the prayer, "Long live the sultan!" My son, it is my wish that zeal will be observed in presenting this petition to the sultan in regard to this matter.[7]

This memorandum sent from the Office of the Ministry of War was presented to the sultan, and he issued an order proclaiming that the ceremony should be performed in the exact same manner as was therein spelled out.

Observances of the ceremonial connected with the Imperial Depiction were also mentioned by Miss Pardoe in her memoirs of İstanbul. One of these was the presentation of the sultan's portrait to the sultan's imperial bodyguard in Üsküdar and another was to the Gunners Barracks in Taksim. The additions made by Mahmud II to the Selimiye Barracks in Üsküdar and the Taksim Barracks had modernized these structures and raised them to a standard congruent with the reforms carried out in the military sphere. The installation, therefore, of the sultan's portrait in these barracks was of significance. Yet, according to Miss Pardoe's memoirs, at the time the sultan's portrait was presented to the imperial guardsmen in Üsküdar, some of them shouted aloud that the making of a likeness of any human being was in violation of Islamic law and, moreover, that this sin had been committed with fanfare and display and, pointing out that the esteem being extended to the picture was comparable to that shown to the person himself, protested "We are becoming Giaours—Infidels."[8]

Again as related in Miss Pardoe's memoirs, when the residents of İstanbul, who delighted in watching each ceremonial attended by the sultan, learned that the Imperial Depiction was to be presented to the Taksim Gunners Barracks, located next to the Grand Champs de Morts, groups of men and women took their places along the route where the ceremonial procession would pass hours in advance. Because of the ceremonial of the Imperial Depiction, the shoreline at Dolmabahçe was densely crowded with caiques belonging to pashas and high-ranking officers of the fleet while the hillsides were covered by the troops. In the ceremonial procession which pro-

[6] Renda, "Portrenin," 411, 502.
[7] Mehmed Memduh, *Tanzimattan Meşrutiyete I: Mir'ât-i Şuûnât* (İstanbul: Nehir Yayınları, 1990), 16.
[8] Pardoe, *The City*, 2:235.

49 Artist unknown. *Sultan Mahmud II.*
Oil on canvas. 190 x 135 cm. Topkapı
Palace Museum, İstanbul.

IX Sultans, artists, and the role of the embassies

ceeded toward the barracks by passing the Military College,

> [The Guardsmen] were succeeded by the Military Staff of the Army, and the Field Officers of the different regiments; the Majors rode first, and were followed by the superior ranks in regular succession, until the gorgeous train of Pashas brought up the rear. The pashas were succeeded by about thirty musicians: and then followed a detachment of Infantry marching in double files, between whose ranks moved the open carriage of the Sultan, drawn by four fine gray horses, each led by a groom; and bearing the portrait of His Highness carefully enveloped in green baize. Said Pasha, the Sultan's son-in-law, preceded the carriage, dressed in a Hussar uniform, and mounted on a noble Arabian; and it was followed by the Seraskier and Halil Pasha riding abreast; succeeded by a squadron of cavalry.[9]

The sultan's portrait served two general purposes. One was its' installation in government offices

50 David Wilkie. *Sultan Abdülmecid*, 1840. Oil on board. 70 x 54 cm. Topkapı Palace Museum, İstanbul.

51 Hermann Kretzschmer. *Portrait of Sultan Abdülmecid*, 1840. Oil on canvas. 74 x 58.5 cm. Stiftung Schlösser und Gärten Potsdam-Sanssouci.

[9] Pardoe, *The City*, 2:238.

[10] Mehmed Memduh, 155. Mehmed Memduh states that the portrait was in the seaside mansion in H. 1318 (1910–1). Sultan Abdülmecid also came from time to time to this mansion during his sultanate. İstefenaki Bey was in the eyes of the realm, a man worthy of respect until his death. His son, Aleko Bey, was like himself in possession of high rank and included among the imperial dignitaries and awarded various appointments, such as ambassador to Vienna; subsequently, while serving as governor of Eastern Rumelia, he was promoted to the rank of vizier.

and military barracks. It was also used with the purpose of rewarding the members of the dynasty or anyone who had demonstrated their usefulness to the realm. According to Mehmed Memduh, İstefenaki Bey to whom had been awarded a portrait of Mahmud II, was a faithful servant who possessed outstanding honesty and loyalty greater than that of any ordinary Muslim and had earned the trust of the empire and was rewarded by a flood of the sultan's favors and blessings. Sultan Mahmud II, accompanied by princes Abdülmecid and Abdülaziz, honored the seaside mansion of İstefenaki Bey in Arnavutköy by his presence and awarded him with his large scale portrait.[10]

Of all the nineteenth century sultans who incorporated the art sphere in the Westernization program of the period of imperial reforms, Abdülmecid occupies a place of distinction. He, clearly, maintained continuity with the leadership in the plastic arts initiated by his father. Abdülmecid expressed interest in different branches of art, such as architecture, painting, music, theater, and opera and, during his sultanate; Dolmabahçe Palace became transformed into a setting for the application of European aesthetics. Though the sultan himself expressed no preference for any particular branch of the fine arts like a dilettante of the Western nobility, he was patronized all areas; and, more important, he undertook in the name of the empire artistic leadership for the changing elite. During his reign, Western influence was broadly diffused in the artistic life of the empire. Just as in the earlier period, under Abdülmecid, Western Orientalist artists, draftsmen, and painters traveled to Ottoman territories and İstanbul in particular. The memoirs penned by travelers were illustrated by draftsmen and were reproduced as engravings in bound volumes or albums. Works in oil and watercolor by Western artists who visited imperial territories exhibited an increase relative to the previous years.

From his youth, Sultan Abdülmecid had had his portrait painted by various Western and native painters. The German artist, Johann Hermann Kretzschmer (1811–90) who had been to İstanbul, executed a portrait of Abdülmecid in 1840 the first year of his sultanate. At the request of the king of Prussia, Friedrich Wilhelm IV, the artist made a copy of the portrait for the Berlin court.

Sir David Wilkie (1785–1841), who arrived in İstanbul in October 1840, requested permission to paint a portrait of Abdülmecid while he was in

ill. 51

İstanbul. Abdülmecid, who at that time was having his picture painted by a Prussian artist, sat for the first time for Wilkie on 12 December 1840. [11] Though Wilkie at first had wanted to depict the sultan seated on his throne and receiving people being presented to him, in the end, he rendered him sitting on a couch, wearing on his head a fez peculiar to the reign of Mahmud II, without aigrette, but with a long tassel, and in formal dress with a cape and white gloves on his hands, which endowed him with a more approachable mien. The artist considered presenting the painting as a present to Queen Victoria of England, which, as his notes indicate, had received the approval of the sultan. [12] However, as the work progressed, Abdülmecid, pleased by the painting, requested one copy of this painting for himself on 27 December. The sultan sat for the last time for this copy, now in the Topkapı Palace Collection, on 3 January 1841. In his diary, Wilkie states that the sessions numbered four in all, two to three hours each, and that the sultan during the sitting and at all times was a gentleman and that he interested himself in the painting to the extent that from time to time he would rise and come beside the artist and make suggestions and even take the brush in hand to make small revisions. As a reward for his work, Abdülmecid presented the artist with a gold and enameled snuffbox with a floral motif in diamonds on the lid. [13]

At the time Wilkie petitioned for permission to paint the sultan's portrait, the Prussian artist at work at the Court must have been Hermann Kretzschmer. In the portraits executed by both Wilkie and Kretzschmer in 1840, Abdülmecid was in the first year of his reign: they both captured the tenderness of his seventeen years and was depicted with the same shape of beard and the same fez and apparel peculiar to the reign of Mahmud II and with the identical medal suspended from his neck.

Wilkie's arrival in İstanbul in the fall of 1840 coincides with the war between the Ottoman Empire and Egyptian governor general, Mehmed Ali Pasha of Kaválla. The artist, who wished to travel in the Holy Land, was required to wait for months in İstanbul until the security of the roads was established. In the meantime, he executed portraits, drew ordinary Ottoman subjects, and painted scenes from everyday life. After the artist had sketched out the main lines of the paintings, he sent them to England by post to be completed

in detail on his return. At the end of the war, Wilkie executed a series of scenes from the New Testament in Jerusalem and on his return trip stayed for a time in Cairo and at the request of Mehmed Ali Pasha executed his portrait. On the return journey to England, he became ill and lost his life; his death was met by deep sorrow in England. [14] While Wilkie was in İstanbul, he executed fifty-nine drawings of the local city scene, which were later published as engravings; six of these pertain to Pera. [15] The artist felt at ease among the Ottomans and shared their ideas. In one letter he sent from İstanbul he states that "by judging the human relations and customs of less developed nations according to our own criteria and by forgetting that the Easterners had developed civilizations before us, we may be doing them an injustice. Even if today they are very much behind us they have given us number of elements which permitted the advancement of our civilization." [16]

Our information is limited concerning direct personal relations between the Ottoman sultans and Western artists. For this reason, the letters written by the artist, Charles Doussault, who executed a portrait of Abdülmecid in the Old Çırağan Palace in December 1846, to his friend, Billecocq, a former French minister plenipotentiary, are of importance. Doussault who occupies a place among those French Orientalist artist who traveled often in the East, exhibited his canvases representing his travel memoirs in the Paris Salon between 1834 and 1870. A student of Achille Devéria, Doussault's interest in the Ottoman Court may be attributed to his teacher. A lithograph by Devéria dated 1829 that depicts Abdülmecid's father, Sultan Mahmud II, in traditional dress is in the Topkapı Palace Museum. Doussault apparently came to İstanbul from Bucharest in order to execute the sultan's portrait with a letter of recommendation by Billecocq. On the day after completing a tiring and dangerous journey on the Black Sea in winter, the artist without taking time to recover from the journey went to the Old Çırağan Palace to see the Sultan with the embassy interpreter Mathurin-Joseph Cor. [17] In his letter, Doussault indicates that they were taken into the waiting room in the palace where while they were smoking a long pipe with the first court chamberlain, Şevket Efendi, the sultan, who had received notice of their arrival, wanted his portrait begun immediately begun, but because they had

ill. 50

[11] A preliminary study for the portrait exists in pencil, colored chalk, and watercolor, signed and dated 1840. Gerald Ackerman, *Les Orientalistes de l'école britannique* (Paris: ACR, 1991), 306.

[12] The first painting executed by Wilkie for Queen Victoria is in the Buckingham Collection, British Royal Palace.

[13] Edip Emil Öymen, "İngiliz Malı Fırçadan İki Osmanlı," *Euroclub* (Sonbahar 87): 45–6.

[14] Ackerman, *Les Orientalistes de l'école britannique*, 304–7.

[15] Allan Cunningham, *The Life of Sir David Wilkie* (London, 1843), 3: 341.

[16] Ackerman, *Les Orientalistes de l'école britannique*, 304.

[17] Joseph Cor-Mathurin served as chargé d'affaires in the French embassy in 1848. Jean–Michel Casa, *Le palais de France à Istanbul/İstanbul'da Bir Fransız Sarayı* (Istanbul: Yapı Kredi Yayınları, 1995), 111.

come to the palace by horseback on the winding roads of Beşiktaş and through mud in the rain he had pleaded that they were not in a state to be received. With the discomfort that he gave by the inappropriateness of the situation and the rejection of the sultan's request, the artist claiming as an excuse that because he had not expected to be received into his presence he had not brought paper, pencil, and paints obtained an appointment for the next day. The next day, with the court chamberlain and an interpreter, Doussault was brought into a room with some dozen windows that all looked onto the palace gardens. Doussault was unable to find a place providing suitable lighting because the light streamed in on all sides. He was shown a number of apartments, arcades, and halls appropriate for Ottoman use in the palace, but in all of them the lighting situation was the same.

> While it was unclear how this problem would be resolved, they put me in one section that formed an apartment, this was the sultan's library. The library was lighted by two large windows. From these windows from the top of a dome of green, the entrance to the Marmara Sea in the distance, the Tower of Leander and Seraglio Point surmounted with pavilions and elegant minarets could be seen. The shelves loaded with richly bound volumes lined the walls of this room where I could conveniently illuminate my model in an appropriate manner. Looking at the always extraordinary and novel view of the Bosphorus after a quarter hour's wait in which I idled, the sultan entered in the company of the servant who had brought us here. He was dressed in a very simple manner without any distinction. After wishing Cor kind greetings in a few words, he looked at the drawings that I had made in Wallachia [Transylvania] and Syria, which he had requested that I bring with me. The hall of Colonel Blarember in Bucharest attracted his notice for a long time. This poor sultan had never seen a European hall and perhaps would never see one. However strange the customs of the East appears to us, our customs must seem equally curious to him. Prior to this first session, one large obstacle had bothered us. No one could seat himself in the presence of the sultan. While waiting, I had made the decision to draw while standing but

[18] *L'Illustration* (14 Oct. 1854): 261.

> he himself ordered that, a chair be brought for me and insisted that I be seated and asked me to tell them about all my requirements. ...
> At the end of the session and on his way out, he had just taken a few steps when, noticing that my drawings on the desk were in a disorderly array, he came back and put them inside their case.[18]

At the second session, the sultan, who had previously seemed preoccupied and somewhat withdrawn, was more at ease and natural. One day, in the middle of one of the painting sessions, the artist received an immediate summons to come to the Palace, where he encountered the sultan who had just returned from the mosque in his ceremonial clothes. The artist was unable to disguise his astonishment in the presence of this splendid costume. Abdülmecid indicated that he had an even more elaborate costume covered with diamonds and that, if the artist wished, he could wear that; he added, however, that diamonds were more appropriate to women. When Doussault asked Abdülmecid about his preferences regarding the portrait, he replied "I desire that it would resemble me as much as possible; but, for the rest, you are the artist and I leave it completely up to you." Impressed by this reply, Doussault states in his letter that sensitivity like this toward art and a sensibility of this kind were absent in many a noble gentleman and bourgeoisie and that, as the portrait proceeded, a variety of subjects were discussed, such as the diamond mines in Brazil, his geographical curiosity, and the history of the Ottoman Empire by Joseph von Hammer and, on being informed that a third sitting would be necessary to complete the painting, the sultan responded "Take as long as you like—however

long you wish." In Doussault's rendering, the sultan has placed an overcoat over his shoulders, which allows the diamond ornamentation of the costume to be exposed, and the artist noted in his letter that at the ceremonial held on the holiday that fell two days later, the sultan wore his coat in a manner identical with that in the portrait. The drawing appearing in the 14 October 1854 issue of *L'Illustration* provides an idea about the painting executed in 1846. The sultan stands in front of a Western-style armchair on his left. Utilizing a scheme that had been widely used in the West for depiction of rulers since the eighteenth century, he is presented to the viewer beside a curtain draped to one side. All the elements of the decor are of European type and this conforms to the world view of the sultan. Abdülmecid, in ceremonial attire, rests one hand on his sword.

Abdülmecid evidently sat for his portrait for a number of European artists during the early years of his reign. According to the information contained in the catalog for the *Salon des Artistes vivants* held by the National Museum of the Louvre (15 May 1848), Abdülmecid had sat in 1847 for his portrait for the Italian Luigi Rubio (1795–1882).[19] Another portrait depicting the sultan standing and in uniform belongs to the Viennese artist, Franz Sterrer (1818–1901).[20] In a piece of news appearing in the 28 January 1848 issue of *Journal de Constantinople*, this artist resided for a time in İstanbul and received a commission to execute a portrait of the sultan. The painting, which was completed in six sessions, was painted in the Old Çırağan Palace. The article reports that the portrait closely resembles the sultan and that the artist was generously rewarded by the sultan. Baron H. Testa, the chief dragoman of the Austrian embassy who accompanied Sterrer to every session, was presented with a cigarette box studded with diamonds.

According to Baronne Durand de Fontmagne, another artist who executed fine portraits of the sultan was Charles-Émile Labbé,[21] who was resident in İstanbul in 1856.[22] A record from the year 1858 located in the Ottoman Archives of the Turkish Prime Ministry indicates that, in exchange for certain paintings presented to the Court, the French artist Labbé was paid fifty thousand francs after the court consulted the French embassy about their value. Labbé neglected other work and stayed on in İstanbul for more than two years in the hope that the Court would hire him as an artist. Apparently,

[19] Abdülmecid's portrait by Luigi Rubio was sold by auction at Etude Tajan in Paris on 13 April 1992.

[20] Franz Sterrer was trained at the Academy of Vienna. He settled at Ecully near Lyon. The artist married a French citizen in Istanbul. *Thieme–Becker.*

[21] Charles-Émile Labbé died in Algiers in 1885. Exhibiting paintings in the Paris Salon Exhibition between 1836 and 1876, his work titled *Pleasure* is owned by the Périgueux Museum. *Bénézit.*

[22] Durand de Fontmagne, *Un Sejour à l'ambassade de France à Constantinople sous le Second Empire* (Paris: Librairie Plon, 1902), 81.

52 Charles Doussault. "Portrait of Sultan Abdülmecid," *L'Illustration* (14 Oct, 1854).

IX Sultans, artists, and the role of the embassies

through the intervention of the French ambassador, the artist was granted a sum of fifty thousand francs out of the generosity of the Court.[23]

Greatly interested in Eastern subject matter, the British artist, Willis Maddox (1813–53) executed a portrait of Mehmed Ali, the Ottoman ambassador to London, which was exhibited at the Royal Academy in 1850. Gaining approval of his work, Maddox was invited to İstanbul to paint a portrait of Abdülmecid where he executed portraits of several people of the Court, but he succumbed to a feverish disease in İstanbul in 1853 before having a chance to paint the sultan's portrait.[24]

Miner Kilbourne Kellogg (1814–89), who indicates in his notes that he was the first American artist to visit İstanbul, came to the city in 1844 on the invitation of the American ambassador, Dabney Smith Carr. Here he painted a portrait of the archeologist Layard, one among the British and Americans with whom he made acquaintance in the circle of Sir Stratford Canning and his wife.

Arriving in İstanbul in 1851 and accounted the earliest American Orientalist, Walter Gould (1829–89) lived in Florence and although he made but one trip to the Ottoman Empire, he executed scenes of İstanbul until the end of his days. The independence movement initiated by Hungarian nationalists in 1848 was suppressed by Russian troops and their leader, Lajos Kossuth, along with a number of other Hungarians took refuge in Ottoman territories. Sultan Abdülmecid settled Lajos Kossuth and his followers at Kütahya. Despite diplomatic pressure by Austro-Hungary and the Russian Empire, the refusal by the Court and the Sublime Porte to turn over the refugees generated much sympathy among the European public toward the Ottoman ruler. Lajos Kossuth became the center of attention during the two years he dwelled at Kütahya and achieved certain popularity in the West. Gould, who was confident of his ability in the sphere of portraits, came to the Ottoman Empire in the spring of 1851 hoping to execute a portrait of Kossuth and to earn some money by making a lithograph and engraving of this portrait and reproducing it. The prominent British ambassador to İstanbul, Sir Stratford Canning, took the artist under his protection and secured a letter of recommendation for him from Alî Pasha, addressed to Süleyman Bey, the governor general responsible for the Hungarians in exile. Reaching Kütahya after an exhausting and sleepless four-day journey on

[23] BOA, Hariciye İradeleri, no. 8258, H. 24 Şevval 1274 (7 June 1858).

[24] Ackerman, *Les Orientalistes de l'école britannique*, 326.

[25] Ackerman, *Les Orientalistes de l'école américaine*, 94–6.

[26] For a documented list of the awards and medals see citations by Cezar from BOA, Hariciye İrade, *Sanatta*, 123–5.

[27] Gérard de Nerval on his visit to Topkapı Palace saw miniature portraits of the sultans in one of the halls and that had been executed first by the Venetians and later by artists from other parts of Italy and that the last one, of Abdülmecid, belonged to Camille Roger, a French artist. Gerard de Nerval, *Voyage en Orient*, 2 vols. (Paris: Charpentier, 1862), 2:357.

horseback, the artist was greeted warmly by Kossuth. Gould managed to render a successful portrait after three or four sittings. Returning to İstanbul in mid-August 1851 Gould was requested by Lady Canning to make a portrait of her husband, and the grand vizier made a similar request. The artist indicates in his letters that, although he was very pleased to receive commissions from such influential personages, this would mean a loss of time for him due to the need to wait for them to find a convenient time for the sittings.[25] Danish painter Hermann Anton Melbye (1818-75) came to İstanbul as an attaché of the Danish embassy and worked for the Sultan in 1853.

Records reveal that, during the reign of Abdülmecid, European artists received gifts and awards in exchange for their presentation of paintings to the Court.[26] Among the Orientalist artists who came to the Ottoman Empire in these years were those who had achieved renown in the Western art circles with their paintings of Orientalist subjects, such as the following, by country: German: Carl Haag (1820–1915), Adolf Schreyer (1828–99), and Maximilian Schmidt (1818–1901); Belgian: Jan-Baptiste Huymans (1826–1906); French: Narcisse Berchère (1819–91); British: William Holman Hunt (1827–1910) and Edward Lear (1812–88); and Italian: Ippolito Caffi (1809–1866), Giovanni Brindesi and Raffaele Carelli (1795–1854). During the same period, the name of Camille Rogier (1805–70), a leading illustrator appears among the foreigners who came to İstanbul.[27]

Architect Gaspare Fossati (1809–83), Amadeo Preziosi of Malta, Pierre Guès, and Giuseppe Schranz of Malta, who served as art instructors in the Imperial Military College and the Imperial Military Cadet School, were leading artists who resided in İstanbul for extended periods. Coming to İstanbul in 1840, Horace Vernet stayed only for a brief period. Another British artist who visited İstanbul the same year was John Frederick Lewis (1805–76). Lewis executed scenes from the daily life of various Ottoman figural types. Richard Dadd (1817–86) visited İstanbul in 1842. In the same year, Austrian Hubert Sattler (1817–1904) was also in İstanbul. While on his way to Iran in an official capacity, the French artist, Eugène Flandin, stopped in İstanbul in 1842. Another French artist in the city was Félix Ziem (1847–56). Ziem, who specialized in views of Venice and İstanbul, became renowned as an artist of the two cities.

The Crimean War, which coincided with the reign of Sultan Abdülmecid, drew a number of draftsmen and artists to the region, the paths of the great majority of whom led through or terminated in İstanbul. Among them was the Italian artist, Carlo Bossoli, the Frenchman, Constantin Guys (1802–94). The French artist and draftsman, Alexandre Bida (1823–95), known for his meticulous drawings, came to İstanbul for the first time in 1843 and then again in 1855 when he drew for the periodicals *Le Tour du Monde* and *L'Illustration*.[28] Another of the artists who passed through İstanbul on their way to the Crimea was Adolphe Yvon (1817–93), who had received a commission from Napoleon III. Yvon exhibited his paintings of İstanbul during Abdülmecid's reign in the 1873 Paris Salon.[29] Théodore Frère (1814–88) dwelled in the city for eighteen months starting in 1851. Fabius Brest, a native of Marseilles who delineated the picturesque parts of İstanbul and the Bosphorus, came to İstanbul in 1847[30] and it is known that he was still in the city in 1856.[31] The geographer, Xavier Hommaire de Hell, and Jules Laurens (1825–1901), who conducted scientific studies on the geography and historical aspects in the environs of the Black Sea and Caspian Sea, found an opportunity to become acquainted with the city in 1846.[32]

The earliest dated pictures executed in İstanbul by Amadeo Preziosi, who resided in the Ottoman Empire until his death, are dated to the fall of 1842. Lord Curzon, the private secretary of British ambassador, Lord Stradford Canning, first commissioned from him a series of paintings representative of the typical character of İstanbul and other commissions followed. Preziosi, whose name became known among foreign visitors to the city for his depictions of the life of İstanbul, and his studio became a place where travelers and art lovers resident in the city, whether foreigner or Ottoman, would stop in. The Prince of Wales and Empress Eugenie purchased paintings by him when they came to İstanbul. In terms of subject matter, the artist's works may be classed into two categories—figural types and views of Constantinople. Reflecting the cultural diversity of the people of İstanbul, the artist preferred to provide a setting from the everyday scene for the models in his works; and when these became very popular, he went to Paris and had them published as lithographs. In his watercolor series (1852–6), he depicted thirty-two male and two female fig-

ures from different regions of the empire. The artist concentrated on the dress and physiognomy of the types he had chosen but abstracted them from their natural environment. Charles Newton states that it is possible to see several facets of Orientalism in his art. On the one hand, while Preziosi furnished the French Court with scenes consistent with its conception of the Orient, on the other hand, he was compiling an album containing sensitive portraits of various types selected, no doubt, because they pleased him; in addition, he depicted realistic and colorful scenes that travelers to İstanbul would appreciate and purchase as a souvenir of their trip.[33] In addition, the artist executed quite a few landscapes of İstanbul.

Among the artists presented to the Court in this era, it is noteworthy that the artists who submitted their works to the Court were the lesser-known Orientalist artists. Some had been invited by the Ottoman Court as possible candidates for the position of Court Artist and some had come to the East on their own as adventure-seeking, itinerant artists. The Western artists who hoped to execute the sultan's picture or who wished to present their works to the Court achieved their objective on the recommendation of an ambassador to İstanbul or of an Ottoman embassy in Europe or sometimes on the demand of a foreign ruler.

The embassies in İstanbul played a leading role in facilitating the invitation and introduction of foreign artists to the Ottoman Court in the nineteenth century. Itinerant Orientalist artists coming to the city with the aim of establishing a connection with the Court applied to their own embassies, to gain a formal presentation to the Court and for services like interpreters. The Ottoman embassies in Europe, particularly that at Paris, were involved in the promotion of artistic connections. They presented the sultan's portrait to Western rulers and from time to time informed the Court of the desire by a Western artist to present a painting to the Ottoman sultan.

Among those who made contact with the Court during Abdülmecid's reign was a Roman artist who came to İstanbul in 1848 at the request of the king of Sardinia and the renowned French artist David who submitted to the Ottoman ambassador in Paris[34] a portrait of the French king in three different sizes, one of which intended for the ambassador, Süleyman Pasha, and the other two were to be sent to İstanbul for the sultan and the grand vizier, respectively; records indicate that for

[28] Lynne Thornton, *Women as Portrayed in Orientalist Painting* (Paris: ACR, 1985), 257.

[29] Thornton, 134–5.

[30] *Les Orientalistes provençaux*, exhibition catalog (Marseille: Musée des Beaux Arts, 1982–3), 20.

[31] Fontmagne, 81.

[32] A. Jacques, C. Peltre and E. Yenal, *Jules Laurens'in Türkiye Yolculuğu* (İstanbul: Yapı Kredi Yayınları, 1998), 12–3.

[33] Newton, 97.

[34] Cezar suggests that this artist probably was Maxime David (1798–1870), who is known to have shown an interest in Eastern individuals. Cezar, *Sanatta*, 123.

their merit, both of these artists were rewarded with imperial medals.[35]

Sultan Abdülmecid commissioned a painting from a Prussian artist named Kripchios, which was sent to the Ottoman embassy in Vienna.[36] Sebuh Manas (1816–89) and Rupen Manas (1810-after 1875), Armenian artists who served as interpreters to the Ottoman ambassador at Paris and who appear to have received training there, also executed portraits of Abdülmecid. Some of the likenesses of the sultan sent to European embassies were executed in Paris by Rupen Manas;[37] a large-scale painting executed by Rupen Manas in 1857, which depicts the sultan standing before the entrance staircase to the Palace, was presented to the Swedish queen.[38] Another portrait of Abdülmecid attributed to Rupen Manas may have been executed for one of the European embassies. For the portrait, the sultan wore a fez with aigrette and a dress uniform. As in many others of his pictures, two sunburst (şemseli) medals of the Order of Mecidiye adorn his chest. The sultan has opened the front of his cape, lined in red fabric in order to display them. Just as in Wilkie's picture, he is wearing white gloves.

Todeschini was another artist who came to İstanbul during Abdülmecid's sultanate. An article about him appearing in the 26 March 1859 issue of *Journal de Constantinople* reports, "[t] he distinguished artist, Todeschini, who has worked here for three years has just completed a work of great value. It is a painting depicting the celebrations arranged the previous summer in connection with the marriage of the sultan's daughters. The sultan complimented the artist and rewarded him."[39], The same article cites that a European artist who came to the city could make the members of the Court and their lives the subject of his paintings and that he could be rewarded on this account, which is indicative of Abdülmecid's favorable position toward art.

Under Abdülaziz, the role adopted by the Ottoman Court of nurturing the practice of Western-style art in İstanbul was enlarged. The sultan made a contribution to its development by his special interest in the art of painting and the fact that he was able to sketch what he wanted from the artists to whom he had given commissions represented a positive step. The 1 March 1330 (1914/5) issue of the newspaper of Ottoman artists society (*Osmanlı Ressamlar Cemiyeti Newspaper*) discloses that Abdülaziz had indicated his reserva-

[35] Cezar, *Sanatta*, 123–4.
[36] Cezar, *Sanatta*, 124.
[37] Kevork Pamukciyan, "Manas Ailesi," *İstanbul: Dünden Bugüne İstanbul Ansiklopedisi* (1994).
[38] Renda, "Portrenin," 45.
[39] *Journal de Constantinople* (26 Mars 1859).

53 Attributed to Rupen Manas. *Sultan Abdülmecid*, ca. 1857-8. Oil on canvas. 81 x 60 cm. Collection of Sevgi and Doğan Gönül, İstanbul.

54 Stanislaw Chlebowski. *Sultan Abdülaziz*, 1867.
Oil on canvas. 274 x 165 cm. Topkapı Palace
Museum, İstanbul.

IX Sultans, artists, and the role of the embassies

55 Pierre Désiré, Guillemet. *Sultan Abdülaziz*, 1873.
Oil on canvas. 140 x 93 cm. Topkapı Palace
Museum, İstanbul.

IX Sultans, artists, and the role of the embassies

tions about the composition of a painting by Chlebowski by presenting to the artist sixty-eight of his own rough sketches in red ink. The same article reports that one fine arts magazine published in English praised the sultan's artistic talent and claimed that the quality of his sketches was indistinguishable from those by a trained artist.

Mehmed Memduh, who describes Abdülaziz as a "handsome, mild tempered, quick witted and majestic as well as a courteous and generous sultan," indicates that, by his having appointing the former sheikhulislam Hasan Fehmi as his tutor, he had learned the Arab sciences, that he appreciated artistic works, and that sometimes he had executed sketches in pencil of villages and the naval vessel types.[40]

In his memoirs titled *Constantinople*, Edmondo De Amicis indicates in regard to Abdülaziz that he indulged himself by satisfying a number of minor whims, such as "having a door painted after a particular design, combination of fruits and after giving the most minute directions, would spend hours watching every stroke of the artist's brush, as though that were the main business of life.".[41] Though these may have been simply rumors, nonetheless, the sultan clearly had an inclination toward the fine arts.

During Abdülaziz' sultanate, exhibitions of fine arts were organized, Court commissions were awarded to foreign artists, participation in international exhibitions took place, the Court formed the first comprehensive art collection, the posts of Court Artist and Court Photographer were created, members of the Court visited exhibitions, and works of art were purchased. The sultan took a keen interest in Şeker Ahmed Pasha's second art show, which was opened at İstanbul University (*Darülfünun*) on 1 July 1875, and he had a number of the canvases brought to the Court for his examination. To encourage the exhibition of paintings and to increase their numbers, he promised rewards for the artists.[42] The hanging on the walls of the Palace of the exhibited works purchased by the Court, whose frames bore the imperial emblem, was an important indicator of the support provided for art and the artist and their reward.

Under Abdülaziz, an increase was registered in the number of foreign artists employed by the Court. Artists like Frenchman, Pierre Désiré Guillemet, and the Pole, Stanislaw Chlebowski, received commissions from the Court and made portraits of the sultans. The Italian Orientalist,

[40] Mehmed Memduh, 99.
[41] De Amicis, 1: 290.
[42] *La Turquie* (5 Août 1875), cited in Cezar, *Sanatta*, 432.
[43] Thalasso, "Les Origines," 366.

Alberto Pasini, who came to İstanbul in 1867 and the Russian artist, Ivan Konstantinovitch Aivazovsky (1817–1900), who came to the city in 1874, can also be numbered among the artists who executed a number of paintings for Abdülaziz.

Chlebowski, who worked for nine years under Abdülaziz, depicted the sultan in a full length portrait in 1867 as he stood at the head of the pool in the garden of Beylerbeyi Palace, which had been completed three years earlier. In the background, a groom has brought the sultan's white horse. The painting is characteristic of the rule that in these depictions, the sultans are shown either in the palaces that they had newly erected or those they preferred to the others, along with objects by which the observer can infer the thought and taste of those in their circle.

The French artist, Pierre Désiré Guillemet, who came to İstanbul in March 1865, worked in the Court circle intimate with Abdülaziz and rendered a full-length picture of the sultan. After returning from his European trip in 1867, Abdülaziz, who supported European art of painting, which up to that time was little known in the Ottoman Empire, appointed Guillemet as Court Artist and supported his opening of an art academy in Pera.[43] In the 29 June 1876 edition of the newspaper *La Turquie*, published in İstanbul, the writer of a news article states that he had visited the atelier of Guillemet and that among the oil paintings were quite a few portraits of Abdülaziz that constituted "near replicas" of the sultan. In a painting by Guillemet dated 1873 in the Topkapı Palace Museum, the sultan is depicted standing on a balcony of Çırağan Palace, which had been finished two years previous. The sultan's uniform was ornamented by a sash (*hamail*) over his shoulder and by one medal and three jeweled decorations, among which two were of the Order of Mecidiye with the sunburst pattern (*şemseli*), and one of Osmanî that he himself had issued. During his reign, the Orientalist style of architecture preferred by the sultan was widely applied in İstanbul by the Balyan family of architects. The Çırağan Palace reflects this style in the clearest fashion and represents a palace erected to conform to Abdülaziz' aesthetics. The appearance in the painting of certain architectural elements, such as the stalactite column capitals, the carved marble screens, the mosque in the background, and other details, show that the painter found an Eastern setting appropriate for the painting.

By commissioning Charles Fuller (1830–75), a British sculptor who came to İstanbul in 1869, to execute his marble bust[44] and his equestrian statue, Abdülaziz stands as a pioneer in the field of sculpture. Ferdinand von Miller in Munich cast this latter work, the first example of a statue belonging to an Ottoman sultan, in bronze in 1872. This equestrian statue was installed in Beylerbeyi Palace, a favorite of his erected in his reign. It is likely that the statue erected in El-Tahrir Square in Alexandria by Mehmed Ali Pasha and observed by the sultan on his tour of Egypt and those statues belonging to Western rulers and prominent personages that stood in urban squares and encountered on his 1867 European tour inspired his own commission of this statue. Though this must be evaluated as a leap forward in one sense, at the same time, the statue was on exhibit at the Court rather than in a public square. This position of hesitancy delimits for us the boundary between the general public and the Court in their understanding of Westernization in the field of art.

Abdülaziz went to Egypt in April 1863 and to France in 1867 to attend the International Exhibition held in Paris; and he went on to London and Vienna before returning to İstanbul. However much political and economic reasons may have played a role in his making this journey in which he as the Ottoman sultan played a leading role, the narrative of the trip, the ceremonies held, and the splendid settings served as an additional stimulus to the contemporary fashion of Orientalism.

Abdülaziz' European tour in an era in which the vogue for Orientalist fashion was intense both from the perspective of the sultan and that of those Westerners who encountered him was interesting and in a sense re-animated this fashion. Abdülaziz was the first Ottoman ruler who paid a formal visit to a European country. Departing from İstanbul on a ship named *Sultaniye* on 21 June 1867, Abdülaziz was accompanied by his ten year old son Yusuf Izzeddin and Princes Mehmed Murad and Abdülhamid and his retinue. To avoid any difficulties in Europe, no one from the harem was included. The ship, furnished like a palace in miniature, had two small pavilions built for Abdülaziz and was opened to French visitors in the port of Toulon. Evrémond de Bérard (1825/30-?), a student of the French artist, Picot, delineated the welcome accorded the sultan at Toulon.

[44] The bust of Abdülaziz by Fuller (1872) is in Topkapı Palace Museum.

Abdülaziz who first set foot in France at Toulon reached the Lyon Station in Paris on 30 June 1867. It was difficult for the Ottoman embassy in Paris to meet the demands of those applying for a place in the stands specially erected at the station. On 1 July 1867, the lead articles in French newspapers indicate that in terms of the magnitude of the interest in the sultan no other king or emperor had aroused a comparable degree of curiosity on their visit to Paris. The people of Paris evidently wished to obtain a first-hand glimpse of the supreme symbol of the East, which had for centuries constituted a threat to Europe and at the same time had

56 Evrémond de Bérard. *Procession
of French Fleet in the Port of Toulon in Honor
of Sultan Abdülaziz's Visit,* 1867. Oil on
canvas.136x198 cm. Marine Museum,
İstanbul.

[45] Taner Timur, "Sultan
Abdülaziz'in Avrupa Seyahatı,
II," *Tarih ve Toplum* (Aralık
1984): 16–25.

tantalized them. At the 1867 International Fair, the sultan paid a visit to the pavilions of the Ottoman and other countries and, in particular, the Fine Arts Gallery; he also toured the Louvre Museum, the Invalides, the School of Fine Arts, and the St. Cyr Military School. After a stay of eleven days, the sultan departed for London, accompanied by splendid ceremonies.

Welcomed by Emperor Napoleon III in Paris and by Queen Victoria in London, Abdülaziz toured, as reported in the contemporary press, the museums and observed military maneuvers. Next, the Ottoman sultan went to Vienna for five days and after staying one evening in Budapest boarded the *Sultaniye* to return to İstanbul.[45] In the picture representing Abdülaziz's visit to the Ambras Gallery in the Vienna Museum, the sultan with his Ottoman train is depicted listening to a talk on sculpture of the Roman period. The small child with his back to the viewer is his son, Yusuf Izzeddin.

How great an effect his tour of Western capitals and his exposure to the lifestyle in Western ill. palaces exerted on the sultan can be inferred by his activities on his return concerning architecture and the art of painting. At this juncture when Orientalism was at its peak, Abdülaziz, who had occupied an elevated position as an Eastern sultan in Europe, preferred Eastern eclecticism in the palace he had built by the architect Sarkis Balyan, who fulfilled the sultan's wishes in his execution of the Çırağan Palace. During Abdülaziz' reign, İstanbul became a staging ground for the specimens of Orientalist architecture that were built one after the other. His position as a supporter of Westernization in the art of painting was maintained. This decisiveness on the part of the sultan is apparent in the making of his equestrian statue and the formation of a Western-style painting collection at the Palace. The 1867 European tour further heightened Abdülaziz' interest in the fine arts. A news article appearing in the 8 October 1868 issue of the *Levant Herald* reports that a gallery comprised of paintings representing the Ottoman sultans and important events and battles in Ottoman history was to open in the new Çırağan Palace and that this gallery was intended to constitute the nucleus of an imperial museum.

This tour affected not only Abdülaziz but also his son, Yusuf Izzeddin, and the princes Mehmed Murad and Abdülhamid, who would in the future ascend the Ottoman throne. These effects cannot, however, be said to have been unilateral, because Abdülaziz, who was the first sultan of the Orient to visit Europe, and his tour—exclusive of the political reasons—was evaluated in the framework of the Orientalist fantasies of the West.

Of all the reforming sultans, Abdülaziz expressed the closest interest in painting, in response to which a great number of Orientalist artists came to the Ottoman Empire, by country of origin, the most well known are as follows: American: Sanford Robinson Gifford; German: Maxmillian Schmidt and Leopold Carl Müller (1834-92); British: Walter Charles Horsley (1855–1943); and Frederick Leighton who was in İstanbul in 1864 (1830–96); Swiss: Rudolf Weiss (1846–1933); Italian: Alberto Pasini; French: Léon Bonnat (1833–1922), Charles Emile de Tournemine (1812–1872) and Jean Lecomte du Nouÿ (1842–1923), who was in the city in 1875.

Jean-Léon Gérôme also came to İstanbul in 1871 and 1875, during Abdülaziz's reign. Undoubtedly the leading name in Orientalist art, Gérôme had first been to the city in 1854. The artist, who came to İstanbul for a fourth time in 1879, treated in a great many of his works in the Orientalist mode slave markets, scenes of the bath and the harem, worshippers in the mosque, dervishes, Albanians, and irregular forces. Though it was announced in the *Basiret Gazetesi* on 26 and 27 March 1291 (1875) that Gérôme and Boulanger were coming to İstanbul to pay a visit to Abdülaziz, no evidence has come to light as to whether or not the artist had any contact with the Court on this visit.[46]

One of the important artists invited by the Court in this period was Stanislaw Chlebowski. The Polish artist was invited to the Court sometime after 1864 to depict the chief wars and battles in Ottoman history, and an apartment in Dolmabahçe Palace was converted into a studio for his use; and, at the end of his term, the artist was rewarded with the medal of the Order of Mecidiye, third class.[47]

[46] Cezar, *Sanatta*, 153.
[47] *Osmanlı Ressamlar Cemiyeti Gazetesi* (1 Mart 1330): 162–3.

57 "Sultan Abdülaziz's Visit to Ambras Gallery, Vienna," *L'Illustration* (17 Aout 1867).

The well-known Italian artist, Alberto Pasini, who came to İstanbul in 1867 at the insistence of French ambassador, Nicolas-Prosper Bourée, who served in İstanbul from 1866 to 1870, executed fifty-one oil paintings and numerous drawings. During the time the artist was in İstanbul, a painting for the sultan was commissioned and this led to three additional commissions. The paintings were to be based on the war in Crete, which had just been concluded. The works called *The Assault by the Ottoman Cavalry* (1868), *The War in Crete* (1868), *The Bombing of the Citadel* (1869), and *The Greco-Ottoman War* (1869) are in the Dolmabahçe Palace Collection.[48] Pasini also rendered depictions of venders in the narrow streets, handicraftsmen at work, oxen-drawn carts, and marketplaces. Other subjects painted by him include the mosques of Nusretiye, Kılıç Ali Pasha, St. Sophia, Sultan Ahmed, and Bayezid and the districts of the city, including Pera, Galata, and Tophane, and the Bosphorus suburbs of Tarabya, Büyükdere, Beykoz, and Rumeli Hisarı. The citadel at Rumeli Hisarı also appears in the background of four paintings whose subject was the harem.[49]

Aivazovsky, a Russian artist of Armenian origin and renowned as a landscape and seascape artist, became acquainted with İstanbul during the reigns of Abdülmecid, Abdülaziz, and Abdülhamid II and executed paintings delineating the vistas of the city and Ottoman daily life. Aivazovsky, who was part of a scientific research field trip conducted in Asia Minor, the Archipelago, and the Eastern Mediterranean in the train of Grand Duke Konstantin Nikolaievich, came to İstanbul for the first time with this scientific team during the reign of Abdülmecid in April 1845 and sojourned only briefly. But the paintings of İstanbul he executed in Feodosiya in 1846 by relying on his sketches made during this tour illustrate to what extent the artist was moved by the exotic attractiveness of the capital of the empire. Following this short visit, Aivazovsky came repeatedly to İstanbul, a subject continually reworked in his paintings until his death.

Aivazovsky came to İstanbul twice during the reign of Abdülmecid, in 1857 and 1858, and was rewarded for his presentation of a painting to the sultan with an imperial medal of the fourth class.[50] Conscious that the sultans supported the Westernization movement, the artist made gifts of paintings to various members of the Court.[51] Aivazovsky, who once again came to İstanbul

during the reign of Abdülaziz, stayed two months in mid-1874 as the guest of Chief Imperial Architect Sarkis Balyan. In connection with the arrival of the artist, newspapers like *Şark* and *Levant Herald* printed articles praising the artist highly, noting that he was the artist of Tzar, Alexander, remarking on his superior talent and mentioning that he had been received at the Court on being presented by the Russian ambassador, Ignatiev.[52] Sultan Abdülaziz received Aivazovsky on 21 October 1874. In an article appearing in *L'Orient Illustré* (24 October 1874), it was indicated that the Armenian artist had been accompanied by the chief interpreter of the Russian embassy, Onou, and Sarkis Balyan. It reports that Abdülaziz had praised the talent of the renowned artist and his paintings in the Yıldız Palace.[53] The sultan also thanked Sarkis Balyan for introducing him to one of the distinguished personages of the art world and at the end of the audience, both Aivazovsky and Sarkis Balyan were rewarded with a medal of the Order of Osmaniye, second class. At this time, Aivazovsky received some commissions from the Court, one of which was a portrait of Abdülaziz. On 16 Ramazan 1291 (1875), the newspaper *Şark* reported that the artist named Aivazovsky, who was sojourning in the city, had executed a portrait of the sultan at his own request and that he was staying as a guest of the Chief Imperial Architect Sarkis Balyan and that he was going to return to Russia in ten days' time.[54] In 1874, Aivazovsky, who came to İstanbul at the invitation of Abdülaziz, was commissioned to execute more than thirty paintings for Dolmabahçe Palace. He made preliminary studies for some of these paintings and completed some of them on his return to Feodosiya in 1875.[55] Paintings in the Dolmabahçe Palace Museum, such as *The Ottoman Fleet before Çırağan Palace* (1875), *Seraglio Point* (1874), and *Eyüp in the Moonlight* (1874) are works that derive from this period.

There is a strong probability that Aivazovsky's painting of 1875 depicting the Ottoman Fleet before the Çırağan Palace represents a commission by Abdülaziz, who took a special interest in the fleet. The artist was highly praised for his seascapes. This depiction of the restored Ottoman fleet, which had been destroyed in the battle of Navarino (the Peloponnesus)[56] was of special significance. It served as a witness of the reforms and achievements of Abdülaziz during his reign.

ill.

[48] The titles of the paintings by Pasini in the Dolmabahçe Palace Collection listed in Vittoria Botteri Cardoso, *Alberto Pasini* (Genoa: Sagep, 1991) are *The War in Crete* (1868), *The Bombardment of a Ship* (1868), *The Greco–Turkish War* (1869), and *The Cavalry Assault*; however, the titles recorded in the Dolmabahçe Collection are considered valid here.

[49] Cardoso, 79–85.

[50] Semra Germaner and Zeynep İnankur, *Orientalism and Turkey* (İstanbul: Türk Kültürüne Hizmet Vakfı, 1989), 91.

[51] Gianne Caffiero and Ian Samarine, *Denizler, Şehirler ve Düşler: İvan Aivazovsky'nin Resimleri* (London: Alexandria, 2000), 64.

[52] Cezar, *Sanatta*, n. 2, 152, *Şark* 262 (7 Ramazan 1291).

[53] *L'Orient Illustré* (14 November 1874) reports that a number of Aivazovsky's paintings were kept in the Yıldız Palace in Istanbul.

[54] Cezar, *Sanatta*, 152.

[55] Caffiero, 64.

[56] The Ottoman fleet, which during the reign of Mahmud II was fired on by the English, French, and Russian fleets at Navarin in 1827 was renewed under Abdülaziz.

58 Ivan Aivazovsky. *Imperial Fleet before Çırağan Palace*, 1875. Oil on canvas. 130 x 193 cm. Collection of Dolmabahçe Palace Museum, İstanbul.

[57] Aivazovsky's portrait of Murad V is in the Topkapı Palace Museum, no. 17/123; the portrait of Abdülhamid II is in a private collection in Berlin.

The existence of another painting dated 1873 depicting *The Ottoman Fleet on the Bosphorus* suggests that the artist had received a commission for this same subject prior to coming to İstanbul.

The portrait of Sultan Murad V (1876) and that of Abdülhamid II executed later demonstrates that the artist was employed at the Ottoman Court after the reign of Abdülaziz.[57] Aivazovsky generated a great deal of interest with his exhibition of 1880 in İstanbul, which was followed by shows in 1886 and 1888. The artist was thus a well-known artist in İstanbul in the 1880s. Aivazovsky, who came once again to İstanbul in 1890 presented two paintings to Abdülhamid II and was rewarded with the medal of the Order of Mecidiye.

The advances made in the sphere of art in the eras prior to the long reign of Abdülhamid II were now producing results, so that the fruits of this development were being gathered and institutions were established. The museum in Yıldız Palace in which valuable artifacts, manuscripts, and the portraits of the sultans were exhibited and the opening of the new Imperial Museum (*Müzehane-i Hümayun*) and the Imperial School of Fine Arts (*Sanaayi-i Nefise Mektebi*) were significant cultural events in Abdülhamid II's reign.

The tastes of the nineteenth-century Ottoman Court during his princehood and the fact that he had participated in Abdülaziz's European tour stimulated Abdülhamid's interest in the fine arts. The sultan enjoyed European songs and operas, played the piano, and, as an amateur, painted pictures in watercolor and oil and made portraits. He is known to have employed pieces of mother-of-pearl as a decorative device to accent his landscapes.[58]

Sultan Abdülhamid II liked to gather representatives of art, science and literature at Yıldız Palace and to put them into service at the Court where people of value to the empire could meet with one another.[59] Ayşe Osmanoğlu states in her memoirs that her father had formed a beautiful collection of paintings at the Court, that he liked landscapes and depictions of flowers, and that he had executed a few portraits, one of which was of his mother, Müşfika Kadın, in charcoal.[60] After the reign of Abdülhamid II, although interest in art continued to be maintained by the Court and its circle, effective leadership now originated in the Imperial School of Fine Arts, with its instructors and the increasing numbers of Ottoman artists rather than the Court. The emergence of a native artist like Osman Hamdi Bey, the subject matter of whose paintings was the Ottoman way of life, constituted an interesting development in the context of Orientalism.

Until the opening of the Imperial School of Fine Arts under Abdülhamid II, the İstanbul Salon exhibitions were significant factors in the enlivening of the art milieu. In 1901, the French architect, Alexandre Vallauri, an instructor in the Department of Architecture in the School of Fine Arts, and Régis Delbeuf, the managing editor of *Le Stamboul* newspaper, initiated the establishment of a salon where the artists and sculptors of İstanbul could come together and exhibit their work, and the first İstanbul Salon exhibition was held in a mansion in the Passage Oriental in Beyoğlu that belonged to a French merchant named Bourdon. Ottoman artists who participated in this exhibition included Osman Hamdi Bey, Ahmed Ali Pasha,

[58] Ayşe Osmanoğlu states that her father, Abdülhamid II, presented to her sister, Princess Refia, four works that showed village scenes/landscapes worked in mother of pearl and which had been removed from the surface of a cupboard. Ayşe Osmanoğlu, *Babam Abdülhamid* (İstanbul : Güven, 1960), 27.

[59] *Le Moniteur Oriental* (21 Fev. 1896).

[60] Osmanoğlu, 2.

[61] Thalasso, "Les premiers salons de Constantinople: le premier salon de Stamboul," in *L'Art et les artistes*. Paris: 1906), 3–11.

[62] Thalasso, "Les premiers," 11–4.

Halil Pasha (1857–1939), and Adil (1868–1928); the Levantine artists were E. Della Sudda, Stefano Farnetti, Lina Gabuzzi, Oskan Effendi, a teacher at the Imperial School of Fine Arts, Salvatore Valeri, J. Warnia Zarzecki, and Pietro Bellò and the European Orientalist artists were Fausto Zonaro (1854–1929) and Leonardo de Mango. Adolph Thalasso who reviewed the İstanbul Salon exhibitions stated, "[t]he first impression diffused by the hall was its Oriental color. This was dominant above else. In two-thirds of the paintings, İstanbul revealed her golds and emeralds, her rubies and sapphires." Though the number of works sent to the First İstanbul Exhibition and the artists was limited, the rate of participation was higher than expected and among the participants were French, Italian, Spanish, Russian, Polish, and Greek artists. The "Turkish School" had proved its aesthetic existence, according to Thalasso. In the works of this luminous school, "a kind of impressionism is applied to the sun rays through which the painter tries to awaken in the spectator, the impressions aroused in him not by the actual appearance of the objects but by the effects of light on these objects."[61]

On the initiative of these same individuals, exhibitions were also organized in 1902 and 1903. The 1902 Salon was opened by a humorous lecture given by the French ambassador, Jean-Antoine-Ernest Constans, where he compared the Salon to a newborn infant and entrusted the exhibition to the Italian ambassador, the Marquis of Malaspina. Among the leading artists who participated in this exhibition of three hundred and twenty-five works, were Osman Hamdi Bey, Salvatore Valeri, J. Warnia Zarzecki, Oskan Efendi, P. Bello, Ahmed Ali Pasha, Halil Bey, Fausto Zonaro, and Leonardo de Mango.

The 1903 Exhibition included two hundred and eighty-three works in the categories of painting, engraving, needlework, and architecture. This exhibition was of a relatively lower quality than the first two, and it seems that the renowned artists of the previous years failed to participate.[62]

In his article Thalasso says that he was expecting to see Orientalist paintings at the İstanbul Salon Exhibitions and his expectation was met by the works of Osman Hamdi Bey, Salvatore Valeri, J. Warnia Zarzecki, P. Bellò, Fausto Zonaro and L. de Mango along with Levantine artists. The writer, in reiterating this expectation in regard to the subject of a museum, complains that there is no

National Museum of Painting and Sculpture, no Louvre of the Orient, and no Ottoman Luxembourg.[63]

At this time when Orientalism was experiencing a revival in Europe, Western itinerant artists continued to arrive in İstanbul. Among those arriving in the very lively city of İstanbul in the last quarter of the nineteenth century were quite a few well-known Orientalist artists like the Americans: Sanford Robinson Gifford (1823–80), Jules Guérin (1866–1946), and Francis Hopkinson Smith (1838–1915); Germans: Ferdinand Max Bredt (1860/68-1921); French: Paul Le Roy (1860–1942), Jean-Léon Gérôme,; Italian: Hermann David Salomon Corrodi (1844–1905); British: Frank Brangwyn (1867–1956), American Edwin Weeks (1849–1903); and Dutch: Marius Bauer (1867–1932); other artists who came to İstanbul in this period were Albert Aublet (1851–1938) who came in 1881, Edouard Debat-Ponsan (1874– 1913) in 1882, Austrian Rudolf Ernst towards 1890, and American John Singer Sargent (1856– 1925) in 1891.

The presentation of paintings to the Court by Western artists in order to obtain a commission from the Ottoman Court and to be rewarded with favors and medals continued under Abdülhamid II. Hippolyte Bertaux (1843–1928), a French artist who came to İstanbul after 1885, executed paintings of Selim III and Mahmud II, each mounted on a horse, which are now in Topkapı Palace Museum. The German artist, Wilhelm Reuter (1859–?), received a commission from Abdülhamid II to execute a portrait of Mahmud II.[64] As these examples suggest the great majority of the painting commissions obtained from the Court during the reign of Abdülhamid II were subjects related to history. Polish painter Tadeusz Ajdukiewicz (1852-1912) who was famous for his military subjects came to İstanbul on the invitation of Sultan Abdülhamid and painted several large canvasses.[65] In order to enter into relations with the Court, artists in this period also drew on the assistance of foreign embassies or an Ottoman statesman as intermediary. The painting by Zonaro depicting the Ertuğrul regiment crossing Galata Bridge was presented to Abdülhamid II through the intermediary of Grand Vizier Ferid Pasha of Vlorë (Albania).

The Italian artist, Salvatore Valeri , who came to İstanbul in the early 1880s on the recommendation of British ambassador, Lord Dufferin, was appointed instructor to the oil painting studio in

[63] Thalasso, "Les premiers," 14.

[64] Renda, "Portrenin," 461.

[65] Martina Haja, Günther Wimmer, *Les Orientalistes des écoles allemande et autrichienne* (Paris: ACR, 200), 188.

the newly founded School of Fine Arts. Valeri, who offered private instruction to Abdülhamid II's sons, was rewarded with the title "Tutor to the Princes." After Valeri had established this connection with the Court, he appears to have obtained further commissions to paint the pictures of members of the imperial dynasty, such as Prince Burhaneddin, Abdülhamid II' son and Princess Nemika, Abdülhamid II's granddaughter. English painter Margaret Murray Cookseley (?-1827) also came to İstanbul following an order to paint one of the Sultan's sons.[66]

A talented French artist, Léon François Prieur-Bardin, whose residence in İstanbul coincided with Jean-Antoine-Ernest Constans' term as ambassador (1898–1909), inspired by the enchanting vistas of İstanbul, executed a painting of the entrance to the port of the city from the Bosphorus, which was presented to Sultan Abdülhamid II. The sultan later presented this painting to his son-in-law, Damad Kemaleddin Pasha, the husband of Princess Naime.[67] It is noteworthy that the sultan may not have always kept the paintings presented to him but instead presented them as gifts to important personages, for this may have represented an effort to increase familiarity with the art of painting among the Court circles.

At the end of Mehmed Reşad's reign (1909-18), one of Sultan Abdülmecid's sons, the Viennese portrait artist, Wilhelm Victor Krausz (1870–1916) executed portraits of Said Halim Pasha, Enver Pasha and Talad Pasha in İstanbul, which were exhibited in the Imperial School of Fine Arts in 1916. One portrait of Sultan Reşad by Krausz is in Topkapı Palace Museum. On 31 March, Abdülhamid II was dethroned and Prince Reşad on becoming sultan took the name Mehmed. The reason for this change of names derived from the establishing of a resemblance between the entrance of Mehmed II on his conquest of İstanbul in 1453 and Reşad's entrance into the city with the operation troops.[68] Krausz, taking Gentile Bellini's portrait of Mehmed II as a model, the depiction the figure within an arch is for this reason, meaningful.

ill. 59

ill. 132

ill. 176

[66] Ackermann, *Les Orientalistes de l'école brittanique*, 317.

[67] N. Said Duhani, *Beyoğlu'nun Adı Pera İken* (Istanbul: Çelik Gülersoy Vakfı, İstanbul Kütüphanesi, 1990), 30.

[68] Sakaoğlu, *Bu Mülkün* , 534.

59 Salvatore Valeri. *Prince Burhaneddin.*
Oil on canvas. 97 x 62.5 cm.
Topkapı Palace Museum, İstanbul.

X Court artists

In the wake of the original reform initiative aimed at Westernization, the position of the Court Artist appears to have become more regularized. The Court Artist—just as in the West—typically, occupied a place in the circle close to the ruler as aide-de-camp, assigned to protocol relations, and, as part of his duties handled matters relating to foreigners making application to the Court. In this context, both Ottoman artists and European painters were given a place at the Ottoman Court. The awarding of such appointments was initiated by Abdülmecid and continued under Abdülaziz and Abdülhamid II, after whom official status of this kind for the artist seems to have lost its former importance. Factors effective in the decline of the position of Court Artist include the restrictions imposed on Court expenditures under the First Constitutional Monarchy, the active role in the İstanbul art scene played by the instructors and former students of the Imperial School of Fine Arts, and the fostering of photography by the Court.

In the post-Tanzimat period, students in the Imperial War Academy were also selected to fill the position of Court Artist. In this modern, imperial military institution, the curriculum included art classes, and youths talented in Western-style art received special support and appointments from the Court. Osman Nuri (Pasha) (1839–1906), a fourth-year student in the military, gained entrance to the Court as an aide-de-camp and Court Artist, and, after rising under the reigns of Abdülmecid and Abdülaziz to the rank of full colonel, he returned to the Imperial War Academy.[1]

In 1861, Ahmed Ali (Şeker Ahmed Pasha) (1841–1907), a student in the War Academy, was sent to Paris at the command of Abdülaziz, and, on his return, received an appointment as "Artist to the Sultan". Ahmed Ali organized art exhibitions with works by both Ottoman and foreign artists in the Sultan Ahmed Vocational School and the University (*Dârülfünun*) while still a student

and initiated the formation by the Ottoman Court of an art collection in the Western sense. Concurrently, he was requested to handle matters of protocol. Thus, as related by de Blowitz in his *Une course à Constantinople*, the aide-de-camp, Şeker Ahmed Pasha, was assigned the duty of showing one member of the Belgium government, M.Olin, through the imperial palaces of Dolmabahçe, Beylerbeyi and Topkapı palaces on his visit to İstanbul.[2]

On the death of Şeker Ahmed Pasha toward the end of Abdülhamid II's reign, the post of Artist to the Sultan was awarded to Hüseyin Zekai Pasha (1860–1918), another graduate of the Imperial War Academy. One painting of the imperial fleet in the Bosphorus by Hüseyin Zekai Pasha, executed while still a student, was presented to the Court, and, receiving the approbation of Abdülhamid II, the artist was rewarded with an appointment as aide-de-camp. The military origins of these artists who contributed so greatly to the development of Turkish painting and their employment by the Court as painters of the Sultan suggests an interesting parallel with the earlier organization of court artists and artisans affiliated to the Imperial Army (*Ehl-i hiref*).[3]

One sign of the interest shown in art by the Court is the establishment by Abdülhamid II of a museum in Yıldız Palace in the last quarter of the nineteenth century. According to a sketch of the museum dated to the 1880s, now held by the Topkapı Palace Museum, among the various kinds of works of art on display, one section was devoted to portraits of the sultans and landscapes.[4]

That both native and European artists assumed positions at the Ottoman Court after the inauguration of the reform period bears significance from the perspective both of their inclusion in the Westernization program and of the status accorded to Western artists who came to İstanbul. Ottoman landscape and still-life artists were active in İstanbul in the 1870s and succeeding years,

[1] It is thought that Osman Nuri Pasha earned Abdülaziz's approval because his paintings treated the subjects of ships and marine subjects. The sultan is known to have been closely interested in both seamanship and navigation. The paintings executed on the ceilings of Beylerbeyi Palace during his reign and certain furnitures with a mooring rope motif are reflections of this interest.

[2] De Blowitz, *Une course à Constantinople* (Paris: Librairie Plon, 1884), 112.

[3] Zeynep İnankur, "Official Painters of the Ottoman Palace," *Art turc: actes de 10ième congrès international d'art turc* (Genève: Fondation Max van Berchem, 1999), 382–83.

[4] Renda, "Portrenin," 532–53.

60

X Court artists

whether appointed to service at Court or in the military schools, such as Şeker Ahmed Pasha and Süleyman Seyit (1842–1913), who had been trained in the West. Despite the existence of trained Ottoman painters working in the Western style, the continued granting of the title of Court Artist to Westerners may be attributed to the commissions awarded for the depiction of scenes from Ottoman history, which required crowded figural compositions. Since no other institution or individual was available outside the Court who would award these commissions, this circumstance led to the emergence of official art in the Ottoman Empire.

European painters appointed to the Ottoman Court in the nineteenth century primarily executed commissions for the execution of portraits of the sultans, parades by the newly instituted military

bodies as witness to the military reforms, the imperial fleet, and scenes devoted to Ottoman history. One indication that, indeed, a distinction was made between figural and non-figural paintings is the presence in the Ottoman imperial art collection of, on the one hand, the above-mentioned paintings by European artists of historical subjects and, on the other, landscapes,[5] seascapes, interiors, still

ill. 61
ill. 62
ill. 63
ill. 64

[5] This landscape painted in 1886 by Şeker Ahmed Pasha was a gift to Ahmed Midhad Efendi on the birth of his son, Süleyman Uluyazman.

60 Şeker Ahmed Pasha. *Self-portrait.* Oil on canvas. 116 x 84 cm. Museum of Painting and Sculpture, Mimar Sinan University, İstanbul.

61 Şeker Ahmed Pasha. *Landscape*, 1886. Oil on canvas. 78 x 100 cm. Collection of Mine and Güven Kemal Persentili, İstanbul.

61

62 Hüseyin Zekai Pasha. *The Imperial Loggia in St. Sophia Mosque*, 1905 / 1906. Oil on canvas. 100 x 81 cm. Museum of Painting and Sculpture, Mimar Sinan University, İstanbul.

X Court artists

lives, and renderings of the imperial gardens, pavilions and summer palaces— by Ottoman artists.

In the second half of the nineteenth century, artists such the Frenchman, Pierre Désiré Guillemet, the Pole, Stanislaw Chlebowski, and the Italians, Luigi Acquarone and Fausto Zonaro, were working at the Ottoman Court. Though Guillemet, Chlebowski and Zonaro painted portraits and Ottoman historical events commissioned by the Court, they were, at the same time, affected by and took advantage of living in an actual Oriental setting and from working at the Ottoman Court in which Westerners took a close interest. Distinct from these commissioned works, the paintings they executed of Ottoman life played a part in making their reputation as Orientalist artists.

Adolphe Thalasso in his book titled *L'Art ottoman: les peintres de Turquie* praises Guillemet, named as Court Artist to Abdülaziz, for founding in Pera the first art academy offering training in the Western style in İstanbul in 1874. On his return from Paris in 1867, Abdülaziz, a supporter of the art in the Western manner, commissioned Guillemet to paint his portrait. The portraits by Guillemet of the women of the Court may have been accomplished by relying on sketches of the live models drawn by his wife, who was, like her husband, also an artist. The 1875 issue of *Revue de Constantinople* reports that among the numerous paintings in Guillemet's studio were two splendid canvases that were going to be sent to the palace and portraits of the sultan.[6] Guillemet, as someone resident in İstanbul and known to have possessed a personal relation with the sultan and intimate knowledge of the Ottoman Court, conveys an air of authenticity in his portraits through the articles of clothing and accessories.

Another artist with connections to the Court was Stanislaw Chlebowski. In 1865, he received an invitation from Sultan Abdülaziz, and an apartment was converted into a studio for his own use at the Court.[7] The artist was successful both with large canvases and Orientalist paintings. An article appearing in the March 1865 issue of *Journal de Constantinople* informed readers that the Polish artist, Chlebowski, in possession of a diploma from the Fine Arts Academy of St. Petersburg, had four paintings ready to submit to the sultan and that those who wished to view the paintings could come to the Galatasaray Barracks,

[6] *Revue de Constantinople* (1875), 541.
[7] Taha Toros, "İstanbul Varşova Köprüsünde Koskoca Bir Tarih Var," *Milliyet Gazetesi* (14 Ocak 1982).

63 Şeker Ahmed Pasha. *Still Life with Melon*, 1893. Oil on canvas. 74 x 102.5 cm. Museum of Painting and Sculpture, Mimar Sinan University, İstanbul.

64 Hüseyin Zekai Pasha. *Still Life*. Oil on canvas. 140 x 140 cm. Private Collection, İstanbul.

65 Stanislaw Chlebowski. *Pitched Battle
at Varna*. Oil on canvas. 300 x 400 cm.
Military Museum, İstanbul

X Court artists

starting on 19 March for eight days. Descriptions of the paintings contained in this same article indicate that one depicted Sultan Abdülaziz preparing to mount his horse in the company of high-ranking officers and troops of the imperial guard unit, that another one delineated the uniforms of the different units in the Levent Çiftlik Military Encampment; that yet another rendered a general view of the military camp at sunrise, and that the final painting delineated the sultan reviewing a maneuver at Emirgan.[8]

Lady Brassey, a visitor to İstanbul and Chlebowski's studio in 1869, relates that the artist was at work on a very large painting showing Mahmud II's entrance as victor into İstanbul.[9] Lady Brassey states that Chlebowski had a portofolio of sketches in red ink, done by the sultan, just to show roughly what he wishes the picture to be. These studies, especially the battle scenes, although composed of just a few strokes in many cases, were extremely spirited and showed great talent..[10]

On Lady Brassey's final visit to the artist to thank him for the present he had made her of an original sketch by the sultan, he told her about his life in the Palace, which seemed almost like that of a state prisoner and complained that he was always hard at work.[11] Chlebowski continued to work at the Court until 1875, when he was forced to resign due to his deteriorating health. A record in the Dolmabahçe Palace Archives dated 11 March 1876 discloses that the artist's duties were terminated in 1875 and that, in response to his request of five thousand liras for the paintings he had executed for the Court, he was by order of the sultan paid only fifteen thousand piasters.[12]

In 1858 prior to coming to İstanbul, Chlebowski had visited Munich and, later, Paris, where he attended the studio of the renowned Orientalist artist, Jean-Léon Gérôme, in the School of Fine Arts. Apart from genre scenes of Orientalist subjects and portraits,[13] he executed works relating to Ottoman history, the principal ones being *The Entrance into Constantinople by Sultan Mehmed the Conqueror* in the Cracow National Museum, painted in Paris and Cracow between 1876 and 1884, *Pitched Battle at Varna*, and *The 1683 Siege of Vienna*.[14]

In the years when Orientalist subjects were met with interest in Western artistic circles, it was evident that Chlebowski, whose work had attained a position of distinction at the Ottoman Court, was himself influenced by the milieu in which he

lived. The artist produced for the Ottoman Court at the request of the sultan, large-scale paintings with historical subjects and executed, for his own pleasure, Orientalist paintings. But his paintings on Ottoman historical events differ from specimens of Western art that depict similar events. For, in Chlebowski's case, it is because the subjects of these paintings are drawn from Ottoman history that they contain Eastern types and Eastern dress and accessories.

Starting in 1865, Chlebowski rendered several portraits of Abdülaziz. Another canvas by Chlebowski is an imaginary painting which represented the thirty-two sultans of the Ottoman Dynasty in front of Sultan Ahmed Mosque:[15] The champion of this interesting work executed between the years 1864 and 1876 is Sultan Abdülaziz. Works like *Panorama of Constantinople*, *Excursion in Constantinople, Kağıthane,* and *Turkish Women at the Mosque* are typical Orientalist paintings, however, and were executed in İstanbul during the same period.[16]

ill. 241

Another artist employed by the Court was Luigi Acquarone, originally of Genoa but who trained in Florence, where he resided for many years. Arriving in İstanbul in 1841, Acquarone was awarded an appointment as artist to Abdülhamid II in 1881.[17] The artist, who worked in both oils and watercolors but was particularly successful in the latter medium, had a studio in Rue Linardi in Beyoğlu. The few works (portraits, still lives and landscapes) attributed with certainty to the artist reveal that he worked in the academic tradition. Acquarone entered the first art exhibition ever arranged in the Ottoman Empire, organized by Şeker Ahmed Pasha and held in the Sultan Ahmed Vocational School on 27 April 1873, with two portraits in charcoal. Paintings by the artist were also included in an exhibition opened in Petit-Champs Municipal Theater in 1877. The earliest dated work by Acquarone in the Court collection is dated 1871.[18] His works in the İstanbul Painting and Sculpture Museum—*The British General* (1888) and *The Farewell* (1889)—may have originally been part of the Court collection. The full-length portrait of Infantryman Ferik Fuad Pasha and the oil portrait of Court Chamberlain Mehmed Emin Bey, an imperial servant of thirty years, by Acquarone, who now bore the title "Chief Artist to His Majesty, the Sultan" (*Serressâm-ı Hazreti Şehriyari*), reveal that he received portrait commissions from dignitaries in Abdülhamid II's circle.[19]

8 *Le Journal de Constantinople* (29 Mars 1865).

9 Undoubtedly, Mehmed II was intended.

10 Lady Brassey, *Sunshine and Storm in the East* (London: Longmans, 1881), 96.

11 Brassey, 124–5.

12 Dolmabahçe Sarayı Arşivi, D.2413, S. 269, cited in Sema Öner, "Tanzimat Sonrası Osmanlı Saray Çevresinde Resim Etkinliği (1839–1923)," Ph. D. dissertation (Mimar Sinan Üniversitesi, 1991), 271.

13 İnankur, "Official," 383.

14 Tadeusz Majda, "European Artistic Tradition and Turkish Taste: Stanislaw von Chlebowski, the Court Painter of Sultan Abdülaziz," *Hacettepe Üniversitesi, Edebiyat Fakültesi, Sanat Tarih Bölümü, Uluslararası Sanatta Etkileşim Sempozyumu Bildirileri* (Ankara : Türkiye İş Bankası, 2000), 177.

15 Majda, 178.

16 Majda, 176–81.

17 For a record indicating that Acquarone and Zonaro were Court painters see Milli Saraylar Arşivi Belgeleri, D.2539, sıra no.103 cited in Sema Öner, "Sultan II. Abdülhamid'in Saray Ressamları: Luigi Acquarone ve Fausto Zonaro," *Hacettepe Üniversitesi, Edebiyat Fakültesi, Sanat Tarih Bölümü, Uluslararası Sanatta Etkileşim Sempozyumu Bildirileri* (Ankara: Türkiye İş Bankası, 2000), 186–7.

18 Öner, "Sultan II Abdülhamid," 186–91.

19 Court Chamberlain Mehmed Emin Bey was the grandfather of the archeologist, Prof. Dr. Muhibbe Darga. Mehmed Emin Bey, whose father, a silkworm merchant named Darugazade Abdürrahim Effendi, was known also to have had close ties with Fausto Zonaro, and who commissioned a portrait from Zonaro. Personal interview by Prof. Dr. Muhibbe Darga.

65

66

Granted a salary of fifteen liras, the artist was appointed as an art instructor at the Imperial School of Fine Arts on 27 March 1889.[20] Acquarone, honored by being awarded the medal of the Order of Mecidiye, third class, the silver medal of Merit, the Ottoman medal of Fine Arts, the Italian medal of Fine Arts, and the Persian medal of the Lion and the Sun, died in 1896, following a protracted illness.[21]

Replacing Acquarone in the same year, another Italian, Fausto Zonaro, was appointed with a salary of thirty-five liras .[22] Receipt of the title "Court Artist" constituted a turning point in the artistic life of Zonaro: it was gained through the patronage of Ferid Pasha of Vlorë, the last grand vizier under Abdülhamid II, who took an interest in Zonaro's work and in the artist himself as an individual and a friend. Ferid Pasha of Vlorë, an intellectual and a connoisseur of refined taste, was a rare Muslim who owned a number of paintings by European artists. The purchase by Ferid Pasha of paintings by Zonaro served to boost the artist's morale and to encourage him to present his paintings to the Court. Thalasso in an article in *Figaro Illustré* states that Zonaro, after presenting the sultan his painting of the Ertugrul regiment passing over Galata Bridge, through the mediation of Grand Vizier Ferid Pasha, was rewarded with a medal of the Order of Mecidiye, first class in 1896, and honored the same year by the title "Court Artist."[23]

As patrons of art, certain Ottoman officials of high rank, like Grand Vizier Ferid Pasha, provided artists with as many opportunities as Western ambassadors, by acquainting them with the milieu in which they lived and providing opportunities for them to learn about the Ottoman way of life in a more intimate manner. Zonaro sold paintings to prominent personages outside the Court and played a role in the formation of an art market in İstanbul. These sales were significant from the perspective of collectors and shed light on the artistic milieu and tastes of the period: two portraits from his preliminary studies for the painting *The Assault (The Battle of Domokos)* executed in 1898 for Abdülhamid and *The Itinerant Barber* were sold to Münir Pasha, the ambassador to Paris; *The Petition Writers* to Sir O'Connor, a former British ambassador to the Sublime Porte; the *Portrait of a Gypsy Girl*, to the Royal Italian collection; *The Odalisque* to the Royal Greek collection; a study for the painting titled *Fishermen at*

ill. 66

[20] BOA, İrade Dahiliye, no. 88088.

[21] To secure a source of income for the family of Acquarone a salary of two hundred and fifty kurush was allocated by the Palace. Dolmabahçe Palace Archive, no. 539, sıra no. 182 cited in Aykut Gürçağlar, "Fausto Zonaro ve Çağdaşlarının İstanbul'u," Master's thesis, Istanbul Teknik Üniversitesi, Mimarlık Fakültesi, 1991, 16. Further, Sabuncuzâde Luis Alberi in his study of Abdülhamid II's *"saray-ı hümayun ressamı"* indicates that after the artist's death an interpreter was sent to his wife to announce that a salary had been assigned to the family. Sabuncuzâde Luis Alberi, *Sultan II. Abdülhamid'in Hal Tercümesi* (İstanbul, 1997), 43–4.

[22] Dolmabahçe Palace Archive, no.539, sıra nos. 103 and 105 cited in Gürçağlar, " Fausto," 14.

[23] Thalasso, "Zonaro," 27.

66 Fausto Zonaro. *Self-portrait.* Oil on canvas. 75 x 60 cm. Comune di Masi. Padova.

67 Fausto Zonaro. *Entrance by Sultan Mehmed II, the Conqueror, into İstanbul,* 1908. Oil on canvas. 98 x 75.5 cm. Collection of Dolmabahçe Palace Museum, İstanbul.

Dawn and the painting *At the Entrance to the Spice Bazaar* to Captain Zampolli, a military attaché in the Italian embassy at İstanbul; and the paintings *On the Bridge* and *Impressions of the Galata Bridge* to the comedian Ermete Novelli. The painting titled *The Mosque of Valide Sultan* was commissioned and purchased by Prince Mavrocordato, a former Greek minister plenipotentiary to İstanbul; and *Women Boarding a Caique* is owned by M. Huber of İstanbul. The works titled *Wildflower* and *Girl Daydreaming* were purchased in 1908 by Prince Abdülmecid, a

son of Sultan Abdülaziz. This list is adequate to suggest the select quality of the circle of patrons Zonaro acquired during his residence in İstanbul.

Two years after Zonaro became Court Artist, he presented to the sultan the composition titled *The Assault (The Battle of Domokos)*, a work that had involved extensive preparation and which depicted the heroism of the Ottoman troops; and, as a token of his immense pleasure, the sultan awarded him the Ottoman medal and, moreover, allocated to him a house in Akaretler in Beşiktaş district, which the artist converted into a studio.[24] The artist, in an interview in 1912 with a critic for the magazine *Caffaro*, revealed that he had written a letter to the sultan in 1909 expressing his desire to paint his portrait and that Abdülhamid II had immediately accepted and granted him three sittings.[25] Besides the portrait of the sultan, members of the Court had commissioned numerous portraits from Zonaro. It is evident that his wife, Elisa, also made an important contribution, particularly in the case of the paintings of the women of the Imperial Harem.

Of the art exhibitions held in İstanbul in the years 1894–5 and 1905, the artist participated in both the First and Second İstanbul Exhibitions, of which the latter was notable for the fact that all thirty-four of his paintings shown were variations on theme of the "Orient." At the art exhibition organized in İstanbul in September, 1907 at the command of Sultan Abdülhamid II on the occasion of the thirty-first anniversary of his accession to the throne, Zonaro received great acclaim for his paintings *Fishermen at Sunrise, In the Caique, Odalisque, A Dervish Playing a Reed Flute, The Petition Writers, The Rifai Dervishes,* and *The Harmony of the Easterners.*

Zonaro, a keen portrayer of Ottoman history, religious life, and people is characterized by A. Thalasso as "this great artist, the possessor of an astonishing and tireless production, a master of the 'Turkish School'" and "one of the greatest Orientalists not only of the present day and of Turkey, but for all time and of all nations."[26] This may be attributed to the fact that the artist lived like an Ottoman subject in İstanbul for many years, that he occupied the position of Court Artist, that he produced a great many works and held exhibitions, that his studio was open to everyone, that he gave private lessons, and that his works were contained in both Ottoman and foreign collections—in short, that Zonaro made a great contribution to the art world of the Ottoman Empire for eighteen years, from 1891 to 1909.

Starting in the year 1896 and repeated every year thereafter, the artist, the "chief Artist to His Majesty, the Sultan," presented a painting to Sultan Abdülhamid II. This explains why such paintings of his, like *Viewing the Transport Overland of the Fleet by Sultan Mehmed II, Sultan Mehmed II Riding His Mount through the Stream to Encourage His Troops, Entrance by Sultan Mehmed II, the Conqueror, into Constantinople, The Assault (the Battle of Domokos)*, and a copy of Bellini's *Portrait of Sultan Mehmed II*, are in the galleries of Yıldız Palace. These examples are equally interesting from the point of view that this sultan, like his predecessors, seems to have appreciated works on Ottoman history. The artist apparently also took an interest in the arrangement of the paintings in Dolmabahçe Palace.[27]

In 1908, Zonaro executed a painting to celebrate the drawing up of a constitution for the Ottoman Empire. The first strokes of his brush on the canvas for this large-scale composition called *The Symbol of Freedom* were made in early October, in the presence of Prince Abdülmecid, a son of Abdülaziz and a painter himself. In November of the same year, Zonaro opened an exhibition of three hundred of his paintings, the cause of a tremendous sensation, in which representatives of Union and Progress Party displayed a great interest. Furthermore, field marshals, generals, court chamberlains, British and Italian ambassadors were among the first to honor the exhibition by their presence. Zonaro, who staged frequent exhibitions in Europe between 1891 and 1911, showed a number of canvases with Ottoman subjects at exhibitions arranged by Società degli Amatori e Cultori di Belle Arti in Rome in 1895–6 and 1903.

Regrettably, with the outbreak of the War of Tripoli in 1911 between Italy and the Ottoman Empire, the artist, with his wife and four children, was forced to leave İstanbul and sell at a low price the three hundred paintings in his museum-like studio in Akaretler.[28] Subsequently, Zonaro settled in San Remo, where he spent his last years. On the proclamation of the Second Constitutional Monarchy and with the departure of Zonaro, the tradition of Court Painters ended.

[24] Thalasso, "Zonaro," 29.
[25] R.Falchi, ed., *Le Tra Stagioni Pittoriche di Fausto Zonaro*, exhibition catalog (San Remo:Villa Ormondi, 1994–1995), 60.
[26] Adolphe Thalasso, *L'art ottoman: les peintres de Turquie* (Paris : Librairie Artistque Internationale, 1910), 36.
[27] Falchi, *La Tra*, 49.
[28] Pamukciyan, "Fausto," 25.

XI The Ottoman imperial art collection

Though there is some truth in the supposition that the idea of an imperial collection composed of Western-style paintings was first conceived in Dolmabahçe Palace during the reign of Sultan Abdülaziz, nonetheless, it is a fact that an accumulation of paintings and portraits of the sultans had already existed prior to this in Topkapı Palace. Thus, Henri Blanc, touring Topkapı Palace in May, 1854, noted in his journal that a beautiful collection of pictures was located here in the corridor leading to the Women's Quarters and that hanging in the corridor, fully illuminated by windows overlooking the garden, were designs of several ships of the French fleet and numerous French lithographs.[1] In 1852, Théophile Gautier mentions in regard to his tour of Topkapı Palace that landscapes, mirrors, and a specimen of calligraphy by Mahmud II embellished the walls of the interior and notes the similarity between calligraphy and design. Gautier also refers to two drawings in pastel in one of the rooms by Michel Bouquet—*Bucharest Harbor* and *A Vista of Constantinople*, as seen from the Tower of Leander—and indicates that none of the pictures contained any figures.[2] A mechanical clock also located in this same room was observed to bear a depiction of Seraglio Point with caiques and sailing craft. Incidentally, the writer states that, while in the Library of Ahmed III, he was shown a large parchment scroll said to contain a kind of family tree, with miniature portraits of all the Ottoman sultans in oval medallions.[3]

Keeping in mind the architectural character and the interior decoration of Dolmabahçe Palace, we may assume that the hall interiors had been embellished by paintings. Works presented to the Court during the reign of Abdülmecid by the numerous European artists coming to İstanbul may also have been hung on these walls. Nevertheless, the first time a group of paintings was purchased by the decision of a sultan occurred during the reign of Abdülaziz, and this

action represents a sign of a new awareness. In 1861 Gérôme has painted a canvas for the sultan Abdülaziz named *Socrates Seeking Alcibiades at the House of Aspasia*. This neo-greek style painting is yet another demonstration of the interest shown by the Court for images of Western style.[4]

On his return to İstanbul, Abdülaziz, having been exposed to the numerous artworks in European palaces, took the first step in forming an art collection by commissioning paintings for Dolmabahçe Palace, furnished in the Western fashion. Şeker Ahmed Pasha, an aide-de-camp in the train of the sultan, played a key role in bringing to the Ottoman Empire this collection of Western art, whose records are preserved in the Dolmabahçe Palace Archives. The fact that when Şeker Ahmed Pasha was in Paris, he became acquainted with Gérôme and worked in his studio was an influential factor in the purchasing of the pieces of art. Through the assistance of Şeker Ahmed Pasha and the mediation of A. Goupil & Co., owned by Gérôme's father-in-law, the works of the leading artists of the era—for the most part French—such as Alfred Eloi Auteroche (1831–1906), Adolphe William Bouguereau (1825–1905), Gustave Boulanger (1824–88), Auguste Bonheur (1824–84), Charles Chaplin (1825–91), Pierre–Auguste Cot (1837–83), Alfred de Dreux (1810–60), Kuwasseg, Victor Leclaire (1830-85), Georges Washington (1827–1901), Jan Baptiste Van Marcke (1797–1849), Victor Huguet (1835–1902), Giuseppe de Nittis (1846–84), Henri Joseph Harpignies (1819–1916), Eugène Fromentin (1820–76), Charles Daubigny and Adolf Schreyer were delivered to İstanbul in the years 1875–6, and, over time, the collection was enlarged by works purchased by or presented to the Court. As a whole, these paintings represent a mix of landscapes and horses, alone or mounted, works by Orientalist artists and portraits of European rulers.

The paintings of horses and horses with riders executed by Eugène Fromentin, Adolphe

---

[1] Blanc, 56.

[2] Michel Bouquet (1807–90) exhibited in the Paris Salon Exhibition starting in 1846 cited in Gautier, *Constantinople*, 253.

[3] Gautier, *Constantinople*, 254.

[4] Gerald M.Ackermann, *Jean-Léon Gérôme* (Paris: ACR, 1986), 210. Why the painting exhibited in the Paris Salon of 1861 has never reached the Court is still to be investigated. According to the art dealer Goupil's registers, it has been sold in 1863 for a sum of 15.000 francs before being purchased in 1865 by Robert Isaacson.

Schreyer, Georges Washington, Alfred de Dreux, Victor Huguet, and Gustave Boulanger, seem likely to have been specially commissioned for the Ottoman palace by a horse fancier, such as Sultan Abdülaziz, who was the first Ottoman sultan to order his equestrian statue and who himself drew sketches of horses.[5] Works on Arab horses and mounted riders in the Dolmabahçe Collection constitute a rather sizeable group.

Dolmabahçe Palace occupies a place in the memoirs of a number of travelers who came to İstanbul; yet, few passages refer to the interior of the palace—and, in particular, to the art collection. For this reason, the impressions of Vicomte René Vigier, who left İstanbul in September 1885 and who collected his memoirs in the book titled *Un Parisien à Constantinople*, are of importance. Though Vigier provides interesting information about the art collection, he criticizes what he sees as negative changes in the cultural life of the Ottoman Empire and presents Dolmabahçe Palace as a concrete example of this phenomenon. On his visit to Dolmabahçe, the halls of the palace were furnished, the writer indicates, with European-style pieces while the walls were covered with pictures by French painters shown in the annual Salon exhibitions in Paris. On his tour, Vigier chanced upon a charming canvas titled *Spring*, poetical and filled with youth, by a French artist named Pierre-Auguste Cot.[6] But Vigier describes the various canvases found in one long gallery as insipid and poor, and adds that, in the light of certain German lithographs on exhibit, he concludes that the sultan apparently took pleasure in displaying the defeats of the French.[7]

Steady enrichment of the imperial art collection, originally composed of the first group of paintings obtained through Goupil, artworks presented to the Court by Europeans—both as gifts and as formal commissions from artists like Chlebowski, Aivazovsky, and Zonaro—and works by Ottoman artists, continued during the reign of Abdülhamid II. The painting *Fire at the Paris Opera* by Rudolf Ernst who came to İstanbul at the end of the eighties was added to the Palace collection at this time.[8] Contemporary photographs reveal that Orientalist paintings were included among the specimens of European pictorial art on the walls of the villas of Büyük Mabeyn and Şale on the grounds of Yıldız Palace.

Mary Mills Patrick provides this information about the painting collection of Abdülhamid II, as follows:

[5] Semra Germaner, "Oryantalist Resimlerde Arap Atları Fantazyalar," *P Dergisi* 11(Güz 1998): 36–51.

[6] Pierre–Auguste Cot (1837–83), sculptor, was a student of Duret, L., Cogniet, Cabanel and Bouguereau. *Bénézit*

[7] Vigier, 205–6.

[8] Haja, 286.

[9] Mary Mills Patrick, *Under Five Sultans* (New York: The Century, 1929), 173.

[10] Cox, 19.

[11] Zeynep İnankur, "Halil Şerif Paşa," *P Dergisi* (Yaz 1996): 71–80.

During the early eighties the Sultan he remained at Dolma Bagtche, although the suspicions and fears that possessed his mind constantly increased while he was still living in the palace, he developed one of the finer sides of his nature, his love of good pictures. There were some paintings in his collection that were really works of art. When Lew Wallace was an American minister in Constantinople, Sultan Hamid took great pleasure in showing him his gallery, and he wished to present Mrs. Wallace with one of his most beautiful pictures.[9]

Samuel C. Cox, another American minister plenipotentiary, mentions in his memoirs the imperial painting collection in his description of the "very wide and long" audience room in Yıldız Palace, as follows:

Its floor is covered with a Turkish carpet. In the centre of the room is a long buhl table. There is a small table behind the Sultan, on which he leans while "audience" goes on.... The furniture in the room is not a prominent feature. Most of it is from Paris.... On the walls hang superb oil paintings. The first on the Sultan's left represents a moonlight view of Stamboul and the Seraglio Point.... It is by the celebrated Russian artist Alvasowski [*sic*]. On the same side of the room is an exquisite night scene of the small Asiatic palace at the "Sweet Waters." It is by Ghickson. Who he is, connoisseurs know. On the other side of the room are three artistic paintings. The best of these represents *The Midnight Sun in Norway*. The other two are naval engagements.[10]

Though at the end of the nineteenth century, the primary mover in active support of pictorial art through the purchase of paintings and the formation of a collection was the Ottoman Court, distinguished and wealthy bureaucrats adopting the principles of reform in the empire and who were in favor of Westernization also began to form art collections, among whom the most prominent were those involved in foreign affairs.

Halil Şerif Pasha, the son of the Egyptian prince, Büyük Şerif Pasha, and one of the most colorful personalities of the reform era, attained the chief prominence among contemporary collectors.[11] In 1856, Halil Şerif, appointed to the Ministry of Foreign Affairs, went to Athens in September 1856 and to St. Petersburg in September 1861 as minister plenipotentiary. Around 1865, Halil left Russia for Paris. Though the reasons behind his departure for Paris are somewhat unclear, the fortune he inherited from his father that year probably played a large part in his decision. This change in his financial circumstances marked the beginning of his career as an art collector. The Pasha, thanks to this fortune, immersed himself in a life of total luxury, and both the weakness he exhibited for a life of ease, gambling, and beautiful women and the feasts he gave soon gave him a reputation as one of the leading personalities of Paris. Halil Şerif was at the same time very interested in literature and art and possessed refined tastes. As Théophile Gautier observed, "his painting collection was the first ever to be formed by a child of the Islamic religion."[12]

Halil Şerif became the owner of a collection comprising half a dozen paintings by Courbet, along with the works of painters like Delacroix, Rousseau, Boucher, Gérôme, Corot, Greuze, Watteau, Chassériau, Diaz, Decamps, and Gerard Terborch. Halil Şerif also showed an interest in pictures with Orientalist subjects and bought works like Horace Vernet's *The Slaying of the Mamlukes*, Marilhat's *A Street in Cairo*, and Ingres' *Turkish Bath*. Because of the luxurious life led by Halil Şerif and his love of gambling, his material situation grew steadily worse and, in order to meet his debts, he was compelled to auction a great proportion of his painting collection in October 1868. In the foreword to the sale catalog of this auction, which created a great sensation in the press of the day, the writer, Théophile Gautier, had this to say

> The number of works in this gallery is not
> great—at most, a hundred paintings—but
> everything has been carefully selected, and
> in this casket of paintings there are among
> the precious stones no bits of rubbish, no false
> pearls. Every artist is presented by one of his
> purest diamonds. A sure taste, a perfect sense
> of quality, a sincere passion for the beautiful
> have guided the owner of this rare collection[13]

Besides Halil Şerif Pasha, who occupied a distinguished position in the West as an art collector, Grand Vizier Said Halim Pasha; Ferid Pasha of Vlorë, an intellectual and art lover of refined taste; Salih Münir Pasha, ambassador to Paris; and the last Ottoman caliph, Prince Abdülmecid, were Muslims unusual for their ownership of a number of works by European artists.

[12] Francis Haskell, "A Turk and His Pictures in Nineteenth–Century Paris," *Past and Present in Art and Taste* (New Haven: Yale University Press, 1987), 175.

[13] Théophile Gautier, "La Collection Khalil Bey," *L'Illustration* (11 Janvier 1868).

XII Artist from the House of Osman: Prince Abdülmecid, the Caliph

68 Spiridon. *Portrait of the Caliph, Prince Abdülmecid*. Oil on canvas. 42 × 34 cm. Museum of Painting and Sculpture, Mimar Sinan University, Istanbul.

Prince Abdülmecid (1868–1944), the son of Sultan Abdülaziz—the last heir to the Ottoman throne (1918–22) and the last caliph (1922–24)—possessed among all the members of his lineage the closest affinity for art and earned a reputation as an artist.[1] Under the First Constitutional Monarchy, as a member of the House of Osman he played an effective role in promoting art by gathering artists about him, serving as benefactor to them, and both purchasing and executing paintings himself.

The professional level at which Prince Abdülmecid devoted himself to his art owed much to the importance accorded to art by the Court during his apprenticeship period. His special education was received in the School for Princes, whose curriculum was overseen by Abdülhamid II, where he learned French and how to play the piano and painted under the tutelage of Sami Pasha and his close friend, Fausto Zonaro.

While still a prince, he formed friendships with artists and literary figures and acted as their patron. He served as honorary president of the Ottoman Artists Society, founded in 1909, and provided financial underwriting for the publication of the Society's newspaper. Through Prince Abdülmecid's active intervention, the famous Ottoman painter Avni Lifij was sent to Paris in 1909 for training; moreover, he extended support for the artists working in the studio established in Şişli district in 1917. Paintings shown by the prince at the 1918 Vienna Exhibition were, in addition to his self-portrait, *Goethe in the Imperial Harem*, *Beethoven in the Imperial Harem*, and *Portrait of Sultan Selim I.*

A former member of Prince Abdülmecid's train, Ismail Baykal reports in his memoirs that the prince reserved Wednesdays for painting and that no visitors were admitted while the artist was at work in his villa in Bağlarbaşı. We also learn from the same source that he frequently received visits by leading dignitaries of the empire, poets, liter-

ill. 68

[1] Princess Neslişah Abdülmünim Osmanoğlu donated a portrait by Spiridon of Caliph and Prince Abdülmecid as a gift to the Museum of Painting and Sculpture, Mimar Sinan University.

[2] İsmail Baykal, "Abdülmecid Efendi ve Sarayında Cereyan Eden Bazı Olaylar," *Yakın Tarihimiz* (1963), 247–8.

68

ary figures, and artists and that he maintained close associations with artists, in particular[2]: among the associates who should be recalled are Abdülhak Hamid, Şehabeddin Süleyman, Münir Nigar, Yunus Nadi, the philosopher Rıza Tevfik, Celal Nuri, Ubeydullah Efendi, İbnülemin Mahmud Kemal, Ahmed Refik, Falih Rıfkı, Abdülhak Şinasi, Halil Edhem, Necip Asım, and Süleyman Nazif.[3] Those whose portraits were delineated by the prince were Recaizade Mahmud Ekrem (1911) and Abdülhak Hamid Tarhan (1917).

After the proclamation of the First Constitutional Monarchy, one of the prince's—or, as he was referred to by his contemporaries, "The Noble Artist" (San'atkâr-i Necib)—greatest pleasures consisted in the presentation of paintings as gifts to his friends, chosen from among the distinguished intellectuals of the empire. In 1910, Prince Abdülmecid, who counted among his intimates the leading poets and writers of the day, presented to Tevfik Fikret a painting titled *The Fog*, inspired by a poem of the same name by this poet. Similarly, after reading a book written by Ahmed Refik for popular consumption on the Tulip Period, he executed a large-scale composition set in Topkapı Palace, peopled by the figures of Sultan Ahmed III and Nevşehirli İbrahim Pasha and their intimates, and in one margin of which he inscribed a few lines from the historian's work.[4]

The friendship between Prince Abdülmecid and Pierre Loti (1850–1923), the romantic writer and admirer of Constantinople, began in İstanbul in 1910 and was in later years cultivated through correspondence. As we learn from this correspondence, the prince, adhering to his custom established with other literary associates, presented several paintings to Pierre Loti. Among them were two paintings dated 1912, now preserved in the author's home in Rochefort, in the Charentes-Maritimes region of southwest France, titled *Sunlight on Seraglio Point* and *The Bosphorus*.[5] Nedim Gürsel, in an article on this residence, mentions a letter from Prince Abdülmecid containing a description of the paintings. In the letter, now held in the private archives of Pierre Viaud, the writer's son, Prince Abdülmecid relates that

69
70

> [a] sad and melancholy scene I witnessed and relived over and over for thirty-two years is treated in the first painting, *Seraglio Point*. This is an İstanbul no longer accessible, as viewed from my window, where entered the assassins

[3] Taha Toros, "Mecid Efendi Köşkü," *Sanat Dünyamız* 31 (1984): 7.

[4] Reşad Ekrem Koçu, "Abdülmecid Efendi," *İstanbul Ansiklopedisi*, 1958 ed.

[5] These two paintings were reproduced in the article by Alain Quella–Villéger, "Aziyade ve İstanbul Aşığı" *P Dergisi* (Yaz 1997).

69 Prince Abdülmecid. *Sunlight on Seraglio Point*, 1912. Oil on canvas. 43.8 x 54.3 cm. House of Pierre Loti. Rochefort.

70 Prince Abdülmecid. *The Bosphorus*, 1912. Oil on canvas. 43.8 x 54.3 cm. House of Pierre Loti. Rochefort.

◄ **69**

◄ **70**

[6] Nedim Gürsel, "Pierre Loti'nin Evinde," *P Dergisi* (Yaz 1997): 102.

[7] "Pierre Loti ve Claude Farrère'in Abdülmecid Efendi'ye Mektupları," *Hayat Tarih Mecmuası* (1 Aralık 1965): 46.

[8] In an interview we conducted with Princess Neslişah Abdülmünim on 25 March 2001, she mentioned a portrait of Sultan Abdülaziz executed by Prince Abdülmecid.

71
▼

[9] "Pierre Loti ve," 46.

[10] "Pierre Loti'nin Abdülmecid Efendi'ye Mektupları", *Hayat Tarih Mecmuası* (1 Kasım 1965): 12-3.

[11] Based on comments by İsmail Baykal'ın "Abdülmecid Efendi ve Sarayında Cereyan eden Bazı Olaylar," Gülsen Sevinç indicates that the photograph was taken in the painting room of the villa because the painting titled *The Dethronement of Abdülhamid II* was in the villa. Gülsen Sevinç, "Ressam Şehzade Abdülmecid Efendi'nin 'Sultan II.Abdülhamid'in tahttan indirilişi' adlı tablosuna dair çözümlemeler,". *Türkiye'de Sanat* (Eylül–Ekim 2000): 20.

71 Prince Abdülmecid's Art Studio. 19.5 x 26 cm. Dolmabahçe Palace Photograph Collection, İstanbul.

hired to kill my dear father, Sultan Abdülaziz—the memory of whom is now fading from my mind. My father was murdered in front of this window. The other painting is a landscape of the Bosphorus that extends as far as Yuşa Hill. For years, this panorama, fully garbed in splendor and vibrant color, represented my only consolation. In this beautiful place, it also became my pleasure to make the acquaintance of a distinguished writer, an outstanding friend of the Ottomans and Muslims.[6]

In his letter of May 1913 to Prince Abdülmecid, Pierre Loti remarks on these two paintings and expresses the closeness he felt to İstanbul and his artist friend in a romantic fashion.

Of the two paintings, I liked best and viewed with a growing sense of delight *Seraglio Point*, as it lies beneath an overcast, winterish sky. I viewed this scene for two full winters from the bridge of the ship I captained. Your majesty, imprisoned in their palaces, viewed the same scene. This picture possesses an inestimable value for me. This is not just because it is a work of a human being who bears the spirit of a genuine artist nor is it because it has a great historical value. But it conveys such a sweet sadness....It is impossible for me to find words to express it.[7]

In the same letter, Pierre Loti goes on to say that

The photographs are also priceless—in particular, those photographs of His Majesty, Sultan Abdülaziz Han, that confirm the state in which he appears in the great painting at Çamlıca.[8] I have noted the source on the back of the frame of each one, so that my children will not forget where I got it and that they may preserve it like a sacred donation.[9]

In his letter of 20 March 1920 acknowledging receipt of the two portraits sent to him by the prince, Loti informs the artist that he especially liked the meaningful expression of the figure wearing a fez, which "was dedicated by His Majesty in his masterful Turkish," and that he was going to reserve a place of honor for this painting.[10] One photograph showing the artist at work captures Prince Abdülmecid seated before his paintings in the art studio of his villa in Bağlarbaşı.[11] On

ill.

the left-hand side is an unfinished painting, *The Dethronement of Abdülhamid II*, and on the right is *Portrait of Selim III* while in the center is the painting titled *Counsel/History Lesson* (1912), which was shown at the 1914 Salon exhibition of Paris. In a photograph of the painting published in the 1 May 1329 (1914-5) issue of *Şehbal*, Prince Abdülmecid can be seen in front of a map of the Balkans giving advice to two children, a girl and a boy. The photograph is captioned: "Forget the cause of your personal tragedies, but never pardon insults to the Motherland." Pierre Loti played a role in the inclusion of this painting in the Paris

Prince Ömer Faruk Efendi and his daughter *Princess Dürrüşehvar*, and scenes of life at the Court (*Goethe in the Imperial Harem* and *Beethoven in the Imperial Harem*). These latter paintings portray members of the Court who have adopted Western culture and reflect their interest in romantic literature and music. The painting by Caliph and Prince Abdülmecid titled *Beethoven in the Imperial Harem* is a valuable record documenting the existence of artifacts peculiar to Western culture, like a statue,[13] a bust, a landscape painting, and Western musical instruments, in the context of the life, tastes, and preferences

ill. 73

ill. 134

72 ►   **73** ▼   **◄ 74**

Salon. In the writer's letter dated 19 February 1914, he informs Prince Abdülmecid that the painting will be exhibited in Grand Palais, notes the terms of the acceptance of the painting, and advises that the painting be sent to Rifat Pasha in the Ottoman embassy in Paris; he adds that, in order to be accepted in the Exhibition, it must obtain approval by a "terrifying" jury.[12] *Counsel/History Lesson* was included among the pictures under the headline "Les Salons de 1914" in the 2 May 1914 issue of *L'Illustration.*

Prince Abdülmecid's paintings include figural compositions of members of his family, such as those of his wife *Şehsuvar Kadınefendi*, his son,

[12] "Pierre Loti'nin" 14.

[13] The equesterian statue of Sultan Abdülaziz was commissioned in 1871 from C.F.Fuller and was cast in Munich.

72 Prince Abdülmecid. *Şehsuvar Kadınefendi, Wife of Prince Abdülmecid.* Oil on canvas. 228 × 143 cm. Topkapı Palace Museum, İstanbul.

73 Prince Abdülmecid. *Princess Dürrüşehvar, Daughter of Prince Abdülmecid.* Oil on canvas. 180 × 135 cm. Dolmabahçe Palace Museum, İstanbul.

74 Prince Abdülmecid. *Beauty at the Court: The Coffee Server,* 1895/1896. Oil on canvas. 160 × 90 cm. Private Collection, İstanbul.

ill. 72

of the Court circle. According to his grand daughter, Prince Abdülmecid bore great admiration for Beethoven and used to like very much drawing charcoal sketches while listening to his music.[14] These two artworks embody concrete images of the Westernization effort by the Ottoman Court. That a member of the dynasty executed these works imbues them with a documentary character. Another work demonstrating the importance accorded by the artist to documentation is his painting whose subject is the dethronement of Abdülhamid II.

ill. 74

In *Beauty at the Court: The Coffee-server*, Prince Abdülmecid depicts a female figure in a white silk dress before a door with mother-of-pearl inlay, one leaf of, which is open, holding a portable coffee hearth; her head is uncovered and a hair ornament of a crescent and star is visible among her tresses; over one shoulder is draped a shawl, and at her waist is a wide belt. As effective and as striking as the monumental figure of the woman in this painting are the Orientalist images: the Islamic arabesque, Kufic-style calligraphy, the figure of a gazelle, and palm branches springing from a vase. Above the doorway appears an inscription of the formulaic Islamic benediction (*besmele*), on the upper right side of the door that of "*Allahu lâilâhe illâ Huvel-belâgul-kulub*" and below it "*lâ gâlibe illâ Allâh.*"[15] Its static composition, the use of a large-scale figure, and the Islamic artifacts recall the Orientalist paintings by Osman Hamdi Bey.

During the years he occupied the post of caliph (1922–4), no changes occurred in the private life of Prince Abdülmecid, the last Ottoman heir, and he continued to pursue his art as in the past.[16] Besides compositions with large-scale figures, he also executed portraits and still lifes —his principal interests—and seascapes. The artist's signature resembles the imperial Ottoman monogram and reads "Abdülmecid bin Abdülaziz Han."

ill. 75
ill. 76

On the abolition of the caliphate in 1924, Prince Abdülmecid, forced to leave İstanbul, settled in Nice, where he established a residence in Cimiez district and spent final years of his life in Paris. The attic of the large mansion in which he dwelled with his family in Nice was remodeled and converted to a studio. The artist usually reserved Thursdays for painting when he would work the entire day. He used to select the best among the seascapes and still lives and submitted them every year to the Salon d'Automne.[17] One self-portrait is owned by the Musée Masséna in Nice.[18]

When Prince Abdülmecid left İstanbul in 1924, Cevad Pasha was appointed proxy. Cevad Pasha exhibited the paintings in Prince Abdülmecid's villa in Bağlarbaşı for sale at Sümerbank. After Prince Abdülmecid informed his private secretary Muazzez Keramet by telegram on 27 June 1939 that he was moving to Paris for health reasons, he thanked him for protecting his property and requested that certain items, like his father's sculptures, the grand piano, certain written materials, and other items of sentimental value, be preserved while the remainder should be sold. Among these latter items, he indicated that the work by Pujol[19] was valuable, and that if it needed to be restored, he could send the necessary materials from Paris, but if this was not possible and if there was an art museum in İstanbul, it should be donated as a gift.[20]

[14] Princess Neslişah Abdülmünim Osmanoğlu. Personal interview. 25 March 2001.

[15] On the sofa on the first floor of Prince Abdülmecid's villa in Bağlarbaşı over the door and on the wall and on the cornice in the room in the northeast corner of the sofa there are couplets of two lines each in *ta'lik* style.

[16] Baykal, 279; Princess Neslişah Abdülmünim especially stressed that Abdülmecid Efendi during his caliphate continued to paint and that he was a person of broad views, open minded and possessor of Western thought: Princess Neslişah Abdülmünim Osmanoğlu. Personal interview. 25 March 2001.

[17] Princess Neslişah Abdülmünim Osmanoğlu. Personal interview. 25 March 2001

[18] Princess Neslişah Abdülmünim Osmanoğlu. Personal interview. 25 March 2001

[19] This must be a painting of Alexandre Denis Abel de Pujol (1785-1861). Pujol was a member of the Academy in Paris and was the teacher of many Orientalist painters icluding Gabriel Decamps.

[20] Salih Keramet Nigar, *Halife İkinci Abdülmecid* (İstanbul: İnkilap ve Aka, 1964), 44.

75 Prince Abdülmecid. *Breakfast Tray.* Oil on canvas. 47 x 56 cm. Collection of Mine and Güven Kemal Persentili, İstanbul.

76 Prince Abdülmecid. *Still Life with Fish,* 1924. Oil on canvas. 57 x 75 cm. Collection of Güner and Haydar Akın, İstanbul.

XIII Ceremonials

As a group, nineteenth-century Western painters of Constantinople shared no single perspective toward the Ottoman Empire, because these "[a]rtists approached the East from different backgrounds and with different aims. Their interpretations differed according to whether they were English or French, academic, romantic or realist painters, and whether their work was intended for exhibition or for illustrating a book."[1] Further-more, what is notable—and characteristic for İstanbul—is the scant evidence for the existence of an ideological dimension to these paintings. Apart from imaginary paintings of the harem, the bath, and the slave market—in which case the bias is non-specific and applicable to the Orient as a whole—the canvases typically executed by Orientalist painters in İstanbul highlight the natural and historical beauties of the city and its cosmopolitan structure, a convergence of different races, religions, and languages. The only aspect that may possibly be interpreted as ideological is the Westerner's tendency to insist on rendering İstanbul as an Oriental city of the past, nearly timeless, and showing no signs of modernization.

Paintings of İstanbul by Orientalists contain the same subjects that are most frequently worked in their diaries: ceremonials, the harem, the bath, the slave market, dervishes, and vistas of the city, the coffeehouse, and open-air recreation areas. Ceremonials as portrayals of Court life and protocol assumed great importance for travelers and artists coming to İstanbul and constitute a distinct subject in Orientalist art. These imperial ceremonials were organized according to Court Protocol (*Teşrifat-ı Kadime*) and the most important of these represent the following principal occasions: religious holidays (the Feast of Ramadan, at the conclusion of the month of fasting, and the Feast of Sacrifice); the Sultan's Procession for the Girding of the Dynastic Sword after accession (*Kılıç Alayı*) and that to the mosque for Friday

[1] McLauchlan, 14.

77
▼

77 Levnî, *The Arrival of the Sons of Ahmed III to Okmeydanı for their Circumcision Ceremony*, ca.1720. *Surname-i Vehbî* . Miniature. Topkapı Palace Museum Library (H.3593), Istanbul.

Prayer Service (*Selamlık Alayı*); the Night of Power (*Leyl- i Kadir*), commemorating the revelation of the *Koran*; and the annual veneration of the sacred relics of Islam, including the Mantle of the Prophet (*Hırka-i Şerif*). These ceremonial events, closely described in travel books by Westerners and eagerly delineated by draftsmen and artists, were greeted with interest in the West, particularly in regard to the special attire worn by the sultan and by the various groups in attendance and the significance of the various aspects of its procedure. In fact, graphic treatments of these ceremonial scenes by European draftsmen appeared as early as the sixteenth century. The woodcut (1553) by Pieter Coeck van Aelst in *Les moeurs et fachons de faire de Turcz avecq les regions y appartenents* depicting the procession of Sultan Süleyman I through the Hippodrome is one of the best known examples on the subject.

The eighteenth century witnessed the mounting of more imposing ceremonials, both in Europe and in the Ottoman Empire. In this era when pomp and display had come to assume a central position in the life of a ruler, the sultans commissioned depictions of these ceremonials as a permanent record of the leading role they had played in such ceremonials. Painters and master draftsmen in the West and miniature illuminators in the Ottoman Empire produced the most successful artistic portrayals of eighteenth-century ceremonial scenes.

Of the "Bosphorus Artists"—those granted appointments in the eighteenth century by European embassies and rendered various features of the city and its life in İstanbul—Jean-Baptiste Van Mour, Louis-François Cassas and Antoine-Ignace Melling were the most successful in transferring the Ottoman ceremonial scenes to their canvases. Ceremonial pictures executed with enthusiasm by Western artists in İstanbul in the nineteenth century traced the changes wrought in the intervening period in everything from architecture to dress. Renderings of ceremonial scenes in drawings, prints, watercolors or oils offered an exotic variation on a subject widely employed in eighteenth-century European art. For the European artist, processions to the mosque on Fridays or on holidays possessed a special added importance, because they provided an opportunity to observe the sultan at close range. In his *Recueil de cent estampes représentant différentes nations du Levant tirées sur les tableaux peints d'après nature en 1707 et 1708*, Van Mour expressed the pride he felt in

[2] Jean–Baptiste Van Mour, *Recueil de cent estampes représentant différentes nations du Levant tirées sur les tableaux peints d'après nature en 1707 et 1708*, ed. Şevket Rado (İstanbul: Apa, 1979), 1.

the fact that his portrait truly resembled the figure of Sultan Ahmed III and averred that it had not been done from memory, for he had frequently observed the sultan on his way to the chase and the mosque.[2] These pictures are rare depictions of the sultan amid the throngs of his subjects; however, as they make clear, the troops and the subjects in these ceremonials wherein the sultan occupies center stage served as little more than extras for this dramatic subject.

These delineated scenes of the imperial processions to the mosque on holidays and Fridays and for the girding of the dynastic sword visually reproduce for the viewer not only the ceremonial procedure, but also the route and the squares through which these processions passed and the architectural features of the mosques visited by the sultan. Held ever since the very first years of the founding of the empire, these ceremonials—regardless of the seeming loss of their former brilliance primarily as a result of the changes occurring in the armed forces under Mahmud II and his successors—still retained their power to fascinate great numbers of Western travelers, as is confirmed by the many surviving engravings and paintings. The execution by Western painters of the ceremonial scenes of the nineteenth century may have represented the outcome of a personal decision by the artist or of a commission from the Court to document change, in particular, those in the military organization under Mahmud II and succeeding sultans.

Holiday ceremonials

Among the most important of the ceremonials in Topkapı Palace that form the subject of paintings and engravings were those conducted both on the eve of and the day(s) of a religious holiday. These ceremonials in observance of holiday celebrations (*Tehniyye-i Iydiyye*) were performed in three phases—Eve Celebration (*Arife Muayedesi*), the exchange of greetings on the holiday itself (*Muayede Resm-i Hümayunu*), and the holiday procession (*Alay-i Iyd*). In his article on the subject topic, Zarif Orgun describes the imperial state levee held on the holiday in the following manner, thus:

> Those who in accordance with imperial protocol were to appear at the reception would begin to arrive at the Court after midnight of the day preceding that of the holiday itself.

Great torches were lit along either side of the road leading from the Middle Gate to the Public Hall Council and the imperial band would play until morning. The chief of the çavuşes of the Palace (*Çavuşbaşı*) and lieutenant of the gatekeepers (*Kapıcılar Kethüdası*), standing guard with their silver staffs until the dawn, would greet the members of the council of state in the prescribed manner. Those who came to the Court after midnight to take part in the holiday ceremonial were the viziers, sheikhulislam, janissaries, Muslim preachers (*Hoca*), commissioners (*Emin*), doctors of Islamic theology (*Ulema*), and Islamic college professors (*Müderris*). The readying of the throne before the Gate of Felicity (*Babü's-saade*) and the ceremonial organization was under the direction of the master of ceremonies

(*Teşrifatî Efendi*). The ceremonial throne, sheathed in gold and set with gems, would be brought from the sultan's Privy Treasury and positioned before the Gate of Felicity. … Before the sultan seated himself on the throne, the princes, garbed in robes of honor (*Hil'at*) would come to stand on the left-hand side of the throne and the halberdiers with tresses (*Zülüflü baltacılar*) and janissary security officers (*Ocak zabitleri*) would assume their places behind them in the direction of the gate to the Court. Opposite the throne and to the left would line up in a row the commander-in-chief of the janissaries, custodian of the sultan's symbols of sovereignty (*Miralem Ağa*), the keeper of the sultan's hounds (*Sekbanbaşı*), the master of ceremonies, head gatekeeper (*Kapıcıbaşı*), officers of the imperial chase (*Şikâr-î hümayûn ağası*), and the Elite (*Müteferrikalar*); and, opposite the throne and somewhat to the right was the chief of the corps of halberdiers, and lieutenant of the gatekeepers with their silver staffs. Following the morning prayer service, the sultan would enter the privy chamber (*Has Oda*)), specially decorated for the occasion, where he would don his robe of honor. In the Inner Court, the second assistant to the chief of the black eunuchs (*Haznedarbaşı*), the head butler (*Kilercibaşı*), the agha of the Palace and, standing in a line opposite them, the pages of the Gate (*Kapı Gılmanı*), and the stewards of the janissary barracks would await the appearance of the sultan. After the sultan had been robed, the agha of the Gate of Felicity would inform him that the throne was ready and when the sultan emerged from his private apartment the janissary aghas, or officers, standing outside the door, would kiss the hem of his robe. They were followed by the sultan's prayer leader (*İmam-ı Sultan*), and the chief imperial physician (*Reisültıbba*), and the prayer leader at this juncture would offer a brief prayer for the continuance of the House of Osman and, after the recitation of the Exordium of the *Koran*, the sultan would continue on foot to the Gate of Felicity. On reaching the throne, the sultan would be greeted by applause from the halberdiers and prayers would be offered, and once he was seated on the throne, the imperial band would begin to play….

▲
78

78 Attributed to Kostantin Kapıdağlı.
Holiday Reception of Sultan Selim III,
ca. 1789. Oil on canvas. 152 x 206 cm.
Topkapı Palace Museum, İstanbul.

[P] personages of protocol waiting in the courtyard would each come before the throne in strict accordance with the official etiquette and submit to the sultan their congratulations and vows of devotion. The ceremonial would be concluded by the kissing of the hem of the sultan's robe by the master of ceremonies.[3]

[3] Zarif Orgun, "Kubbealtı ve Yapılan Merasim," *Güzel Sanatlar Dergisi* (Ocak 1949): 104.

The painting depicting *Holiday Reception Ceremonial of Selim III* in the Topkapı Palace Museum shows the sultan seated on the golden holiday throne, placed before the Gate of Felicity as was traditional. The throne stands on a costly Palace carpet. To the left of the sultan, Grand Vizier Koca Yusuf Pasha, the sheikhulislam, the admiral of the fleet (*Kaptan Paşa*), the chief black eunuch of the Imperial Harem (*Kızlarağası*) and other chief officers are shown in the act of pray-ing. To the right of the sultan stand two sword-bearers (*Silâhtar*) and the princes in their robes of honor. Beneath the portico, halberdiers with tresses and the eunuchs of the sultan's palace and, near the courtyard, the running footmen (*Peykler*), guardsmen in attendance on the sultan in processions (*Solaklar*), and high-ranking impe-rial officials are arranged in ceremonial order. With their silver staffs in hand, the chief of the corps of halberdiers and the chief of the Palace door keepers would show the way to those guests arriving at the reception. Those personages appearing in the painting are in the act of coming before the sultan's throne to submit their felicita-tions and devotion, in strict conformance with the rules of imperial protocol.

Renda believes that this painting may be a work by Kostantin Kapıdağlı, who worked at the Court

79 Louis-François Cassas. *Sultan's Holiday Procession*, ca. 1784. Pen and quill and India ink, gouache, and watercolor on paper. 45 x 60 cm. Musée Bertrand, Châteauroux.

in the late eighteenth century and executed various portraits of Selim III and landscapes in the apartments of the empress mother in the Imperial Harem of Topkapı Palace. Moreover, the clearly indicated presence of Koca Yusuf Pasha, who served his second term as grand vizier in 1791–2, permits the inference that the painting should be dated to the final decade of the eighteenth century.[4] Assumed to have been commissioned by Selim III, this work is both a memento and a record for the Ottoman Court. Comparison of this painting with ceremonial scenes in miniature illuminations reveals it to be a transitional work that, interestingly enough, possesses qualities of both types. A singular specimen in the Topkapı Palace Collection, this composition suggests that Kapıdağlı may have borrowed the style of representation and composition of Van Mour, who painted ceremonials taking place in the courtyards of the Palace in the early eighteenth century. Renda, indicating that this kind of holiday reception was frequently executed in the studios of İstanbul, states that an album held by Biblioteka Uniwersytecka in Warsaw contains a painting exhibiting a similar composition.[5]

Holiday processions

On the conclusion of the ceremonial of the Holiday Reception in Topkapı Palace, the sultan would enter the Imperial Harem apartments and exchange holiday greetings with his mother, favorite wife, children, and the other women of the Imperial Harem and then change his costume for the Holiday Procession to the mosque. At this juncture, an imperial procession (*Mevkib-i Hümayun*) would be drawn up in the first court. The sultan would mount his horse before the Throne Gate of Imperial Harem, brought to him by the master of the horse (*Mirahor Ağa*) and the officers who walked at the stirrup of the sultan, and, exiting from the Gate of Salutation (*Babü's-selâm*) accompanied by a round of applause and the offering of prayers, he would head for the mosque where the holiday worship service was to be held. After attending the worship service and performing his prayers in the loggia reserved in mosques for the sultan and other members of the imperial dynasty, he would return to the Palace in procession.[6]

The subject of the Holiday Procession exerted the greatest fascination on artists both in terms of the ceremonial order and the sumptuous cos-

[4] Renda, "Ressam," 145–6.
[5] Renda, "Portrenin," 470.
[6] Necdet Sakaoğlu, "Osmanlı Sarayında Bayram," *Skylife* (1 January 2000): 32.

tumes. One depiction of the Holiday Procession of Abdülhamid I is by Louis-François Cassas, resident in İstanbul during the reign of Abdülhamid I (1774–89) and primarily a painter of panoramic vistas and architectural monuments. In this work, unusual for Cassas because of its subject matter, Abdülhamid I is portrayed in his passage from Topkapı Palace to the mosque of Sultan Ahmed in formal procession. Surrounded by his personal processional guardsmen, the sultan, mounted on a dappled horse in gold trappings, is wearing a special turban (*katibî*), set off by a tall jeweled aigrette. Following the sultan on horseback are the imperial sword-bearers and the chief black eunuch of the Imperial Harem. Preceding the pro-

cession are the running footmen, and the sultan's processional guardsmen, with a solemn demeanor and wearing enormous headdresses of white feathers. The expectant crowd of subjects, drawn back at the side of the road, bow in the presence of the sultan's grandeur as a sign of respect. This ceremonial scene—fascinating the European observer by the splendor of the ceremonial costumes and the awesome mien of the sultan and the troops at his side—signified a culture unlike any in the West.

Another depiction of the Holiday Procession of Selim III, as seen from the mosque of St. Sophia, is by Antoine Ignace Melling and contained in his album *Voyage pittoresque de Constantinople et des*

80 Antoine- Ignace Melling. *Sultan's Holiday Procession*. Engraving. *Voyage pittoresque de Constantinople et des rives de Bosphore*, (1819).

80

rives du Bosphore. In this engraving of the ceremonial procession shown as it issues from the Imperial Gate of Topkapı Palace (*Bab-ı Hümayun)*, the chief black eunuch, one of the most esteemed functionaries of the Court, has just exited the gateway. The sword-bearer, in advance of the chief black eunuch, carries the sultan's sword and follows Selim III. The Palace pages, wearing a headdress of white feathers, form a veritable white cloud surrounding the person of the sultan, who can be distinguished by the tall plume of egret feathers affixed in his specially styled turban (*tuğlu*), ornamented with diamonds. Each of the Palace pages boasts a special costume and bears a headdress adorned by plumes or gilded and holds in his hand a very long halberd. Also part of the scene are the janissary corps in ceremonial dress and headgear who line the route of the procession and spectators in a variety of costume, among whom are women in outdoor mantles (*ferace)*, with their heads and faces covered by a sheer material, lined up in rows along the side of the road. Europeans also can be distinguished making their way through the crowd. The monumental fountain of Ahmed III, built to meet the water needs of the neighborhood, stands in the center of the square.

Melling, who executed various drawings of this subject, delineated in his engravings the members of the procession together with individuals composing the crowd and rendered with lively veracity the scattering of gold coins among the onlookers by the chief black eunuch. The artist discloses in *Voyage pittoresque de Constantinople et des rives du Bosphore* that,

> [t]he sultan's bodyguards and the pack
> of pages with very tall white feathers
> on top of their heads form a dense mass
> in the immediate vicinity of the sultan. When
> standing at close range, one can only see the
> waving of plumes; for this reason, it is necessary to withdraw a certain distance in order to
> clearly observe the sultan's visage."[7]

As this statement indicates Melling, like Van Mour and other artists, took down sketch notes during the ceremonial, taking advantage of this opportunity to capture a close likeness of the sultan.

[7] Antoine Ignace Melling, *Voyage pittoresque de Constantinople et des rives du Bosphore* (Paris: Treutel et Wurtz, 1819).

Procession of salutation

The ceremonial performed at midday on Fridays in connection with the attendance by the Ottoman sultan at the communal worship service in the mosque was the Procession of Salutation. Up to the mid-seventeenth century, such processions constituted a splendid spectacle, until they became relatively less dramatic after the reign of Mehmed IV (1648–87), and on the abolition of the janissary corps in 1826.

Typically, the chief sword-bearer would be informed by a palace servant about the mosque the sultan had selected for that week. The chief sword-bearer would have officials announce to those in the Inner Service who was required to join in the imperial procession to the district and site of this mosque: the mutes (*Bizeban)*, running footmen, lackey footmen and the corps of heralds and messengers under the grand vizier as chief of the Imperial Council. On the day of the Procession, under the command of the chief officer of the janissary corps, forty men of the Sultan's Private Apartments, appareled in ceremonial dress and mounted on decorated horses, fifteen assistant functionaries, and forty to fifty sergeant at arms in the bodyguard of the sultan would proceed half an hour in advance to the mosque to oversee the preparation of the sultan's loggia in the mosque. Two assistant functionaries, each bearing an aigrette as part of their headgear, would ride past, followed by two chief officers of the Sultan's Private Apartments, each assigned to carry one of the sultan's imperial headdresses (*Destar-ı Hümayun)*, with which they would acknowledge the crowd lined up on either side of the route and who would respond by a crying out of their salutations. This portion of the Procession of Salutation was called the Veneration of the Turban (*Sarık Alayı)*. The grand vizier and other imperial dignitaries also joined the Procession. The sultan rode in the Procession of Salutation on horseback. The subjects lined up along the route greeted the sultan's appearance with applause and shouts of "May fickle Fortune bring you prosperity and good fortune" and "Long live the Sultan!" Representatives of foreign countries were also invited to this ceremonial.

In 1826, after the abolition of the Janissary corps, the Procession of Salutation underwent a complete change, including the elimination of one portion of the Inner Palace servants participating in the Procession, and a new protocol was adopted. One special Procession of Salutation occurred during the reign of Mahmud II. It was performed on the completion of Nusretiye Mosque on Friday, 21 February 1241 (1826).[8] This mosque was called Nusretiye meaning Victory because it was finished just after the sultan's triumph over the Jannisaries.

As is disclosed by the frequency of their descriptions in travel books and letters of the Procession of Salutation ceremonial, members of European embassies and foreign travelers were keen to attend these ceremonials. Both as a religious ceremony connected with Islam and as an official ceremony defined by protocol and, further, as an opportunity to observe the sultan at close range, the Procession of Salutation was an event that select foreigners visiting İstanbul put at the top of their must-see list.

Théophile Gautier, whose visit to İstanbul coincided with the reign of Sultan Abdülmecid, reports that European guests would be informed by hotel interpreters one day in advance or on the day of the ceremonial which mosque the sultan planned to attend. Thus, the writer, who was staying at the Hotel de Byzance, learned that Abdülmecid was going to leave from Çırağan Palace to attend the nearby Küçük Mecidiye Mosque and indicates that, on arriving at the mosque to view the Procession of Salutation, he encountered British, Americans, Germans, and Russians.[9] Gautier put down his views on the subject, as follows:

> The Commander of the Faithful visits a different mosque every week—St. Sophia, Süleymaniye, Osmaniye, Sultan Bayezıd, Yeni, Lâleli, and the others—following a prearranged route. This was not simply for the purpose of worshiping at a mosque on the day prescribed by the fundamental tenets of the *Koran*, but also it was a required duty of the sultan as the leader of Islam; moreover, this official act of religious observance served a political purpose: though he might spend the entire week secluded in a corner of the palace or in one of the summer palaces scattered along the shores of the Bosphorus, by showing himself to his subjects the sultan demonstrated that he was alive. Before the eyes of everyone, the sultan, who passed through the city in front of his subjects and the foreign ambassadors, virtually signed a record attesting to his existence as a kind

[8] Hafız Hızır İlyas Ağa, *Tarihi-i Enderun/Letaif-i Enderun (1812–1830)* (İstanbul: Güneş, 1987), 269.

[9] Gautier, *Constantinople*, 176.

[10] Gautier, *Constantinople*, 175.

[11] De Amicis, 1:286.

[12] Knut Hamsun and H. C. Andersen, *İstanbul'da İki İskandinav Seyyah* (İstanbul: Yapı Kredi Yayınları, 1993), 42.

of necessary precaution against palace intrigue to disguise the sultan's natural or sudden death. Even serious illness could pose no obstacle to the making of this public appearance. Despite being so ill, he had difficulty staying in the saddle and had to cosmetically disguise the paleness of his face, Mahmud I, the son of Mustafa II, nonetheless, participated in the Friday Procession of Salutation, but, in the course of his return, he expired midway between two of the Palace gates.[10]

Artists, having obtained the opportunity of viewing the sultan up close in the Procession of Salutation, also observed these ceremonials with a professional interest. On his visit to İstanbul in 1874, Edmondo De Amicis remarks in his description of one of Abdülaziz' Procession of Salutation to the Bezmialem Valide Sultan Mosque at Dolmabahçe that "[a] few long-haired individuals wandering about the outskirts of the crowd own portfolios under their arms I took to be artists animated by a faint hope of being able to make a hasty sketch of the imperial features."[11]

Knut Hamsun, who arrived in İstanbul in 1899 motivated by an interest and love of the genuinely mystical and the pure, indicates that in order "to observe the ceremonial procession outside the mosque that was unique to Oriental lands," he had had to expend two days attempting to obtain permission to observe the "Cérémonie du Sélamlik," which was finally granted on the basis of a letter from the embassy addressed to "Palais Impérial de Yıldız."[12]

Abdülhamid II, who laid great importance on the Procession of Salutation, conducted the ceremonial after his accession in one of the following mosques—Beşiktaş and those in the vicinity, Sinanpaşa, Dolmabahçe, Kılıç Ali, and Nusretiye. With the completion of Hamidiye Mosque in 1886 on the tenth anniversary of his accession, he commenced making the Procession of Salutation ceremonial to this mosque, whose construction exhibits an eclectic Orientalist style and which is situated adjacent to the Yıldız Palace. Joining in the procession were the princes, all the civil and military dignitaries, the sultan's aides de camp, and a division of armed forces composed of various military bodies. While it had been customary for sultans to lead the Procession of Salutation mounted on a horse, Abdülhamid II now appeared in a carriage drawn by four horses.

During his reign, Western travelers and the majority of the guests were in constant attendance at the Procession of Salutation. As reported by Sermet Muhtar Alus, the procession was watched from the terrace of the Ceremonial Observation Point that was specially constructed for the German emperor Wilhelm II's first visit to İstanbul in 1889. In 1901, this privilege was withdrawn, and permission was now granted to foreign guests only on condition that they could submit a diplomatic card from their own embassies and that they had no binoculars or cameras on hand as they observed the procession from the side of road in their carriages.[13]

As an artistic theme, the Procession of Salutation, unique to the Ottoman world, generated attention. Samuel S. Cox, in his memoirs collected under the title *Diversions of a Diplomat in Turkey*, states that Osman Hamdi Bey was commissioned by a man named Elliot F. Shephard of New York to make a painting of *The Sultan's Procession of Salutation* wherein Abdülhamid II was depicted in an open carriage in the company of Namık Pasha and Osman Pasha, the hero of Pleven.[14] The painting by François Dubois on the subject depicts Sultan Mahmud II's exit from the

[13] Sermet Muhtar Alus, "II. Abdülhamid'in Cuma Selamlıkları," *Resimli Tarih Mecmuası* (Ağustos 1951): 912.

[14] Cox, 34.

81 82

XIII Ceremonials

Imperial Entrance Gate with his new military corps. Painted in a broad perspective, three important landmarks of İstanbul—St. Sophia Mosque, the Imperial Gate, and the fountain of Ahmed III are encompassed by this work.[15] This wide angle of vision permits the inclusion of both the Procession of Salutation and all the people who have come to witness the ceremonial. To the right of the sultan is shown the new military ensemble (*Muzıka-yı Hümayun*) formed to replace the traditional imperial military band (*Mehterhane*). Those who have come to observe the sultan and

[15] François Dubois's painting exhibits a close similarity both in terms of perspective and composition to an engraving by L'Espinasse titled *St. Sophia, Bab–ı Humayun and the Fountain of Ahmed III.* Mouradgea D'Ohsson, *Tableau générale de l'empire othoman*, 3: Pl. 138.

[16] Pardoe, *The City*, 1:5,6.

[17] Sedad Hakkı Eldem, *İstanbul Anıları* (İstanbul: Aletaş Alarko, 1979), 90.

the Procession of Salutation form a great, bustling crowd, and we may deduce from the presence of the itinerant venders wandering through the crowd that they have been waiting a long time. Women also can be seen seated in a carriage drawn by oxen standing in the shade of a tree before the fountain of Ahmed III. This painting represents not simply an observance of a ceremonial, but also the introduction of the new army corps to the local inhabitants. Another depiction by Lewis, which shows a Procession of Salutation of Mahmud II departing from the Sultan Ahmed Mosque to return to Topkapı Palace, was made into a lithograph, based on the sketches made by Cole Smyth who was in İstanbul in 1835–6.

After the changes instituted in dress regulations by Mahmud II, these ceremonials seem to have become relatively less elaborate. The sultan and the other officials participating in the Procession of Salutation wore fezzes and uniforms, but the women and men who came to observe the procession continued to appear in traditional costume. This alteration in dress made by Mahmud II aroused disappointment among Europeans who made their way to Constantinople with the aim of finding the exotic East. Miss Pardoe reveals in her memoirs the sadness she felt at seeing the splendid muslin and cashmere turbans replaced by the ugly and meaningless fez and protests that a bad caricature of European dress, lacking in elegance, had been adopted.[16]

The painting by Speranza Fecir depicts the arrival of Abdülmecid who spent the winter of 1840 in Topkapı Palace to Sultan Ahmed Mosque with the Procession of Salutation. The date of this painting corresponds to the first year of his reign and possibly commemorates his first Procession of Salutation. The sultan's troops and guards appear in the procession, along with a large crowd of subjects in the foreground, including European women with their children; one foreign diplomat wearing a wig has just alighted from his carriage with an imperial servant appointed to attend him at his side while in the background can be spotted Muslim women in their carriages and, on the right-hand side, curiosity seekers viewing the scene from a terrace. Monuments shown include the obelisques in the Hippodrome, the mosque of Sultan Ahmed and, on the right-hand side, the building housing the Office of the Registry of Landed Property (*Defter-i Hakani*).[17]

The sultans traditionally joined in the

83 ▼

84 ➤

83-84 John Frederick Lewis. *Return of the Sultan from the Mosque. Illustrations of Constantinople* (1837).

85 Sperenza Fecir. *Procession of Salutation.*
1840. Oil on canvas. 114x 152.5 cm.
Museum of Painting and Sculpture, Mimar
Sinan University, İstanbul.

Procession of Salutation either on horseback if the district in which the mosque to be visited was located within the city proper or by caique if it was by the seaside. Processions of Salutation to the mosques erected along the shores of the Bosphorus in the eighteenth and nineteenth century in baroque and eclectic styles represented scenes conducive to instilling a yearning for the picturesque in the Orientalist artists. As is evident in the works by Amadeo Preziosi and Luigi Querena,[18] when a mosque along the Bosphorus formed the locus of the imperial visit, they preferred to employ a broader perspective, so as to reflect the splendor of the ceremonial by carefully delineating the mosque to be visited, the sultan's caiques, and the boats carrying the members of the Court and those of the subjects. Since the Bosphorus occupied prominence as a main artery

[18] Luigi Querena, born in Venice in the second half of the nineteenth century, exhibited paintings in Venice from 1854 to 1879. *Bénézit.*

of the city in the nineteenth century, it was natural for it to serve as a venue for the leading Court ceremonials. In pictorial specimens of this type, although the sultan himself is not visible, the vivid rendering of the ceremonial scene conducted on the water in the presence of animated crowds in the context of the Bosphorus served to enrich the Orientalist subject matter.

In the watercolor by Amadeo Preziosi titled *Approach of Sultan Abdülmecid to Beylerbeyi,* the imperial caique of Sultan Abdülmecid prepares to dock at Beylerbeyi Mosque after having embarked from Dolmabahçe Palace. Waiting on

ill. 88

the quay of the mosque are the sultan's troops, arranged in ceremonial order and, on the shore, a cluster of subjects while a great crowd of men and women have come by caique to greet the sultan: the whole clearly conveys the excitement of the moment experienced by those present. Dated to ca. 1843–50, another water color by Preziosi, held by the Victoria and Albert Museum, that depicts the Friday Procession of Salutation of Abdülmecid is titled *The Imperial Caiques before Nusretiye Mosque*; the scene is composed of the mosque of Nusretiye, a structure combining the baroque and Empire styles, and the imperial caiques as they near the wharf.

87 Based on a photograph by Sebah & Joaillier, the painting by Querena dated 1875 portrays a Friday Procession of Salutation during the reign of Abdülaziz. The neo-baroque mosque of Ortaköy which juts out from the shore of the Bosphorus forms one of the principal elements of the picture, finely detailed and exposing its splendid aspect. On the landing stage of the mosque is a formation of soldiers in blue uniforms boasting trim in narrow, red bands of fabric cut on the bias. The scene of everyday life as it is acted out in front of the mosque and on the water furnishes the main theme of the painting.

86 In front of the monumental structure, thirteen pairs of rowers pull at the oars of the imperial caique with gold inlay decoration and a red marquee edged in gold fringe reserved for the sultan's use. The tall prow bears the symbol of the Ottoman Empire—a golden falcon with outspread wings. Because the sultan would return to the Court in a different caique, a second caique was kept ready in front of the mosque. The rowers wear shirts of white, raw silk crepe, close-fitting trousers, and a red fez with a tassel of blue silk. The rowers of the two, smaller caiques ornamented in gold gilt inlay with seven pairs of oars, which traditionally preceded the imperial caique, are shown conversing with each other as they await the departure of the sultan from the mosque. Delineated immediately beside the imperial caiques at the shore are women in mantles with veils, seated in light rowboats, and two fishing vessels with sails. On the right-hand side of the painting, accurately reflecting the lively traffic on the Bosphorus is the large, heavy type of rowboat ordinarily used for mass transportation on the water and here filled with men and women. These vessels that carried both passen-

86-87 Luigi Querena. *Imperial Caiques before the Mosque at Ortaköy*, 1875. Oil on canvas. 69 x 104 cm. Collection of Azize Taylan, İstanbul.

88 Amadeo Preziosi. *Approach of Sultan Abdülmecid to Beylerbeyi*. Watercolor. Topkapı Palace Museum, İstanbul.

gers and freight to the villages on the Bosphorus were capable of holding fifty to sixty passengers of both sexes and without regard for religious affiliation on a predetermined route along the Bosphorus and the Golden Horn. A festive air is contributed to Querena's painting by the flags decking the steamships passing through the Bosphorus and the caiques filled with people, and the sultan's summer palace of Beylerbeyi on the opposite shore adds an accent of grandeur. In this work, the artist has moved beyond a formal depiction of the Procession of Salutation ceremonial to a rendering of a segment of daily life.

The dynastic sword procession

The ceremonial conducted soon after a sultan's accession to the throne of the House of Osman in Eyüp was called the Procession of the Dynastic Sword. Within the first two to seven days of his accession and following the swearing of oaths of allegiance at the Court, the sultan would issue from the Palace on horseback after the morning prayer service to board—the water route generally being chosen—the imperial caique that would take him

to the suburb of Eyüp on the Golden Horn. Here, at the İmam Landing Stage, where he would be saluted by viziers and top-ranking dignitaries waiting to see him off as he proceeded to make his way, again on horseback, to the tomb of Ebû Eyub El Ensarî, a Companion of the Prophet. After visiting the tomb, the sultan would enter the courtyard situated between the tomb and the mosque and be girded with the dynastic sword; generally, it was the sheikhulislam who had the honor of performing this duty. This symbolic act completed, the sultan would again remount and make his way to the Palace, following the overland route from Edirnekapı at the city walls and visiting in turn the tombs of his ancestors along the way; other members of the procession included the grand vizier, the sheikhulislam, the military judges (*Kazasker*), the chief of the descendants of the Prophet (*Nakibüleş-*

89-90 Pavlo Verona. *Procession of Abdülmecid and Retinue on Return from Eyüp and Girding of Dynastic Sword*, after 1839. Watercolor. 83 x 67 cm. Topkapı Palace Museum, İstanbul.

89 90

raf), and other imperial servants. This ceremonial marked the sultan's initial appearance before his subjects, and it was customary to scatter coins minted in the name of the new sultan and to sacrifice rams to be distributed to the poor. In addition, in the course of the return route between the tomb gate and the entrance gate to the Palace, the chief of the Palace doorkeepers and the master of the horse would collect the petitions that his subjects wished to present to the sultan.[19]

The painting signed "The Work of [Your] Humble Servant, Pavlo Verona" (*Amel-i Bende-i Pavlo Verona*) takes as its subject matter the Procession of the Dynastic Sword on the return journey to the Palace from Eyüp. Abdülmecid is shown passing with his retinue before the Tomb of Şah Sultan, a sister of Selim III, adjacent to which is a monumental fountain and an elementary school. The purpose of delineating Abdülmecid in front of the tomb of Şah Sultan is to emphasize the practice of visiting ancestral tomb on the day of the Dynastic Sword Procession. The young sultan is shown advancing in the center of the procession on a white horse with a saddle ornamented by gold needlework, wearing on his head a fez surmounted by an aigrette and a large, long cape in dark blue. After the dress reform, the first ruler to appear in the Procession of the Dynastic Sword in his new ceremonial attire was Abdülmecid. After sailing to Eyüp in the imperial caique, where he was greeted by his subjects, imperial officials, and members of the dynasty and Court gathered in the vicinity of the tomb, Abdülmecid was girded with the sword of Caliph Omer by the chief of the descendants of the Prophet, Military Judge Abdurrahman Efendi. The new sultan, in procession with the prescribed train, next paid a visit to Sultan Mehmed II's tomb and from there returned to Topkapı Palace, passing through the districts of Atpazarı and Bayezıd, via the principal artery of Divanyolu. Tents had been pitched at Eğrikapı for the ambassadors of the European states, and as the sultan passed by, he sent his chamberlain to inquire after their well-being.[20]

Procession of the imperial gifts to the sacred cities

One event that attracted the presence of both natives and foreigners was the annual departure of the caravan to Mecca and Medina, by which presents

[19] *İslam Ansiklopedisi* and Cemal Kafadar, "Eyüp'te Kılıç Kuşanma Ceremonialsi," in *Eyüp: Dün/Bugün* (İstanbul: Tarih Vakfı Yurt Yayınları, 1994), 54–5.

[20] Haluk Y. Şehsuvaroğlu, "Osmanlı Padişahlarının Kılıç Kuşanma Merasimi," *Resimli Tarih Mecmuası* (Temmuz 1950): 271–2.

were sent in the name of the reigning Ottoman sultan. Each year at the beginning of the pilgrimage period, money and gifts were sent to the people of Mecca and Medine, primarily, from two sources. The more important of these was the Ottoman sultan, who possessed the title "Servant of the Sacred Cities, Mecca and Medina," (*Hadimü'l-Haremeyni Şerefeyn*) and the other was the Egyptian Viceroy, and their parcels of gifts were known respectively as the Sacred Imperial Litter (*Mahmil-i Hümayun*) and the Sacred Egyptian Litter (*Mahmil-i Mısri*). The ceremonial held in honor of the sending of the Ottoman sultan's gifts was called the Procession of the Imperial Gifts to the Sacred Cities (*Sürre Alayı*). This procession traveled by mule and camel caravan until the year 1864 and, thereafter, by ship until the construction of the Hejaz railroad when it began to be sent by train.

The Procession of the Imperial Gifts to the Sacred Cities as a subject for Orientalist paintings was directly inspired by the ceremonials conducted prior to 1864. The organization and command of the ceremonial procession was assigned to the commissioner of the Procession (*Sürre Emini*), an imperial official respected for his piety and uprightness and who was entrusted with the delivery of the Imperial Gifts in the company of a great many members of the imperial retinue and guards. Those whose presence was required in the ceremonial, which began in the Palace, were informed the day previous by invitations from the chief black eunuch and the minister of domestic affairs, and the admiral of the fleet was alerted that he should dispatch a war galley with sails and oars to the Kireç Kapısı landing stage for the transport of the Sacred Litter across the Bosphorus to Üsküdar. On the day of the ceremonial, the guests invited to the Palace would witness the submission to the chief of the procession of both the purses of money and their registers, carried into the presence of the sultan on the shoulders of the imperial black eunuchs, and an imperial rescript addressed to the Emir of Mecca. At this juncture, robes of honor would be presented, passages from the *Koran* and poems praising the Prophet Muhammad would be recited, and the steward of the imperial stables would parade the camel bearing the Sacred Litter in front of the Public Audience Hall. Gifts for the Sacred Cities included rare carpets, chandeliers and candelabra set with rare gems, copies of the *Koran*, framed sacred inscriptions, curtains, silver curtain hoops, and quantities of incense. The robe reserved for commissioner of the Procession, embellished with diamonds, pearls and gilt needlework, and a selection of the most brilliant of the gifts being sent to the Hejaz, like bejeweled swords and rosaries of pearls, would be carried by the camel with the Sacred Litter, which, with its chain of silver and halter of silk, would be decked out in the showiest manner possible. The camel bearing the Sacred Litter and the mules of the Procession would exit by the Imperial Gate, passing the Kiosk of Processions (*Alay Köşkü*) on their way to Hocapaşa, by way of the Bahçekapısı road to the Kireç Kapısı Landing Stage, where it would board the galley, to the accompaniment of prayers and blessings, and set out for the Hejaz overland after first crossing to Üsküdar.[21]

What rendered this ceremonial spectacle interesting in the eyes of Westerners and prompted a great many artists to handle the subject was the tie between the Procession of the Imperial Gifts to the Sacred Cities and the religion of Islam, the costly gifts and the fact that they were being sent by the sultan, who was, in his same person, the caliph, and the ethnic diversity of the participants of the procession. One transposition to canvas of this event is the rendering by French artist, Jacques-François Martin (ca. 1720–?), whose portrayal of this processional type, called *The*

91 "Camel Bearing Sacred Litter Ready to Depart for Mecca," *L'Illustration* (Jan.-Juin 1901).

92 Stefano Ussi. *The Departure of the Camel Bearing the Sacred Egyptian Litter for Mecca*, 1873. Oil on canvas. 300 x 520 cm. Dolmabahçe Palace Museum, İstanbul.

[21] Mehmet Zeki Pakalın, *Tarih Deyimleri ve Terimleri Sözlüğü* (İstanbul: Milli Eğitim Bakanlığı Yayınları, 1983), 280–3.

93 François Dubois. *Parade of Mahmud II's New Troops*. Oil on canvas. 86 x 153 cm. Dolmabahçe Palace Museum, İstanbul.

Sultan's Caravan to Mecca, represents no actual procession but rather a Turquerie—a carnival-like procession staged in front of the San Pietro Basilica by French artists of the Académie de France in Rome in 1748.[22] Joseph-Marie Vien (1716–1809) drew costume designs of the participants in this event.[23]

In nineteenth-century depictions, however, the artists, unaware of that segment of the ceremonial taking place at the Palace, treat the subject in a desert context, either as passage through a desert or a caravan halt in the desert. Now part of the Dolmabahçe Palace Collection, a painting by Stefano Ussi (1822/32-1901) dated 1873 and titled *The Departure of the Camel Bearing the sacred Egyptian Litter for Mecca*, pictures the camel caravan bringing presents to Kaaba, as it sets out from Cairo, with pilgrims and the special battalion of the Ottoman army assigned to protect

[22] Boppe, 164–5.
[23] Boppe, 170–3
[24] Juler, 258.

ill. 92

the caravan during the entire journey. Containing a rich visual content, this rendering of the Islamic world captures the religious enthusiasm of the mounted Ottoman troops, waving banners and offering prayers as they advance in front of the camel loaded with gold in the middle of the caravan, and those who, on the left-hand side of the painting, are offering food and drink to the pilgrims in pitched tents.

Ussi's interest in the Orient began with his arrival in Egypt to participate in the ceremonies for the opening of the Suez Canal in 1869. The artist acquired fame in the palace of Viceroy İsmail Pasha. The khedive, having seen the painting he had executed for Nubar Pasha titled *A Bedouin at Prayer*, commissioned a picture from Ussi delineating *Mahmil-i Mısri*. Thus this painting of the departure for Mecca of the camel bearing the Sacred Litter is that originating in Egypt.[24] This, the largest painting in the art collection of Dolmabahçe Palace, is very spectacular, and it possesses a custom-made frame exhibiting a direct link to the religious content of the subject matter. On the outer margin of the frame is inscribed in a floral Kufic script a portion of the sura, "The Imrans," in the *Koran*. A cartouche at mid-point in the inner margin of the frame at the top reads "1289" (Hegira, i.e., 1873).[25] The painting was entered in the 1873 Vienna International Exhibition.[26] Since the Ottoman Empire also entered this exhibition and whose commissioner was Osman Hamdi Bey, who was known for his Orientalist canvases, Ussi's painting may have possibly entered the Dolmabahçe Palace collection by this route. On the other hand, this painting might have been a gift from the Egyptian khedive, having been commissioned at a time when Egypto-Ottoman relations had been restored under Sultan Abdülaziz.

Military ceremonials

Paintings of military ceremonials executed subsequent to the proclamation of the imperial reforms that reflect the Westernizing current in the Ottoman Empire noticeably tend to emphasize modernization in the military sphere. The Ottoman military organisation, involved in the attempt to modernize, not only initiated the training of a generation of "Military Artists" who introduced perspective into Ottoman painting, but the army itself also became the subject matter of these works of art. In a sense, these paintings, which serve as indices of change and Westernization, inform us that the picturesque of Orientalism had come to an end. These examples no longer represented a decision by an artist who hoped to delineate on his canvas the mysterious exoticism of the East, but rather commissions by Ottoman administrators desirous of validating this movement by a recorded display of their successful implementation of Westernization.

The existence in the Dolmabahçe Palace Collection of the work *Parade of Mahmud II's New Troops* by François Dubois suggests that it was a Court commission. The name given to the new military organization established to replace the janissary corps abolished by Mahmud II in 1826 literally signified "The Victorious Army of the Prophet Muhammed" (*Asakir-i Mansure-i Muhammediye*). To accommodate the "Victorious" troops, whose numbers became rapidly augmented, additions were made to the barracks in the suburbs of Üsküdar and Levent, a new barracks was constructed in the district of Davudpaşa, and those in the districts of Selimiye and Rami were repaired. Starting in 1828, this military body began to wear the fez as headgear and a uniform type of costume was designed. The members of this unit, who were

[25] Öner, "Tanzimat," 274.
[26] Juler, 258.

trained by foreign specialists, were assigned wartime as well as peacetime duties, such as the securing of law and order in the city and, and even the duties of a fireman. The painting depicting the new Victorious troops on parade in the Hippodrome must have been intended to introduce and display the organization of the new army. This work affords a panoramic view of the Hippodrome, which constituted the most centrally located area in town that could accommodate the passage of an army in formation and which was the only square of this size in the city. The dress of the soldiers and the fezzes on their heads indicate that its date of execution falls after 1828. This work and another one by François Dubois depicting the exit from the Imperial Gate by Mahmud II in the company of the

◀ 94

◀ 95

94 Fausto Zonaro. *Ertuğrul Cavalry Regiment Crossing Galata Bridge*, 1901. Oil on canvas. 117 x 202 cm. Dolmabahçe Palace Museum, İstanbul.

95 Fausto Zonaro. *Ertuğrul Cavalry Regiment Crossing Galata Bridge*. Gouache on cardboard. 10 x 19 cm. Collection of Suna and Inan Kıraç, İstanbul.

96 Fausto Zonaro. *Emperor Wilhelm on Quay at Dolmabahçe Palace*, 1898. Oil on canvas. 77 x 110 cm. Dolmabahçe Palace Museum, İstanbul.

new troops implies that the artist was resident in İstanbul during the reign of Mahmud II and that he received commissions from the Court.[27]

ill. 94   The painting by Fausto Zonaro dated 1901 and titled *Ertugrul Cavalry Regiment Crossing Galata Bridge* is at once a painting of a military ceremonial and a depiction of a scene from contemporary daily life while the features of its composition make it obvious that it is based on a photograph. This canvas, which is in the Dolmabahçe Palace Museum, is the second specimen of a work of the same name by Fausto Zonaro, an artist who came to İstanbul in 1891 and shortly thereafter received

[27] The French artist Dubois, who was active in the art world 1814–61 achieved renown for his paintings employing historical subject matter: Germaner and İnankur, 111.

[28] Zonaro was allocated a salary of thirty five liras as Court Artist on H. 4 Zilkade 1313 (17 Nisan 1896). Dolmabahçe Sarayı Arşivi sıra no 105, cited in Gürçağlar, "Fausto Zonaro," 92.

[29] Thalasso, "Fausto," 27.

the title of Court Artist. The painting was presented to Abdülhamid II in 1896 through an intermediary, Grand Vizier Ferid Pasha of Vlorë.[28] Subsequently, Abdülhamid II as a gift gave this painting to Paul Deschanel, a French politician and then president of the Parliament, on his visit to the Ottoman Empire.[29] A small-scale work in gouache of the same name, which is now contained in a private collection in İstanbul, may have been the sketch of the first painting presented to the Court.   ill.

The Zonaro painting in the Dolmabahçe Palace Collection portrays Abdülhamid crossing Galata Bridge with his imperial bodyguards in parade formation. With the aim of expanding the visual field, a deep perspective dominates the composition and the cavalry with unfurled banners, mounted on pure white, excellently groomed horses, emerges from a background containing a faint silhouette of Yeni Mosque. On the sidelines, Zonaro and his wife can be spotted among the town residents on the bridge intent on watching the parade and in a state of wonderment. The perceptible outweighing of the Orientalist elements by the European figural types and the modern organization of the troops depicted in the painting underscore the gradual loss by Constantinople of its Eastern identity: the accent in the picture is on the westernizing aspects of life in the empire rather than on Orientalism.

Fitting into the context of paintings of ceremonials are some interesting oil paintings by Court Artist Zonaro covering the visit to İstanbul of Emperor Wilhelm, which can be inserted into the category of record. Since the primary intention implied by these paintings was to document, their execution was based on photographs. However oil paintings were still in demand also for documentary purposes because the photographical techniques of the era did not yet permit large-scale reproductions. The renderings of the German emperor, Wilhelm II, who came to İstanbul on three separate visits (1889, 1898 and 1917) and who, with his wife Victoria, was lodged in the Şale Kiosk on the grounds of Yıldız Palace, are among those works taking as subject matter the visits by members of the European houses of royalty to the Ottoman sultan. For their second visit in 1898, the emperor and his wife traveled by private train as far as Venice, where they embarked on the yacht *Hohenzollern* and anchored in İstanbul on 18 October. Following a short period of rest in Dolmabahçe Palace, they were brought to the Şale Kiosk at Yıldız Palace by four-horse carriages.

96 In the painting delineating the emperor and empress and their retinue as they leave by the sea gate of Dolmabahçe, about to embark on the imperial caique, the ornate imperial caiques with decorative gold inlay can be seen docked at the quay. While awaiting their illustrious guests, the rowers are trying to stay the caiques against the current with hooked poles. Affixed to the prow of the caique the emperor is to board is the symbol of the Ottoman Empire—a falcon of gold with outstretched wings. A white shirt of raw silk crepe and a red fez with tassels top the costume of the rowers. The backdrop consists of a vista of İstanbul including Dolmabahçe Mosque.

97 The painting in watercolor by Zonaro depicting the Emperor and his wife in a four-horse carriage standing before the Şale Kiosk closely resembles

a hand-colored photograph. The presentation of a partial view of the villa in the background and the breadth of the visual angle tend to confirm this supposition. The perspective employed in both pictures also indicates that the artist based himself on photographs—very likely those taken on the sightseeing excursions arranged for the emperor and his wife. We may infer that Court Artist Zonaro was requested to enlarge and hand-color some of them.

97
▼

97 Fausto Zonaro. *Emperor Wilhelm and Wife at Yıldız Palace*, 1899. Watercolor. 43 x 76 cm. Dolmabahçe Palace Museum, İstanbul.

XIV The harem

My Dear, we Turkish women are wholly unknown in Europe. I may even claim that less is known about us than about the women of China and Japan…

The things they make up about us are unimaginable. So be it. They believe that we are slaves, that we are shut up in chambers [and left to die], that we live in a cage and even, probably, that we are bound in chains and kept under guard by savage, black slaves who are fully armed and that they stuff us in sacks from time to time and throw us into the sea [to drown]. They think that we live in a communal state, competing with countless other wives, and that every Turkish husband has a harem of his own—that is, at least eight to ten wives. They also suppose that we live in our cages, dressed in costumes of pink or light green satin, and dance and sing songs, partaking in poetic fashion of rose confitures, narghiles, and even pipes of opium…

You, however, know very well what we are in fact: we are—God be praised! —not unlike all other women…. We more or less resemble you—[only] perhaps a little more naive, slightly simpler, and somewhat childlike…[1]

Just as Princess Seniha, daughter of Sultan Abdülmecid, commented above in her letter to Madame Simone de La Cherté on 30 December 1910, Ottoman women and their life in the harem were what Westerners deemed of greatest interest, but, at the same time, this latter aspect represented the least known institution.

The main factors contributing to this circumstance were that the harem was closed to the outside world,that it constituted a forbidden city, and that domestic and foreign sources on this subject were inadequate. Nevertheless, the harem retained its primacy as the subject matter most frequently depicted in Orientalist paintings, because for Westerners the harem represented a microcosm of the East and stood as the most potent symbol of exotic thought and Otherness. Though the chief referent of the word harem in Orientalist art was the women's quarters within the Ottoman Palace, in actuality, *harem* signifies something sacred that is forbidden; by extension, it came to refer to both the domestic quarters to which the entrance of outsiders is prohibited and the women dwelling in these quarters.

One of the subjects most cherished by Orientalist artists was the life of the Eastern woman, closed off from the outside world. The West became fascinated by the Oriental harem because of its air of mystery and erotic connotations, and, for numerous Western artists, the harem scenes in Orientalist paintings were a means of satisfying the repressed desires of the buyers. The East served as an ideal milieu for artists unable to treat this kind of subject in a Western Christian context: they were able to respond to the unexpressed desires of the prospective purchasers and, by the same token, they were also freed from all ethical considerations by laying stress on the fact that these peoples were non-Christian and that their moral values were peculiar to this very different society. According to Rana Kabbani, the author of *Europe's Myths of the Orient,*

> Such portraits, in wishing to convey the East, described more accurately, Europe. They portrayed the repressiveness of its social codes, and the heavy hand of its bourgeois morality. The gaze into the Orient had turned, as in a convex mirror, to reflect the Occident that had produced it.[2]

Another reason why the scenes in the harem that served to expose the Oriental woman in all her splendor, appealed to Western viewers was the impossibility of their ever being permitted to enter this space. In consequence, the majority of the

[1] Claude Farrère, "Prenses Seniha'nın Yedi Mektubu," *Hayat Tarih Mecmuası* (Eylül 1971): 55–6.

[2] Kabbani, 85.

harem paintings themselves are essentially derived from written sources, and non-Muslim models were employed in their execution, supplemented here and there by the imaginative powers of the artists as in the case of Giuseppe Aureli (1858-1929) who had never been to the Near East.

The harem of the Ottoman Palace was the most intriguing of all the Eastern harems. But very few first-hand sources on the Imperial Harem are available. Besides Ottoman sources—whose count does not exceed ten[3] —the memoirs and letters of Western women travelers, spouses and relatives of ambassadors, diplomatic corps and governesses who had the opportunity of entering an Eastern harem like Lady Mary Wortley Montagu, Elisabeth Craven, Baronne Durand de Fontmagne, Julia Pardoe and Marie Adelaide Walker constitute quite reliable sources.

The first thing that comes to mind when the word "harem" is mentioned is the Topkapı Palace.

[3] The principal works on life in the harem by Ottoman women are Melek Hanım, *Harem'den Mahrem Anılar*; Leyla Saz, Şair Leyla (Saz) Hanım: *Anılar, 19.Yüzyıl Saray Haremi*, Princess Mevhibe Celâlettin, as told to her granddaughter, Sara Ertuğrul Korle, *Geçmiş Zaman Olur Ki*; Safiye Ünüvar, who acted as instructor to princes and princess, *Saray Hatıralarım*; Nevzat Vahdettin, the fourth wife of Sultan Vahdettin, *Yıldız'dan Sanremo'ya*; Ayşe Osmanoğlu, daughter of Abdülhamid II, *Babam Abdülhamid*; Şadiye Osmanoğlu, *Hayatımın Acı ve Tatlı Günleri*. In addition, Ressam Naciye Neyyal'ın *Mutlakiyet, Meşrutiyet ve Cumhuriyet Hatıraları* represents a source containing very interesting information on the Palace and the Palace circles.

98 Guiseppe Aureli. *Imperial Harem.* Oil on canvas. 33 x 47 cm. Güner and Haydar Akın Collection, Istanbul.

The Imperial Harem (*Harem-i Hümayun*) of the Topkapı Palace represented the Ottoman harem of the most compelling interest due to its magnitude, its complexity, and its witnessing of Court intrigues and power struggles. The Imperial Harem was situated in the third courtyard of Topkapı Palace. As indicated by Çağatay Uluçay, the Imperial Harem of Topkapı Sarayı was located between, on the one side, the apartments of the chief of the black eunuchs (*Kızlarağası*), the

99 Courtyard of the Favorites. Topkapı Palace Museum, İstanbul.
100 Marble Pool. Topkapı Palace Museum, İstanbul.

99 ➤

100
▼

ill. 99

head gate keeper (*Baş Kapı Gulamı*), and the female superintendent of the Imperial Harem, second in command to the empress mother (*Hazinedar Usta*) and, on the other side, the Circumcision Room (*Sünnet Odası*), the Revan Pavilion and the pavilion of the sacred relic, the Mantle of the Prophet (*Hırka-ı Saadet*). Between these two boundaries were arranged close to four hundred chambers. The central portion of the Imperial Harem surrounded the private apartment where the ruler slept and that of the empress mother. Adjacent to the courtyard of the empress mother were located the apartments of the concubines (*Cariyeler Dairesi*), of the empress mother (*Valide Sultan Dairesi*), of the imperial wives (*Kadın Efendiler*) and of the Princes (*Şehzadeler Dairesi*)[4] Thanks to the regime secured by the black eunuchs, the superintendent, and the assistant mistress, strict authority was maintained over

[4] Çağatay Uluçay, *Harem II* (Ankara: Türk Tarih Kurumu Yayınları, 1992), 7–8.

the daily affairs of the ruler and of those in the Imperial Harem. Due to this rigid control, the Imperial Harem preserved its air of mystery for centuries. This inaccessibility and secrecy aroused great curiosity among Westerners. As early as 1630, the French traveler, Jean Baptiste Tavernier, a visitor to Constantinople on several occasions, states in his book on life in Topkapı Palace that no chapter could be devoted to the Imperial Harem because no definite information was available, and he goes on to state that

> No Christian convent of nuns—regardless of how dismal and whatever the level of strictness in its adherence to the rules—prevents the entrance of males to this extreme degree. Despite his knowledge regarding the Inner Palace down to the smallest detail, the chief of the white eunuchs, active in the Inner Service

XIV The harem

101 Jean-Léon Gérôme. *The Terrace of
Seraglio*, 1886. Oil on canvas. 82 x 122 cm.
Private Collection.

for more than fifty years and who related to me
the information here, was unable to describe
any aspect at all of the Women's Quarters. At
the entrances to the Imperial Harem, the black
eunuchs keep guard and only the sultan and,
when necessary, the doctor may enter—outside
of whom no male and no woman other than
those who dwell here may be admitted.[5]

The Imperial Harems of the nineteenth century
were located in the palaces of Beşiktaş, Çırağan,
Dolmabahçe, Beylerbeyi, and Yıldız. On the construction of the Beşiktaş and Çırağan palaces by
Mahmud II, Topkapı Palace declined in importance and, under Abdülmecid, its occupants were
removed to Dolmabahçe Palace; during the reign
of Abdülhamid II, however, Yıldız Palace
assumed primacy. During this period, Topkapı
Palace became a residence for retired Harem ser-

[5] J. B Tavernier, *Topkapı
Sarayında Yaşam* (İstanbul:
Çağdaş Yayınevi, 1984),
152–3.

vants, both the females and the black eunuchs.
But this palace remained constantly alive in the
imagination of Westerners and remained a symbol
of the concept of harem and of the Orient. While
describing the architectural features of Topkapı
Palace in his *Memoirs (1616-1685)*, Sir George
Courthope fabricated the following story, so as to
make his relation account more interesting: imagining the sultan before the pool of porphyry he
had seen in the Palace, it is recounted that

> He [i.e., the sultan] putteth in his Concubines
> stark naked and shooteth at them with certain
> pellets that stick upon them without any
> damage to their bodies. And sometimes he lets

the water in such abundance upon them…that being above their heights they all bob up and down for life; and when his pleasure is satisfied with the sport, he lets down the water, and calls the Eunuchs who wait upon his women, to fetch them out if alive.[6]

Stereotyped views like this established such a secure place in the European imagination that some two hundred years later the French artist, Jean Léon Gérôme, could execute a painting of the Imperial Harem that displayed a similarly fantastic character. In his painting titled *The Terrace of the Seraglio*, Gérôme employed as the setting the fourth court of the Palace and very likely drew on photographs taken by his friends, the Abdullah Frères. The artist shifted the location of the Imperial Harem from the interior to the exterior, to the head of the marble pool with great jets before the Revan Kiosk in the compound of the Topkapı Palace. The main elements composing this typical Orientalist depiction of the Imperial Harem are the concubines, in a state of nudity or semi-nudity, refreshing themselves in the pool while the sultan, positioned to their rear, gazes at them and a black eunuch keeps watch over them. This type of black figure, in the act of guarding the Imperial Harem or the gates to the Palace and of preventing access to these areas, frequently appears in Orientalist paintings.[7] What is noteworthy is that despite the passage of centuries the fantasies of Western males regarding the Imperial Harem underwent little or no alteration.

Albeit a rarity, certain Western males did actually obtain an opportunity of observing the women of the Imperial Harem. One of these was Thomas Dallam, who built the organ sent by the British queen, Elisabeth I, as a gift to Mehmed III and who came to İstanbul in 1599 in order to set it up. Dallam was able to see the Harem women briefly with the help of a page:

> When he had showed me many other things which I wondered at, than crossinge throughe a litle squar courte paved with marble, he poynted me to goo to a graite in a wale, but made me a sine that he myghte not goo thether him selfe. When I came to the graite the wale was verrie thicke, and graited on bothe sides with iron verrie strongly; but through that graite I did se thirtie of the Grand Sinyor's Concubines that weare playinge with a bale in

6 Sir John Courthope, *Memoirs (1616–1685)* (London, 1907), 123, as cited in Kabbani, 19.

7 Paintings of this type, for example, are Ludwig Deutsch's *The Nubian Guard, Outside the Palace* and Jean–Léon Gérôme's *The Harem Guard*.

8 James Theodore Bent, ed., "The Diary of Master Thomas Dallam, 1599–1600," *in Early Voyages and Travels in the Levant*, cited in John Freely, *Inside the Seraglio* (London: Penguin, 1999), 98–9.

9 Uluçay, 12.

another courte. At the first sighte of them I thoughte they had bene yonge men, but when I saw the hare of their heades hange doone on their backes, platted together with a tasle of smale pearle hanginge in the lower end of it, and by other plaine tokens, I did know them to be women, and verrie prettie ones in deede.Theie wore upon theire heades nothinge bute a little capp of clothe of goulde, which but cover the crowne of her heade; no bandes a boute their necks, nor anythinge but faire cheans of pearle and a jeull hanginge on their breste, and juels in their ears; their coats weare like a soldier's mandilyon [cloak], some of reed sattan and some of blew, and som of other collors, and grded like a lace of contraire collor; they wore britchis of scamatie, a fine clothe made of coton woll, as whyte as snow and as fine as lane [muslin or lawn]; for I could desarne the skin of their thies throughe it. These britchis cam doone to their mydlege; some of them did weare fine cordevan buskins, and som had their leges naked, with a goulde ringe on the smale of her legg; on her foute a velvett panttoble [a shoe] 4 or 5 inches hie.[8]

The foundation stone of the Imperial Harem and of the dynasty was the concubine. The structure of the harem in Topkapı Palace is generally likened to a pyramid: the empress mother (*Valide Sultan*) at the summit; then the royal consorts (*Haseki, Kadın*); followed by the favorite concubines (*İkbal*) and concubines (*Odalık*); the female superintendents, administrative officers of the Harem (*Usta*) and the assistant mistress (*Kalfa*). As Uluçay indicated in his study on the Imperial Harem, the concubines in the early period were comprised of females captured as prisoners of war or presented as gifts to the sultan from imperial servants or purchased for the Harem by the imperial customs controller. Most of them were from the Caucasia—Circassia, Abkhasia, and Georgia. Despite the prohibition enacted by the Ottomans in the nineteenth century against the taking and selling of female slaves, Caucasians continued on their own volition to present their daughters to the Court.[9]

Yıldız Palace was vacated and the Imperial Harem dispersed on Abdülhamid II's being exiled to Thessalonica in 1909. In *The Fall of Abd-ul-Hamid*, Francis McCullagh describes the subsequent events as follows:

One of the most mournful processions of the many mournful processions of fallen grandeur that passed through the streets during these days was one composed of the ladies from the ex-Sultan's Harem on their way from Yıldız to the Top-Kapu Palace [the Seraglio]. These unfortunate ladies were of all ages between fifteen and fifty and so numerous that it took thirty-one carriages to convey them and their attendants. Some of them were sent to the Old Seraglio in Stamboul, but this old palace of the early Sultans had fallen into such a state of disrepair that it was found to be unsuitable for them and they were sent back again to Yıldız. Finally, they were all collected in the Top-Kapu Palace in connection with one of the strangest ceremonies that ever took place even there. It is well known that most of the ladies in the harems of the Turkish Sultans were Circassians, the Circassian girls being very much esteemed on account of their beauty and being consequently very expensive. As Abd-ul-Hamid's Seraglio was no exception to this general rule, the Turkish Government telegraphed to the different Circassian villages in Anatolia, notifying them that every family which happened to have any of its female members in the ex-Sultan's Harem was at liberty to take them home, no matter whether the girls had been originally sold by their parents or had (as was the case in some instances) been torn from their homes by force. In consequence of this, a large number of Circassian mountaineers came in their picturesque garb into Constantinople, and on a certain fixed day they were conducted in a body to the Old Palace of Top-Kapu, where, in the presence of a Turkish Commission, they were ushered into a long hall filled with the ex-Sultan's concubines, cadines and odalisques, all of whom were then allowed to unveil themselves for the occasion. The scene that followed was very touching. Daughters fell into the arms of their fathers whom they had not seen for years. Sisters embraced brothers or cousins, and in some instances relatives met who had never met before, and were only able to establish their relationship by means of long and mutual explanations. The contrast between the delicate complexions and costly attire of the women and the rough, weather-beaten appearance of the ill-clad mountaineers who

had come to fetch them home was not the least striking feature of the extraordinary scene; and in some instances the poor relatives were quite dazzled by the beautiful faces, the graceful manners, and the rich apparel of their kinswomen. The latter seemed all very glad, however, to get away; and as a rule they lost no time in packing their trunks and departing, sometimes after a very affectionate leave-taking of the other odalisques. The number of female slaves thus liberated was two hundred and thirteen. Clad in Circassian peasant dress, they are now in all probability milking cows and doing farm work in Anatolia... This joyful reunion in the Top-Kapu Palace had its sad side, however, as more than one of the men did not find the face he sought. Some of the girls had died, some had been put to death by Abd-ul-Hamid, and others of them after Abd-ul-Hamid's fall, had been brought with him to Salonica by the ex-Sultan or quietly drafted into the harems of imperial princes who had taken a fancy to them. Moreover a good many of the women, especially those who had already passed their first youth, were disheartened to learn that nobody came to fetch them. Apparently their relatives had died or migrated, or did not relish the prospect of bringing back into their miserable mountain huts women no longer young, who had contracted expensive tastes and forgotten the language of their childhood...[10]

Many Western writers have compared the strict regimen and organization of the life of the concubines in the Imperial Harem to that of nuns in convents. The female slaves in the Harem were required to follow a planned curriculum. Giovanni Angiolello, a former Palace page in the Inner Service during the reign of Mehmed II, disclosed that the education of the women in the Harem consisted in the most senior of the women teaching the newcomers to speak properly and to read, to learn Islamic law, and, in addition, those who displayed an aptitude were taught to sew, to do needlework, to play the harp, to sing, and to learn by heart the ceremonials and customs.[11]

Paintings of the harem executed by Western artists fall into a variety of groupings, according to whether they are realistic or imaginary and whether the atmosphere of the harem is domestic, complete with house and family, or fantastic

[10] Francis McCullagh, *The Fall of Abd-ul-Hamid* (London, 1910), 276–8, cited in N. M Penzer, *The Sultans' Harem* (Istanbul: Elya Publishing, 1998), 20.

[11] Giovanni Maria Angiolello, *Historia Turchesa (1300-1514)*, ed. I.Ursu (Bükreş, 1909), 128, cited in Leslie Peirce, *Harem-i Hümayun* (İstanbul: Tarih Vakfı Yurt Yayınları, 1993), 188.

102 Franz Hörmann, Hans Gemminger,
and Valentin Mueller. *Scene from Turkish
Harem*, 1634. Oil on canvas.
130.81 x 193.58 cm. Collection of Sevgi
and Doğan Gönül, İstanbul.

XIV The harem

and loaded with erotic images. The harem ordinarily depicted in such scenes is the Imperial Harem or those of imperial elite.

Guillaume Antoine Olivier, dispatched by the French government to Constantinople as the head of a team of specialists in 1792, states in his discussion of the harem in his book of travels that Ottoman women above a certain social level very seldom left the home.

> It is not considered proper for young women to appear frequently on the street even if their faces are veiled. For the woman is exempted from attending the mosque and may bathe whenever she wishes in the excellent bath in her home, and has slaves, servants, and intimates at her beck and call to perform all services. The main occupations of the Turkish women in the harem are to please their husbands and to keep them for as long a time in the women's quarters as their duties will permit, to bear children and take care of them, to occupy herself with her personal adornment and beauty and a few domestic chores, to pray at the times prescribed in the *Koran*, to welcome guests to the home with coffee and cigarettes....[O]ne of the things she likes most is to don her most expensive and elaborate dresses when receiving guests and to display all her jewelry and to put on high airs.[12]

Life in the harem and harem entertainments

Because the harem was an extremely circumscribed milieu, amusements with music and dance performed among themselves played a very important role in the lives of its occupants. A good illustration of how these women entertained themselves is contained in a painting of 1634 titled *Scene from Turkish Harem*, which today forms part of a private collection. The painting is one of a series of oil paintings commissioned in 1628 by the Austro-Hungarian ambassador to the Sublime Porte, Hans Ludwig von Kuefstein. Studies on these paintings have focused on the names of the artists, Franz Hörmann, Hans Gemminger, and Valentine Mueller. An inscription on the painting reads: "Because it is not the custom for distinguished Turkish ladies to leave the house or to meet foreigners, they invite each other to their houses and entertain themselves with dance,

[12] Guillaume Antoine Olivier, *Türkiye Seyahatnamesi* (İstanbul: Ayyıldız, 1977), 89–90.

[13] Thévenot, 138.

comedy and other such entertainment." As Lady Mary Montagu noted in *The Turkish Embassy Letters*, these kinds of occasions were quite popular in the harem.

In the upper portion of the above-mentioned painting there is a balustrated gallery surrounded by a sofa on three sides. A hilly landscape is visible through the grilled windows. Carpets cover the floor. A parrot is perched in a cage suspended from the ceiling, and a small, crouching monkey is attached to the balustrade by a leash. Both animals were at that time very fashionable in Europe as an exotic animal. On the left, four musicians including one black are playing a rebec (*rebab*), a tambourine with cymbals (*def*), and a dulcimer (*santur*) and in the center and on the right two women are shown dancing and holding an embroidered muslin scarf in their hands. In the lower portion is depicted a welcoming scene: despite the differences in the women's dresses, it appears to be a sequence of five scenes. In the first, the hostess greets with open arms a guest whose face is veiled by a long, white muslin veil; in the second, she is embracing the guest; in the third, she removes her guest's veil; and in the fourth and fifth scenes the guest is dancing to the rhythm of her hostess' tambourine. The guest wear on her head a cap that tapers toward the crown. Jean Thévenot, who was in the Ottoman Empire in the years 1655 and 1656, states in his memoirs that when the women went outside the home, they put on a rather tall cap of gilded cardboard, whose crown was broader than the base and that they covered their heads and their foreheads down to their eyes with their loose outer garment and that a veil covered the remainder of their whole face.[13] Most of the women in the painting are wearing a robe (*entari*) over a chemise of white silk gauze (*bürüncük*) and a cardigan with short sleeves. The hostess greeting her guest wear a fur-lined over garment (*kaftan*) a type reserved for the wealthy and muslin is wound like a turban around her cap (*terpuş*). In the lowest portion, six women whose heads are bared are performing a dance with a quicker step than the one pictured above. The skirts of two of the women holding castanets (*çalpara*) are billowing as if from whirling. They are smaller in scale compared with the figures above. The floor is also carpeted. The ornamentation and decorative richness of the room is furnished by the pillows on the divan and the carpets.

102

XIV The harem

Women's costume of similar description appears in a work titled *Portrait of a Turkish Lady*, executed in 1832 by French artist Fidel Gudin. The young woman who wears a long conical cap (*arakçin*) of silver brocade (*seraser*) is attired in a pair of white silk ankle length trousers (*şalvar*), a transparent ankle length under tunic, whose hem and sleeve cuffs display colorful needlework and which provides for a generous exposure of the bosom; completing her costume is a red cardigan with short sleeves and a patterned sleeveless over garment lined with ermine fur and on her feet are tall, ornamented clogs. This painting is a near replica of the painting of a woman contained in the book by George Sandys titled *Relation of a journey begun An. Dom. 1610. foure bookes containing a description of the Turkish Empire, of Aegypt of the Holy Land, of the remote parts of Italy, and islands adioyning.*[14] Apart from slight differences of detail in the costume, Gudin has also turned the woman's head to the right and in place of a rose, she holds a scarf with needlework.

The female subject of the *Portrait of Young Woman*, a work by an unknown artist of the French school in the second half of the eighteenth century, is clothed in a robe with deep decolletage, an outer caftan faced with ermine fur, a belt studded with jewels, and accessories, all conforming to the fashion of the reign of Ahmed III. Her dark red velvet headdress (*hotoz*) is draped with a scarf edged in needlepoint lace. A pair of beaded ornaments is attached to the sides of her *hotoz*. Both the costume and the type of *hotoz* with one-sided brim curving over one shoulder closely resemble the model in the female portraits by Levnî, court painter to Ahmed III.

Another example of harem entertainment is rendered in a painting attributed to Van Mour but which lacks a signature and is undated; known as *Amusements in the Harem, or Dancers in the Harem*, it is believed to date to the Tulip Period. Trees are visible beyond the latticed windows. On the divan extending the full expanse of the windows are seated the women of the harem, who are watching two women dancing in the central area. Precisely in the center of the bay window is a woman, seated apart from the others, garbed in different apparel and assuming a posture different from that of the other women. A rare specimen—here, the sultan, or the man of the house—is seated on the right and engaged in conversation with

[14] George Sandys, *Relation of a journey begun An. Dom. 1610. foure bookes containing a description of the Turkish Empire, of Aegypt, of the Holy Land, of the remote parts of Italy, and islands adioyning* (London, 1621), 68.

103 Fidel Gudin. *Portrait of a Turkish Lady*, 1832. Oil on canvas. 82 x 66 cm. Collection of Ayşegül and Ömer Dinçkök, İstanbul.

104 Artist unknown. *Portrait of Young Woman*. Oil on canvas. 87.5 x 73 cm. Collection of Sevgi and Doğan Gönül, İstanbul.

105 Jean Baptiste Van Mour. *Dancers in the Harem*. Oil on canvas. 78 x 108 cm. Collection of Azize Taylan, İstanbul.

one of his wives; ordinarily, harem paintings never contain any male figure. A slave girl standing immediately before this couple is waving a fan. Two slave girls stand to the rear of the couple, hands folded together in an attitude of respect. On the right-hand side of the room, food is being prepared and while one slave girl is occupied with arranging filled serving vessels on a large tray, another one is bringing in a plate of food, and yet another one is taking a plate of fruit from a black, female servant. On the left-hand side, musicians, seated cross-legged in front of a black eunuch, are playing a tambourine, cymbals, and a lute as an accompaniment to the dancing slave girls. The women are wearing above their loose-fitting trousers an undertunic of white silk gauze revealing décolletage, over which is worn a robe and a belt with a golden buckle studded with precious stones. On their heads are caps typical of the fashion of the period. The woman seated in the center and the one conversing with the sultan are dressed in an identical manner, but with the addition of an outer caftan lined with ermine fur.

These kinds of amusements with dance and music were very popular in the harem. Music and dance groups of slave girls were common in the Imperial Harem, and the leading male instructors of the day tutored the musicians. Women were active in music not only in the Palace, but also in the residences of the wealthy Ottoman elite. In the home of the grand vizier's agent (*Kahya Bey*) visited by Lady Mary Montagu in Edirne in 1718, a similar entertainment was performed. When Lady

106

Montagu arrived at the house, she was received in a large hall in which the water from a white marble fountain flowed into three or four basins and whose ceiling was ornamented with a design of a profusion of flowers spilling out of gilt baskets. Fatma, wife of one grand vizier's agent, who was reclining against white, satin pillows on a divan, raised three steps and covered with Persian carpets, commanded shortly after her guest's arrival that the slave girls should play and dance.

> Four of them immediately [began] to play some soft airs on instruments, between a lute and a guitar, which they accompanied with their voices, while the others danced by turns. This dance was very different from what I had seen before. Nothing could be more artful or more proper to raise certain ideas; the tunes so soft, the motions so languishing, accompanied with pauses in so artful a manner that I am very positive the coldest and rigid prude upon earth could not have looked upon them without thinking of something not to be spoken of. I suppose you may have read that the Turks have no music but what is shocking to the ears, but this account is from those who never heard any but what is played in the streets...[15]

The reign of Selim III represented a golden age for Ottoman music. According to Ziya Şakir, the sultan gathered at the Court the greatest music masters of the era and organized music and dance ensemble composed of female slaves in the Imperial Harem. The sultan allocated the Serdab Kiosk for the performance of musical programs (*Küme Fasılları*), but, on those evenings when no concert was scheduled, he would listen to the Harem ensemble in the Imperial Hall (*Hünkar Sofası*). This hall contained a canopied platform **ill. 106** reserved for his use, where he commonly accompanied them on his *tanbur*, an ancient form of lute. At these musical gatherings, the program included dancing after the performance of compositions in a slow tempo and songs. Female slaves of the Harem would present dances, such as *curcuna*, *köçekçe*, *tavşan*, and *kalyoncu*, each of which required a separate costume. The love of music of Selim III was taken up by his nephew, Mahmud II, which explains the latter's continuation of the practice of arranging concert programs by the Harem ensemble in the Imperial Hall, over which he would personally preside.[16]

[15] Lady Mary Wortley Montagu, *The Turkish Embassy Letters* (London: Virago, 1996), 88-91.

[16] Ziya Şakir, "Saray Harem Musikisi ve Harem Bandosu," *Resimli Tarih Mecmuası* (Aralık 1953): 2760.

106 Imperial Hall. Topkapı Palace Museum, İstanbul.

Western music first entered the Imperial Harem during the reign of Abdülmecid.[17] Abdülmecid, who was a lover of Western music and who himself played the piano, kept the musical ensemble but also founded a Harem band. Leyla Saz, the daughter of the Court physician, İsmail Pasha, relates in her memoirs that Sultan Abdülmecid reserved one section of the ground floor of the Old Çırağan and Dolmabahçe palaces for music lessons. All the instructors were male. The musicians, who were the senior slaves of the Imperial Harem, would come to the lessons in their everyday dress but worn with a veil; the dancers, however, were not veiled. The Western music orchestra and band would rehearse together twice a week while the Ottoman music ensemble rehearsed only once. There was a special private room for the dance lessons, but, on the general rehearsal day, all would meet in the Great Hall of Honor, where performances were presented by

[17] Music of the nineteenth century Ottoman Court was performed by the London Academy of Ottoman Court Music under the direction of conductor, Emre Aracı, on a CD issued in the year 2000 titled *European Music at the Ottoman Palace.*

[18] Leyla Saz, *The Imperial Harem of the Sultans* (İstanbul: Pera, 1994), 42-4.

[19] Osmanoğlu, 25, 66–7.

the ballet troupe and orchestra. Western music was taught by written musical symbols, but Ottoman music was acquired through hearing only. At the grand reception in honor of the birth of Abdülmecid's son, Prince Vahideddin, the sultan's orchestra and the Imperial Harem orchestra, the latter stationed behind a screen, took turns playing. Among the pieces played by the Harem orchestra were the *Wilhelm Tell Overture* and selections from *La Traviata.*[18]

Articles appearing in contemporary newspapers also refer to Sultan Abdülmecid's interest in Western music. For example, it is stated in the 21 August 1845 issue of *Journal de Constantinople* that the sultan had for some time expressed a wish to listen to the famed pianist Meyer, resident in İstanbul, and who, having received an invitation from the Court, played several pieces in the presence of the sultan. This interest in Western music persisted. Princess Ayşe Osmanoğlu, in her biography of her father, Abdülhamid II (*Babam Sultan Abdülhamid*), asserts that her father preferred European classical music to Ottoman classical music and quotes his opinion that "Ottoman classical music is beautiful, but it always exudes an air of melancholy. European classical music is different—it gives joy." The princess goes on to say that whenever a foreign ensemble came to İstanbul the ambassadors would send word to the Palace and submit their recommendation. By this means, numerous foreign artists came to perform for the sultan and foreign musicians who played in the Imperial Military Band, also took part in the presentation of many operettas and operas. Because Abdülhamid II had little fondness for Ottoman classical music, he put an end to the regular performance in the Palace of dances like *köçekçe, tavşan, matrak* and *kalyoncu,* so that now they were seen only on holidays.[19]

In addition to depicting the performance of dance and music in the Imperial Harem, Western painters also rendered important ceremonials. Now in a private collection and similar to a work by Van Mour titled *The Greek Wedding* in the Rijksmuseum is the painting known as *After the* ill. *Wedding: the Feast of Trotters (Paça Günü).* In a nineteenth-century Ottoman work on customs and ceremonials (*Osmanlı Adet, Merasim ve Tabirleri*), the author, Abdülaziz, states that the Feast of Trotters always took place on a Friday, and that this day was accorded nearly the same level of importance as the wedding day. For this

107

107-108 Artist unknown. *After the Wedding: the Feast of Trotters.* Oil on canvas. 53.5 x 78 cm. Collection of Sevgi and Doğan Gönül, İstanbul.

XIV The harem

reason, the groom was required to leave home early on that morning. If the groom was living in the household of his father-in-law, he would have delivered to the house on that morning a dozen or more sets of trotters prepared the day before, plus four or five large platters of boiled cream, the amounts varying according to the size of the household and the number of guests. On that day, only close relatives and families of standing would attend. The bride would wear what was called the "Trotters' Day" dress. As the crowd of the previous day would no longer be present, the service had to be very scrupulous for the remaining select guests. The most elaborate tableware would be set out that day for the service of the trotters with sauce and the boiled cream to display the wealth and power at the disposal of the family. Following the meal, entertainment would be provided by musicians and dancing girls.[20]

In this composition, heavy green velvet curtains have been hung on both sides of the room. Spread over the divan is a white cover of fine stuff, whose edges are ornamented by needlework. Of the women seated on the divan, the one in the very center—as is signaled by the red cloth in front of her—is the bride. She holds in her lap the gifts of a belt and a pearl necklace. The presentation of a costly belt by the bride's father or her nearest male relative was an ancient custom. The red veil embroidered in gold hanging at the rear on the left and the fur lined violet caftan with gold needlework on the right belong to the bride. The other women seated next to the bride wear caftans lined with ermine fur, robes, and shifts of white silk gauze and their caps are wound about with a length of silk fabric and decorated by pearls. On the large tray on the elevated platform are flower-filled vases. On the left is shown the welcoming of the guests and assisting the first guest in taking off her head scarf (*neskep*). The costumes conform to the style of the mid-eighteenth century. In this period, "the length of the skirt rose above the ankles and the neckline became deep enough to reveal the breasts, while the right front panels of the open fronted dresses were cut diagonally at the waist level to have an overlap over the left panel."[21]

Another painting from the eighteenth century belongs to Antoine de Favray, a "Painter of the Bosphorus". Auguste Boppe claims that the artist was very little acquainted with the local Muslim community and that many of his canvases were

peopled by Greek figures, both of which facts can be linked to the lessened frequency of contacts by the Muslim community with the embassies and the lack of esteem accorded de Favray by the Court because he was a knight of Malta.[22] As a result, it is unclear whether the figures in his painting titled *A Turkish Woman and her Child*, executed in 1769, are ethnically Turkish or Levantine or possibly even European. The young woman seated on a divan in a costume entirely in keeping with the vogue of the day exhibits a generous décolletage, whose basic component is a pale green robe, patterned in gold, all of whose edges are decoratively finished in gold needlework, with buttons down the vertical front opening. Her frilled under shirt of silk gauze partially covers her exposed bosom, and her waist is encircled by a belt with a gold buckle in seashell form whose edges are studded with diamonds, the outermost layer consists in an outer robe of white fur with half sleeves. The length of white muslin wound about her red cap is knotted in front in an ornamental fashion. A printed scarf is also wrapped around her daughter's red cap. The child rests one of her hands on her mother's shoulder and, with the fingers of her other one,

ill. 108

ill.

[20] Abdülaziz Bey, *Osmanlı Adet, Merasim ve Tabirleri* (İstanbul: Tarih Vakfı Yurt, 1995), 1: 131–2.

[21] Filiz Çağman, "Women's Clothing," *9000 Years of the Anatolian Woman*, exhibition catalog (İstanbul: Topkapı Sarayı Museum, 1993), 256

[22] Boppe, 116.

109 Antoine de Favray. A *Turkish Woman and her Child*, 1769. Oil on canvas. 97 x 76.5 cm. Collection of Ayşegül and Ömer Dinçkök, İstanbul.

XIV The harem

110-111 Artist unknown. *Scene from Imperial Harem*. Oil on canvas. 39.5 x 49 cm. Collection of Sevgi and Doğan Gönül, İstanbul.

holds up her pendant of red stone, as if to draw her mother's attention. The successful rendering of the bonds of intimacy and affection between the mother and child interjects a sentiment seldom portrayed in paintings intended to introduce Ottoman types and costumes.

In a painting from the era of Turquerie by an artist who, in all likelihood, had never been to the Ottoman Empire titled *Scene from the Imperial* **ill. 111** *Harem*, the sultan is depicted before a curtain draped to either side. A bed can be made out in the background. The sultan is wearing a fur-lined caftan and his headgear is accented by three plumed aigrettes and a gold crescent studded with gems. He holds a golden mace (*şeşber*) in his

10 111

112-113 Jean Baptiste Van Mour. *An Armenian Home*. Oil on canvas. 38.5 × 60 cm. Collection of Suna and Inan Kıraç, İstanbul.

hand. Slave girls attired in very colorful and rich **ill.** costume are lined up before the sultan. A black dwarf servant appears in the right-hand corner. The painting represents a stereotypical harem scene, a product of a Westerner's imagination—eye-catching but greatly lacking in authenticity.

The serving of coffee and having one's fortune read was a principal preoccupation of harem life. The harem scene painted by Van Mour and titled *An Armenian Home* is similarly represented by a **ill.** group of women in a richly appointed interior. Three of the women are standing and occupied with the serving of coffee and food. The rest, including a child, are seated on a divan drinking coffee and telling fortunes. The women are dressed in attire typical of the eighteenth century—bared neckline and caftans lined with ermine, **ill.** with a colored cloth wound like a turban around their cap, ornamented with strings of pearls. This composition, whose decor closely resembles that in *Dancers in the Harem* by the same artist, **ill.** underscores domesticity rather than eroticism.

114-115 Salvatore Valeri.
The Harem, 1888. Oil on canvas.
102 x 76. Collection of Yüksel Pekiş
Behlil, İstanbul.

XIV The harem

Salvatore Valeri, an instructor in the Imperial School of Fine Arts and the art tutor to the sons of Abdülhamid II—having been rewarded by the sultan with the title "Prince's Tutor"—executed in 1888 the painting titled *The Harem* which, since it is rendered with the eye of someone familiar with this kind of setting, is much more realistic. Here is presented an authentic Ottoman home, including all its traditional accessories—the framed inscriptions on the wall, the turban stand with crescent and star motif, the table with mother-of-pearl inlay, the reed mat and carpet on the floor, the water pipe (*nargile*), and the backgammon case. The cover of one of the volumes lying on the desk reads "Volume Two." A framed inscription of a Hadithe reads, "The lord of the tribe is the one who serves them [i.e., its members]," which figuratively implies the role of the male in the Harem. The other framed inscription, pear shaped, reads "The Letter, Elif," that is, the first letter of the Ottoman alphabet and symbolic of beauty. Seldom depicted but whose presence is ever palpable, the man of the house makes an appearance here in his nightdress, smoking a water pipe, which contributes a realistic touch. The costume of the young woman standing barefooted is quite modern and European in style. One figure whose presence is a constant in this kind of setting is the female musician, here seated cross-legged on the carpet, strumming a lute. Both the décolletage, whereby one breast of this woman is partially exposed, and the sleeveless dress on the other woman represent an attempt by Valeri to respond to the expectations of Western viewers.

One notable characteristic of the majority of Orientalist depictions of the harem is that the female occupants are never engaged in any task. As Rana Kabbani has observed, these women "do not embroider, or cook, or sew, or pray- they hardly perform any duty at all. They simply prepare and adorn themselves for the absent male, and they wait."[23] The stress on the lack of activity in these kinds of harem paintings is striking. This misrepresentation, apparent in the depictions of harem women by Western artists, also occurs in the area of literature:

> The grace of a Turkish woman seems to consist entirely in those attitudes of repose which display to their best advantage the charming curves of her figure....Nor is the practice

of such arts as these the only occupation by which they seek to enliven the deadly monotony of the greater number of lives passed in a harem....They do everything in their power to combat ennui: the whole day is often nothing but a prolonged struggle with this dreaded enemy. [They] spend hours at a time watching the movements of the ships on the Bosphorus Strait or Sea of Marmara...or weave interminable romances of love and liberty and riches as they watch the smoke from their cigarettes curl upward in blue wreaths. Tired of their cigarettes, they betake themselves to the chibuk and inhale the "blond hair of Latakia," then a cup of Syrian coffee and a few sweetmeats, or some fruit or an ice, which they spend half an hour in eating; then comes a little more smoking, the narghileh this time, perfumed with rosewater, and after it a piece of mastic gum, which they suck to get rid of the taste of the smoke; then some lemonade to do away with the taste of the mastic. They dress and undress, try on all their costumes, make experiments with all the colors in their little boxes, put on and take off patches cut like stars and crescents; and arrange a dozen or so mirrors and hand-glasses in such a way that they can see themselves on all sides...[24]

[23] Kabbani, 84.
[24] De Amicis, 44-5.

▲
116

116 "The Harem," Samuel S. Cox, *Diversions of a Diplomat in Turkey.*

XIV The harem

These lines by Edmondo De Amicis serve as an accurate précis of the male-centered harem paintings so far examined. By contrast, Leyla Saz, the author of one of the rare memoirs of the Imperial Harem, states in reference to harem life in Çırağan Palace that the "[r]eading of the Koran, newspapers, literary works, and particularly book[s] on history as well as handicrafts and music were the principal distractions of the sultan's wives and favorites."[25] Leyla Saz's statement that the sultan's wives were very closely involved in the education and raising of their children speaks of a way of life quite unlike that described by De Amicis.

Gendered interpretations on the subject of the harem were also evident in contemporary artworks. One artist who made this explicit in her paintings is a French artist whose pseudonym was Henriette Browne (1829–1901). Presenting a feminist position, Browne, whose real name was Sophie de Boutellier, generated broad notice at the 1861 Paris Exhibition because of two of her realistic harem portrayals. Having been to İstanbul for two-weeks in connection with the appointment of her diplomat husband, Jules de

[25] Saz, 102.

[26] Théophile Gautier, *Abécédaire du Salon de 1861* (Paris: Libraire de la Sociéte des Gens de lettres, 1861), 72–7, cited in Reina Lewis, *Gendering Orientalism: Race, Femininity and Representation* (London: Routledge, 1996), 132.

[27] Olivier Merson, *Exposition de 1861: la peinture en France* (Paris: Libraire de la Sociéte des Gens de lettres, 1861), 275–6, cited in Lewis, 137.

Saux, Browne now met with great success in both England and France with her authentic depictions of an Ottoman harem: *A Visit: Harem Interior, Constantinople, 1860* and *A Flute Player, Harem Interior, Constantinople, 1860,* both displayed the following year in the gallery of Ernest Gambart in London.

In her examination of the works by Henriette Browne and other now-forgotten female Orientalist artists (*Gendering Orientalism*), Reina Lewis indicates that Henriette Browne's paintings render the Otherness of the East and, at the same time, point up parallels between domestic life in the Orient and in Europe. Browne's works garnered admiration because their creator had personally visited an Eastern harem, and her realistic representations posed a challenge to the traditional harem fantasies. The factual content of Browne's harem delineations served as a protest against the assertion by Théophile Gautier that "[o]nly women should go to Turkey—what can any man see in this jealous country?",[26] shaking the foundations of stereotyped fantasies and invalidating the portrayals by the leading male Orientalist artists. This is evident, for instance, in the disappointment expressed by Olivier Merson after having viewed Browne's harem paintings in the 1861 Exhibition, as follows:

> Having been able to clear the threshold of the harems, she [i.e., Browne] painted from nature those strange and jealous interiors, … This then is the harem. Instead of diamond palaces and rejuvenated Alhambras, marble basins and gushing fountains, sumptuous rugs and naked odalisques rolling about in their pearled costumes, on piles of cushions or mosaics, we see a room that is austere and somber, lacking ornamentation, with colonnettes and white-washed walls, a mat unwinding on the flags, a divan dominating all around, and populated with silent women, bored, … somnolently graceful,…chaste in the muslin of their long robes…which outline their fragile and languid bodies. I confess that these paintings disturb our Oriental dreams a little.[27]

The viewer of *A Visit* may infer from the size of the masonry structure in which the scene is set that this must have been the reception hall of a palace harem. The room is very plain, with only a few furnishings. The pointed horseshoe arches,

117 Henriette Browne. *A Visit: Harem Interior, Constantinople, 1860.* Oil on canvas. 89 x 115.5 cm. Christie's, London.

118 Alberto Pasini, drawing based on painting by Henriette Browne. "Tandır," *Tour du Monde* (Quatrième Année, Premier Semestre 1863).

the ornamented column capitals, the ewer on the table, and the reed mat comprise the principal elements. Absent is the profusion of articles and accessories of luxury and wealth habitually appearing in Orientalist paintings. The scene presents the reception of visitors. To welcome her guests, the hostess has risen to her feet. The visitors, all in colorful outdoor mantles are accompanied by a little girl, have not yet removed their veils and outerwear. The child, whose face bears a shy expression, is holding on to her mother's hand. Some of the women of the harem are standing and some are seated on the divan, engaged in observing the newcomers. A black servant, who has entered with the guests, is carrying a cushion and while she is ascending the staircase turns her head to look at something below, invisible to the viewer. On the right, a women in blue whose

XIV The harem

hand rests against a column for support is leaning forward and looking at the same point. These kinds of visits usually took place in the most spacious and richly appointed hall. The female slaves, after having greeted the guests, would show the way and present them to the hostess, seated on the divan. Once the guests were seated, coffee, followed by a beverage of sweetened fruit juice, would be served as refreshments. As conversation got underway, fruit and nuts of the season would be brought in on silver dishes and trays, and female slaves would play music and dance to entertain the guests. Because these halls were difficult to heat, this kind of gathering would be held in smaller chambers in cold weather, and both open and covered braziers would supply heat.

ill. 119

The covered brazier (*tandır*) was one object that captured the interest of foreigners. In his work on traditions and customs in the eighteenth-century Ottoman Empire, Mouradgea D'Ohsson explains that *tanndour* was a corruption of the Arabic *tennur* meaning 'oven' and that Muslim women spent their days in winter seated around the covered brazier—working, dining, and receiving guests and engaging in conversation—and that he had no doubt that if Europeans had become acquainted with this method of heating "they also would have adopted it, because the warmth generated by the tandır [was] very agreeable and present[ed] much less danger than the raging heat issuing from a fireplace."[28]

ill. 118

The location of the great reception hall pictured in *A Visit* is unknown. But the memoirs of Marie Adelaide Walker, an artist and writer who came to İstanbul in 1856, provide a clue. Walker states, in connection with her notice that she had painted the portrait of a daughter of Sultan Abdülmecid married to the son of a prominent statesman, and that she herself had presented another Western woman to this palace. The woman in question was Henriette Browne. Walker claims that this palace on the shore of the Bosphorus was where Brown had executed the studies on which she based her paintings that, shortly afterwards, graced the walls of the art exhibition halls in Paris and London.[29] Though Walker fails to provide the name of the princess, it is very probable, both on account of her personal description and the information supplied about the palace, that the woman was Princess Fatma, the wife of Ali Galip, son of Mustafa Reşid Pasha, who served under Sultan Abdülmecid, and that the palace, very modern for

[28] D'Ohsson, 4: 174–5.

[29] Mrs. [Marie Adelaide] Walker, *Sketches of Eastern Life and Scenery* (London: Chapman and Hall, 1886), 1: 10.

119 Alexandre Bida. "Storyteller in the Harem," *Tour du Monde* (Quatrième Année, Premier Semestre 1863).

120 Sandor Alexander Swoboda.
Shopping in the Harem. Oil on canvas.
36 x 54 cm. Dolmabahçe Palace Museum,
İstanbul.

the time, was the Baltalimanı Palace on the shores of the Bosphorus, which is of masonry.

The subject of the painting titled *A Visit* is an Orientalist version of the afternoon visit, which occupied an important place in the life of the European bourgeoisie. In contrast to the women who, in the harem paintings by male artists, sit idly, dreaming in their own world, here possess a social relation to each other. As the hostess in the center of the composition is in the act of welcoming her guests, the others are waiting to greet them. The Browne harem, indicates Lewis, is a space shaped by the daily round of its female occupants, a space defined in relation to the house; and the importance of the absent spouse,

120

XIV The harem

her husband, has been reduced to inconsequentiality. The inclusion of a small child in this entirely decent and innocuous domestic setting defuses the sexual intensity of the harem atmosphere and highlights the resemblance between the home life of the Europeans and the Ottomans, in opposition to the fantasies of Western Orientalists.[30] This setting is no longer the habitat of the semi-nude females in the paintings by Delacroix, Ingres, or Gérôme, nor is it a setting made colorful by luxurious accessories, laden with eroticism, and divorced from the outside world: it is a quiet, upright social milieu dominated by females, places where visitors from the outside world are frequently welcomed or where musicians con-

[30] Lewis, 156.

on a divan in the Imperial Harem and looking at the jewels in the coffer brought for their perusal by a peddler of women's goods. Their costumes conform to the fashions of the first half of the nineteenth century: one of the women is wearing on her head a fez with a shallow crown, ornamented by beads, and the other two have bound their heads in a printed scarf with sequins. The dress of the woman in the right-hand corner is of a shiny, red fabric, typical of the fabrics imported from Europe in this era. The viewer may observe a tambourine and a rose water sprinkler in a wall recess and three cups and a coffeepot on a table with inlaid mother-of-pearl next to the divan. According to Sermet Muhtar Alus, female venders

1 ▶

▲ 122

▲ 123

tribute an animated accent. Browne's paintings are extremely significant, both as an expression of first-hand acquaintance with Ottoman life in the palaces as domestic residences under the reign of Abdülmecid and also as an exposition of what might almost be termed a deliberate counter thesis to the Orientalist stereotype of the harem.

The women of the harem and fashion

In the painting titled *Shopping in the Harem* by the Hungarian artist, Sandor Alexander Swoboda (1826–96), three members of the Court are seated

121 Follower of Jean Baptiste Van Mour. *Interior with Oriental Female.* Oil on canvas over board. 35.5 x 26 cm. Collection of Ayşegül and Ömer Dinçkök, İstanbul.

122 Follower of Jean Baptiste Van Mour. *Interior with Oriental Female.* Oil, canvas on wood. 35.5 x 26 cm. Collection of Ayşegül and Ömer Dinçkök, İstanbul.

123 Artist unknown. *Esclave du Grand Seigneur.* Oil on board. 35 x 24 cm. Private Collection, İstanbul.

20

124-125 "Costume Design," *L'Elégance Parisenne'*(1873—1874). Archives, Topkapı Palace Museum, no. 10739/7 and 10739/6.

126 "Costume Design," *La Saison* (1873-1874). Archives, Topkapı Palace Museum, no. 10739/3.

fell into two categories. One was the Muslims comprised of emigrants from the Balkans or Gypsies. Aged between forty and sixty, they covered their heads with a length of cambric that draped over their shoulders like a cape, their over garment was full-length and loose-fitting, and they carried their cloth-wrapped bundle under one arm. The second category of female venders was made up of Austrian and Czech Jews, whose numbers probably increased after the reform proclamation.[31] Women of the dynastic family employed intermediaries to make their purchases. With a written list of the goods desired in hand, a servant would place the order and when they were delivered to the Palace, the princesses would select those things they liked and return the remainder. A book on the life of a nineteenth-century Ottoman princess Refia contains detailed information of the subject of purchases by members of the dynasty.[32] The cour physician's daughter, Leyla Saz relates that, occasionally, the members of the Imperial Harem would go to the Grand Bazaar, but, because it was improper for them to enter the shops, they would wait in the adjacent mosque of Nuruosmaniye in the section reserved for the imperial family. After the servants had placed the princesses' order with the shop-

[31] Sermet Muhtar Alus, *Masal Olanlar* (İstanbul: İletişim Yayınları, 1995), 85–6.

[32] Ali Akyıldız, *Mümin ve Müsrif Bir Padişah Kızı: Refia Sultan* (İstanbul: Tarih Vakfı Yurt Yayınları, 1998), 53–4.

[33] Saz, 115.

keepers, the goods would be delivered by the shopkeepers to the black eunuchs for presentation to the princesses for their approval.[33]

The contents of depictions of females in the harem offer detailed information on women's fashion and what was worn at home. Ottoman costumes and albums acquainting the West with these costumes had been enthusiastically received since the Renaissance. Prominent among those executing works in this sphere are Nicolas de Nicolay, Melchior Lorichs, and Pieter Coecke van Aelst. In the eighteenth century, many artists produced paintings of Westerners in Eastern costume. One of these was Van Mour. The artist executed a series of paintings rendering a variety of individual Ottoman types and costumes that served to [ill.] influence many artists and was widely imitated. Women in the eighteenth century continued with [ill.] minor changes, to don the traditional style of clothing with loose-fitting trousers, silk undergarments, a cardigan, a robe and a caftan. For instance, the painting by an unknown hand but which is inscribed "Esclave du Grand Seigneur", [ill.] limns a woman wearing a blue robe, patterned in gold. Buttons are employed to close the bodice while the skirt overlaps in a manner conforming to eighteenth-century fashion. The generous decolletage permits a glimpse of her undershirt. A sash of white muslin with gold tassels encircles her waist and over her robe is worn a green, velvet outer garment with long sleeves. Gold-colored bands outline the neckline and the cuffs of both the robe and the outer caftan. Her hair is styled

XIV The harem

127 Chusseau-Flaviens. "Les désechantées chez le couturier," *L'Illustration* (19 Mars 1910).

with short bangs over her forehead. A long length of white muslin, pierced by diamond brooches, binds her conical cap; a tassel in pink accents the crown of the cap.

The growing frequency of contacts with the West and Westerners introduced changes in female costume, "first, the accessories of the costume—the edging, lace, gilded trim, broad and shiny—made inroads and then technical applications, like pleats, corsages, and collars. A transitional period of some twenty-five years, beginning in the 1850s, was marked by traditional costumes trimmed with Western notions, but which was succeeded after the second half of the 1870s by two-piece outfits—a long skirt topped by an upper garment—a wholly authentic European style."[34]

Despite the dearth of surviving specimens, two tailor registers in Topkapı Palace Archives and the orders recorded in it permit the assignment of a firm dating for this change. The first register covering the years 1854–6 and 1871 indicates on the first page that it contains records for articles tailored for Mahinev Hanım, Imperial Wife Three. The name of the tailor is Koço Uzun Terzi Dimitri Angeli. A study on this register by Hülya Tezcan discloses that the costume at this time still consisted of the traditional components—loose-fitting trousers, robe and cardi-

[34] Hülya Tezcan," On Sekizinci Yüzyılda Osmanlı Kumaş Sanatı," *P Dergisi* 9 (Kış '97): 85.

[35] Hülya Tezcan, "Osmanlı İmparatorluğu'nun Son Yüzyılında Kadın Kıyafetlerinde Batılılaşma," *Sanat Dünyamız* 37 (1988) 48–9.

[36] Tezcan, "Osmanlı," 49–50.

[37] Saz, 162.

[38] Dodd, 389.

gan.[35] The transformation to a fully Europeanized women's costume, that is, the one-piece dress or the skirt and jacket, occurred during the reign of Abdülaziz. Coincidentally or no, the French empress Eugenie's visit to İstanbul at this time seems to have made a deep impression on the sultan and the Court. The Empress Mother Pertevniyal, at the reception arranged in Eugenie's honor and the Head Consort, at a reception arranged in honor of the Prince of Wales and his consort who were in İstanbul in the same period, are known to have worn European-style dresses. The second register in the Topkapı Palace Archives also derives from this era. As indicated by Tezcan, the register consisting of seven leaves, dating to 1873–4, presents a diverse array of women's dress patterns and were collected from various French fashion magazines, like *L'elégance Parisienne, La saison,* and *Penelope.* ill. 124 Inscribed on the patterns are instructions to the tailors from the women of the imperial family and to ill. 125 which are attached fabric samples. The samples are ill. 126 plain and include colors like lilac, pale pink, light green, light blue, straw yellow, and canary yellow. It is easy to detect the influence of Paris fashion in the instructions to the tailors. Another fashion indicator of the period is the increase in the numbers of Armenian and Greek tailors, whose patrons are among the Court élite and the wealthy and for whom they stitched costumes in the latest European mode.[36] A number of tailoring shops and clothing stores were located in Beyoğlu. On the welcoming ceremony held on Sultan Abdülaziz's return from Europe, Leyla Saz reports that "[a]t this period, the young ladies and young girls had completely abandoned the old dresses with three tails, or trains, and the baggy pants underneath; fashion now demanded skirts with a single train which was caught up and attached to the belt—there were now petticoats instead of şalvars, or the baggy pants, previously worn. The headdresses had also changed with the times and now usually matched the costumes; there were earrings with jewels, medallions and elaborate hairstyles, garnished with precious stones."[37]

Anna Bowman Dodd, a visitor to the Ottoman Empire in 1850, states in her work, *In the Palaces of the Sultan,* that the changes in fashion were connected with Abdülaziz's trip to France and that the Ottoman women who came to La Grande Rue (Beyoğlu) to purchase a broad array of imported goods from Le Bon Marché unwittingly carried out a remarkable revolution in Ottoman life.[38] Chusseau-Flaviens' photograph "Les Désechantées ill. 127

chez le couturier", published in the 19 March 1910 issue of the magazine *L'Illustration*, represents a good example of this change. The photograph refers to Pierre Loti's novel *Les désechantées: roman des Harems turcs*. In this work, published first in serial form in *Revue des Deux Mondes* and then as a book in 1906, Loti takes as his subject two well-educated girls and their cousin from an upper-class family, and through the personalities of these girls explores contemporary Ottoman women's traditional life style and how it was restricted by its norms and their opposition to them.

128 ➤

128 *Princess Fatma, Daughter of Sultan Abdülmecid*. Ruben 1266. Engraving. Topkapı Palace Museum Library.

129 Pierre Désiré Guillemet. *Portrait of a Lady of the Court Playing the Tambourine*, 1875. Oil on canvas. 98 x 79 cm. Collection of Suna and Inan Kıraç, İstanbul.

Marie Adelaide Walker, who rendered on canvas a number of İstanbul harem scenes, came to the city around 1855 and executed portraits of a number of very prominent individuals, such as Princess Fatma and Serfiraz Hanım, who ranked as the second of Sultan Abdülmecid's Favorite Concubines.

Residing in İstanbul for many years and serving as an instructor in the Turkish Girls' School established in 1870 near the Yerebatan Cistern, this artist must be the same as the "Madam Walker" who participated in the Paris Salon exhibition of 1867, the Imperial School of Fine Arts exhibition in the suburb of Tarabya in 1880, and the exhibition of the ABC Club in Tepebaşı district in 1881. Walker, who also served as art tutor to Miss

129 ➤

Serviçen, submitted a portrait of Sultan Abdülaziz to the Paris Salon Exhibition and showed a painting of a black serving fruit at the exhibition of the Imperial School of Fine Arts. During her period in residence, Walker employed as one of her models, Princess Fatma, Sultan Abdülmecid's daughter. **ill.** Walker, who was referred as a "portrait painter" (*tasvirci*), rendered the princess' portrait in the harem of the summer palace (at Baltalimanı) on the Bosphorus. The dress worn by the princess for this important event displayed, laments Walker, no trace of Eastern elegance or splendor. She adds that, although Princess Fatma owned some very beautiful clothes, for her sittings, she had posed in an extremely unbecoming French silk dress, simply for the sake of fashion in the European mode and that the ease, elegance, and stunning brilliance of Eastern attire had disappeared through the influx of Western fashion. Several years after this incident, Walker was summoned by this same princess to her winter palace in order to convey her wish that the dress in the painting be redone in the style of a dress shown in a fashion maga-

Another anecdote, related by Charles White as an illustration of how greatly Westerners admired traditional Ottoman dress and how interested were the foreigners who came to İstanbul in having their portraits painted in such costume, concerns a dinner at which White was a guest in the Emirgan villa of Rıfat Pasha, at that time the minister of foreign affairs (*Reis Efendi*). Among the guests was the artist, John Frederick Lewis, then

130 Pierre Désiré Guillemet. *Portrait of a Palace Slave*, 1875. Oil on canvas. 98 × 79 cm. Dolmabahçe Palace Museum, İstanbul.

131 Pierre Désiré Guillemet. *Portrait of a Young Lady of the Court*, 1875. Oil on canvas. 98 × 79 cm. Dolmabahçe Palace Museum, İstanbul.

zine recently arrived from Paris. During her stay in the palace, Walker, who found these European-style clothes aesthetically unpleasing, also made drawings in a small sketchbook of the classical Ottoman clothing of the women of the Court. On being informed of this situation, the princess immediately ordered that the sketchbook be brought to her and, crossing out the sketches so furiously that she nearly ripped the pages out of the book, sent her a message that she should never again depict women in clothes like these, otherwise, Westerners should believe that the women of her palace wore clothes of very poor taste.[39]

[39] Walker, 1: 15–6, 311–2.

resident in Cairo but who was at that juncture on a visit to the British embassy. After dinner, Lewis brought out his portfolio for the perusal of Rıfat Paşa and about whom a group immediately clustered, including Ali Efendi, at that time the ambassador to London. After studying the drawings one

by one—each more wonderful than the other in its faithfulness of line and color to reality—the minister of foreign affairs withdrew one of them. It was a portrait of the wife of his family's British physician, who was depicted in a Turkish costume, and "[u]pon seeing this, one of the spectators observed, 'Mashallah! a Turkish woman! How came you to obtain such a model for your pencil? Oh you are a fortunate man, a devourer of hearts.' 'This good fortune has not befallen me,' rejoined Mr. Lewis; 'it is the wife of Dr. Macarthy.' 'In a Moslem dress?' exclaimed the other. 'Yes,' interposed the Reis Effendi; 'the lady is the good doctor's property, but the dress belonged to my house.' No sooner had the Pacha uttered the last words, than all Turkish eyes were averted, as a mark of respect, to the portrait of garments belonging to his harem."[40]

The works titled *Portrait of a Young Lady of the Court* and *Portrait of a Palace Slave* in the Dolmabahçe Palace Collection and *Portrait of a Lady of the Court Playing the Tambourine* in a private collection are all by Pierre Désiré Guillemet. In the second painting, dated 1874, is represented a young woman with henna-tinted fingers and blond, plaited hair, who is holding a small brazier and an ashtray. The woman has a dark blue scarf bound about her head and tied in the front forming a bow, to the edge of which is attached a gold crescent; earrings dangle from her ears and a pendant is suspended by a chain at her neck.[41] Her costume of the three-skirt panel type with deep V-shaped décolletage is trimmed by a broad edging of needle point lace. At her waist is a colored sash of muslin. In the third portrait executed one year later, a woman playing a tambourine is wearing a robe of four skirt panels in a patterned fabric, with a V-shaped front opening and a narrow, standup collar while the edges of the collar and sleeve cuffs display needlework trim; visible beneath her robe is a shift edged in lace, and at her waist is a belt with two large stones in a silver setting. The woman's hair falls to her shoulders, and on her head is a crown of blue fabric, ornamented by flowers, to front of which is attached a white feather.

In the painting titled *Princess Nemika*—the grand daughter of Abdülhamid II as a young girl— Salvatore Valeri presented his model in European-style clothing. The princess' lilac-colored dress has a triangular lace insert at the upper bodice terminating in a high standup collar and its hemline and

ill.
ill.
ill.

ill.

[40] Charles White, *Three Years in Constantinople* (London: Henry Colburn, 1845), 139–40.

[41] It contains her manumission document, ıtk-name : Çağman, 210.

cuffs trimmed in lace are adorned with tiny bunches of white flowers, setting off the bow of her long white sash is a sprig of lilac. Non-Ottoman written sources of the day also reveal that the women of the Turkish Court were expressing an interest in European fashion. The caption beneath a photoengraving by L. Sabbatier in one issue of *L'Illustration* (21 February 1912) reads "*Elegance jeunes Turques*", accompanied by the following text:

33

Women's fashions in Turkey are as caught up in the process of change as are their ideas, and thanks to our engraving documented by the photographs and original sketches forwarded to us by Izzet Melih, the author

of the contemporary dramatic piece *Leyla*, it is apparent from the various poses that the classic veil (*peçe*) has been transformed to an envelope of sheer stuff and the traditional çarşaf has been abbreviated ... to a short cape; the two elegant ladies in the foreground who are taking a Parisian friend sightseeing represent the fashion of the day—or of tomorrow. It is obvious that the insubstantial face covering pleased our artist for it has been rendered quite transparent in order to show the smile beneath the veil. We are truly indebted for this charming exaggeration. However, to be frank, we have no idea how such a young Turkish woman, modernized to this degree and lacking

133

132 Salvatore Valeri. *Princess Nemika.*
Oil on canvas. 184×100 cm. Topkapı
Palace Museum, İstanbul.

133 L. Sabbatier. "Elegances Jeune
Turques," *L'Illustration* (21 Fev, 1912).

134 Prince Abdülmecid. *Beethoven in the Imperial Harem.* Oil on canvas. 155.5 x 211 cm. Museum of Painting and Sculpture, Mimar Sinan University, İstanbul.

135-136 Prince Abdülmecid. *Goethe in the Imperial Harem.* Oil on canvas. 132 x 173 cm. Ankara Museum of Painting and Sculpture, Ankara.

XIV The harem

a carriage, possess the courage to walk on the Muslim streets or even through the European crowds of Pera.

An article by Laurence de Laprade on daily life and fashion in İstanbul after the declaration of the Second Constitutional Monarchy titled "L'Elégance Française en Orient" appeared in *Figaro Illustré*, the leading periodical of the day. The subject was the fashion show held in the Pera Palace Hotel by Laferriere, a renowned couturier and fashion house of Paris. The writer draws a parallel between the way Ottoman intellectuals were influenced in the past by the ideas of the French Enlightenment and the way French fashion would now teach the Ottomans about the modern way of life and execute a "Bloodless Revolution." Laprade states that the French were not newcomers to the Ottoman Empire and that those who are masters on the art of living like Laferriere had been waiting "for a conquest where no weapon would be employed other than aesthetics." Laferriere had for many years garbed the beauties of İstanbul; however, these clothes had always been kept under cover, either in the harem or by the loose-fitting outer garment. But, the newly created constitution had changed all this, and a new Europeanized Ottoman woman was being born, so that, at last, their clothes would be exposed to the light of day. The writer concludes his piece by introducing the collection prepared by the designer, keeping in mind this new urbanity in the Orient.[42]

Two paintings by the caliph, Prince Abdülmecid, titled *Goethe in the Imperial Harem* and *Beethoven in the Imperial Harem* constitute one of best sources for the changes that had been wrought over the centuries in the Imperial Harem. These paintings were executed in his villa in the Asian district of Bağlarbaşı. The poetess, Nigar Hanım (*Şair Nigar*), frequently visited this villa and her diary entry for 8 November 1917 reads: "Every evening, I spend some time surrounded by the prince's precious paintings in a state of spiritual exuberance, listening to the musical ensemble composed of piano, two violins, two violas, and two cellos in the company of the artists—the prince and his wife, and six stewardesses of the Imperial Harem."[43]

ill. 134 A setting of closely similar character is rendered in the painting *Beethoven in the Imperial Harem*. Here, Prince Abdülmecid is shown wearing the khaki uniform prescribed for all military personnel

[42] Laurence de Laprade, "L'Elégance Française en Orient," *Figaro Illustré* (1908): 5.

[43] Şair Nigar, *Hayatımın Hikayesi* (İstanbul: Ekin Basımevi, 1959), 86.

[44] Aykut Gürçağlar, "Halife Abdülmecid Efendi' ve 'Harem'de Beethoven'in Düşündürdükleri," in *Hacettepe Üniversitesi, Edebiyat Fakültesi, Sanat Tarih Bölümü, Uluslararası Sanatta Etkileşim Sempozyumu Bildirileri* (Ankara: Türkiye İş Bankası, 2000), 139.

[45] Arnold Höllriegel, "Die türkische Kunstausstellung in Wien," *Wochen–Ausgabe des Berliner Tageblatt* (5 Juni, 1918): 7.

after the proclamation of the Second Constitutional Monarchy, his cape and calpac of lambs' wool have been tossed to one side while he listens to a trio by Beethoven, his favorite composer. Playing the violin is Şehsuvar Kadınefendi, his Principal Wife, on the piano is Hatça Kadın, whose real name was Ophelia, and, of the two young women standing on the left-hand side, the woman closer to the viewer is Mehisti Kadınefendi, the second wife of Abdülmecid.[44] All the women are in European dress. The furnishings and accessories in the room—the bust of Beethoven on a marble base, the musical notes fallen on the floor, the seascape painting on the wall, in which can be made out the silhouette of Seraglio Point, and the bronze equestrian statue of Abdülaziz by C. F. Fuller, visible at the back of the room between two windows—reflect a thoroughly Westernized mode of life. Moreover, this also represents one of those rare depictions in which the man of the house makes his appearance in the harem. In *Goethe in the Imperial Harem*, Caliph   **ill.** Abdülmecid wishes the observer to infer from the copy of Goethe's *Faust* held in the hand of Şehsuvar Kadınefendi that this was a woman who could read in a foreign language and whose hair style and clothes were indistinguishable from those of   **ill.** any European. This message was so manifest that when the painting was shown in the Ottoman Artists show in Vienna in 1918, Arnold Hollriegel admitted in an article titled "Die turkische Kunstausstellung in Wien" in the weekly supplement of *Berliner Tageblatt* that he was astounded to discover that a prince of the Ottoman house had executed large-scale oil paintings that constituted propaganda for German culture.[45]

Another painting by Caliph Abdülmecid titled *Boarding the Caique for an Excursion on the*   **ill.** *Bosphorus*, dated to 1922, shows members of the Imperial Harem with parasols, veils, and out door mantles in front of an ocher-colored mansion at the edge of the Bosphorus, who are getting into the caique with the assistance of black eunuchs. The landscape panels on the walls in the entryway of the seaside mansion are in the nineteenth-century style. The caique culture of İstanbul was wholly unique: one went to the Bosphorus in pri-   **ill.** vate caiques and the type of caique varied according to the rank of those who boarded them. Abdülhak Şinasi Hisar describes the caiques of the Bosphorus in his work on the special culture of seaside mansions on the Bosphorus, thus:

◄ 138

137 Prince Abdülmecid. *Boarding the Caique for an Excursion on the Bosphorus*, 1922. Oil on canvas. 183 x 254 cm. Dolmabahçe Palace Museum, İstanbul.

138 Albert Mille. "Caique on the Bosphorus," *Figaro Illustré: Constantinople* (Oct. 1908).

XIV The harem

The caiques were neither Venetian nor Arab nor Persian nor were they European: they were nothing other than Turkish and of the city of İstanbul, a précis of the Bosphorus sense of pleasure. Thus, it was a refined and special instrument of civilization and had come to occupy the position of assistant in a seaside mansion. A well-maintained house caique was in itself a work of art. Running along the margin of the sides of most of these caiques, whose classic color was orange, was a pair of parallel, gilt bands with the intervening space in lavender or in the color of the waters—a medium blue or a light navy blue. The furnishings of covering and pillows were of velvet or broadcloth in one of the colors popular in those days—crimson, dark cherry, light blue, or brown.

The rowers' outfits were always of identical cut, with open, crescent-shaped necklines to reduce perspiration, white loose-fitting trousers, white stockings on their feet and light, flat-heeled shoes with the backs pressed down and on their heads fezzes of identical shape. Over their cream-colored full-sleeved shirts of a cotton-silk blend, they might add a vest or a girdle of satin in a color matching that of the caique furnishings. If the caique was one reserved for the exclusive use of the women, a covering in a blue matching that of the waters would trail in the water at the back of the craft.

Even the manner of boarding and alighting from these caiques over time settled into a traditional form. The women while boarding or disembarking would lightly rest their hand—like a bird who alights and suddenly flies off—on one of the strong shoulders proffered for use as a support by the foremost boatman standing on the dock. In the meantime, the rear-most boatman would attach the hook to a convenient point in the rocks

[46] Abdülhak Şinasi Hisar, *Boğaziçi Yalıları* (İstanbul, ÖtükenYayınları, 1978), 23–4.

[47] Çelik Gülersoy, *Kayıklar* (İstanbul: Türkiye Turing ve Otomobil Kurumu Yayınları, 1983), 76.

to secure the craft from drifting away from the wharf.[46]

The subject of women and caiques was a combination popular with foreign artists. In a painting by Zonaro titled *In a Caique*, four women are moving over the water in a light rowboat being propelled by a single rower wearing a blue vest with gold needlework. With the ease gained by being on the open sea, the women have uncovered their faces, in full enjoyment of the boat excursion while in the background can be seen the Golden Horn and the port of İstanbul, dense with steamships. Such light rowboats were "the luxury sea-cabs of the day, taking on passengers at the various landing stages."[47] Even though a light rowboat like this might be hired from time to time, well-to-do families commonly had caiques of their own built to suit their needs, with their length and the number of rowers proportional to the social position of their owners. ill. 139

Zonaro in his painting titled *Women Boarding a Caique*, now in the Dolmabahçe Palace, shows an Ottoman family boarding a caique at Aya Kapı on the Golden Horn. In the background are the Galata Tower, steamships, sailing craft and caiques, the Unkapanı Bridge, and, further distant, the opposite shore of Asia Minor. Three women wearing outdoor mantles and double veils (*yaşmak*) and a young unveiled servant dressed in light colored clothes is followed by three veiled women with veil who are about to board after having settled on the fee of passage with the boatmen, sporting long, thick mustaches and wearing white, loose-fitting trousers and red fezzes. ill. 140

139 Fausto Zonaro. *In a Caique*. Oil on canvas. 37 x 61 cm. Collection of Suna and Inan Kıraç, İstanbul.

140 Fausto Zonaro. *Women Boarding a Caique*. Oil on canvas. 56 x 83 cm. Dolmabahçe Palace Museum, İstanbul.

XV The bath

In Ottoman life, the bath occupied a position of centrality. In Islam, equal importance is laid on a clean body and a pure heart, and flowing water is considered cleaner than still water. In this context, the bath tradition attracted the attention of Westerners, who frequently noted that it constituted an Ottoman institution.[1] The bath represents a setting, in addition to the mosque, the marketplace, and the coffeehouse, where all segments of the population could come together. The baths in

[1] The Turkish bath became fashionable in various European cities at the end of the seventeenth century.

[2] Ahmet Refik (Altınay), *Kafes ve Ferace Devrinde İstanbul* (İstanbul, 1998), 101.

İstanbul were divided into two classes—private, that is, those in palaces and mansions, and public. Undoubtedly, the most illustrious of the private baths was the Bath of the Imperial Sovereign (*Hünkâr Hamamı*) and the Bath of the Empress Mother, (*Valide Sultan Hamamı*), erected in Topkapı Palace by Chief Imperial Architect Sinan. As for the public baths, the majority was reserved for women's use in the daytime, but there were also double baths with separate facilities for males and females. Those restricted to women in the residential areas were called *avret* and those for males in the marketplace and trade markets were called *rical*. In time, because of water shortages, the decision was made to prohibit the building of additional baths in the city and a firman issued in 1768 reads, in part:

> [H]ereafter whether in [the metropolis of] İstanbul and the annexes of Üsküdar and Galata or whether in the towns of Eyüp on the Golden Horn and those on the Bosphorus, no permission or license will be granted for the erection by the chief architects and others of double and single public baths, and [in the name of] the honored Imperial Rescript, it is [henceforth] strictly prohibited and forbidden.[2]

Despite the fact that the bath occupied a very significant position in the daily life of Ottoman males, few Orientalist paintings depict the men at the bath. Rather, Westerners chose the women's bath as a subject, because in their eyes it was, like the harem, symbolic of the sensuality of the East. The bath pictured in an eighteenth-century print by Le Barbier represents a detailed and objective delineation of its architecture and associated etiquette and conveys the sense that this place was a component of the woman's daily round and is far removed from the erotic. In contrast, Gérôme, who executed the greatest number of paintings of the bath as subject matter in the nineteenth cen-

141   **142**

141-142 Bath of the Sultan. Topkapı Palace Museum, Istanbul.

tury, exhibits an approach in works like *Steam Bath*, *Nude Bather*, *Harem Bath*, and *The Grand Bath at Bursa*, that focuses on the nudity of the female and her feminine quality. The fact that the bath was a place where women were totally nude served greatly to stimulate interest. Foreign women travelers who gained access to the bath devoted detailed descriptions to them. The most well known, contained in a letter dated 1 April 1717 refers to the women's bath at Edirne. In her letter, Lady Montagu laid particular stress on the nudity and beauty of the women.[3] Miss Pardoe, who entered a public bath for women in İstanbul roughly one hundred and eighteen years after Lady Montagu's experience, was of the opinion that, because she had encountered none of the unnecessary and wanton exposure described by Lady Montagu, the diplomat's wife had either participated in some strange ritual or else Ottoman women of the capital have become more sensitive and fastidious in their ideas of propriety.[4]

[3] Montagu, 58–9.

143
▼

144 Fausto Zonaro. *The Welcome. Déri Séadet ou Stamboul Porte du Bonheur,* (1908).

acceptance of sexual excesses and her interest in the lives of the rich and powerful to the exclusion of ordinary folk. As Mellman indicates, the correlation made between class and morality is altogether characteristic and explicative. Criticism concerning the behavior and mores—especially those related to gender—of the nobility is an important element of the urban elite culture of which Miss Pardoe was a member and the newly emerging middle-class ethos. Miss Pardoe's focus on nudity may be interpreted as a sign of the conservatism of the Victorian period.[5]

Despite this cleavage between Lady Montagu and Miss Pardoe, there is one point on which they both agree: the Turkish bath is "the terrestrial paradise of Eastern women"[6] and "'tis the women's coffee house, where all the news of the town is told, scandal invented etc."[7] For women, whose domestic life was rather insular and monotonous, the bath represented both an opportunity to get out of the house and a way of whiling away a pleasant interval from morning till evening. According to Mrs. Harvey, the author of *Turkish Harems and Circassian Homes*, when the bathing session was over in the bath, in the late afternoon, a club-like atmosphere would begin to form. The women reclining on mattresses would converse with each other, smoke a pipe, and drink coffee and eat fruit while their servants would dry their hair, comb it, and dress it with henna.[8] Women came not simply to bathe and amuse themselves, but they also came for selecting a wife for their son. In addition, the bath served as the setting for the festive bridal-bath party held several days before the marriage of a bride-to-be, and a bathing party also marked the fortieth day after childbirth and the end of the period of confinement. Ercüment Ekrem Talu reveals in his article on "Women's Baths in Old İstanbul" that certain baths acquired popularity because of such things as the quality of its' water and the cleanliness, manners, experience, and cheerfulness of the bath matron and the bath stewardesses and attendants. The bathing ritual, according to Talu, began on a predetermined day when

> [e]arly in the morning the servants would
> prepare the cloth bundles of the bathing
> accessories. Each one held a silk waist wrapper,
> a cotton bath wrapper from Bursa, a large
> towel, one towel each for the head, the face,
> and the feet, a loofah and a coarse scrubbing

Touching on the inconsistencies between the descriptions given by the two women, Billie Melman concludes in her study titled *Women's Orients: English Women and the Middle East, 1718-1918* that, although what Montagu described in her letters was a treasure trove for males unable to enter the harem, her sensuous descriptions of the Ottoman female had become a source of embarrassment by the Victorian Age. Montagu was criticized because of her general

4 Pardoe, *The City,* 1: 137.

5 Billie Melman, *Women's Orients: English Women and the Middle East, 1718–1918* (Ann Arbor: University of Michigan Press, 1998), 100.

6 Pardoe, *The City,* 1: 130.

7 Montagu, 59.

8 Mrs. Harvey, *Turkish Harems and Circassian Homes* (London: Hurst–Blackett, 1871), 78.

cloth, a printed scarf edged in needlework lace, henna for the hair, the palms, and the nails, kohl for the brows, a bar of hard, Cretan soap, a mirror, and a silver or German-silver bath dipper. In a separate bundle was placed pairs of bath clogs with inlaid mother-of-pearl and slippers of broadcloth. In yet another bundle would be tucked one clean outfit of under-clothes—all of which bundles were handed over to the male servant of the mansion, who was, without exception, an Armenian of Van, Erzurum, or Haçin and who would go in advance of the bathing party. The bath stewardess who recognized which male servant belonged to which household would at once issue instructions to prepare a dressing room on the upper floor to receive the ladies whose arrival was imminent and for whom a private compartment would be made ready.[9]

In his studio in Akaretler neighborhood, Zonaro executed a triptych on the subject of the bath. The first panel is called *Welcome!* Three women in street coats and veils are shown at the entrance to the bath. The lead female holds a small boy wearing a fez by the hand. A young, semi-nude girl, standing in clogs and a pair of slippers and wearing a wrapper around her waist, is inviting them to enter. The second panel *The Bath* presents the three women and the small child in the act of bathing, and the third panel called *Pleasure (Keyif)* depicts them seated on divans, relaxing after the bath. These paintings, sold in London in 1904, were later reproduced in a book titled *Déri Séadet ou Stamboul Porte du Bonheur*, whose text was written by Adolphe Thalasso.

One of the earliest paintings rendered on the subject of the bath by a Western artist is that executed in pastels by Jean-Etienne Liotard called *European Woman and Her Slave at the Bath*. This painting, depicts a young female servant standing before a marble bath basin (*kurna*). Both of the female subjects are in Ottoman dress, with fingers tinged with henna, and on their feet to insulate them from the heated floor are high clogs (*nalın*). The woman holds in her hand the stem of a long pipe and in the bath dipper held by her servant is a comb of ivory and a bowl for henna. It may be interesting to compare this painting by the Genevan artist with one done around the same time (1741–2) by an Ottoman artist, Abdullah Buhari. This latter,

[9] Ercüment Ekrem Talû, "Eski İstanbul'da Kadın Hamamları," *Resimli Tarih Mecmuası* (2 Şubat 1950): 66.

145 Jean-Etienne Liotard. *European Woman and Her Slave at the Bath*, 1742-3. Pastel on paper. 71 x 53 cm. Musée d'art et histoire. Geneva.

called *Bathing Female* delineates a nude female in the bath. Seated before a marble basin and pouring water with a bath dipper over her head and displaying henna-tinged fingers, toes, and heels, the woman is richly adorned with earrings, a ring, a bracelet, and an arm-bracelet; and her legs are covered by a light blue bath wrapper with a red border.

Without a doubt, the most famous painting of an Ottoman bath by a Western artist is *Turkish Bath* by Jean-Dominique Ingres. Ingres executed a painting of Turkish women in the bath for Prince Napoleon. However, the subject of the painting was regarded as offensive by the prince's wife, and it was returned to the artist. Ingres transformed the nearly square canvas of the rejected painting into a circle and sold it to Halil Şerif Pasha in 1868.[10] Halil Şerif Pasha, whose financial position was ruined by his luxurious style of life and weakness for gambling, was forced to sell it at auction along with other paintings of his collection. Théophile Gautier, who comments on this painting, as follows, wrote the foreword to the catalog for this auction, which caused a great sensation in Paris at the time:

> Ingres, the painter of odalisques … is
> represented by his painting of the Turkish Bath.
> This painting conforms admirably to its shape
> and is a magnificent pretext to render all types
> of women unveiled within a circular frame.
> The great artist has drawn these beautiful
> bodies in diverse postures to emphasize their
> attractiveness—from the rear, side, profile,
> foreshortened, standing, reclining, and bending
> to highlight their rich body lines and expose the
> nape of their necks defined by the fine turban,
> with their shoulders damp with perspiration;
> commingling the rosy pallor of the sultana's
> skin, softened by the silvery steam of
> the sweating room, with the underlying marble
> of the ancient goddess.[11]

[10] See in this regard Ruth Bernard Xeazell, *Harems of the Mind* (New Haven: Yale University Press, 2000), 28.

[11] Gautier, "La Collection."

Ingres' Orientalism may be classified as "armchair-Orientalism," for the artist had never been to the Orient but drew on the graphic works he had observed and the written texts he had read to formulate the odalisque theme, the foundation of his paintings with Orientalist subject matter. This was an ideal theme for the artist to convey the rhythmically flowing contours of nude female. One of his two main sources for the *Turkish Bath* was the

146 Jean-Dominique Ingres. *Turkish Bath*, 1862. Oil on canvas. Diameter 100 cm. Musée du Louvre, Paris.

147 Abdullah Buhari. *Bathing Female*, 1741-2. Watercolor and gilt on paper. 16.2 x 10.8 cm. Topkapı Palace Museum Library (no. y. y. 1043), İstanbul.

women's bath in Adrianople (Edirne) described by Lady Montagu in her letters. Ingres copied into his sketchbook this portion of Montagu's book in French translation: "[T]here were two hundred women.... The first sofas were covered with cushions and rich carpets, on which sat the ladies, and on the second their slaves behind them...[and] ...stark naked....Yet there was not the least wanton smile or immodest gesture amongst them."[12] The other source of inspiration for Ingres was an engraving in the book titled *Les quatres premiers livres des navigations et pérégrinations orientales* by Nicolas de Nicolay, who had come to İstanbul with the French ambassador, Gabriel d'Aramon, in 1551. Here, Nicolay had depicted a woman on her way to the bath with her black female servant. The text beneath the legend *"Turque Allant au Baing"*, informs the reader that the servant carried a copper vessel on her head in the shape of a small bucket, in which was contained clothing and a depilatory drug.[13] Ingres employed these two figures without alteration in the background, except that here the woman's head is bound with an orange cloth but the greater proportion of her body is shown unclothed.

As is evident in *The Turkish Bath*, Ingres, like other Orientalist artists, generally added to his composition the figure of a black servant for the purpose of contrast to heighten the beauty of the nudes in the bath. Edouard Debat Ponsan rendered in *Massage, Scene from a Turkish Bath*, a nude white woman being given a massage by a black servant. Lying on the heated marble slab, entirely relaxed, the woman with her well-tended body and the strong, worn-out body of the black woman who, through her activity forms a contrast that is reiterated by the horizontal and vertical elements and the light and dark colors. These kinds of female-centered paintings typically imply a master whose existence is never shown but always implied. Having been to İstanbul in 1882 to execute a large-scale panorama of the city, Debat-Ponsan here covers the walls of the bath with tile patterns he copied from those in Yeni Mosque.

[12] Montagu, 58–9.
[13] Rouillard, 277.

148 Nicolas de Nicolay. *Turque Allant au Baing*, 1567. *Les quatres premiers livres des navigations et pérégrinations orientales.*

149 Edouard Debat Ponsan. *The Massage, Scene from a Turkish Bath*, 1883. Oil on canvas. 127 x 210 cm. Musée des Augustins, Toulouse.

XVI The slave market

The male and female slaves of the Court and its circle and the wealthy families of Constantinople can be divided into two groups. One group was composed of the youths of both sexes selected from Caucasia, who were renowned for their beauty, and the other group was comprised of the black and Abyssinian slaves procured from Africa, who were mainly employed for physical and menial tasks. The slave trade from the early eighteenth century was conducted by auction in the central courtyard of the Slave Caravansary (*Esir Hanı*), which was located between Nuruosmaniye Mosque and the Grand Bazaar. In his description of eighteenth-century Istanbul, İnciciyan stated that this caravansary had numerous chambers and that, although in former times slaves of Georgia, Abkhasia, and other nations had been sold here, in his day, there were sold only male and female slaves from Africa.[1] This caravansary was dismantled in 1847. C. W. Vane, the Marquis of Londonderry, who saw this slave market in 1842, penned this description:

> At the door of a great court, near the mosque bazaar stands the head slave-master, by whom you are admitted. Around the court are cells, in which the negroes and negresses, as well as all white slaves, are deposited, and where they eat, drink, sleep and cook. Before each miserable abode is a square or oblong raised wooden platform; on which, in the day the slaves are ranged and seated.[2]

Slaves were also sold in the neighborhoods of Karabaş (Tophane district) and Avret Pazarı (Aksaray district), the district of Çemberlitaş, and in the vicinity of the mosque of Mehmed II (Fatih). The slave markets of İstanbul, as indicated in the history by Lutfî (*Tarih-i Lutfî*, VIII: 133), were abolished in 1846, but the sale of slaves continued in certain districts like Tophane and Fatih until 1908.

Nearly all the European travelers who touch on the subject of slavery in the Ottoman Empire indicate that they were very well treated and that the traditional Ottoman exploitation of male and female slavery was very different from that in the West. The Marquis of Londonderry states that foreign travelers are agreed that the form of slavery in the Ottoman Empire was at its most humane and that it bore no resemblance at all to the horrible reality created by greed and cruelty in Europe and the United States.[3] Baronne Durand de Fontmagne, cousin to the wife of Edouard Thouvenel, the French ambassador to İstanbul, states in her book titled *Un Séjour à l'ambassade de France à Constantinople sous le second empire.* that, although the slaves in the harem were purchased from slave dealers, the terms of servitude were very pleasant and that "slavery in this country meant a sort of adoption of young girls by taking them from their families at a tender age and that when they were adults they were married to the young men of the family or those of other harems."[4] Fontmagne, in regard to a visit she paid to the seaside mansion of Fuad Pasha, reports that the pasha had presented to her a very beautiful young woman and informed her that "[t]his woman is my daughter-in-law. She is Circassian. We purchased and raised her as a bride for our son. As you see, our conception of slavery is very different from yours."[5] Jean Henri Abdolonyme Ubucini also affirms that slaves were treated very well in the Ottoman realm and that the slave market, open also to Europeans, had been closed by the government in [1847]; further, he stated that, during the period in which he had been resident in İstanbul, the number of slaves had been considerably reduced and that both the change in living conditions and the regulations that the government had imposed had made the sale of slaves more difficult, so that their prices had risen considerably.[6]

Apart from the bath and theme of the harem where the female formed the centerpiece, the

1 P. G. İnciciyan, *XVIII.Asırda İstanbul* (İstanbul: Baha Yayınları, 1976), 35.

2 C.W.Vane, Marquess of Londonderry, *A Steam Voyage to Constantinople by the Rhine and the Danube in 1840–41* (London: Henry Colburn, 1842), 1: 296–7.

3 Vane, 298.

4 Fontmagne, 288.

5 Fontmagne, 299

6 Jean Henri Abdolonyme Ubicini, *1855'de Türkiye* (İstanbul: Tercüman, 1977), 2: 60.

150 Alexandre Bida. "Circassian Slave
Market," *L'Illustration* (11 Aout 1849).

XVI The slave market

third subject of interest on the part of Orientalist artists and Western observers was the slave market. Orientalist painters like Gérôme and William Allan depicted the slave markets in a manner differing from Western writers, who tended to treat the subject in terms of the social dimension. The portrayal in these paintings of the sale of the female slaves closely resembles those of the bath—both represented opportunities for the display of the nude female body. The beautiful slaves sold in slave markets, some of whom rose to high positions in the Court after entering the Imperial Harem, invariably, constituted a subject of fascination to Westerners. Chlebowski in his painting of 1879 titled *Slave Purchasing, Constantinople* has depicted such a scene. The setting is a covered market next to a shop. Here is a shop where such objects as carpets, horse trappings, a saddle, brass vessels, daggers, clay pipes with long stems, and guns, very likely of Caucasian manufacture, were sold. A sign above the shop reads, "What wonders God wills" (*Maşallah*). The slave dealer in Caucasian garb is raising the white veil covering the face of a young slave seated on a divan next to the shop to reveal to the man, whom all signs indicate is a prominent customer, a naked girl whose head is bowed in a shy manner. Behind the customer is a black servant who has accompanied him; and who holds in his hands what is likely to be the clothes in which the slave girl will be attired—a caftan with gold needlework and a pink parasol. According to Leyla Saz, the person who bought a slave had the right to look at the slave's face and to examine her chest, arms and her legs, but only up to her knees.[7] The foreign artist, however, ordinarily renders these slaves in a naked state and, consequently, conveys an imaginary scene to the Western world.

[7] Saz, 60.

151 Stanislaw Chlebowski. *Slave Purchasing, Constantinople*, 1879. Oil on canvas. 93 x 72 cm. Collection Berko, Knokke-le-Zoute.

XVII Dervishes

The theme of the prayer service in a mosque is rather rare in Orientalist art, because Christians were required to obtain special permission to enter or to work in Islamic places of worship. Furthermore, an imperial rescript had to be obtained merely to visit a mosque.[1] In consequence, Orientalist artists like the Austrian, Rudolf Ernst, executed paintings of mosque interiors by relying on photographs. It was not so difficult, however, to enter the Sufi lodges of as the Mevlevî and Rıfaî orders; renowned Orientalists, such as Jean-Léon Gérôme and Albert Aublet, for instance, produced works delineating the rituals performed in the lodges.

Nearly all Western travelers devote a chapter in their memoirs on Constantinople to Sufi dervishes. The lodges most frequently attended were the Rıfaî lodge in Üsküdar and the Mevlevî lodge in Galata. The Galata lodge (*Galata Mevlevihanesi*), the most important of the five Mevlevî lodges located in İstanbul, represented the first large establishment in the city of the Mevlevî order. Each of the İstanbul Mevlevî lodges was characterized by a complex of structures for "worship, education, the accommodation of guests and other social services."[2] Mevlevî lodges were built on sites remote from the city center, outside the city walls. The Mevlevî Lodge of Galata was founded in 1491 by İskender Pasha, a vizier under Bayezid II, on his own hillside plot overlooking Galata and became known as Kulekapısı, or Tower-gate Mevlevî Lodge because its location was beyond the city walls. Experiencing decline by the time of the reign of Abdülhamid I, the Galata Mevlevî Lodge regained its former importance under Selim III. Selim III, himself a Mevlevî, chose, asserts Ekrem Işın, to counter the opposition being voiced to his reforms in the military and administrative sphere by Bektaşi dervishes through a revival of the Mevlevî order. Thanks to his support, the Galata Mevlevî Lodge enjoyed a strong recovery, with the result that the influence of the order on the social

culture persisted without a break until it was closed in 1925.[3] The meetinghouse where the Mevlevî rituals were performed was a wooden structure whose exterior façade was plain; but whose interior (*Semahane*), which one Western observer described as "a combination of ballroom and theater", was on an octagonal plan.[4]

Foreign travelers to İstanbul were certain to observe the rituals of the Mevlevî dervishes—otherwise known as the "whirling" dervishes. Following attendance at their ritual, a great proportion of them would move on to a Rıfaî lodge to witness the rituals of the Rıfaî dervishes, whom they termed the "howling" dervishes. Miss Pardoe, who twice viewed the ritual in the Mevlevî lodge in Galata, made many unsuccessful attempts to attend the lodges of the Rıfaî dervishes, but she finally gave up, reportedly, because they very jealously protected their secrets.[5] The Rıfaî order was established by Seyyid Ahmed Rıfaî in Iraq in the twelfth century. The first restricted appearance of the order in İstanbul was in the late sixteenth century, the order became widely popular once the Rıfaî main lodge (*Asitane*) had been established by Sheikh Mehmed Hadidî in the Tavaşi Hasan Ağa neighborhood in Üsküdar in 1730. During the Rifaî ritual, the sheikh seated himself on a throne of sheepskin, with the dervishes, also seated, arranged on either side of him in a semi circular formation. After the sheikh had recited the Exordium of the *Koran* and a short prayer, the dervishes would rise to their feet and, standing in opposing rows, commence their invocation. As described by Baha Tanman, the dervishes, in the heat of their enthusiasm and having attained a state of rapture, would stab skewers called *topuz* into various parts of their bodies, cool a red hot piece of iron by licking it, and lie atop sharp swords. These demonstrations were deemed irrefutable proof, or *burhan*, that the dervish possessed the capacity to accomplish extraordinary acts.[6]

ill.

[1] *Lettres sur le Bosphore, au relation d'un voyage à Constantinople pendant les anneès 1816, 1817, 1818 et 1819* (Paris: Locard et Davi, 1822), 133.

[2] Ekrem Işın, *İstanbul'da Gündelik Hayat* (İstanbul: Yapı Kredi Yayınları, 1999), 301.

[3] Işın, 305.

[4] James Sullivan, *Diary of a Tour: In the Autumn of 1856 to Gibraltar, Malta, Smyrna, Dardanelles, Marmora, Constantinople* (London, 1857), 39.

[5] Pardoe, *The City*, 2: 60.

[6] M. Baha Tanman, "Rıfaî Âsitanesi," *Dünden Bügüne İstanbul Ansiklopedisi*, 1994 ed.

152 Amadeo Preziosi. *Mevlevî Dervishes.*
Stamboul Souvenir d'Orient.

XVII Dervishes

The Rıfaî rituals performed in the lodge in Üsküdar also served as artistic subject matter. Zonaro's painting titled *Rıfaî Dervishes* was exhibited in İstanbul and various cities in Europe and met with high acclaim. Adolphe Thalasso describes the scene depicted on the canvas as "the moment when the fanatical devotees had attained a state of sublime ecstasy and the trance-like expression on their faces was lighted by a paradisiacal joy."[7] Similarly, the artist in a watercolor study for this painting—the large oil painting alluded to by Thalasso—concentrated only on the facial expressions of the dervishes; several such studies of the dervishes are today scattered among various collections. Noteworthy among the native and foreign visitors who figure among the observers in *Rıfaî Dervishes* are Zonaro, his wife, Elisa Pante, and their daughter. What is interesting is that Zonaro placed himself apart from the visitors and depicted himself as a dervish. Gerard de Nerval, who visited this place when he came to İstanbul in the 1840s, states that the meeting place

[7] Thalasso, *L'Art*, 35.
[8] Nerval, *The Women*, 2: 243.
[9] Tanman, "Rıfaî."

was a very large wooden hall with galleries and, in contradiction to Miss Pardoe's statement, indicates that foreigners encountered no obstacles in gaining access here.[8] In the painting, "in front of the dervishes in the act of performing the invocation in the standing position in rows, accompanied by a reed flute player and a singer, the sheikh can be seen walking on the backs of those seeking cures, who are lying face down and aligned on the axis of the pulpit."[9]

It is possible to distinguish the sheikh with his black cloak (*Hırka*) and his headgear (*Rıfaî Tacı*). Hung on the wall of the meeting hall are framed inscriptions of religious expressions in Arabic, such as "*Eşhedü enlâ ilâhe illâllah ve eşhedü enne Muhammeden abduhü ve Resûlüh*", the *Besmele* and the names of the Prophet and his caliph Ali. In view of the fact that the central Rıfaî lodge in Üsküdar burned in 1942, Zonaro's painting possesses importance as documentary evidence. The artist's wife, Elisa Pante, made a large oil painting based on a photograph taken in the studio while Zonaro

was working on this painting, which is, at present, in Villa Contarini at Torino. The 12 April 1908 issue of the Armenian journal *Luys*, published in İstanbul, contains an article on Zonaro by the artist, Rafayel Şişmanyan, who states that he viewed this painting in the artist's studio in Akaretler prior to its being completed.[10]

[10] Rafayel Şişmanyan, *Luys* (12 Nisan 1908):516–26, cited in Pamukciyan, "Fausto Zonaro," 26.

153 Fausto Zonaro. *Rifaî Dervishes*, 1910. 100 x 201.3 cm. Oil on canvas. Christie's, London.

154 Fausto Zonaro. *Rifaî Dervishes*. 32.5 x 48.5 cm. Watercolor on paper. Collection of Sevgi and Doğan Gönül, İstanbul.

153

154

XVIII Vistas of Constantinople

Written and graphic depictions of Constantinople in the nineteenth century "were constructed with certain constant elements, not unlike 'variations on a theme'."[1] Their primary elements were the silhouette of the Historical Peninsula, the port, the shores of the Bosphorus and its villages, the monumental mosques and archeological remains in the city proper, the marketplaces where was manifested the lively and colorful life of the city, the fountains, the mosque courtyards, the coffeehouses, and the excursion spots. Views of the city were the predominant subject selected by foreign artists and each of them possesses high importance, both as a work of art and as a historical record. For the period prior to the emergence of the photograph and the oil painting by Ottoman artists, our knowledge concerning the city is necessarily based on these pictures and engravings. The now vanished geographical and social topography has survived to the present through the works of these artists who pictured its monuments, figural types, and ceremonials within the scenes of daily life At the same time, besides the landscapes of Constantinople by artists who had never visited the city, which were executed simply by looking at photographs and engravings and which were specially aimed at the creation of an Oriental atmosphere, there were artists like Fabius Brest who, although they had been to the city, did not hesitate to construct, at times, a veritable collage by assembling in a single painting a medley of the picturesque corners of the city they had found pleasing.

ill. 155

It is notable that the European artists who discovered the picturesque in the nineteenth century in the harmony between Islamic architecture and natural beauties, delineated İstanbul from certain angles. Selected for their panoramas of the city, in particular, were the hills of İstanbul overlooking the port and the Bosphorus. The most preferred viewpoint, on the Asian shore, were Mount Çamlıca, the hills of Üsküdar and Bulgurlu

[1] Edhem Eldem, "Ottoman Period Istanbul," *İstanbul: World City*, exhibition catalog (İstanbul: History Fundation of Turkey, 1996), 133.

[2] Zeynep Çelik, *The Remaking of Istanbul: Portrait of an Ottoman City in the Nineteenth Century* (Seattle: University of Washington Press, 1986), 3-4.

Peak and, on the European shore, the hillsides of Pera. The palaces and seaside mansions of this century, which were situated along the shores of the Bosphorus, endowed the city with an even more picturesque appearance and stimulated Eastern exoticism. The majority of the landscapes lay out before the eyes of the viewer the panorama obtained on entering the city by sea and the port of İstanbul.

In the early nineteenth century, Constantinople projected the appearance of an Ottoman Islamic city. The main settlements consisted in the city proper and the suburbs of Galata and Üsküdar. As indicated by Zeynep Çelik in her study on the Ottoman capital city in the nineteenth century, the city's commercial center lay in the area between Divanyolu and the port and in the marketplaces that were located in between. Members of different ethnic groups and faiths worked side by side in this commercial district, but they resided in neighborhoods grouped on the basis of religious adherence. Muslims, who constituted the largest group, were concentrated in the center of the Historical Peninsula while Armenians, Greeks, and Jews tended to dwell along the shores. The principal square in the city center was the Hippodrome (*At Meydanı*) and, apart from this, the main areas where everyone could freely congregate were the courtyards of the monumental mosques and their complexes. Thus, these areas served both sacred and mundane functions. With their impressive dimensions and regular plans, these monuments formed a strong contrast to the irregular and dense street network.[2]

These characteristics can be observed in the canvas executed in 1844 called *Panorama of Constantinople from Süleymaniye Mosque* by the Austrian artist and traveler, Hubert Sattler. Executed in an extremely detailed manner, the Büyük Valide Caravansary, one of the largest of the commercial buildings, on the left-hand side is the most conspicuous, with secondary importance

ill.

155 Fabius Brest. *View of Constantinople*, 1873. Oil on canvas. 54 x 84 cm. Collection of Koç Holding, Istanbul.

156 Hubert Sattler. *Panorama of Constantinople from Süleymaniye Mosque*, 1844 Oil on canvas. 84.4 x 132 cm. The Fine Arts Society, London.

accorded to the Yeni Mosque and the Spice Bazaar attract attention. On the right-hand side, the Nuruosmaniye Mosque, the earliest example of Ottoman baroque, occupies the peak of the second hill. The Grand Bazaar serves as a bridge between the first and second hills, with the mosques of Sultan Ahmed and St. Sophia visible beyond. The contrast between the monumental masses of the mosques, their domes, and vertical minarets and the dense but horizontal accent of the domiciles surrounding them constituted for the foreign artists one of the most interesting features of the city. Hubert Sattler traveled through Greece, Syria, Asia Minor, Egypt and Sinai Peninsula in 1842 and, at the end of his travels, he mounted a traveling exhibition—a "cosmorama"—by means of which he generated revenue through an admission charge as well as popular interest in European cities.

Three main developments of the nineteenth century significantly altered the appearance of the city. The first of these was Westernization, which introduced new aesthetic forms. The second was the transformation of İstanbul into a very important commercial and finance center despite its having become, politically, "The Sick Man of Europe"; and, as a concomitant, a very cosmopolitan life style came into being in the city. The third change was that demographic increase no longer increased the density of the settlement center but rather encouraged urban sprawl.

At the outset, the Westernization movement was focused on the areas of technology, science, and education and was aimed at developing the military power of the state. Acquiring a new dimension with the proclamation of the Imperial Reforms rescript, "[t]he structure of the Western thought was imported and this situation resulted in more radical changes."[3] Westernization also affected the physical appearance of the city; certain districts of İstanbul assumed a more European and cosmopolitan appearance. These changes can be detected in the works by Western artists who came to the city in the nineteenth century. In fact, the first modification in the settlement pattern of İstanbul began in the Tulip Period in the early eighteenth century

Though prior to the Tulip Period, the construction of very large and medium-sized mosque complexes represented the norm, structural activity concentrated on works of

secular architecture in the Tulip Period—palaces, public or private gardens and public fountains….A society that had been customarily inward looking, thus, became acquainted for the first time with a life way that was outward looking.[4]

The view from Galata and Pera

Regardless of these changes, the duality of the domed mosques and the horizontal development of the residential areas retained its validity. However, certain important developments gradually modified this silhouette. The city began to spread beyond the city walls and the importance of the shores of the Bosphorus and the Golden Horn and Üsküdar began to increase; and the Western-influenced styles, materials and monumental dimensions of the military barracks and schools erected at the end of the century endowed the city with a new visage. By late century, almost half of the population of İstanbul dwelled outside the city walls and on the shores of the Bosphorus and the Golden Horn and in Üsküdar. Old İstanbul remained within the ancient walls of Theodosius and maintained its traditional Islamic character. By contrast, the commercial center of Galata acquired a Western character and spread in the direction of Pera. This ancient Genoese neighborhood, enclosed by walls since the fifteenth century, was a district where non-Muslims and Europeans lived and with its caravansaries, storage buildings, and trading establishments composed one of the city's most important commercial centers. Galata, whose history, way of life, and demographic composition closely resembled those of Europe played a key role in the Westernization of the city and in contrast to the Historical Peninsula, which preserved its traditional Islamic character; it rapidly adopted a Western appearance. As one American visitor to the city wrote in 1895, "In Galata, the East seems transformed as if by a magician's wand….Galata/Pera is sneered at as the Giaour City... And so it is: a Western city stranded in the East."[5]

Occupying the highest point in the district of Galata, Galata Tower was a subject chosen by numerous artists. One of these was the Swedish ambassador to Constantinople, Carl Gustaf Löwenhielm (1790–1858). Löwenhielm, who had entered the army in 1808 as a military attaché,

[3] Çelik, 32.
[4] Doğan Kuban, *Istanbul: Bir Kent Tarihi* (Istanbul: Tarih Vakfı Yurt Yayınları, 2000), 309.
[5] Edwin Augustus Grosvenor, Constantinople (Boston, 1900), 2: 93, cited in Andrew Wheatcroft, *The Ottomans: Dissolving Images* (London: Penguin, 1995), 149.

157 Carl Gustaf Löwenhielm. *Galata Tower*, 1824. Watercolor on paper. 35 x 24 cm. Swedish Palace, İstanbul.

XVIII Vistas of Constantinople

158 Carl-Gustaf Löwenhielm. *Landscape from the Top Story of the Swedish Palace in Pera*, 1824. Watercolor on paper. 24 x 35 cm. Swedish Palace, İstanbul.

started to gain in importance in the seventeenth century on the construction here of foreign embassies, and it eventually became a locale populated by Europeans and non-Muslim Ottoman subjects. The move to this area by wealthy Ottomans who had lived on the Historical Peninsula prior to the nineteenth century represents an important indicator in the development of the city. The large mansions, the covered shopping arcades, the patisseries, large stores and the theaters lining the Grand Rue de Pera, the main artery of Pera in this century, were identical to those in any European city. In Léon Verhaeghe's book titled *Voyage en Orient* on İstanbul in the 1860s when he was resident there states:

> As soon as you reached the Grand Rue de Pera, European influence dominated the scene, and you might imagine that you were in any other place than Turkey. I have never encountered in any other place such a profound distinction between neighborhoods that you might believe they were different cities. Europeans feel at home in Pera: there they settle, live and enjoy themselves just as they please.[6]

Thus, two distinct cities had emerged in İstanbul, one Turkish-Islamic and the other European, and the urban growth was in favor of the latter. Naturally, Orientalist artists who came to the city in search of exoticism almost never pictured Galata and Pera, which scarcely differed from their own country, but they frequently took advantage of the gardens and terraces of the embassy buildings here and Galata Tower in order to obtain very beautiful panoramas of İstanbul. The view of Seraglio Point executed by Löwenhielm, looking from the top floor of the Swedish Palace, is a fine example of this. The painting identified as *View of Constantinople* by the Austrian artist, Luise Begas Parmentier (1840-83), delineates Tophane, Kılıç Ali Pasha Mosque, and the dome of a now ruined bath, the sailing and steam vessels in the port, Seraglio Point, and the shores of Üsküdar in the late nineteenth century and, in the foreground, the shelter fabric of both wooden and masonry construction interspersed by trees. Louis Bunuel, who came to İstanbul during the Crimean War, noted the colorful appearance of the painted wooden houses in this area, made more charming by the shade of cypress and pine trees.[7]

[6] Léon Verhaeghe, *Voyage en Orient 1862–1863* (Paris: Librairie Internationale, 1865), 39.

[7] Louis Bunuel, Jerusalem, la côte de Syrie et Constantinople en 1853 (Paris, 1853), 366, cited in Çelik Gülersoy, "Son 400 Yılda Tophane Semti," in *VIII. Türk Tarih Kongresi Kongre Bildirileri* (Ankara: Türk Tarıh Kurumu Yayınları, 1983), 3: 1638.

ill. 157

was dispatched to St. Petersburg where he participated in battle as aide-de-camp to the czar, and, in 1824, he was appointed to İstanbul as minister resident of the king. Having had art lessons as part of his military training, Löwenhielm made numerous drawings and water color sketches of the city and its pattern of life during the three years he resided in the city. In one of these, Galata Tower is shown within the ancient Galata walls and surrounded by the neighborhood that developed around it. This version of the tower belongs to that from the reign of Selim III after the fire of 1794. When the tower was renovated, a timber bay-windowed belvedere (*cihannüma*) was added and the lead-covered conical roof was redone. One other aspect worth noting is that the people of this area, who were non-Muslim Ottoman subjects and Levantines, are wearing Oriental costume. The residents here only began to appear in Western-type dress in the second half of the nineteenth century.

Pera on the hills above Galata, which at one time were covered with vineyards and gardens,

The development of a shoreline city

The first important change that Westernization brought to the urban dimensions of Constantinople was the discontinuity in the horizontal growth of the city and the onset of the erection of structures other than mosques in possession of very different but equally monumental appearance. These were barracks and palaces, built by the military and the sultan and his circle, and the majority of which were constructed in Western architectural styles. The departure in the eighteenth century of the Court and its circle from the traditional center was a signal event that served both to demonstrate the westernizing trend and to determine the development of the city. Palaces, seaside mansions, and mosques began to be erected along the shores of the Golden Horn and the Bosphorus and "a shoreline city concentrated along the edge of the sea replaced the ancient configuration of İstanbul, which had been bounded by the city walls."[8] The settlements on the shores and hills of the Bosphorus were gradually enlarged by the

[8] Kuban, *İstanbul: Bir*, 313.

159 Luise Begas-Parmentier. *View of Constantinople*. Oil on canvas. 60 × 90 cm. Private Collection, İstanbul.

159
▼

palaces, seaside mansions, and villas built one after another as can be seen in the painting by Aivazovsky titled *Eyüp in the Moonlight* .In the ancient suburb of Eyüp on the Golden Horn, the elegant wooden palaces were being replaced by manufacturing factories. One possible reason why Aivazovsky depicted the Golden Horn in the moonlight was to preserve its picturesqueness by disguising the factory chimneys.

The new construction that would change the traditional silhouette of İstanbul began with Mahmud II's repair of Beşiktaş Palace and his removal here. The sultan, who spent the greater proportion of his time in this palace, abandoned Topkapı Palace, and, having made the decision to build a palace in which he could reside permanently, he personally occupied himself with its construction. In *The Beauties of the Bosphorus* by Miss Julia Pardoe relates an anecdote connected with the building of the palace. While Mahmud II was still undecided as to whom he should

[9] Julia Pardoe, *The Beauties of the Bosphorus* (London: George Virtue, 1838), 18–9.

160 Thomas Allom. *Sultan's New Palace on the Bosphorus. Constantinople and the Scenery of the Seven Churches of Asia Minor* (1838).

161 Ivan Aivazovsky. *Eyüp in the Moonlight.* Oil on canvas. 92.5 x 71 cm. Dolmabahçe Palace Museum, İstanbul.

appoint as the builder of the palace, one intimate recommended a certain Armenian architect. When the sultan met with the architect on the site where the palace was to rise—pointing to Topkapı Palace—he asked him what he thought of it. When the architect replied that he had never had the opportunity of visiting it, the sultan commanded that the architect be shown through the palace. When they met again and the architect told the sultan that he had toured many palaces in the West, but that he had never seen any as beautiful as Topkapı, the sultan replied, "In that case, the European are liars when they claim that these depictions represent the palaces of their own sultans and who send me such stuff," upon which he took out a roll of papers and showed the architect various views of royal palaces in Europe. He asked the architect "whether or not he had seen any of these palaces and whether or not they truly bore no resemblance to these drawings," to which the architect responded, "They do resemble them, Your Excellency, I have seen most of them." Then the sultan exhorted,

> You are unsuited to the undertaking [the project] which I contemplate; for none, save a rogue or a fool, could class that place fitted only for deeds of blood and mystery [again pointing to Topkapı] that place hidden beneath high walls, and amid dark trees, as though it could not brave the light of the day; with these light, laughing palaces open to the free air, and pure sunshine of heaven. Such would I have my own, and such it shall be.[9]

These words by Sultan Mahmud II serve to indicate to us the high level of receptiveness he bore toward Westernization and to Western architecture and how determined he was to leave Topkapı Palace.

However, the final abandonment of Topkapı Palace occurred in 1856 on the completion of Dolmabahçe Palace and the transfer of the seat of the empire by Abdülmecid, the son of Mahmud II. Abdülmecid tore down the Old Beşiktaş Palace and, in its place, had Dolmabahçe Palace erected, which was followed by the building of Beylerbeyi in 1865 and that of the present Çırağan Palace in 1872. This development on the Bosphorus influenced the mosques as well as the palaces. Mosques that had dominated the silhouette of this Historical Peninsula for centuries were, in the

XVIII Vistas of Constantinople

162-163-164 Martinus Rørbye. *Petition Writer in front of Kılıç Ali Paşa Mosque in Tophane*, 1837. Oil on canvas. 95 x 130 cm. Christie's, London.

nineteenth century, built on the shores of the Bosphorus. One of these mosques was the Nusretiye built for Mahmud II in the baroque-Empire style by Kirkor Balyan in 1826. The district of Tophane in which the mosque was built may be regarded as the entrance to the Bosphorus. Here, from the nineteenth century, besides Nusretiye, were situated the Tophane Clock Tower and the Tophane Pavilion; and, from the eighteenth century, Tophane Fountain, the Gunners Barracks (no longer extant), and the Kılıç Ali Pasha Mosque complex of the sixteenth century. Naturally, this impressive whole formed the subject matter for numbers of foreign artists. Von Moltke in a letter of 4 January 1836 mentions in reference to Kılıç Ali Pasha Mosque the petition writers in the courtyard…

> There are shops in this courtyard that sell
> elegant things. Beneath one of the vaults sits
> a Turkish petition writer, a sheaf of thick paper
> on his knee and a reed pen in his hand.
> In voluminous coats and yellow slippers,
> the women wrapped so that only their eyes are
> showing are explaining to him what with
> vigorous gestures of the hands and the Turk,
> without the slightest alteration in his visage,
> writes the secrets of the harem, a bill of
> complaint, a petition to the sultan, or a death
> announcement and he folds the paper in a
> masterful manner, wraps it in a piece of muslin
> on which he presses a seal with red wax and
> whether it is a letter of joy or news of a death
> he receives twenty *para*, one fortieth of a
> piaster, in exchange.[10]

Finding the petition writers in the courtyard of Kılıç Ali Pasha Mosque interesting when he came to İstanbul in 1834, the Danish artist, Martinus Rørbye (1805–48) painted a picture of them. In front of a Persian medallion rug draped over the iron balustrade of the courtyard, an aged petition writer with white muslin twisted around his red headgear, bearded, and wearing glasses is seated and is writing something on the paper in his hand. To his left is a man holding a money purse in his hand and wearing a red fez and a dark red robe with hood and opposite him is a woman who has taken off her yellow shoes, with her legs drawn up close to her body. In her hand, the woman has a wick to warm the seal. Behind her, a black servant in a green street coat is waiting.

162

164

[10] Helmuth von Moltke, *Moltke'nin Türkiye Mektupları* (İstanbul: Remzi, 1969), 31.

[11] Robert Walsh, *Constantinople and the Scenery of the Seven Churches of Asia Minor/Drawing from nature by Thomas Allom*, 1:21.

[12] Müller-Wiener, *Bizans'tan*, 176–7.

Attached to the rug on the wall is a written announcement bearing the imperial monogram of Sultan Mahmud II.

ill. 163

Its historical monuments were not the only reason this district attracted the notice of foreign artists and travelers. The Tophane landing stage and the open area behind it was the place where foreigners who arrived in the city by ship generally disembarked. In the text of *Constantinople and the Scenery of the Seven Churches of Asia Minor*, Robert Walsh observed, "what has rendered Tophane so distinguished is, that it is the great point of embarkation, either for the Bosphorus or the Sea of Marmara. In a country where there are no carriages, nor properly speaking, roads to run them upon, water is the great medium of conveyance. This then is the resort of a continual moving mass, of all nations and costumes."[11] Müller-Wiener states that between the landing stage and Tophane, which was enclosed by high walls, stood old plane trees until the early years of the nineteenth century and that around Tophane Fountain was a row of coffeehouses where would gather captains, merchants, travelers, and sailors; here, transport agreements were drawn up, travelers found ships to take them to their destinations, caiques were hired for tours of the Bosphorus and horses waited beside the fountain for those who found the road up to Pera too steep and difficult.[12] The fountain was erected by Mahmud I in 1732. On each of its four façade there is a spigot and a basin within an arch flanked by tall niches and the whole surface is richly ornamented with foliate decoration, potted fruit trees and a double band of poetry which, at one time, had been painted and gilded. Around the fountain, the most lively and crowded weekly market of Pera was set up, selling watermelons, melons, pumpkins, cauliflower, artichokes, fruits and vegetables and all kinds of fish and dried fruits and nuts.

Etienne Raffort (1802–95), a French artist who was both a painter and a master of zincography and lithography, placed Nusretiye in the background of his painting called *Tophane Fountain* while in the left foreground stands the Tophane Headquarters of the Field Marshal; this building in the neoclassical style burned in 1864 and another was built in its place. The ornamentation in relief on the Tophane Fountain is finely detailed and naturalistic. Covered in the reign of Mahmud II, the roof of the fountain is a flat one with a para-

ill. 166

pet. The small shops in which a wide variety of goods were sold, the women in street coats in different colors and with children, a fruit seller weighing fruit whose large baskets are lined up on the ground, a man observing this market scene sits cross-legged and smokes a water pipe, an old timer who is driving his donkey loaded with goods, an Armenian in a black robe and black turban, a porter carrying a large basket on his back, a cluster in conversation sitting beneath a tree, the people waiting to fill their water jugs at the fountain, a black seated on a flat-woven covering on which two barrels are standing in front of him, the portable display stands set up beneath awnings in the shape of an umbrella behind the fountain, soldiers, street dogs playing with each other, and the historical landmarks standing at the margins of this open area—all these details demonstrate the degree to which this square affected foreigners coming to İstanbul.

Pierre Guès, born in the Ottoman Empire, was appointed as art instructor in the War College and the War Academy in 1846, and who served here for forty years, looked at the same view from a slightly different angle and from a greater distance.[13] Guès very likely possessed a special relationship with this square because his father had been invited to İstanbul during the reign of Mahmud II and appointed to the Tophane Cannon Foundry and the Shipyard. In his *Tophane Fountain*, shops no longer exist between the fountain and Nusretiye Mosque and the area between the fountain and the mosque has been turned into a drill field, of which only the fence is visible. On the left-hand side, in front of the Office of the Field Marshal building are two red and white striped sentry boxes. As Mustafa Cezar indicated in an article on the Tophane district, when the police organization was established in 1846, it was under the direction of the Tophane Office of Field Marshal.[14] This allows us to suggest that this picture must have been executed during the time that this building also served as the headquarters for the police organization. In the square, a number of soldiers can be spotted who have issued from the Tophane barracks wearing long frock coats and red fezzes. Most of them are engaged in conversation by the fountain and before the stands with green awnings set up in front of the building, which stands to the rear of the fountain.

In contrast to the stamp of reality borne by the

[13] Cezar, *Sanatta*, 390.

[14] Mustafa Cezar, "400 Yılın Önemli Eserlerinin Diz Dize Olduğu Semt: Tophane," *Mozaik* (Eylül 1996): 32.

165-166-168 Etienne Raffort. *Tophane Fountain*, 1849. Oil on canvas. 92 x 134 cm. Collection of Emine Renda, İstanbul.

167 Pierre Guès. *Tophane Fountain*. Oil on canvas. 39.5 x 57 cm. Topkapı Palace Museum, İstanbul.

paintings of Raffort and Guès, the painting titled
ill. 170 *View of Constantinople* by Jacob Jacobs presents a
fanciful version of the landing stage of Tophane
and its environs. The sea is filled with light rowboats, heavy market rowboats, and sailboats, and
the concentration of sea traffic in the port area in
front of Yeni Mosque attracts particular notice.
Here, the Tophane Fountain has been moved to a
position quite close to the shore, a double staircase has been added in front of its facade, Nusretiye Mosque has been shifted from the left-hand
side of the fountain to the right, and Süleymaniye
Mosque stands higher than in actuality while
Galata Tower and Yeni Mosque have been pulled
closer together. A red carpet has been spread out
on the landing stage, and the sultan, newly alighted from his caique with marquee and wearing a
caftan lined with fur and a turban with a aigrette
set with jewels, is advancing through a crowd of
men and women who are greeting him by pros-
trating themselves on the ground and standing at
the very front is an *évzoni* soldier. On the staircase
in front of the fountain, women are lined up with
a black eunuch of the imperial harem among them
and a camel drover in a striped caftan whose
camel is tied by an iron ring to stair railing is
observing the sultan with interest.

[15] This work by Raffort *Le Port de Constantinople* is con-
tained in Joubert, *Tableau Historique, Politique et Pittoresque de la Turquie et de la Russia* (Paris, 1854).

[16] Hagop Mintzuri, *İstanbul Anıları: 1897–1940* (Istanbul: Tarih Vakfı Yurt Yayınları, 1993), 28.

of the square of Eminönü, a commercial site that
extends from the shore inwards, were found a
variety of landing stages and large public weighing machines for wholesale commodities. Prior to
the building of the bridge, passenger transit rowboats passing from Eminönü to Karaköy on the
other side of the Golden Horn secured connections between the two shores. Afloat on the sea is
a lively display of numerous sailboats, launches,
barge lighters, rafts, fishing boats, light rowboats,
and heavy market rowboats.

The British landscape artist, Tristam J. Ellis
(1844–1922), who drew on the Golden Horn and
İstanbul as the subjects for his paintings, treats a
scene of daily life on the sea in his painting titled
Constantinople. In the painting, a market boat   ill.
loaded with large baskets of grapes at the back is
heading directly for Tophane from the Asian
shore of the Bosphorus. The market caiques,
which the public used for mass transportation
vessels and for the carrying of all kinds of cargo,
disappeared when transportation lines shifted to
the land. Hagop Mintzuri describes in his memoirs
the oars of these market boats, which were so
long and heavy, he reports, that with each and
every stroke the rower had rise to his feet to pull
on them.[16] This is confirmed by Tristam J. Ellis'
powers of observation, for in his painting of such

The Port

For their depictions of İstanbul as an exotic port
city, the artists chose as a vantage point the
heights above Galata, Pera, and Beşiktaş or, to
view the inner port, Kasımpaşa or the hillsof
Eyüp. Some preferred a panoramic composition,
and some focused on lively, picturesque areas of
the city, such as the entrance to the Golden Horn,
the port area, the Tophane landing stage, and the
shores of the Bosphorus. These close-up takes
also exhibit a documentary quality concerning the
social and work life of the city's inhabitants.

From the perspective of Western artists, the port
represented the most unusual section of İstanbul,
and the combination of the view of the city from
the sea and the picturesque richness produced a
subject widely exploited. Paintings of the port
may be grouped into panoramic vistas and scenes
of life activities. In his painting of the port of
Constantinople shown at the 1849 Paris Salon,
ill. 169 Etienne Raffort depicted Yeni Mosque and
Eminönü, one of the chief landing stages in the
nineteenth century.[15] Lining the seaside boundary

▲
169

169 Etienne Raffort. "Port of Constantinople," *L'Illustration* (14 Juillet 1849).

170 Jacob Jacobs. *View of Constantinople.* 1842. Oil on canvas. 170 x 250 cm. Koç Holding Collection, İstanbul.

171 Tristam J. Ellis. *Constantinople*, 1895. Watercolor on paper. 55 x 100 cm. Private Collection, İstanbul.

XVIII Vistas of Constantinople

172 François Prieur-Bardin.
Constantinople. Oil on canvas.
100 x 152 cm. Private Collection, İstanbul.

173 Adolf Kaufmann. *The Golden Horn.*
Oil on canvas. 76.5 x 113.5 cm.
Dolmabahçe Palace Museum, İstanbul.

[17] Tinayre, 18–9.

a vessel carrying two veiled women and one man in the prow, the four rowers are standing and pulling on the oars with all their might. Coming from behind, a light rowboat is shown passing the market boat. Both private and public mass transportation vessels are depicted side by side. As always, the port is filled with sailing vessels of all types. A foggy and faint silhouette of İstanbul in the distance supplies the setting for the action.

The grayish blue silhouette of the Historical Peninsula, comprising the Serasker Tower and the domes and the minarets of the mosques of St. Sophia, Yeni, Süleymaniye and the other mosques, with sailing or steam ships and rowboats in the foreground, was employed as the background for many landscapes of İstanbul, and this view came to symbolize the city itself. Marcelle Tinayre in his collected memoirs of the Ottoman Empire describes the characteristic silhouette of İstanbul in an artistic manner, thus

> Against the pale sky, the city rises just like
> a theater set. Seemingly two-dimensional, its
> silhouette breaking, curving, ascending in
> slender minarets and swelling in vast domes,
> is cut out by a pair of unseen scissors.
> The starting point of this silhouette is the dark
> cypresses of Eyüp, it continues on to the
> furthest point of the Old Palace on the right,
> with its crenellated medieval towers, and
> terminates between the waters of the Golden
> Horn and Marmara on the left. There is no
> vibrant color: whites, browns, a faint reddish
> color, a few pinches of green. In the humid air,
> the ships' smoke tangled, like a ragged
> transparent gray cloth, is still and without
> movement. And İstanbul in the distance, nearly
> unreal, swimming suspended in the vapor.[17]

In the early twentieth century, as artistic subject matter, İstanbul contained a wealth of new opportunities for narrative by virtue of its being an Oriental city with its settings full of light and color, and, especially, its intimate relation to water. In the paintings of the port of İstanbul by Zonaro and Prieur-Bardin, the silhouettes of the mosque of St. Sophia, the Office of Public Debts (*Düyun-u Umumiye*) building, and Yeni Mosque composing the background reveal that Orientalist artists benefited from the experience of the Impressionists in observing light and color and that, from time to time, created a specific atmos-

172 ➤

173 ➤

phere similar to theirs. In Ziem's study on the İstanbul harbor, which focuses on the relation between color and light rather than on line and form, it may be said that the rough sketch has acquired an appearance of a finished work.

In his painting with the rendering of a foggy İstanbul silhouette in the background, the Austrian artist, Adolf Kaufmann (1848–1916) ill. 173 wished to display the different types of boat collected at the mouth of the Golden Horn—sailing ships, steam ships, fishing boats, and both heavy and light rowboats—as a demonstration of the lively life on the water in the port. Unlike ordinary landscapes of İstanbul, however, this work delineates not an Oriental city, but rather the atmosphere of a cold, Northern European city. This oil painting from the Dolmabahçe Palace Museum Collection, registered under the name *The Golden Horn*, may be the same as the painting called *Entrance to the Port of Constantinople*, which was executed for Abdülhamid II. The presence of this work in the Palace collection strengthens this possibility.

Prieur-Bardin has also depicted the lively atmosphere of the port, but this time from the Bosphorus. On this canvas can be seen a passenger ship of the ill. 176 Messageries Maritimes company and in the background, near the Tophane landing stage, the patrol boat of the French embassy, La Mouette.

174 Felix Ziem. *Landscape, Constantinople*. Oil on canvas. Private Collection, İstanbul.

175 Fausto Zonaro. *Landscape, Constantinple*. 48.5 x 97 cm. Oil on canvas. Dolmabahçe Palace Museum, İstanbul.

176 François Prieur-Bardin. *Tophane and the Bosphorus*, 1899. 90 x 150 cm. Oil on canvas. Private Collection, İstanbul.

Bridges over the Golden Horn

Mahmud II's preference for the Beşiktaş Palace to the Topkapı Palace exerted an impact on the development of the city, with the result that the shores of the Bosphorus increasingly gained in prestige; at the same time, the weekly procession by the sultan to the Old City for the Friday worship service by sea led to the building of a bridge over the Golden Horn, thereby adding to his convenience and number of choices about means of transportation. In 1836, what later became known as the Old Bridge (*Cisr-i Atik*) was built between Azapkapı and Unkapanı. In his report of 5 September 1836, Moltke stated

> The latest event in İstanbul is the construction of a bridge in the port by Captain Ahmed, the field marshal in command of the guards [Hassa Müşiri]. This is the first bridge since that violent winter provided a means of transit between Galata and İstanbul in the time of Emperor Theodosius. It is 637 paces long and 25 paces wide and a forest of the best timber was pounded into the bottom to found it. Now, the sultan can go from his palace in Beşiktaş by carriage directly to the entrance to the bridge....[T]he other day Sultan Mahmud II became the first to go by carriage from Galata to Bayezid Mosque. The bridge was opened by a religious ceremonial in which the sultan, by touching his hand to the knife that would slaughter thirteen rams at the bridge entrance, executed a ritual of sacrifice.... [F]or the people of [Old] İstanbul and Beyoğlu (if we discount the boatmen) this bridge is a perfect gift.[18]

This bridge of wooden structure, intended to connect the two sides of the Golden Horn, was built in the Imperial Maritime Shipyard and is supported by the poles pounded into the bottom and wooden pontoons. For the passage of small boats, there were, at both ends, broad arched gaps. Because no transit fee was charged for passage over the bridge, it became popularly known as "The Good Deed"(*Hayratiye*). In the foreground of one *View of Constantinople* by an unknown hand and now in a private collection, the Azapkapı Gate at the imperial shipyard and Azapkapı Mosque erected by Chief Imperial Architect Sinan for Sokollu Mehmed Pasha are finely detailed. To the rear of this is shown the

dense architectural fabric around the Old Bridge, **ill. 179** Süleymaniye Mosque, and the perimeter of the **ill. 180** mosque and Valens Aqueduct. The austerity of the architectural fabric in the background is enlivened by the sailboats and caiques on the sea, the men gathering the nets on the wooden landing stage and transformed into a scene of daily life. Except for a few details, this oil painting is nearly identical to the engraving captioned *Constantinople from Kasımpaşa*[19] by Thomas **ill. 182**

178
▼

[18] Moltke 65.

[19] Doğan Kuban in connection with this engraving by Allom states that this is the only record showing how the Sokollu Mehmed Pasha Mosque (Azapkapi) and the Imperial Shipyard wall are joined and that despite the quite accurate drawing of the mosque the minaret is not rendered correctly.. Doğan Kuban, *İstanbul Yazıları* (Istanbul: Yapı Endüstri Merkezi, 1998), 51.

177-178-179-180 Artist unknown. *View of Constantinople.* Oil on canvas. 50.5 x 76 cm. Collection of Yüksel Pekiş Behlil, İstanbul.

XVIII Vistas of Constantinople

Allom, who was in İstanbul during the reign of Mahmud II, and illustrated the book by Robert Walsh *Constantinople and the Scenery of the Seven Churches of Asia Minor/drawing from nature by Thomas Allom.*

After 1838, Galata gradually gained in importance and, after the removal of the sultans to Dolmabahçe, inner city communication became concentrated on the axis of Eminönü-Karaköy. The horse drawn carriages imported from Europe in this period became common and thus emerged the need for a second bridge to provide for the new conveyances between the two shores."[20] This second wooden bridge, which was called the New Bridge (or, Galata Bridge), was supported by pontoons attached to the landing stages of Karaköy and Eminönü and built in 1845 by Abdülmecid's mother, Bezmialem and renovated several times. Edmondo De Amicis claimed that the best way to observe the procession of the people of İstanbul was to stand for an hour on this bridge: "It is an ever-changing mosaic, a kaleidoscopic view of race, costume, and religion, which forms and dissolves with a rapidity the eye and brain can with difficulty follow."[21] The water color by Amadeo Preziosi called *Galata Bridge* depicting sellers of crisp ring-shaped rolls covered with sesame seeds, porters, cavalrymen, dervishes, women with parasols, and men in turbans confirms De Amicis' assertion. The bridge was constructed, so that it could open in the middle and provided passageways for small boats to pass under, forming a raised portion on the bridge, which can also be seen in the painting. Hubert E. H. Jerningham in his book titled *To and From Constantinople* supplies the following recommendation of the verity of Preziosi's work:

[20] Gülsün Tanyeli and Yegan Kahya, "Galata Köprüsü," *İstanbul: Dünden Bugüne İstanbul Ansiklopedisi* .

[21] De Amicis, 1 :48.

[22] Hubert E. H. Jerningham, *To and From Constantinople* (London: Hurst and Blackett, 1873), 329–30.

[23] İlhan Tekeli, "19.yüzyılda İstanbul Metropol Alanının Dönüşümü," in *Modernleşme Sürecinde Osmanlı Kentleri* (İstanbul: Tarih Vakfı Yurt Yayınları, 1999), 28–9; and Sedad Hakkı Eldem, "Boğaziçi Anıları," in *İstanbul Armağanı 2: Boğaziçi Medeniyeti* (İstanbul: İstanbul Belediyesi Kültür İşleri Yayınları, 1996), 44–5.

[24] Ekrem Işın, *İstanbul'da Gündelik Hayat* (İstanbul: Yapı Kredi Yayınları, 1999), 227; and Müller-Wiener, *Bizans'tan,* 159.

For an excellent rendering in watercolors of the life, which is visible on the bridge, no one who visits Constantinople should fail to see Mr. Preziosi's studio. With an admirable talent for water-coloring in general, he above all been gifted with the power of seizing to the life the particular Eastern hue which pervades all things Eastern, and of preserving therefore to the traveler the true recollection of what he most admired.[22]

The Bosphorus

The growth of the seaside district of Galata, where the center of the city had shifted, occurred in three directions: along the seashore from Tophane to Ortaköy; from Taksim toward Şişli; and from Dolmabahçe to the interior toward Teşvikiye and Nişantaşı. After the removal of the imperial palace to the Bosphorus, a new prestige ordering based on proximity to the Court emerged: first, the palaces of Dolmabahçe and Çırağan, second, the palaces of Feriye where the princes resided, succeeded by the seaside mansions of the princesses and their husbands, built in the suburb of Ortaköy on the former sites of Jewish and Armenian seaside mansions. Also, situated between Defterdarburnu and the landing stage at Kuruçeşme were the palaces of the sultan's daughters, along with the seaside mansions of the ministers of state.[23] However, over time, this order was revised, particularly, because of the development of ferryboat service.

The traditional means of communication was by sea. For many years, the city had been served by rowboats; but after 1851, when the Imperial Ferry-Boat Company (*Şirket-i Hayriye*) was established, the number of routes was increased. Ferryboat service began with runs between Eminönü and Galata, the Golden Horn, and the Bosphorus. These ferryboats operated by steam or side-wheel paddle connected the different shores of the city to each other and contributed to the development of residential areas. After service began in 1854, the ferryboats served not only as a means of transportation between the Bosphorus and the center of İstanbul, but they also furnished a setting for political discussion and social intercourse among the colorful figures of the Sublime Porte who met in the boat salon and over time served to unite the urban culture.[24] In a painting showing the ferryboat on the Eminönü-Bosphorus

ill. 183

181 Amadeo Preziosi. *Galata Bridge,* 1856. Watercolor on paper. 29 x 39 cm. Collection of Oya and Bülent Eczacıbaşı, İstanbul

182 Thomas Allom. *Constantinople from Kasımpaşa. Constantinople and the Scenery of the Seven Churches of Asia Minor,* (1838).

183 Artist unknown. *Kabataş Landing Stage and Ferryboat of Imperial Ferryboat Company.* Oil on canvas. 100 x 152 cm. Private Collection, İstanbul.

184 Leonardo de Mango. *Pendik*, 1908. Oil on canvas. 11 x 29 cm. Collection of Duran Tamtekin, İstanbul.

line as it docked at the Kabataş landing stage, we see those waiting in front of the wooden station at the landing stage that projects over the sea, constructed in the founding stages of the Company, as the ferryboat crew throws its anchoring rope to the the quayside hand on the landing stage in the foreground with the Dolmabahçe Mosque, the Clock Tower and Dolmabahçe Palace rendered in a deep perspective looking toward the Bosphorus. The side-paddle wheel boats and steamships have taken the place of the sailboat on the Bosphorus.

The commencement of the ferryboat service as well as the suburban trains on the European side from Yeşilköy and Bakırköy and, on the Asian side, Kızıltoprak, Erenköy and Bostancı encouraged the development of these residential districts. Thanks to these developments in urban transportation, the artists also found it convenient to visit the suburbs of İstanbul and paint more pictures. For example, that by Leonardo de **184** Mango called *Pendik* possesses the quality of a historical record for this suburb, which today has undergone great changes.

Bosphorus Landscape by Fabius Brest depicts a **185** typical village of the Bosphorus and whose houses were built with a ground story of masonry and an upper story of wood, with bay windows, where we see villagers in front of the shops with white awnings doing some shopping, the mosque, the fishing boats on the shore and the caiques. Brest came to İstanbul in 1847 and later visited Algeria. He exhibited his landscapes from Asia Minor and the Bosphorus, views of the port, coffeehouses, and street scenes in the Paris Salon between 1850 and 1896. In 1906, his paintings were included in a retrospective Orientalist exhibition arranged in Marseilles (Exposition Colonial de Marseilles).

Brest who depicted another *Bosphorus* **186** *Landscape* in the evening hours offers a slice of the daily life in the Bosphorus villages—the mosque hidden behind a plane tree, men conversing beneath a tree, a rowboat with passengers disembarking, a sail boat, houses of masonry and wood with bays. Both paintings reflect no place in particular but the artist has observed and absorbed the unique atmosphere of the Bosphorus settlements in an accurate manner. The settlements on the Bosphorus trace the shoreline because the only means of transportion was **187** by sea. In *Caiques and Sailboats on the Bosphorus*

by Felix Ziem, the artist has delineated the sea traffic on the Bosphorus, accented by a scattering of minarets, large sailboats moving along the shores of the Bosphorus or anchored, the light rowboats, and a steamship.

Because the land roads in İstanbul were narrow and inconvenient, for many years the sea had been the most utilized means of transportation. Until ferryboat service began in 1851, the heavy two-oared boat (*pereme*), the light rowboat (*piyade*), and the market boat (*pazar kayığı*) secured communications among the shores of İstanbul. Starting in the eighteenth century, the Bosphorus villages, far from the city center, acquired the character of summering places, and the building of seaside mansions (*yalı*) along the entire extent of the shore and villas on the hillsides developed and animated this area. The sea-

Λ
185

185 Fabius Brest. *Bosphorus Landscape*. Oil on canvas. 30 x 49 cm. Private Collection, İstanbul.

186 ▼

186 Fabius Brest. *Bosphorus Landscape.*
Oil on canvas. 34 x 49 cm. Collection
of Oya and Bülent Eczacıbaşı, İstanbul.

[25] Pardoe, *The Beauties,* 41–2.

[26] Philip Mansel,
*Constantinople: City of the
World's Desire* (London:
Penguin, 1997), 118.

side mansions and villas were the wooden summerhouses of the prosperous and those from the Court circles. Later on, prominent non-Muslims and embassies were included in this group. To the rear of these seaside mansions were situated very beautiful gardens and woods, and a perfect harmony was created between the blue of the sea and the green of nature. As reported by Miss Pardoe, due to the prohibition by the Turks against non-Muslims employing their own favorite colors, Armenians and Greeks painted their houses a dull red or lead gray while the Jews used black.[25] On the construction of seaside mansions in masonry, the shores of the Bosphorus over time assumed an altered visage and, with the founding of Imperial Ferry-Boat Company, experienced its liveliest and most brilliant period.

Fabius Brest, who very much enjoyed life on the Bosphorus, depicted in his painting titled *Sailboats* **ill.** *on the Bosphorus* the caiques and fishing boats on the shore, with their nets being gathered and whose baskets are filled with fish. Because these boats sail on the open sea, they are very strongly built with both ends rising in a high curve and wide bodies and are also equipped with sails. Fishing was one of the most important means of earning a livelihood in the villages on the shores of the Bosphorus, and these fishermen were very skillful. As related by Philip Mansel, when the French Minister of the Marine wished to rejuvenate French fishing, twelve paintings were commissioned in 1732 from Jean-Baptiste Van Mour to illustrate the methods by which the fishermen on the Bosphorus caught fish.[26] As can be seen in the picture, the shores of the Bosphorus began gradually to be filled with seaside mansions, but the hillsides still lacked settlement and were bare.

De Mango, who came to İstanbul in 1883, where he settled and lived until his death in 1930, **ill.** depicted a sailing vessel in front of a silhouette of the Seraglio Point, one of the picturesque components of the İstanbul shores.

It would be interesting to compare these views with the *Beykoz Summer Palace from Yalıköy,* one **ill.** of the earliest paintings of the Bosphorus by an Ottoman artist, Tevfik, a figureless depiction where the emphasis is on the contemporary architectural features. The Beykoz summer palace was the first summer palace of masonry to be built on the Bosphorus and its architects were Nigoğos and Sarkis Balyan. Construction was initiated by Khedive Mehmed Ali Pasha in 1855, which was

187 Felix Ziem. *Caiques and Sailboats on the Bosphorus.* Oil on canvas. 54 x 81 cm. Collection of Suna and Inan Kıraç, İstanbul.

188 Fabius Brest. *Sailboats on the Bosphorus.* Oil on canvas. Private Collection, İstanbul.

189 Leonardo de Mango. *Sailboat*, 1925.
Oil on plywood. 41 x 28 cm. Güner and
Haydar Akın Collection, İstanbul.

XVIII Vistas of Constantinople

completed by his son, Said Pasha, and presented to Sultan Abdülaziz as a gift. When Empress Eugenie came to İstanbul, she was welcomed in this summer palace and a tent in Oriental style in the shape of a kiosk was put up at Sovereign's Green (*Hünkar Çayırı*) in Beykoz and hunting parties were organized. The villa is in two stories, each of identical height. The row of windows on the third story belongs to the light well over the two-storied central hall. The garden of the summer palace is terraced and descends toward the shore. This splendid masonry structure in which members of the imperial house resided creates a contrast with the modest, wooden homes along the shore.

Aivazovsky's painting titled *Entrance to the Bosphorus from the Black Sea* is one of his romantic landscapes treating the theme of full moon and the sea. Here, the artist has depicted the Byzantine Yoros Castle at Anadolukavağı and the lighthouse at the point. The artist has here endowed the citadel, deserted in the nineteenth century and fallen into a ruined state, with its former sound state.[27] A short distance beyond the lighthouse, a large sailing ship can be seen entering the Bosphorus. A fishing boat drawn up to the shore has fishing nets spread over it, and the fishermen a little beyond have lighted a fire in a sheltered corner and are relaxing and smoking pipes.

Old İstanbul

Galata Bridge is one of the most prominent indicators of Westernization in the city and of the shift of the city center within the walls to the Galata shore. In former times, the most desirable districts in the city were located on the Historical Peninsula, but the Galata shore became important when the sultan moved to Dolmabahçe Palace. Despite this development, the Sublime Porte and the market district on the Historical Peninsula continued to maintain their importance. The splendid entrance to the Sublime Porte appears in the small painting dated 1887 by Emile Godchaux. As an expression, the "Sublime Porte" is employed to designate the office of the grand vizier and the structures in which this office was located. Under Mahmud II and his successors, a series of building activities were undertaken to accommodate the administrative reforms. One of these was the entrance gate to the Porte. To the Ottoman citizen, this gate stood for the empire, the place where they assembled, where soldiers

[27] The lighthouse, which fell into ruins and no longer exists, can be seen in the plate of the engraving by Thomas Allom. Walsh, 1: Pl. 52.

190. Tevfik. *Beykoz Summer Palace from Yalıköy*. Oil on canvas. Private Collection, İstanbul.

191 Ivan Aivazovsky. *Entrance to the Bosphorus from the Black Sea*. Oil on canvas. 94 x 133. Collection of Danielle and Hasan Kınay, İstanbul.

and diplomats came and went, and where beggars, venders, and travelers to the city contributed to making this one of the liveliest spots in İstanbul. Godchaux's work depicts the magnificent gate with its baroque covering and gilt inscription and those waiting in front of it.

On the Historical Peninsula in the nineteenth century, Western influence was not yet much in evidence and the exotic urban façade of traditional life remained intact—a locale that Western artists never wearied of painting. Felix Ziem's *St. Sophia and the Walls of Constantinople* and his other Bosphorus paintings were described by his childhood friend, Nicolas Fétu: "Let ourselves be captivated by the enchanting symphony of light, let ourselves be carried off on the wings of ecstasy before the incomarable splendor of Ziem's memories of the Orient. This is an opium dream transferred to canvas in which the colors and figures at their most intense level waver between the real and the imagined."[28] Occupying the spotlight in this painting are the primary, vibrant colors; the relation between light and color has become the main concern of the artist.

ill. 194   In his painting titled *Seraglio Point*, Leonardo de Mango reveals that even Seraglio Point could be affected by time and modernization in the city

ill. 193

[28] Félix Ziem, *Journal (1854–1898)* (Arles: Actes Sud, 1994), 96.

and that, in order to make way for the passage of the railway line, a portion of the city walls that had stood for centuries as a symbol of İstanbul and some seaside kiosks belonging to Topkapı Palace were demolished.

One of the busiest thoroughfares on the Historical Peninsula was Divanyolu, which extended between the districts of Sultan Ahmed and Beyazıt. This had been the main artery of the Byzantine city of Constantinopolis. The markets situated between Divanyolu and the port made this area as one of the most active in İstanbul. Fabius Brest's painting titled *Shopping on Divanyolu* delineates the Koca Sinan Pasha Mosque complex built by Davud Agha. Within the complex, enclosed by a marble wall with an iron balustrade, is a medrese, monumental fountain, and tomb. The most interesting of these is the tomb on a floor plan of sixteen sides, built of colored stone. However, Brest chose not to show the red and

ill.

192 Emile Godchaux. *The Sublime Porte*, 1887. Oil on canvas. 22 X 41 cm. Private Collection, İstanbul.

▲
192

193 Felix Ziem. *St. Sophia Mosque and the Walls of Constantinople*. Oil on canvas. Private Collection, İstanbul.

194 Leonardo de Mango. *Seraglio Point*. Oil on cardboard. 30 x 55 cm. Private Collection, İstanbul.

195 Amadeo Preziosi. *Divanyolu*.
Watercolor on paper. Topkapı Palace
Museum, İstanbul.

196 Fabius Brest. *Shopping on Divanyolu*,
ca. 1855-9. Oil on canvas. 49 x 34 cm.
Topkapı Palace Museum, İstanbul.

197 Fabius Brest. *At the Mosque*. Oil on
canvas. 33 x 49 cm. Private Collection,
İstanbul.

white stonework on the tomb and the framing of
the windows on the façade of the fountain; instead,
he highlighted the colorfulness and animation of
the passersby and shoppers. One characteristic of
Brest, who executed many paintings of İstanbul, is
his ability to convey in a very successful manner,
life in the historical environs of İstanbul.

Amadeo Preziosi in his painting titled
Divanyolu now in the Topkapı Palace Museum
also furnished, as was his custom, a glimpse of
İstanbul life by depicting Divanyolu and people
walking or running, children, a camel drover, and
a beggar beside the walls of the mosque complex.

Besides the marketplaces, one of the principal
social settings for the residents of İstanbul was the
courtyard of the mosques and mosque complexes.
These spaces, which "joined the religious and the
worldly functions",[29] captured the interest of the
artists because of the architecture and colorful
crowds and many foreign artists made pictures
depicting the façade of a mosque or its courtyard

ill. 195

[29] Çelik, 4.

and the people there. The painting by Brest titled
At the Mosque is an extremely picturesque view of
the society that passed through here and the people from different walks of life, the street dogs, the
tomb stones and, in the background, the mosque,
and the fountain for ritual ablutions. Despite the
small proportions of the figures, the artist, who
was very keen observer, successfully renders the
variations in costume. In these kinds of picturesque and exotic views, which foreigners occasionally found interesting as here, Brest did not
hesitate to combine the real and the imaginary.
Thus, certain features of this mosque are reminiscent of Zal Mahmud Pasha Mosque in Eyüp.

The panoramic vista titled *Süleymaniye Mosque
and Tomb from Serasker Tower* by Franz von Alt
(1821–1914), an Austrian artist, is a copy of the
engraving by Bartlett contained in Miss Pardoe's
The Beauties of the Bosphorus. In this view, executed looking from the Serasker, or Beyazıd Fire
Watching Tower and with Süleymaniye Mosque as
the central compositional element, subsumes an
area enclosed by walls that are supported by triangular piers. Formerly, the first imperial palace,
the Old Palace (*Eski Saray*) was situated within
these walls. After the janissary corps was abolished in 1826, this site was given to the ministry of
war (*Bâb-ı Seraskerî*). The building on the left is
the residence of the minister of war. This building
was later demolished and in its place, the Office of

ill.

ill.

XVIII Vistas of Constantinople

the Ministry of War was erected. The site where the Bekir Agha squadron and the Süleymaniye Barracks came to be situated was still vacant at this time. The area enclosed by walls in front of the north wall of the Palace compound was later used as an ammunition dump. Behind the walls stretches the Süleymaniye Mosque complex and, lower down by the shore, the cluster of ship masts indicates the port area. On the opposite shore at the end of the Unkapanı Bridge, we may note the Azapkapı Mosque, the walls of Galata district, and Petit Champs des Morts. The painting successfully conveys the relation between the central position of the Süleymaniye Mosque and its articulation with the texture of the city.

The Hippodrome, or At Meydanı, was "the only open space [in İstanbul] that was consciously preserved,"[30] for "its urban spatial design was not part of a Turkish Islamic urban concept."[31] The Hippodrome, inaugurated by Roman emperor, Septimus Severus, occupied a pre-eminent place in Byzantine life. An emperor newly acceded to the throne would show himself in the emperor's loggia and numerous emperors and generals celebrated their victories here. However, as the name implies, it was, above all, a square in which were held various kinds of circuses and chariot races. Most of the monuments on the spina, which divided the racecourse into two halves, were damaged during the Latin Occupation 1210-61. During the Ottoman period, this square became known as Atmeydanı and preserved its character as the most important square in the city. The mosque of Sultan Ahmed I was erected on the site of palaces built here in the sixteenth century by leading personages like Sokollu Mehmed Pasha and Semiz Ahmed Pasha. The Hippodrome was the scene of imperial festivities, celebrations of imperial weddings, the Processions of Salutation and Holidays; jereed matches and open-air markets. Gerard de Nerval describes a holiday ceremonial he witnessed in the Atmeydanı.

[30] Kuban, *Istanbul Bir*, 338.
[31] Kuban, *Istanbul Bir*, 339.

> The following morning was the first day
> of Bairam. Guns from all the forts and ships
> roared forth at daybreak, drowning the call
> of the Muezzins who hail Allah from the tops
> of a thousand minarets. This time the feast was
> to be at the Atmeidan... The square is oblong,
> and still keeps its old shape of a hippodrome,
> with the two obelisks round which the chariots
> used to turn in the days of the Byzantine

198 Franz von Alt. *Süleymaniye Mosque and Tomb from Serasker Tower*. Oil on canvas. 76 x 106 cm. Collection of Cenap Pekiş Egeli, İstanbul.

XVIII Vistas of Constantinople

contests between *greens* and *blues*. The best preserved obelisk, whose pink granite is covered with hieroglyphics that are still distinct, is supported by a marble pedestal round which are bas-reliefs which represents the Greek emperors surrounded by their court, battles and ceremonies. They are not very well done, but their existence proves that the Turks are not so much the enemies of sculpture as we, in Europe, usually suppose....On one side of the square is the mosque of Sultan Ahmed [I]. There His Highness Abdul-Mejid was to come for the great prayer of the Bairam.[32]

The painting executed by Brest in 1882 called *The Hippodrome* demonstrates how lively the square was on ordinary days too; portable display stands covered by green awnings have been set up between the obelisk and the Serpent Column. A very colorful crowd is strolling about the square, shopping or merely passing through and among the crowd are donkeys with loaded panniers, carts drawn by water buffalo, riders on horseback and a portable coffeehouse. Brest made a drawing in 1849 that closely resembles this painting and from it, Émile Thérond (1821-?) made a copy, which was published in an article on İstanbul in *L'Illustration*.

Fountains

One of the places in İstanbul that drew the attention of foreign artists because of its picturesque appearance was the fountain. The fountain has always been an inseparable part of İstanbul life. As related by Necdet Sakaoğlu, fountains built against a wall that were strongly harmonious with the neighborhood to which they furnished life were more numerous than the monumental fountains endowed by sultans, empress mothers, imperial white eunuchs, and viziers. The largest fountains generally stood at the main intersections of the city, in landing stage squares, near ceremonial grounds and large marketplaces. Another characteristic of these fountains was the adjacent plane or cypress tree located where the inhabitants could converse and relax. [33] A special type of fountain is the *sebil* which is a charity serving the purpose of distributing drinking water. The building has several ornamented grilled window openings to which are attached by chains metal drinking pots.

[32] Gerard de Nerval, *The Women of Cairo: Scenes of Life in the Orient* (London: Routledge, 1929), 2: 396.

[33] Necdet Sakaoğlu and Nuri Akbayar, "İstanbul Sularına Şehrengiz," *İstanbul* (Ocak 1994): 40, 42.

Discounting the Hippodrome, the concept of public square in İstanbul developed in the Tulip Period with the erection of the fountain of Saliha Sultan in Azapkapı and the fountains of Ahmed III in Üsküdar, and in the square before the Imperial Gate of the Topkapı Palace. Among these fountains, the latter erected by Ahmed III in 1728–9 is undoubtedly the most renowned and formed the subject of numerous Orientalist paintings. One of these is a watercolor by Preziosi. Just as in all of his works, Preziosi here also presents the fountain in the context of the daily life in its environs. The rich motifs in relief and inscriptions on the İstanbul fountains display the fine workmanship and ornamentation of Eastern art and offered an opportunity to the artists to prove their talent in drawing.

For Brest, who liked to interpose the life of İstanbul residents in the segments that he chose from the picturesque corners of the city, the fountain where people came together formed an

ill. 201

ill. 202

201

199 Fabius Brest. *The Hippodrome*, 1882. Oil on canvas. 54 x 81 cm. Collection of Koç Holding, İstanbul.

200 Emile Theodore Thérond. "The Hippodrome," *L'Illustration* (26 Mai 1849).

201 Amadeo Preziosi. *Fountain of Ahmed III*. Watercolor on paper. 26 x 38cm. Collection of Oya and Bülent Eczacıbaşı, İstanbul.

XVIII Vistas of Constantinople

202 Fabius Brest. *At the Fountain*. Oil on board. 21 × 15 cm. Collection of Güner and Haydar Akın, İstanbul.

203 Fabius Brest. *View from Üsküdar*. Oil on canvas. 52 × 75 cm. Private Collection, İstanbul.

appropriate setting for his painting .The artist in a painting called *View from Üsküdar* depicted a ill. 203 fountain at the seashore. Though the fountain is reminiscent of the public square fountain of Ahmed III in Üsküdar, just as in his other works, it does not precisely portray what he actually saw, but has the quality of a caprice. In fact, Brest may be called the master of caprice, because, by fusing even the most picturesque specimens of locales and life ways of İstanbul—just as in this work— with the imaginary, he succeeded in creating in all his paintings an atmosphere unique to İstanbul.

One public square fountain was depicted on the ill. 204 sea shore in a painting by Leonardo de Mango dated 15 August 1908. A typical scene is depicted: those fetching water from the fountain, the water venders, the passersby, the sesame-roll sellers, and a street cleaner, and street dogs. Incidentally, it may be noted that the number of steamboats on the Golden Horn has risen.

203
▼

Üsküdar

The old İstanbul neighborhoods, which were hidden behind the active life—still and peaceful and drawn within themselves frequently, appear in Orientalist pictures. Because the Orientalists particularly wanted to capture scenes of old İstanbul, untouched by the effects of Westernization, the neighborhoods they sought were in the city within the walls on the Historical Peninsula, in the suburbs and villages of the Bosphorus and the Golden Horn, such as Üsküdar and Eyüp, with their narrow and irregular streets and wooden houses. The painting by Brest titled *Üsküdar*, now in Topkapı Palace Museum, is a slice of the introverted and quiet neighborhood life of old İstanbul, with its unpaved streets, mosque, fountain, two-story wooden houses, shops with front awnings, street venders, and street dogs. This district where Muslims were in the majority frequently appears in the paintings of foreign artists and this reason why

ill. 205

204 Leonardo de Mango. *Fountain in the Square*, 1908. Oil on cardboard.
31 x 45 cm. Collection of Danielle and Hasan Kınay, İstanbul.

this was so may explained by the following statement by director of the Imperial Museum, Philipp Anton Dethier: "The high and the low and the poor are here, hand in hand. That is what makes this milieu so picturesque."[34] Üsküdar attracted the notice of foreign artists as much for its neighborhood life as for the beauty of the view from the grassy areas on its hillsides.

Another place that foreign artists went to make paintings on the Asian shore was Salacak, principally, because this vantage point along with the hills of Galata and Pera provided the most beautiful view of the Historical Peninsula. The Italian, Carlo Bossoli, was one artist who usually preferred to paint the Historical Peninsula from the shore of Salacak. Included in his painting of the *Tower of Leander and Seraglio Point* as seen from Salacak is a group of men and women sitting on the shore enjoying the view. This informs us that the historical and natural beauties of the city exerted an affect on both foreigners and the local inhabitants. In another painting by Bossoli, the Tower of Leander is pictured from a closer viewpoint. Here, the light beaming from the tower and the moonlight on the sea creates a very romantic atmosphere: as remarked by Miss Pardoe, the tower was "an object in itself so picturesque that it would arrest the eye though it possessed no legend to attract the sympathy..."[35] Despite its being night-time, there are people on the shore who have come to observe both the moonlight and the Tower of Leander. In a watercolor by Luigi Brocktorff in the Topkapı Palace Museum, a similar view was delineated. Fausto Zonaro, who liked to capture on canvas the picturesque neighborhoods of İstanbul, also executed a view from Salacak.

In Zonaro's *Street Scene, Üsküdar*, the artist very likely included part of the Karaca Ahmed Cemetery in Üsküdar. On one side of the unpaved road is a cemetery and in a row on the other are wooden houses with bay windows. The veiled women walking on the road and the street dogs that were a fixture of the streets of İstanbul and to which foreign travelers always devoted a chapter can be seen. The proximity of the cemetery to the dwellings and the intimacy of the living with the dead of the city and the cypress trees, which are a constant feature of the cemeteries always caught the attention of foreigners.

Nineteenth-century İstanbul remained to a great extent tied to tradition and persisted in building their houses of wood. The cheapness of wood, its

[34] P.A. Dethier, *Boğaziçi ve İstanbul* (İstanbul: Eren, 1993), 91.
[35] Pardoe, The City, 1: 143.

205 Fabius Brest. *Üsküdar*. Oil on canvas. 34 x 49 cm. Topkapı Palace Museum, İstanbul.

206 Fausto Zonaro. *Women on Hillside above Üsküdar*. Watercolor. 28 x 49 cm. Private Collection, İstanbul.

207 Carlo Bossoli. *Tower of Leander and Seraglio Point*, 1848. Oil on canvas. 17 x 26 cm. Collection of Suna and Inan Kıraç, İstanbul.

208 Luigi Brocktorff . *European Shore of Bosphorus from Şemsi Paşa Mosque.* Watercolor on paper. 70 x 59 cm. Topkapı Palace Museum, İstanbul.

XVIII Vistas of Constantinople

209 Carlo Bossoli. *Tower of Leander.*
Watercolor, gouache, pastel on paper.
42 x 30 cm. Collection of Duran
Tamtekin, İstanbul.

XVIII Vistas of Constantinople

210 Fausto Zonaro. *View from Salacak.*
Oil on canvas. 51 x 35 cm. Private
Collection, İstanbul.

211 Fausto Zonaro. *Street Scene, Üsküdar.*
Oil on canvas. Private Collection, İstanbul.

resistance to earthquakes, the easy availability of the material, its ease of construction, and the brevity of the construction period—despite all the firmans and regulation codes issued against its use—led to its continued utilization. However, eventually, starting in Pera and especially in areas where non-Muslims resided, masonry structures began to replace those of wood. Regardless of the advantages of wood as a construction material, its flammability were frequently mentioned by Western artists and travelers and led to their depiction of the tremendous İstanbul fires. Each neighborhood in İstanbul organized its own fire-fighters. These people would register for this work and in the daytime tend to their own occupations while in the evening would gather in their coffeehouses. According to Ref'i Cevad Ulunay's description, the "team," or brigade, who carried the old-fashioned fire pump on their shoulders, were supplemented by a captain, a lantern hold-er, leader of the pump squad, fire hose carriers, and usually a mounted fire pump officer. Their outfits consisted of a felt cap or a napkin bound around the head, undershirts woven of Lisle thread, a girdle round their waist, breeches that reached to the knees and on their feet, flat-heeled shoes or sometimes none at all. If the firefighters were not competing with another team as to who would get to the fire first, they would pass through the crowded streets and in front of the large coffeehouses, adopting a posture of exag-gerated swagger and taking small steps in a des-ignated pattern. This institution disappeared when the fire department organization was estab-lished in 1923.[36]

212   Appearing in an 1870 issue of *L'Illustration* is an engraving of these firefighters and an article about them by Henri Vigne. Vigne indicates that the fire-fighters were independent units, that they had cus-toms, rules, ceremonials, and celebrations, and that when news of a fire reached them they ran like lightning to the place where the fire was, but that when they got there, unfortunately, they started to negotiate about the fee for their service, and as this bargaining went on sometimes it became too late to do anything about the fire, "but once an agree-ment had been reached, you could depend on their power, fearlessness, and bravery....These workers possessed an undaunting courage."[37] In the sketch **214** by Zonaro called *Firefighters*, the firefighters can be seen running across Galata Bridge toward the dis-trict of Galata. Zonaro treated this subject several

[36] Ref'i Cevad Ulunay, *Sayılı Fırtınalar* (Istanbul: Bolayır, 1958), 310–1.

[37] Henri Vigne, "Les pompiers de Constantinople." *L'Illustration* (2 Juillet 1870): 11.

212 "Fire in İstanbul," *L'Illustration* (2 Juillet 1870): 12.

213 Fausto Zonaro. *There's a Fire*. Pastel on paper. Collection of Axa Oyak Sigorta, İstanbul.

214 Fausto Zonaro. *Firefighters*. Oil on canvas. 21 x 33 cm. Güner and Haydar Akın Collection, İstanbul.

times, making slight alterations, and executed sketches in different mediums. According to his grandson, Cesare Mario Trevigne, two paintings in the family collection titled *There's a Fire* were sold in Milan between 1960 and 1970. In the large-scale work in pastel titled *There's a Fire*, which was owned by the insurance company (*İttihad-ı Millî Türk Sigorta Şirketi*) established in the Ottoman Empire in 1918 by the French Union Fire Insurance Company, we may note the firemen of the fire department founded in 1874 with four brigades in their new uniforms, who are trotting behind the fire pumpers carrying their hoses and pumps across the bridge. On the left-hand side of the painting, Zonaro's wife may be detected standing on the sidewalk as a witness to the event. One can discern in the background the silhouette of Yeni Mosque.

İstanbul fires were a prominent feature in foreign newspapers and magazines. The Kemeraltı fire that broke out in Galata in February 1865 was depicted in a sketch by Preziosi that appeared in *L'Illustration*. In the text related to this picture, Dr. Louis Ernst informs us that the fire started in a wooden house, that it spread with rapidity, and that some one hundred houses and part of the Providence Convent of the nuns of St. Benoit in Galata were burned.[38]

ill. 213

ill. 215

38 Louis Ernst, "Incendie de Galata," *L'Illustration* (25 Mars 1865), 181.

39 The same figure with turban and cane in the foreground of this painting was used in the foreground of a painting of Valide Sultan Mosque commissioned from Zonaro by Prince Mavrocordato, the Greek minister plenipotentiary to Istanbul.

Marketplaces

Not all the streets of İstanbul were quiet and peaceful. A painting by Zonaro [39] delineated a street scene in one of the market areas of İstanbul, where most of the structures were of masonry, with men sitting and drinking coffee and smoking the narghile along the entire length of the sidewalk while the street was filled with heavy pedestrian traffic. In the nineteenth century, when, particularly in the Galata and Pera districts, European-style stores selling imports were opening one after the other, the marketplaces that interested the foreign travelers most, architecturally and in terms of the goods sold and the typical Oriental figures and settings, were the Grand Bazaar and Spice Bazaar. Occupying a significant place in the economic life of the city, the Grand Bazaar housed a wide variety of trades. Léon Verhaeghe, who was in İstanbul in the 1860s, summarized this characteristic of the marketplace very succinctly:

ill. 216

> Everything can be found in the Grand Bazaar. Without having to go elsewhere, one can be

215 Based on sketch by Amadeo Preziosi. "Fire in Galata District," *L'Illustration* (25 Mars 1865).

216 Fausto Zonaro. *Street Scene*. Oil on
canvas. 44.5 x 68 cm. Collection of Oya
and Bülent Eczacıbaşı, İstanbul.

217 Amadeo Preziosi. *Grand Bazaar*,
1853. Watercolor on paper. 40 x 54 cm.
Museum of Painting and Sculpture, Mimar
Sinan University, İstanbul.

attired and armed, a house can be furnished,
a set assembled, and the materials necessary
for a house can be stored: the Grand Bazaar
brings together in one place the entire life
of the city—all of its activities and all of
its commerce.[40]

With its origin stretching back as far as Mehmed
II, the Grand Bazaar was established first as a
bedesten and shops were built around it. But as a
result of fires because the shops were made of
wood, the decision was made in 1701 that the
shops should be of masonry and with vaulted covers and, thus, it was transformed into a masonry
structure. According to information dating to a few
years prior to the earthquake in 1894, the bazaar,
composed of sixty-one streets and eighteen
entrances, contained two *bedestens*, four thousand
three hundred and ninety-nine shops, two thousand one hundred and ninety-five chambers, one
bath, one Friday mosque and ten other mosques,
sixteen fountains, eight wells, two ablution fountains, one monumental fountain, one tomb, one
school, and twenty-four caravansaries.[41]

From Carlo Bossoli to Amadeo Preziosi, numerous artists depicted the Grand Bazaar, which
besides being a shopping center that could meet
every need with diverse variety of goods, its random organization and complex plan attracted
Westerners. Edmondo De Amicis claimed that the
Grand Bazaar was not a building, but a true city
with streets, fountains, mosques and squares.[42]
Carlo Bossoli's painting titled *Grand Bazaar* ill.
depicted the broadest street in the market, the
Avenue of the Calpac Makers. On both sides of
the street, the merchants are seated on raised
wooden platforms with their shops, that is to say,
the cupboards (*dolap*), behind them, with shelves
on the walls while in front of them were stalls and
glass show cases.

Preziosi in his painting of 1853 titled *Grand* ill.
Bazaar has depicted the drapery and costume
market—the main attraction for women. To
endow his picture with a more colorful air, as
was his custom, Preziosi added some interesting
figural types: besides the women engaged in
shopping, there was a water seller offering water
to two small children, a youth selling prepared
food on a tray suspended from his neck, and a
dervish. In another painting, Preziosi presents a ill.
close-up look at one corner of the *bedesten* and
creates an atmosphere charming to all Western

[40] Verhaeghe, 490.

[41] Mustafa Cezar, *Tipik
Yapılarıyla Osmanlı Şehir-
ciliğinde Çarşı ve Klasik
Dönem İmar Sistemi*.
Istanbul: Mimar Sinan Üniversitesi, 1985), 148.

[42] De Amicis, 1:129.

218 Carlo Bossoli. *Grand Bazaar*, 1845.
Watercolor on paper. 57 x 44 cm.
Collection of Oya and Bülent Eczacıbaşı,
İstanbul.

XVIII Vistas of Constantinople

travelers by a veritable catalog of all the kinds of goods sold, from cloth to spoons: here, we see a stand with mother-of-pearl inlay, chests, glass and porcelain vases and vessels lined up along the wall, a variety of daggers hanging on the wall, and a framed inscription. Edmondo De Amicis has provided a detailed, written description of his experience in the Bazaar on being exposed to the many treasures on display to which he added: "One must indeed be an uncommonly well-balanced person, a very mountain of wisdom, to be able to withstand the temptations of this place, whence many an artist has come forth as poor as Job, and where more than one rich man has thrown away his fortune."[43]

[43] De Amicis, 1 :155

The second kind of typical marketplace setting in the Ottoman Empire was that in which all the artisans in a single cluster of shops were engaged in the same handicraft. The best example in İstanbul was the Spice Bazaar. This covered market belonged to the nearby Yeni Mosque complex and it was built to earn revenue for the staff and upkeep of the mosque. The foundation of the market in an L-shape was laid in 1597 and opened in 1665. Fabius Brest's picture of the street in the middle of the market is arched and vaulted. The plan of the Spice Bazaar provides for "first, a series of vaulted chambers with one side open. To the

ill. 220

219 Amadeo Preziosi. *Grand Bazaar.* Collection of Ersin Börteçen, İstanbul.

220 Fabius Brest. *Spice Bazaar.* Oil on canvas. 58 x 81.5 cm. Private Collection, İstanbul.

220
▼

221
▼

222
▼

223
▼

rear of these vaulted chambers and almost twice as deep are the shops."[44] Foreigners on entering the Spice Bazaar were struck by the sharp fragrance of the spices, cooking and healing herbs, and perfumes and essences, as well as dyes; and a variety of remedies for ills were available.

As can be seen in the picture by Alexandre Bida (1823–95) published in *L'Illustration* and titled *Shop in Constantinople*, neighborhood shops were generally located beneath the living quarters and were of wood. These shops were built on "a plan suitable to accommodate a bench for the practice of the artisan's trade and the dwelling of the shop owner. In front of most shops, there was a portable display stand."[45]

Apart from the large markets and the neighborhood shops, the residents of İstanbul could also turn to the street venders to meet their needs.

ill. 221

[44] Cezar, *Tipik*, 183.
[45] Necdet Sakaoğlu and Nuri Akbayar, *Osmanlı'da Zenaatten Sanata* (İstanbul, Körfezbank, 2000), 2: 237.

Today, some of the few such venders still to be encounter in İstanbul are, in the winter months, the chestnut roasted sellers and the makers of a beverage made of fermented millet and the sellers of a jellied confection who wait outside school entrance gates and the cry of yogurt sellers can yet be heard in some neighborhoods. The street venders of İstanbul formed the subject matter for both writers and artists. Foreigners who stayed a long time in the city relate in their memoirs that, thanks to these venders, they could meet many of their needs without ever having to leave the house. One could encounter these venders in the marketplaces, the weekly open-air markets and on the streets in every part of the city. Selling all kinds of goods from prepared food to beverages, pencils, notebooks, canes, and toys, they even included the street photographer. A number of foreign artists in the nineteenth century executed their pictures. Depictions of such venders include those by De Mango of the *Grape Seller*, and *Chimney Sweeper* and *Flower Seller* by Salvatore Valeri. Even the

ill.
ill.
ill.

224 Salvatore Valeri. *Flower Seller*,
1889-90. Oil on canvas. 123 x 95.5 cm.
Museum of Painting and Sculpture, Mimar
Sinan University, İstanbul.

⁴⁶ Thornton, 230.

well-known Austrian artist, Rudolf Ernst, known **ill.**
for his paintings on the theme of mosques depicted a vender selling watermelons from his large
basket standing in front of a mosque. Other similar
works by Ernst include a petition writer or a watermelon seller or a flower seller outside a mosque by
means of which the artist treated the religious
architecture in the framework of a scene from life.
Coming to İstanbul in the 1890s, Ernst particularly
focused in his paintings on the mosque and worship scenes that stress the religion of Islam. Lynne
Thornton claims that, despite being an amateur
photographer, Ernst, when denied permission to
take photographs, swiftly rendered rough sketches,
but subsequently drew on published photographs
whose subject matter was Islamic art and architecture.[46] In another work by the artist, a carpenter **ill.**
was depicted cutting a piece of wood with a saw
seated in front of a hearth faced with glazed tiles
and his apprentice who was stirring something in
a large jug—no doubt, glue. A door leaf resting
against one wall whose inlay of mother-of-pearl is

225 Rudolf Ernst. *Watermelon Vendor at
Rüstem Paşa Mosque.* Oil on board.
24 x 18.5 cm. Collection of Danielle and
Hasan Kınay, İstanbul.

226 Rudolf Ernst. *Intarsia in
Mother-of-Pearl.* Oil on board.
24 x 18.5 cm. Collection of Danielle
and Hasan Kınay, İstanbul.

half finished suggests that both of them were working on this door.

Pictures of venders can be encountered illustrating articles about İstanbul in foreign newspapers and magazines. One of these is the picture of a *Pudding Seller*, a *Porter*, and a *Confectioner* printed in *L'Illustration*. In the text by Jean Henri Abdolonyme Ubicini, it is stated that, in İstanbul and in other large cities in the Ottoman Empire, there was an interesting group of males known as "bachelors" and that most of them had come from the interior of the empire, particular Asia Minor. This group, which in İstanbul numbered some seventy-five or seventy-six thousand, was two-fifths Turkish, three-fifths Greek or Armenian. Ubicini indicates that most of the bachelors, who had left their home towns with no definite objective and no particular skill, worked in large cities as porters, water sellers, halwah sellers, liver sellers, or confection sellers and that they chose occupations that required little capital, and when they had earned a little money they would return to their home

227 "Pudding Seller," "Porter," "Confectioner," *L'Illustration* (10 Juin 1854).

XVIII Vistas of Constantinople

towns.[47] In order to generate interest in their future customers, they would wear the local costumes of their own region and some would chant traditional Turkish folk verse as they advertised their goods. Dorina Neave, who lived in İstanbul between 1881 and 1907, in support of her assertion that İstanbul was a very noisy city reported that

> A fishmonger, who had often passed by my side in a very quiet manner, would suddenly cry out just by my ear "Mackerel!" and while fleeing from him I would run into a water seller crying "Water!" or an ice cream seller shouting "Creamy ice cream!" It was as if the sale of the man's product good was dependent on his ability to shout loudest. To this jumble of cries and chorus of shouts was added by the confectioner vender the repeated musical refrain of "Turkish Delight!" For this reason, it was both very exciting and very difficult to pass through a Turkish street.[48]

Apart from the venders, another figural type that foreign artists found interesting was the beggars of İstanbul, who were generally stationed on Galata Bridge, at promenade and excursion spots, at funerals and in cemeteries, and in the mosque courtyards.

ill. 228
ill. 229
ill. 230

[47] Jean Henri Abdolonyme Ubucini, "Les Petits Metiers a Constantinople," *L'Illustration* (10 Juin 1854): 362

[48] Dorina L. Neave, *Eski İstanbul'da Hayat* (Istanbul: Tercüman, 1978), 159–60.

228 Albert Mille. "Turkish Beggar," *Figaro Illustré,: Constantinople* (1908).

229 Salvatore Valeri. *Beggar.* Watercolor on paper. Collection of Güner and Haydar Akın, İstanbul.

230 Salvatore Valeri. *Snake Charmer* (dedicated to Giulio Mongeri), 1911. Watercolor on paper. 48 x 31.5 cm. Collection of Pervin and Metin Kaşo, İstanbul.

Cemeteries

Cemeteries occupied a special place among the views of İstanbul by Orientalist artists. The Muslim way of looking "at death peacefully and without fear"[49] was irreconcilable with the gloom and fear borne by Westerners and the making of cemeteries as the most beautiful greens in the city attracted the attention of Westerners. In their writings, they often mentioned one of the customary sights of the city was the holding of picnics in the cemeteries, where pipes were smoked, cows grazed, and children run about playing. Another unaccustomed sight for foreigners was the gravestone that was carved and painted to reflect the gender, the rank, and the occupation of the deceased. With some exceptions, "grave stones for males were identifiable by the type of headgear worn by the social class to which they belonged; whereas those of females lacked headgear but were ornamented with decorative motifs."[50] In Preziosi's work from 1853 titled *View from Eyüp*, the artist shows the cemetery on the hillside overlooking

the Golden Horn along with the colorful and carved gravestones. Cypress trees are frequently mentioned in connection with cemeteries. Clara Erskine Clement in *Constantinople: The City of Sultans* states that by reason of the fact that the cemeteries of İstanbul both in terms of their location and their use by the public as excursion spots did not call up melancholy or sadness and that the cypress trees in the cemeteries were not a symbol of sadness and death but rather embellishments of both gardens and the city of the dead and the protector of the grave.[51]

[49] Pardoe, *The City*, 1: 98.
[50] Işın, 260.
[51] Clara Erskine Clement, *Constantinople: The City of Sultans* (Boston: Estes and Lauriat, 1895), 16.

231 Amadeo Preziosi. *View from Eyüp*, 1853. Watercolor on paper. 39 x 57.5 cm. Museum of Painting and Sculpture, Mimar Sinan University, İstanbul.

231

232 R. L. Giradet. "Cemetery at Eyüp," *L'Illustration* (26 Mai 1849).

233 Fausto Zonaro. *Tomb of Selami Ali Efendi.* Oil on canvas. 56 x 86 cm. Private Collection, İstanbul.

In terms of gravestones, İstanbul was the possessor of a very rich accumulation. The great cemetery of Eyüp, in particular, with its beautiful gravestones and its atmosphere of the world beyond, produced the impression of a city of the dead. The district of Eyüp is one of the most sacred places in the Islamic world as the grave site of Eyüp el Ensarî, a Companion of the Prophet and the standard bearer and one of the most picturesque places in the city for both travelers and painters with the cypress trees and the gravestones in its vicinity and its wonderful view of the Golden Horn.

Baroness Durand de de Fontmagne discloses in her memoirs her impressions of the Muslim cemeteries she had seen in İstanbul.

> The difference between Muslim cemeteries and ours is the absence of the cross and the ease of wandering through them and the choice according to one's heart the place desired as a setting for one's own death. Neither walls nor gates nor guards. A grove of cypresses, a forest that first struck the eye or a beautiful corner of the Bosphorus.... All these things may be the most suitable place for these spacious tombs. They leave in this state of theirs that is an air full of poetry and dreams rather than depressing...
> The stones placed at the graves of males are ornamented by a quilted turban carved of marble in such a fashion as to indicate the class of the deceased. Occasionally you may see a grave with a red fez...
> The stones placed at the head of female graves are broader than that placed at the foot...
> These stones are ornamented from top to bottom by an inscription. Some are painted or gilded. Among the reliefs of fruit and flowers is inscribed the name of the deceased.
> An empty vase indicates a woman, a flower a young girl; then a verse from the *Koran* and a few words of praise.
> In such a charming environs, the gravestones scattered here and there at the top of a high hill embracing the view—some fallen, some darkened, some gleaming with whiteness, and some with gilded carving—are like a setting of a fairytale world. Death in the cemeteries of Turkey does not frighten one.
> Sometimes several women add color to the scene. When they believe themselves to be alone, they sit at their ease and loosen their veils and outer cloaks in order to eat something.[52]

[52] Durand de Fontmagne, 117-19.

XIX Excursion sites

Outdoor recreation areas granted Westerners an opportunity to gaze at natural beauties as well as at the life ways of the native inhabitants, and these places where their lives briefly intersected were of great interest to them. Though, ordinarily, Western figures seldom appear in Orientalist artworks, they constitute a common element in paintings devoted to such excursion spots.

Residents of Constantinople in the Ottoman period very much enjoyed taking their leisure on meadows in the open air. The qualities most sought after in such areas were the presence of greenery, an occasional shade tree, and a stream. An ordinance publicly issued in 1861 by the government regarding excursion spots in İstanbul incidentally provides us with a record to acquaint us with the names of the principle recreation areas of the period, thus

234

Recreation areas open to the public in İstanbul on Friday and Sunday as well as on the other days of the week are Veliefendi, Çırpıcı Meadows, Bayrampaşa, Üsküdar, Çamlıca, Merdiven Köyü, Haydarpaşa, Duvardibi, Beylerbeyi and Havuzbaşı.

Since, however, areas are reserved for their separate use, males and females should neither commingle nor sit together. In the event this should occur, punishment will be meted out in accordance with Article 254 of the Ordinance. Some excursion areas along the Bosphorus Strait and in Üsküdar are set aside for use by women only on Fridays and by men on Sundays: on Fridays—Kağıthane in the metropolis of İstanbul and Modaburnu and Fenerbahçesi in Üsküdar, Hacıhüseyin Bağı in Beşiktaş, Ihlamur, Küçükçiftlik, Taksimönü in Beyoğlu, Küçük and Büyüksular on the Bosphorus, Çubuklu, the Hünkar landing stage, Arnavutköy Point—but Muslim ladies are prohibited from these places on Sundays. If they do otherwise, they will be punished

[1] Balıkhane Nazırı Ali Rıza Bey, *Bir Zamanlar İstanbul* (İstanbul, Tercüman, n. d.),.219.

[2] Georgina Max Müller, *İstanbul'dan Mektuplar* (İstanbul: Tercüman, 1978), 96–8.

[3] IRCICA, Seyfeddin Özege Collection, no. 4.

according to the provisions of the aforementioned law.

Regardless of the day of the week, Muslim women are strictly forbidden to stop and make free use of the following districts, given the fact that they are not and have never been considered as excursion spots: the now opened areas of Çiftehavuzlar, located between Maşatlık in the vicinity of Bağlarbaşı in Üsküdar and the Bostancıbaşı Bridge, Serbostanbağı and Susuzbağ near Sultantepesi and Arapzade Bağı above Kuzguncuk; Maslak; Şişli; Levent Farms; Pangaltı; and beyond Zincirlikuyu.[1]

In addition to the excursion spots named above, a painting by an unknown artist makes it evident   ill. 235
that water reservoirs were places favored for outings by Europeans, no doubt, because they were located near the summer residences of embassies at Tarabya and Büyükdere. Georgina Max Müller, who came to İstanbul in 1894 to visit her son, a clerk in the British embassy, relates in detail an excursion and picnic held at the Sultan Mahmud II and Valide Reservoirs. While most of the men from the British and German embassies at Tarabya went by horseback, the women journeyed to the reservoirs in carts covered by an awning, but, by the time they arrived, they saw that Ottoman women had already taken the most desirable places.[2] Based on a photograph,[3] this painting delineates the dam of Mahmud II (*Bend-i Cedid*), built at the command of the sultan by Garabed Balyan for the water distribution point at Taksim. An inscription stone appears in the center of the dam structure. Atop the stone there is an oval medallion bearing the imperial monogram. This medallion is surrounded by a sunburst pattern in the Empire style, which was peculiar to the reign of Mahmud II. Of the seven promenading or seated figures, five are foreigners.

Westerners applied the name "Sweet Waters" to the recreation areas along the banks of streams.

234 Amadeo Preziosi. *Excursion to Çamlıca*, 1853. Watercolor on paper. 40 x 59 cm. Museum of Painting and Sculpture, Mimar Sinan University, İstanbul.

Accordingly, the most popular and renowned excursion area, the "Sweet Waters of Europe," as it was known by Europeans, or Kağıthane, were the greens lying between the streams of Alibey on the west and Kağıthane on the east, both of which flow into the northern most point of the Golden Horn. Accessible by both water and overland, "one bank [of the stream] at Kağıthane, starting from the first bridge, was reserved for females and the other

234
▼

[4] Balıkhane Nazırı, 202.

for males, and the area in between beneath an arcade of ball-shaped topiaries was for carriages.[4] Kağıthane, praised as early as the fifteenth century for its natural beauties, witnessed its liveliest era in the eighteenth century. Influenced by the impressions relayed by the Ottoman ambassador, Yirmisekiz Çelebi, in regard to the palaces in the environs of Paris, Sultan Ahmed III and Grand Vizier Nevşehirli Damad İbrahim Pasha ordered

235 Artist unknown. *Dam of Mahmud II.* Oil on canvas. 54 x 72.5 cm. Collection of Pervin and Metin Kaşo, İstanbul.

the construction of pavilions and summer palaces along the banks of Kağıthane above the Golden Horn. First of all, the stream of Kağıthane

was diverted into a straight canal [called the Silver Canal, or *Cedvel-i Sim*] with wharfs at regular intervals on both sides [, leading from Kağıthane village to the site of the proposed sultan's palace]....The new palace was given

235
▼

the name *Sa'dabad*. The water, collecting in a pool due to the stream being blocked by a weir, was led by narrow channels to the other side of the weir where it flowed over a marble cascade and ran into a second, lower pool. A pair of bowers of very delicate construction was situated at the place where the water ran over the top level

236 Antoine- Ignace Melling. *Kağıthane.*
Voyage pittoresque de Constantinople et des
rives de Bosphore, (1819).

237 Luigi Acquarone. *Jereed Match at*
Kağıthane, 1891. Oil on canvas.
62 x 117 cm. Private Collection, İstanbul.

of the cascade. A projection jutted over the water at the head of the dam and on which was erected a marquee-like pavilion with broad eaves and open sides, resting on columns, and whose central portion was occupied by a pool....From this pavilion called the Palace of Gaiety [Kasr-ı Neşad], it was possible to view the stream in its entirety and listen to the water as it flowed....Right before the Palace of Gaiety in the middle of the pool...was a bronze column with jets in the form of dragon heads, a near replica of the ancient Serpent Column in the Hippodrome which was terminated by three intertwined serpents. Forty orange saplings, a gift of the French king, were planted in front of the palace. The spacious grounds belonging to the palace were covered by a grove of lofty trees. Swans swam in the several artificial lakes among the trees. One façade of the palace rose directly above the quay and bay windows projected over the water.[5]

The opening ceremony in 1722 for Sa'dabad—a name signifying 'Place of Happiness'—was accompanied by feasts, dances, horse races, and jereed matches. According to Ahmed Refik, tents were pitched here and at night the area was lit by thousands of oil lamps, candles, and lanterns and the sounds of the harp, rebec, dulcimer, tambur, lute, violin, a double-reed instrument (*zurna*), and loud cries issuing from every tent, along with the blast of fireworks and cannon shot reverberated through the grounds until dawn, and, by day, performances were staged by conjurers, jugglers, masters of fireworks displays, magicians, and greased wrestlers.[6]

236
237
Copied from an engraving of *Kağıthane* by Melling, Luigi Acquarone depicted in an oil painting a scene from a jereed match being played on the grounds near the stream of Kağıthane. The rolling terrain in the environs of the palace had rapidly assumed a beautiful, park-like appearance with walking paths, channels of water, gardens, fountains with jets, and pavilions. A number of these works of beautification was damaged during the revolt of Patrona Halil in 1730.

Sa'dabad represented an extremely significant work of urban design that altered the life style of İstanbul residents through the provision of a recreation area with facilities for them to obtain pleasure from country life and nature and the inauguration of an extrovert lifestyle. Sa'dabad, in

[5] Semavi Eyice, "İstanbul Halkının ve Padişahların Ünlü Mesiresi: Kağıthane," *İstanbul Armağanı 3: Gündelik Hayatın Renkleri* (İstanbul: İstanbul Büyük Şehir Belediyesi Kültür İşleri Yayınları 1997), 82–3.

[6] Ahmet Refik (Altınay), *Lale Devri* (Ankara: Başbakanlık Kültür Müsteşarlığı Yayınları, 1973), 29–30.

[7] "Description de Sadiabath, maison de plaisance du Grand Seigneur," *Mercure de France* (Juin 1724): 1260, cited in Ayda Arel, *Onsekizinci Yüzyıl İstanbul Mimarisinde Batılılaşma Süreci* (İstanbul: İstanbul Teknik Üniversitesi Yayınları, 1975) 26'dan

[8] Eyice, "İstanbul," 85–6.

which nature and architecture were subjected to concurrent treatment, was constructed, so that the imperial family and members of the Court circle could enjoy an amusing retreat. A letter published in *Mercure de France*, as follows, confirms this:

> Turks appear to have undergone a transformation in their temperament and attitude because of this recreation area. As you know, Sir, formerly they were never fond of excursions, but now they have suddenly developed a passion for the out-of-doors—to such an extent that on certain days it is as crowded there [i.e., Kağıthane] as Cours-de-la-Reine or the Champs-Elysées. Both natives and foreigners of every age and of both sexes may go there in complete security. In addition, the representatives of foreign rulers may, on occasion, meet here with the grand vizier or the other viziers, always in good humor and predisposed to please.[7]

ill. 238
The illuminated manuscript *Hubanname and Zenanname* by Fazıl Enderunî contains one of the few works rendering a view of the summer palace of Sa'dabad and environs prior to the revolt of Patrona Halil. The miniature permits a view of women in the foreground amusing themselves while the cascading stream, lying slightly to the rear of the marble fountain *Çeşme-i Nur*, the dragon-headed jets, and the palace and its gardens are visible on the other side of the stream. Rebels active during the reign of Mahmud I destroyed all the pavilions and summer palaces here. G. Jehannet, in İstanbul in 1731, states that Patrona Halil ruined the kiosks on the nearby slopes, but that he left untouched the sultan's palace and the cascades.[8] Despite all these changes, Kağıthane has preserved its renown as an excursion spot. Sa'dabad Palace, having suffered extensive damage, was renovated by Mahmud II in 1809–14, on a completely different plan by Kirkor Balyan, and the new structures and kiosks built in the vicinity sufficed to restore it to its former beauty.

ill. 239
A watercolor executed in 1825 by Löwenhielm, the Swedish ambassador to İstanbul, enlightens us as to the state of the Sa'dabad complex in this period. The summer palace erected by Mahmud II at the Great Dam of the Waterfall [Büyük Çağlayan Bendi] , appears in the background, with the façade that overlooks the water broken up by four bay windows resting on columns standing in the

238 Fazıl Enderuni. *Kağıthane. Hubanname and Zenanname,* (1793). İstanbul University Library (no.1527/24).

water. In front of the palace is the Çadır Pavilion. This bower-like pavilion was re-built on the marble platform on the site formerly occupied by the summer Palace of Gaiety. Closer to the viewer, in the foreground, are three bower-type pavilions on the Great Çağlayan Dam. These pavilions are supported by marble columns, enclosed by a balustrade, and covered by gilded copper over framework. However, Sultan Mahmud II soon afterwards either lost his enthusiasm or had ceased to care about this place. John Auldjo, arriving in İstanbul in 1833, observes in his memoirs that Kağıthane still retained all its liveliness as an excursion spot, but that the deserted palace was rapidly becoming a ruin, with the park being visited only in the springtime, and that the sultan had sent his horses there to graze.[9]

Though the palace at Kağıthane and environs suffered neglect during the reign of Abdülmecid, the grounds, nonetheless, remained popular as a recreation area. Abdülaziz, who enjoyed Kağıthane and who held entertainments here, had a two-story wooden palace in a wholly European style con-

[9] John Auldjo, *Journal of a Visit to Constantinople and Some of the Greek Islands in the Spring and Summer of 1833* (London: Longman, 1835), 69.

structed by Agop and Sarkis Balyan to replace Mahmud II's palace; and he also renovated Sa'dabad (Çağlayan) Mosque, first erected in 1722 and restored during the reigns of Selim III and Mahmud II. In the *View from Kağıthane* by Salvatore Valeri, who came to İstanbul in the 1880s, Çağlayan summer palace is viewed from the same angle employed by Löwenhielm but at closer range. The minaret of Sa'dabad Mosque rises in the background. But the palace appearing in Valeri's picture seems to be the Çağlayan summer palace of Mahmud II rather than that of Abdülaziz in view of the roof covering and the bay windows carried by columns standing in the water. This suggests that the painting may have been executed with the aid of an engraving or a photograph.

Chelebowski, Court Artist under Abdülaziz, executed a vivid depiction of the animation and colorfulness of this excursion spot, much beloved by the sultan. In the foreground can be seen women holding parasols, in streetcoats and veils, approaching the bank of the stream in their caiques and women seated beneath the trees, accompanied by a black eunuch. Pitched tents appear on the left in the background, and venders have set up their stands and await customers. Attended by guards on white mounts, a coupé

ill. 2

ill. 2

ill. 2

belonging to members of an embassy and a European couple on horseback can be noted. Sa'dabad Mosque, built by Abdülaziz, stands in the background.

One other popular excursion spot was the area between the streams of Büyük Göksu issuing from the village of Anadoluhisarı and Küçük Göksu (Küçüksu) flowing from the village of Kandilli, both of which emptied into the Bosphorus. Ahmed Refik states that "what distinguished Göksu and Küçüksu from Kağıthane was the formers' quasi-official status as imperial excursion sites."[10] Those who lived on the European shore of the Bosphorus sailed across in a caique while those who lived on the Asian side would make their way here by ox-cart. Both the summer palace of Küçüksu and the Fountain of Küçüksu possessed a distinctive beauty. The fountain, erected in 1806 by Selim III for his mother Mihrişah Sultan was one of the most famed of all the public square fountains in İstanbul. "The season at Göksu started in the warm months," writes Sermet Muhtar Alus, "and ended when the weather became chilly....On Fridays and Sundays, the entire length of the stream would be completely filled with rowboats and skiffs and the meadows crowded with promenaders; it would be packed with a major proportion of the inhabitants of the Bosphorus and the city of İstanbul.".[11]

As disclosed by an announcement contained in the 5 October 1912 issue of *L'Illustration*, foreigners also held receptions here. The news-piece informs us that the wife of Bombard, the French ambassador, had arranged a pleasant party in the Sweet Waters of Asia on the Bosphorus at the time the most frightening news from the Balkans had been received and when the Italian fleet had begun to cruise the waters near the Dardanelles Strait.

> The guests in their light and elegant caiques, gondolas, and small steam-powered yachts, decked out charmingly with flowers, having arrived at their destination in the small bay of Kandıllı, surrounded the French ambassador's gala caique, which was powered by five pairs of rowers and decorated in a similar fashion with flowers and leaves, with a stylized rose in the bow while the stripes of the Tricolor trailed from the stern, licking the waters of the Bosphorus. On a signal given by the captain of the embassy's patrol boat, Jeanne-Blanche, ten rowers of the great caique swung to their

[10] Ahmed Refik, *Kafes* (İstanbul: Kitabevi, 1998), 84.

[11] Sermet Muhtar Alus, "Göksu ve Alemleri," *Resimli Tarih Mecmuası* (Ekim 1951): 1033.

239 Carl Gustaf Löwenhielm. *Kağıthane*. Watercolor on paper. 38 x 48 cm. National Museum, Stockholm.

240 Salvatore Valeri. *View from Kağıthane*. Oil on canvas. 86 x 117 cm. Dolmabahçe Palace Museum, İstanbul.

oars and…moved to the head of this floral-decked flotilla and just behind them the state caique of the German ambassador and all the other caiques and thus they reached the meadows of the Sweet Waters of Asia next to the sultan's white palace…resembling to perfection a Louis XV bonbonnière. Here, a magnificent table of refreshments was set up and the blue and red uniforms of the servants of the French embassy attracted a curious crowd to this area, which was one of the most popular promenades in the summer. Of a sudden, the authentic music of the indigenous drum and pipe—which destroys the eardrums and with which we have become familiar on the holiday celebrations of Constantinople held in the open air—began to be sounded: it was the guests dwelling in the surrounding villages who had arrived in prehistoric carts drawn by oxen and water buffalo and decorated by flowers and colorful carpets.

A short time later, the oarsmen began to dance the native dances, accompanied by this music. The "princesses" of the imperial dynasty who had come for the day were observing the guests

241-243 Stanislaw Chlebowski. *Kağıthane*. Oil on canvas. 62 x 102 cm. Military Museum, İstanbul.

242 Fausto Zonaro. *Amusements at Sweet Waters of Asia*. Oil on canvas. 65 x 94.5 cm. Collection of Suna and Inan Kıraç, İstanbul.

XIX Excursion sites

from the windows of Küçüksu Kasrı. In this fashion, everyone from the ordinary subjects and the humble rowers to the women of the House of Osman shared in this special festival, which was framed by the elegant and poetic setting of the Bosphorus.

ill. 244   The painting *Excursion to Sweet Waters of Asia* executed by Josef Warnia-Zarzecki (b. 1853) is a copy of the engraving captioned *The Valley of Kucuk Su, the Sweet Waters of Asia* in the book by Allom and Walsh titled *Constantinople and the Scenery of the Seven Churches of Asia Minor.*[12] Walsh describes the scene in the engraving, as follows:

> When parties proceed to those picnics, even the members of a family never mix. The unsocial jealousy of a Turk so separates the sexes, that the father, husband, and brother are never seen in the same groups with their female relatives. The women assemble on one side round the fountain, and the men on the other, under the trees. Between, are the various persons who vend refreshments to both indiscriminately. On the left is the *tchorba-gee* mixing sherbet....On the other side is a vender of *yaourt*. The itinerant confectioner is always a necessary person at these meetings. He carries about upon his head a large wooden tray, and under his arm, a stand with three legs. When required, he sets his stand, and lays his tray upon covered with good things. The first is a composition of ground rice boiled to the consistence of a jelly, light and transparent, called *mahalabie*;...The next is *halva*, a composition of flour and honey, which separates into flakes;...the fourth...is the most highly-prized confection of the Turks, who call it by a very appropriate name, *rahat locoom*, or "comfort to the throat," which it well merits.
>
> However, of all the refreshments sought for, simple water is perhaps the most in request and in all convivial picnics on the grass, the *sougee*, or "water vender," is in the greatest request. He is everywhere seen moving about, with his clear glass cup in one hand, and his jar with a long spout in the other, and the cry constantly heard is *sou, soook-sou*, "water, cold water."...In the illustration is seen one of those magnificent fountains, by which the Turks express their respect for the precious fluid. The front is the reservoir into which the water pours. This is

[12] Walsh, 1: Pl.32.
[13] Walsh, 1: 33–4.
[14] Walsh, 1: 32.
[15] Nerval, *The Women*, 2: 383.
[16] Charles Mac Farlane, *Constantinople in 1828* (London: Saunders and Otley, 1829), 2: 516.

generally surrounded with gilded cups or basins, and a dervish, or other person, stands beside them to dispense the water. Among the fruit sold is the grape. The Turks cultivate a peculiar kind, called *chaoush*; it is large, white, and sweet, and consumed in great quantities....Among the sellers of refreshments, is the *oozoom-gee*, who weighs out his fine fruit at five paras, or less than one halfpenny, per pound.[13]

One portion of the wooden Küçüksu Palace, demolished during the reign of Abdülmecid, can be seen behind the Küçüksu Fountain, which stylistically exemplifies the transitional period between the baroque and Empire styles. Walsh indicates that the sultan in order to practice archery or shooting or to amuse himself with other kinds of sports customarily withdrew to this palace in summer.[14]

Excursions involved lengthy preparations and the cooking of picnic dishes. On reaching the recreation spot and alighting from the carts and caiques, light mattresses topped by coverings would be spread on the ground, and food and drink would be taken out of their containers to set out the meal. Also on the scene were sellers of watermelon, corn on the cob, sesame and walnut halwah, and beverages such as sweetened fruit juice. Musicians and fortunetellers also represented an inseparable element. Until evening, all would promenade, eat and drink, sing songs, and dance folk dances when again food would be eaten and, after coffee, preparations would be made for the return home, and they would set off in their carts and caiques.

Foreign travelers often frequented Göksu and Kağıthane in order to observe the local inhabitants. What was most discussed in the passages in their memoirs devoted to these excursion spots was the beauty detected beneath the veils of the women. As was remarked by Gerard de Nerval, "[i] f the women are more or less hidden beneath their veils, they do not try too cruelly to hide themselves from the curiosity of the Franks."[15] Similarly, in 1828, Charles Mac Farlane, on his return from an outing in İstanbul, relates with astonishment that when he turned his head to look at a group of Muslim women, three of the women in the group, one by one, lifted their veils and showed their faces.[16] The fact that women **ill.** appeared out of doors in this manner and went as a group to the excursion spots, brought their clothing and adornment under public scrutiny: the ferace which was a plain outdoors garment would be transformed...Later it became even more lively with the use of bright and cheerful colors... High headgear with crests, covered with a thin veil would be accompanied by pleated silk parasols, the same color as ferace, with jeweled handgrips.[17]

244 Josef Warnia-Zarzecki. *Excursion to Sweet Waters of Asia*. Oil on canvas. 60 x 80 cm. Private Collection, İstanbul.

[17] Hülya Tezcan, "16–17. Yüzyıl Osmanlı Sarayında Kadın Modası," *P Dergisi* (Kış '98–99): 69.

244
▼

Besides the women they saw at the excursion spots the ox carts also called excursion carriages used for these outings also attracted the interest of the Westerners. On 26 October 1855, Mrs. Edmund Hornby who went to the Göksu excursion spot described her impressions of these carriages/carts as follows:

245 Fausto Zonaro. *Portrait of a Lady.*
Pastel on cardboard. 70.5 x 51.5 cm.
Collection of Sevgi and Doğan Gönül,
İstanbul.

XIX Excursion sites

The most curious-looking equipages at the Sweet Waters are the *araba*s, a huge kind of wagon, made of dark oak, rudely carved and ornamented, and drawn by two white oxen, caparisoned in the most fantastic manner. The collars, four or five feet high, are covered with scarlet tassels, and long crimson cords run from the collar to the tail of the animals, which they hold up most becomingly in a kind of festoon. Round the neck of each ox is a string of blue or many-colored beads, as a charm against the evil eye; and the forehead and each cheek of the gentle animals is slightly tinged with red paint. A handsome canopy of scarlet cloth, (sometimes even of velvet), embroidered with gold and trimmed with gold fringe, protects the veiled ladies, children, and black slaves inside from the sun. The large cushions of the *araba* are often made of the same rich materials; so I leave you to imagine what a mixture of magnificence and extreme rudeness is to be seen here.[18]

Another kind of cart used to travel to places in the countryside was a Balkan type of light covered vehicle open at the sides [*talika*]. Mrs. Hornby compares these curtained carts drawn by horse or donkey to Cinderella's fairy-tale pumpkin carriage.[19]

246 Amadeo Preziosi. *Ox-cart*, 1847. Watercolor and pencil on paper. 46 x 61 cm. Collection of Danielle and Hasan Kınay, İstanbul.

247 Giovanni Brindesi. *Talika.* Hand-colored lithograph. 22 x 33 cm. Collection of Güner and Haydar Akın.

[18] Edmund Hornby (Mrs.), *In and Around İstanbul* (Philadelphia: James Challen, 1863), 69–70.

[19] Hornby, 70.

◄ **246**

◄ **247**

XX Coffee houses

Coffee and coffeehouses made a strong contribution to the dissemination of Eastern influence in the West. First introduced to Europe by travelers to the Orient, coffee was originally employed as a kind of pharmaceutical, and it became increasingly sought for its properties as a stimulant. The earliest coffeehouse in Europe was opened in Venice in 1630, and, due to its popularity, it soon afterwards appeared in London, where by the 1700s, the number of coffeehouses had reached five hundred. The fashion of coffee drinking in France was introduced by several citizens who had formerly been to the Ottoman Empire, but it experienced a surge when Süleyman Agha arrived as envoy in 1669. By the eighteenth century, coffee had become a facet of daily life, and it was customary for men and women of the nobility to extend invitations to gatherings at which coffee was served. In all likelihood, Madame de Pompadour, the mistress of Louis XV, sat as a model for the painting by Carle Van Loo titled *A Princess Having Coffee Served by a Negress*. A treatise on the virtues of coffee titled *Eloge du Café* also appeared in print at this time.[1]

Depictions of the women of the harem drinking coffee constitute a frequent theme in Orientalist harem scenes. Indeed, the ritual of serving coffee did at one time occupy an important place in the homes of Constantinople. In order to carry out this ritual service, one needed both a special coffee set and female servants to prepare and serve the coffee. A wide variety of coffee sets were available, and they served as indicators both of the elegance and the wealth of their owners. The primary component of the ceremony of coffee service was the *sitil*, which is a kind of small brazier, made of copper-gilt, silver, brass or copper. The brazier was carried by a ring from which were suspended three chains attached to the margin of the brazier. Hot charcoal was placed on top of ashes in the brazier. A cover pierced with holes enclosed this fire. The coffee pot would be placed on this cover. In her Court memoirs, Leyla Saz states that while one of the servants bore the brazier, another serving girl would bring the thin porcelain cups, nestled in their holders of gold or silver openwork tracery. The coffee cups were placed on a serving tray covered by a cloth of silk or velvet, embroidered in gold and sometimes with pearls, and one end of which hung down from the tray. Finally, a third serving girl would fill the cups with coffee and place them one by one in their holders. Their presentation to the guest would be accomplished by picking them up, one by one, with the tip of the index finger supporting the base of the holder, balanced by the thumb lightly touching the rim of the cup. The requisites involved of performing this domestic ritual suggest why its practice in this form was exclusive to well-to-do families.[2]

[1] The full title of this work being *Recueil de chansons sur l'usage du café, du chocolat et du Ratafia*, cited in Desmet–Grégiore, 88.

[2] Saz, 108.

248 Jean Baptiste Van Mour, *Turkish Girl Drinking Coffee on a Divan, Recueil Ferriol,* (1712-13).

249 Cornelis de Bruyn, *Woman with a Terpuş, Reisen van Cornelis de Bruyn,* (1698).

250-251-252 Artist unknown. *Lady Drinking Coffee*. Oil on canvas. 112 x 101.5 cm. Collection of Sevgi and Doğan Gönül, Istanbul.

Though the artist of the oil painting titled *Lady Drinking Coffee* is unknown, the source of its inspiration is clear—the engraving by Jean Baptiste Van Mour of *A Turkish Girl Drinking Coffee on a Divan* from the album *Recueil de cent estampes représentant différentes nations du Levant tirées sur les tableaux peints d'apres nature*. Here, however—unlike Van Mour, who delineated the servant standing with her back to the viewer, holding a coffee ewer in one hand and a plate in the other—the artist has positioned the servant figure kneeling and holding only a plate, with her face is turned toward the viewer, and shifted her from the left-hand side of the composition to the right. The lady, sitting cross-legged, is attired in a chemise of white silk gauze, a robe of silk-cotton blend, a belt with a golden buckle, and a red, outer caftan lined with ermine, a sumptuous outfit appropriate to eighteenth-century fashion. However, her headdress bound by a number of colored scarves and draped with a string of beads is excessively large and exaggerated. Both the necklace around the neck of the lady and the headdress are copied from the picture of two women with special headgear in *Reisen van Cornelis de Bruyn* first published in 1698 by Cornelis de Bruyn, a Dutchman like Van Mour.[3] It may be inferred that the posture and the clothes of the woman were borrowings from Van Mour, the jewelry and the headdress from de Bruyn.

The serving of coffee attained the status of a ceremonial among females in the domestic sphere while among males outside the home it led to the creation of a special kind of meeting place. Foreign travelers and artists expressed a keen interest in the coffeehouses of İstanbul. Coffee arrived in İstanbul in 1519, but it became widely known only in the second half of the sixteenth century. In 1554, Hakem of Aleppo and Şems of Syria opened the first coffeehouse in the Golden Horn district of Tahtakale in İstanbul. On the introduction of tobacco soon after that of coffee, they became an inseparable duo, with the tobacco habit accelerating the fondness for coffee even more.

The Ottoman male, whose life had been divided between home, the mosque, and the workplace, now acquired a new activity with the advent of neighborhood coffeehouses opening at the end of the sixteenth century. Adding a new dimension to social life, the majority of these coffeehouses, a setting for discourse and a forum for the discussion of current and other issues, were open all night throughout the month of Ramadan. In time, coffeehouses diversified: one kind, known as *semai*, specialized in the performance of epics and folk songs by minstrels, and another kind provided a haunt for firefighters; others, concentrated in the vicinity of the markets, drew the custom of artisans and tradesmen, and yet others became the special preserve of artists and players. D'Ohsson's work on Ottoman customs and traditions in the eighteenth century reveals that the streets and avenues in nearly every district of İstanbul boasted coffeehouses and that they were built on attractive sites in the form of a kiosk, with most of them affording beautiful vistas.[4] Writing roughly a century after D'Ohsson, Edmondo De Amicis states

> Coffe is drunk on the summits of Galata and Serasker towers, you find it on the steamboats, in the cemeteries, in the barber shops, the baths, the bazaars. In whatever part of Constantinople you may happen to be, if you merely call out "Café-gi!" without taking the

[3] Cornelis de Bruyn, *Reisen van Cornelis de Bruyn* (Delft: Henrik van Krooneveld, 1698), 34.

[4] D'Ohsson, 4:81.

254
▼

253-254 Theodore Frère. *Coffeehouse on the Shore of the Bosphorus.* Oil on canvas. 32 x 62.5 cm. Collection of Yüksel Pekiş Behlil, İstanbul.

[5] De Amicis, 1:106.

255 Artist unknown. *Coffeehouse in Tophane*. Oil on canvas. 62 x 84 cm. Private Collection, İstanbul.

trouble to leave your seat, in three minutes a cup is steaming before you.[5]

Charles Theodore Frère (1814–88), arriving in İstanbul in 1851 for a stay of eighteen months, depicts in his *Coffeehouse on the Shore of the Bosphorus* the open-air section of a coffeehouse situated beneath an arbor, filled with customers. Other customers are seated beyond the arbor on benches, smoking the water pipe and playing backgammon. One male figure, garbed in a yellow robe and white turban, has just alighted from a caique and is making his way toward the coffeehouse.

The coffeehouses of İstanbul can be classified into different types: those containing both summer and winter quarters, those in the open-air and open only in summer, and the movable cof-

ill. 2

ill. 2

feehouse. The movable coffeehouse, that De Amicis, refers to was run by an itinerant coffeemaker, who typically chose a place where he could kneel or sit and who provided low stools for his customers; the only other articles he required were a brazier and a coffee set and a box to place them on. In an article on coffeehouse architecture (*Kahvehane Mimarisi*), Rıfat Uzman indicates that winter coffeehouses had a shoe rack for one's shoes in the entryway, which led to a large space edged by a divan that measured, as in guest rooms in villages, some eighty centimeters wide and twenty-five to thirty centimeters high. At the back of the room was a hearth flanked by built-in cupboards with doors. In the corner opposite the fireplace was situated the principal divan—reminiscent in form of the private area reserved for the sultan in an imperial mosque—enclosed by a railing and with access provided by a narrow stairway of two steps. These special corner divans were reserved for the privileged regular customer. Close by this divan was a small walnut chest with a few drawers. In front of this chest a sheepskin was laid out. This place belonged to the proprietor of the coffeehouse and near it, stood a counter displaying all the utensils and vessels for the making and serving of coffee. The surface of the hood and the mantel of the elegant fireplaces found in these old coffeehouses were ornamented as was the niche with shelves on either side, on which were arranged the coffee cups and cup holders. Finally, in proximity to the niche were tall, narrow built-in cupboards with wooden doors for storage of the pipes with long stems and the mouthpieces for the water pipes.[6]

In a special issue of *Figaro Illustré* (October 1908) on Constantinople, the painter Osman Hamdi Bey contributed an interesting article on the coffeehouses of the city in which he noted that the cupboards and shelves on either side of the fireplace boasted tin boxes of sugar, glass jars of coffee, backgammon sets, and playing cards, plates for serving Turkish Delight candy, packets of Iranian tobacco, which was coarsely shredded, moist and fragrant, specially obtained and brought by caravan for the water pipe habitués from Yazd and Shiraz and he concludes his article, as follows:

> From dawn to dusk, imams, hodjas, soldiers,
> and wealthy citizens entered these
> low-ceilinged places in a steady flow and...

◄ 256

◄ 257

[6] Süheyl Ünver, *Türkiye'de Kahve ve Kahvehaneler* (Ankara: Türk Tarih Kurumu, 1963), 60.

256 Artist unknown. *Coffeehouse in Tophane*. Watercolor on paper. Collection of Ersin Börteçen, İstanbul.

257 Thomas Allom. *Coffeehouse in Tophane. Constantinople and the Scenery of Seven Churches of Asia Minor*, (1838).

258 Amadeo Preziosi. *Turkish Coffeehouse, Constantinople*, 1854. Pencil and watercolor on paper. 40.7 x 58.8 cm. Searight Collection, Victoria and Albert Museum, London.

[7] O. Hamdy Bey, "Les Cafés de Stamboul," *Figaro Illustre: Constantinople* (Octobre 1908).

[8] Walsh, 1: Pl. 59.

no one was ever disturbed by the tradesmen, small shopkeepers, ordinary subjects, or members of even more lowly classes, and one could converse with them for hours in the most democratic, frankest and most sincere manner possible. This democratic manner of thought, innate to Turks, and their avoidance of alcoholic beverages, like wine and liqueur, contributed more than is supposed to the peaceful transformation that put its stamp on the Constitutional Monarchy.[7]

The coffeehouse that comprises the subject of an oil painting by an unknown artist, a second one rendered in watercolor, and that in an engraving contained in *Constantinople and the Scenery of the Seven Churches of Asia Minor* is one and the same.[8] Robert Walsh, who wrote the text for this engraving titled *Coffeehouse in Tophane*, done after a sketch by Thomas Allom, indicates that

ill. 2
ill. 2
ill. 2

[t] he edifice is generally decorated in a very gorgeous manner, supported on pillars, and open in front. Its interior space is defined by a wall-to-wall raised platform, covered with mats or cushions, on which the Turks sit cross-legged. On one side are musicians, generally Greeks, with mandolins and tambourines, accompanying singers... and the loud and obstreperous concert forms a strong contrast to the stillness and taciturnity of Turkish meetings....The coffee is served in very small cups, not larger than egg-cups... Besides the ordinary chibouk for tobacco, there is another implement, called narghile, used for smoking in a caffinet, of a more elaborate construction....In the centre of the room is generally an artificial fountain, bubbling and playing in summer, and round it vases of flowers, with piles of the sweet-scented melons of Cassaba, to keep them cool, and add, by their odour, to the fragrance of the flowers. A frequent addition to the enjoyments of the caffinet, is the medac, or storyteller. There are several of these public characters at Constantinople, who, at festival seasons, are engaged by the caffinet-ghees to entertain their guests. On these occasions, to accommodate the increased company, stools are placed in semicircles in the streets before the caffinet, and refreshment sent from the house. A small platform is laid on the open window, so that the audience within and without may hear and see. On this the storyteller mounts, and continues his narrative sometimes till midnight.[9]

[9] Walsh, 1: 60–1.
[10] Abdülaziz Bey, 1: 305–6.

A pool with jets like these in the central area of the coffeehouse appears in *Turkish Coffeehouse, Constantinople*, rendered in pencil and watercolor by Amadeo Preziosi in 1854. On the divans around the perimeter of the pool are İstanbul residents of every race and occupation, sitting cross-legged and drinking coffee and smoking a clay pipe or the water pipe. Among them is a Mevlevî dervish, an Iranian and some Greek youths, each in their respective characteristic dress, a black servant, and men with turbans and robes. In a high recess on the left is seated a two-person musical ensemble. Preziosi, whose travel memoirs were among the best selling of those foreigners who had been to İstanbul, rightly emphasized in his works in water color the cosmopolitan nature of the city's population and depicted representatives of the different races, religions, and occupations sharing the same setting. The accessories in the pictures by the artist are very rich and detailed. Thus, in this coffeehouse, we see, on the left, stools with seats of woven rushes and wooden clogs and, on the wall a small chest with mother-of-pearl inlay and beyond that a group of narghiles, and, in front of the fireplace with baroque ornamentation, a large earthenware jar and water jugs, clay pipes, coffee cups with holders—nearly every kind of object that might be found in a coffeehouse.

Until the type of barbershop known as *perûkâr* opened during the reign of AbdülhamidII, the workplace of the barber trade was the coffeehouse. The customers were the neighborhood residents while those of the higher classes had barbers come to their homes.

When a customer came the barber would seat him in front of him, open a bundle of clean towels, tie on an apron of silk from Bursa, cover his shoulders with towels with silk borders, and then pour hot water into the polished brass barber jug with spigot, which hung suspended from a wall bracket and wet his head thoroughly and taking the strop razor from its case and stropping it a few times on the strop tucked in at his waist and, uttering the formulaic benediction, would begin to shave the head of his customer. On completing the shave and the shaping of the beard with a pair of scissors, he would sprinkle into his palm a few drops of clove oil from a bottle hanging on the wall and massage it into the scalp well to ward off a chill and then the hair clippings would be shaken into a box standing in one corner of the coffeehouse. The emptying of the filled box of clippings into the sea used to be assigned great importance. Removing the towels after the shave, the barber would hand a small hand mirror inlaid with mother-of-pearl to the customer. After a careful inspection of his work by the customer and attending to any further modifications requested, the barber would extend the traditional blessing of "May you enjoy good health!" (*Sıhhatler olsun*).[10]

Among the duties performed by these barbers were the pulling of teeth, circumcisions, and cupping. Besides the class of barbers who worked in coffeehouses, there were also itinerant barbers,

who set up shop on the street, in the marketplace, or in front of a mosque. In his illustrations of Eastern ethnic types appearing in *L'Illustration*—a publication that played a very significant role in acquainting the West with the Ottoman Empire—Alexandre Bida devoted two to a coffeehouse on the shore of the Bosphorus and an Armenian barber shaving his customer. In De Mango's depiction, the barber has a turban on his head and so that the customer can see that his hands and feet are clean, he has rolled up his sleeves and is barefoot. Reşat Ekrem Koçu states that the barbers and their apprentices were required by an order of the cadi to work barefoot or in clogs with bare feet summer and winter and that this requirement arose because a naked foot could be cleaned more easily than a stockinged foot.[11] Here we see that the barber has spread a large towel over the customer's shoulders and that hanging on the wall are the barber's bowl, mirror, and strop razor.

[11] Reşat Ekrem Koçu, *Türk Giyim, Kuşam ve Süslenme Sözlüğü* (Ankara: Sümerbank Kültür Yayınları, 1967), 34.

259 Leonardo de Mango. *Barber*, 1877. Oil on canvas. 43 x 31 cm. Collection of Duran Tamtekin, İstanbul.

260 Alexandre Bida. "Coffeehouse on the Bosphorus," *L'Illustration* (29 Sept, 1849).

261 Alexandre Bida. "Armenian Barber," *L'Illustration* (29 Sept, 1849).

260

261

XXI The court and photography

Photography was accepted as part and parcel of modernization, and, just as with the westernization of architecture and the art of painting in the aftermath of the nineteenth-century reforms instituted in the Ottoman Empire, it was supported by the Court. The interest shown in photography in the second half of the nineteenth century by the Levantines, servants of the Court, bureaucrats, and high-ranking military officers rapidly developed and spread. Photography, which provided more satisfactory results in transmitting an image than paintings was taken up by members of these elite circles and the "Court Photographer" assumed a place beside that of the "Court Artist." But in this era, when the boundary between painting and photography was still indistinct, the definition of "artist" was applied equally to the photographer.

Constantinople's introduction to photography coincides with the early years of Abdülmecid's reign. Europeans invited to the city in connection with the reform activities, became the first to exploit this new invention. In the framework of Abdülmecid's efforts to modernize the city, French engineer, Ernest de Caranza, presented to the sultan two series of photographs that he had shot in 1852 and 1854.[1]

One of the first photography studios was opened in the 1850s by the Greek Vasilaki Kargopoulo (1827–86) in the district of Pera. Kargopoulo, whose first studio stood next to the Russian embassy on Pera Avenue, later moved to Tünel Square no. 4. Becoming known among the Court circles in 1860, the popularity of photography in İstanbul appears to have steadily grown. Kargopoulo, whose principal clientele was composed of the imperial family, upper-level bureaucrats, statesmen, and military personnel, was awarded an appointment by Abdülhamid II as "Palace Photographer" in early 1879. Kargopoulo, who photographed scenes of the city, panoramas of the Bosphorus, venders, and subjects in ethnic

costume that were enthusiastically received by travelers to İstanbul, was the first Ottoman subject to become a professional photographic artist.[2]

The Briton, James Robertson (1813–88), a master engraver, was invited to İstanbul to work as chief engraver in the Imperial Mint, which had undergone modernization during the reign of Abdülmecid and came into operation in 1843. In the 1850s, Robertson established a partnership with his brother-in-law, Felice Beato, and set up a photography studio in Pera that remained in operation until 1867. Robertson also had a studio in Malta, and he established connections with studios not only in İstanbul and Malta but also in Europe for the sale of his photographs. One quality possessed by his photographs that derived from his being a master engraver was their resemblance to the exotic Oriental engravings contained in nineteenth-century travelogues. Robertson's photographs were published in London in 1853 by Joseph Cundall as *Photographic Views of Constantinople*. An album published in Trieste in 1854 titled *Souvenirs de Constantinople* containing twenty-one plates consisted in photographs by James Robertson. A pioneer in journalistic photography because of the photographs he took in connection with the Crimean War, Robertson remained in İstanbul, photographing various parts of the city and daily life, until he retired and went to Japan in 1881.[3]

The art of photography began to gain popularity in the Ottoman Empire during the reign of Abdülaziz and in 1863; the Abdullah Frères earned official status with their appointment as the sultan's photographers. The Abdullah Frères were influential in the development of the art of photography in İstanbul and became renowned for their photographs with Orientalist content. In order to learn about photography, the invention of the era, Kevork (1839–1918) and Viçen Abdullah (1820–1906) went first to Italy and then to Paris the photography center of the period, and

ill. 2

[1] B. A. Henisch and H. K. Henisch, "James Robertson," *Visions of the Ottoman Empire*, exhibition catalog (Edinburgh: Scottish National Portrait Gallery, 1994), 81.

[2] Bahattin Öztuncay, *Vasilaki Kargopulo Hazret–i Pâdişâhi'nin Ser Fotografı*, (İstanbul: Birleşik Oksijen, 2000), 9–10, 14.

[3] *James Robertson, İstanbul Fotoğrafçısı*, sergi kataloğu (İngiliz Kültür Heyeti ve Edinburgh İskoç Ulusal Portre Galerisi), 8.

262 James Robertson and Felice Beato.
At the Fountain of Ahmed III. Istanbul, ca.
1850s. Albumen Print. Scottish National
Portrait Gallery.

XXI The court and photography

on their return to İstanbul they brought a letter of recommendation to the French ambassador, Marquis de Moustier. Written by Count Olympe Aguado, the letter expressed the desire that "these young men should be recommended to the eminent imperial dignitaries and generals of Turkey inasmuch as they were deserving of every kind of encouragement and assistance."[4] The role played by the embassies in the artists' coming to the attention of the Court is noteworthy.

Photography was included as a branch in the Paris International Exhibition of 1867, to which Abdülaziz had paid a visit. At this exhibition, the Abdullah Frères exhibited a series of photographs, including one of Sultan Abdülaziz; other specimens in this series of photographs included the French foreign minister; a former ambassador to İstanbul, Marquis de Moustier; the embassy secretary de Bonnière; Keun, the Belgian minister plenipotentiary; Davud Pasha, the governor general of Lebanon; the Egyptian Boghoz Bey; the İstanbul Armenian Catholic Bishop Gr. Hassoun; M.Camondo, one of the prominent wealthy Jewish entrepreneurs of Galata; and numerous Levantine women. In addition, the Abdullah Frères exhibited four panoramic vistas of İstanbul. Two of these were taken from the Serasker Tower in Beyazıd, one from the Maritime Arsenal on the Golden Horn, and the final one was from Galata Tower, whose legend read "View of the Golden Horn." Also included in the exhibition were photographs introducing a group of weapons and domestic costumes of Constantinople.[5] All the photographs exhibited by the Abdullah Frères bore a high documentary value, and it is clear that they were greeted with interest by European visitors curious about the exoticism of the East.

The Abdullah Frères, whose İstanbul photographs at the 1867 Paris Salon were met with broad approval, exhibited in their photographic studio and shop window certain photographs as well as paintings by Osman Hamdi Bey, Sarkis Direnyan,[6] and Chlebowski. A small canvas exhibited by Chlebowski was titled *Entrance to a Moorish Bath*, based on a study he brought from Egypt, and which he presented to the Abdullah Frères.[7]

In an article appearing in the 4 July 1874 issue of *L'Orient Illustré*, it is reported that the sultan had invited the Abdullah Frères to Dolmabahçe Palace and had a number of shots taken of himself and on the same date two Ottoman periodicals—the magazine *Mecmua-i Maarif* and the newspaper *Şark*—also note that by order of the ruler it was forbidden for other artists and photographers to copy any pictures of the sultan, the princes and the dynasty produced by others. One of these sources referred to the Abdullah Frères as "His Imperial Majesty's Artists" and in another as "the renowned artists of Beyoğlu."[8]

After stressing the renown of the Abdullah Frères, it is stated in Murray's *Guide de Voyageur* that "one of the most valuable and interesting aspects of Constantinople, the capital of the Ottoman Empire, are the photographs taken by these masterful hands, and it is recommended that all foreigners who visit the city obtain their photographs."[9] Included in the photograph collection of the Abdullah Frères are various vistas of İstanbul and traditional artisans in their workplaces or at their portable workbench, inhabitants in regional dress, members of the imperial house, and miniature illuminations from Topkapı Palace, masterfully enlarged.[10]

Another of the famed photographic studios in Pera was the El-Şark opened on Postacılar Street in 1857 by Pascal Sébah (1823–86). Photographs for the catalog *Costumes Populaires de la Turquie* prepared by Osman Hamdi Bey for the 1873 Vienna International Exhibition were taken here by Pascal Sébah. It is known that Osman Hamdi Bey drew on photographs by Sébah for his Orientalist canvases. The photographs for which he or others served as a model served as sources for Osman Hamdi's principal compositional figures. The works by Pascal Sébah and Osman Hamdi Bey represent one of the finest examples of cooperation between artist and photographer.[11]

One piece appearing in the *L'Orient Illustré* (13 February 1875) contains the assertion that İstanbul was one of the best photography centers in the world and indicates that the methods of Nièpce and Daguerre were employed with success in Pera; and it is noted that Cosmi Sébah (? –1896) and his partners possessed a very beautiful collection of artistic works in their studios at 346 Pera Avenue. It claims that the hand-colored portraits in relief on glossy paper were excellent and that in the near future this chic establishment would become a modern meeting center. Pascal Sébah, who is identified as the winner of medallions and awards at the International Exhibitions of Paris, Vienna, and Philadelphia, opened a studio in Cairo in 1873 and in 1884 formed a partnership with Policarp Joaillier and this photogra-

[4] Engin Özendes, *Abdullah Frères: Osmanlı Sarayının Fotoğrafçıları* (İstanbul: Yapı Kredi Yayınları, 1998), 33.

[5] Salaheddin Bey, 144–5.

[6] Cezar, *Sanatta*, 439.

[7] *Levant Herald* (20 Oct. 1875): 369.

[8] Cezar, *Sanatta*, 151.

[9] Özendes, *Abdullah*, 45.

[10] Özendes, *Abdullah*, 45.

[11] Engin Özendes, *Sébah & Joilliers'den Foto Sabah'a Fotoğrafta Oryantalizm* (İstanbul: Yapı Kredi Yayınları, 1999), 181.

phy studio became known as the Sébah-Joaillier studio as of 1888.

In this period when the boundary between the art of photography and painting was still indefinite, an advertisement in the city guide by Mamboury indicates that artistic portraits in oil, pastel, and water color were executed by enlarging photographs in the photographic studio of Sébah and Joaillier, now located at 439 Pera Avenue, next to the Russian embassy. Moreover, it reported that the studio possessed Oriental costumes for purposes of posing and a large photographic collection of the historical monuments and views of İstanbul.[12] Though this studio was later sold to Agop İskender and Perpanyani, it enjoyed continued renown in İstanbul. Another photographic master who took documentary photographs of the city was Guillaume Berggren (1835–1920), who came to İstanbul from Sweden, and, on becoming captive to the mystery of the East, settled here and opened a studio at 414 Derviş Street in Pera in 1870.

Some portraits taken in the studio in these years were enlarged (by squaring for transfer) in the same studio and executed in oils; on this account, painters also found employment in photographic studios. In this era when the relation between photography and the art of painting was so very intimate, there were photographers who were also painters. The artistic talent of Viçen Abdullah, who executed miniature portraits of Sultans Abdülmecid and Abdülaziz and several top generals, led to his working as a touchup artist with the photographic studio of the German, Rabach, in the district of Beyazıt.[13]

Zonaro and his wife, who came to İstanbul in 1891, were artists who boosted the popularity of photography among Court circles. Zonaro, who was honored in 1896 with the title "Artist to His Imperial Majesty," received numerous portrait commissions. In his execution of the pictures of the harem women, it is obvious that his wife made a sizeable contribution. Elisa, who had been to Paris for eighteen months for instruction in photography, took pictures of the women in the harem on her return to İstanbul, which Zonaro transformed into oil paintings. In acknowledgment of her accomplishments, the sultan gave Elisa the title of "Official Portraitist of the Court." In October 1906, Teresita Menzigher, a journalist for the Italian magazine *La Donna*, requested an interview with Elisa Zonaro. When Menzigher arrived

[12] Ernest Mamboury, *Constantinople Guide Touristique* (Constantinople: Rizzo, 1925), 522.

[13] Özendes, *Abdullah*, 31

263 O. Kürkciyan. *Field Marshal Gazi Ahmed Muhtar Paşa*, 1910. 130 x 89 cm. Oil on canvas. Military Museum, İstanbul.

264 O. Kürkciyan. *Hafız Hakkı Paşa*, 1914. Atelier Phèbus. 130 x 88 cm. Oil on canvas. Military Museum, İstanbul.

XXI The court and photography

265 O. Kürkciyan. *Portrait of Sultan Selim I*. Atelier Phèbus. Oil on canvas. 100 x 72.5 cm. Collection of Sevgi and Doğan Gönül, İstanbul.

[14] *Le Tra,* 38–9.

at the Zonaro residence, she was met by Fausto Zonaro. While waiting for his wife, Zonaro related anecdotes about the paintings on the walls of their home. After Elisa joined them, Fausto Zonaro showed Elisa's photographic collection to Menzigher. These were stunning photographs not only of her husband's paintings but also of the women in the Imperial Harem. For Sultan Abdülhamid II had given permission to Elisa to take photographs in the Imperial Harem whenever she wished. Elisa told the journalist how happy the young women were about her coming to the Harem because they were ignorant of what was happening in the outside world, lonely, and hungry for novelty and how they had given thousands of different poses for the pictures and, afterwards, they had expressed their amazement at the photographs of themselves, like small girls.[14]

Among the leading photographers of Pera and the proprietor of Photo Phébus, Bogos Tarkulyan (? –1940) was a master artist who had taken art lessons for years and who practiced portrait painting. Bogos Tarkulyan earned the approval of Abdülhamid II with his works that constituted the first appearance of hand-colored photographs in the Empire and was rewarded with the title of "Court Photographer." O. Kürkciyan worked in the same studio in the early twentieth century and, in the light of the specimens in the İstanbul Military Museum and those now found in certain private collections, he also executed portraits in oils based on photographs from this studio.

Westernizing activities, in which the Court led the way during the period of reforms in the sphere of artistic activity, were adopted by Ottoman intellectuals, bureaucrats, and, in particular, higher ranking military officers; and the first contact such individuals had with the art of painting was obtained through the commissioning of their own portraits. The introduction of photography and the execution of portraits in oil by the use of enlarged photographs facilitated the task of artists working in this area. In this period when painting and photography were conceived as one, portraits were executed by artists who had received instruction in oil painting in photographic studios. The portraits of field marshal Gazi Ahmed Muhtar Pasha (1839–1918), and Hafız Hakkı Pasha (1879–1915) executed by O. Kürkciyan in the early twentieth century are representative examples. On the other hand, it may be recalled that paintings with Orientalist content

ill. 263

ill. 264

266 Simon Agopyan. *Sultan Mehmed V*,
1914-15. Atelier Apollon. 175 x 75 cm.
Oil on canvas. Military Museum, İstanbul.

were produced in photography studios with an eye towards sales. The portrait of Sultan Selim I, produced by Kürkciyan from an existing representation in the Phèbus Studios, also served as a model for a work by Halil Pasha.[15] In such examples, as in the portrait painting of Sultan Mehmed Reşad V, the name of the photography studio appears along with the name of the artist who produced the canvas.

Poses in ethnic costume and Eastern dress in the top photography studios of İstanbul became common in this period. The poses arranged by the photographers conformed to themes beloved in Orientalist pictures: Gypsy dancers, camels with riders, and Bedouins were popular in Cairo while in İstanbul shots were frequently composed of a woman stretched out on a divan in Oriental attire with a water pipe in her hand and a table inlaid in mother of pearl next to the divan. To attract the attention of Europeans visiting İstanbul, Sébah-Joaillier studio, which turned out pictures of Eastern women, produced a series of the "woman in the harem." Because it was impossible to obtain Muslim women as sitters, the models employed were selected from among those who worked in the brothels of Pera. Compositions were also arranged employing Western female visitors to the empire or even, in a pinch, males.[16] Outside the studio, subjects frequently exploited by the photographer were popular local images, such as palaces, mosques, fountains, coffeehouses, women on excursions in the countryside, firemen, venders, streets, cemeteries, and Mevlevî whirling dervishes. Thus, a parallel can be observed in the choice of subject between photography and the art of painting.

Surviving specimens allow us to infer that the art of photography was popular in İstanbul in the late nineteenth and early twentieth centuries. Travelers to İstanbul used to don Eastern costumes in the photographic studios in Pera and have souvenir photos taken; whereas, the members of the Ottoman Court, top-ranking bureaucrats, and military officers most often had their likenesses taken with their families in single or group photographs. The women of the Court, in particular, expressed an interest in photography at quite an early date. In the list of names in the inheritance inventory of Princess Refia (1842–80), the daughter of Sultan Abdülmecid, Court Artist Abdullah Effendi appears as one of the creditors (with a debt of 2,500 piasters). The estate of the

267 "Adorning in the Harem," *Figaro Illustré, Constantinople* (1908).

deceased princess includes "one album of miscellaneous photographs." Both Princess Refia and others in her retinue had had numerous photographs taken, of which some were indicated in the inheritance inventory as having been framed and inserted in albums.[17] Münevver Ayaşlı relates in her book titled *Dersâadet* that, on going to the palace of Princess Saliha, a daughter of Abdülaziz, immediately after the sultans had been expelled from the Ottoman Empire, she observed that it contained a very rich photograph collection.

There were photographs signed by all the sultans and princes and pictures of all the Processions of Salutation since the invention of photography, and of all the foreign rulers and their wives who had visited the empire. This photograph collection, irreplaceable and a historical treasure, was deemed worthless by the antique dealer who purchased the furnishings and antiques of the Palace and was thrown into the sea.[18]

[15] The painting by Halil Pasha of Selim I is identical with that by Kürkciyan. Taha Toros, "Halil Paşa," *Antik–Dekor* 45: 73.

[16] Özendes, *Sébah*, 166

[17] Akyıldız, 99, 107, and 166.

[18] Münevver Ayaşlı, *Dersâadet* (İstanbul: Bedir Yayınları, 1993), 130.

Exploiting the virtues of photography, Abdülhamid II had photographic albums prepared as documentary records and sent them to the United States and England as gifts. Pictures are rare of Abdülhamid II, although he assigned importance to photography and also took photographs himself, because he granted no permission for the taking of his own photograph.

In addition to portraits, views of picturesque spots in the city were included in the domain of the photographer's interest. Replication of the scenes that had composed the subject matter of engravings and oil painting since the beginning of the nineteenth century in İstanbul was attempted in photography. For instance, in the Nadir Photography studio, located at 473 Pera Avenue, vistas of Constantinople and views in stereoscope, large scale photographs of the Bosphorus and the Golden Horn were available.[19]

Photography's contribution to orientalist art

The top photography studios of İstanbul were active in their attempt to identify those views and images that would satisfy the tastes of the period and, at the same time, supply materials to Orientalist artists. Abdullah Frères furnished photographs to Jean-Léon Gérôme and those taken by Sebah and Joillier were employed by Osman Hamdi. It was an accepted practice for Orientalist artists to draw on photographs in the execution of their paintings. For the itinerant Orientalist artists, who laid much stress on credibility and detail in their rendering of the subject, photography facilitated their task in various respects in the process of depicting the subject selected for any certain work. In Islamic cities where these artists were foreigners, it was either impossible for them to work whether in the open air or in the mosque or where permissions difficult to be obtained. Reliance on the photograph allowed them to complete the painting in a studio without having to deal with these kinds of formalities and without being disturbed while working. Some of these photographs were, as in the case of Osman Hamdi Bey and Gérôme, taken by the artists themselves.

At the beginning of the century, some of the views of Constantinople in oils had been based on executed engravings, but by the second half of the century, the photograph had replaced the engraving. Examples of painted landscapes exe-

[19] Özendes, *Abdullah*, 18.

268 Abdullah Frères. *Marketplace in Üsküdar*, ca, 1890. IRCICA, Yıldız Palace Photograph Collection.

cuted by relying on photographs are quite common. In comparison to vistas delineated from engravings, where the artist's imagination came frequently into play, those landscapes based on photographs are realistic.

Postcards

On the other hand, it is evident that views of İstanbul determined by photographs were disseminated in reproduction as postcards. The demand for these subjects was directly created by European travelers visiting the city. In a sense, one might state that, by the means of the post, postcards insured that the mode of Orientalism in the early twentieth century would reach a mass audience. Illustrated postcards (*Cartes Postales Illustrées*) first appeared on the Western market in 1891. The pioneer in the publication of postcards in İstanbul was Max Fruchtermann, who sold postcards, first at 13 Yüksekkaldırım and later in his shop on Grand Rue de Pera , from the 1890s until 1915. The main publishers of postcards in the city were J. Ludwingsohn, the Sarrafian Brothers, Römmler-Jonas, A. Zellich Fils, Au Bon Marché, and Georges Papantoine. The subjects related to Constantinople among these postcards ranged from portraits of the sultan to vistas of the city, from historical monuments to women wearing the latest fashion at the end of the century.[20] The postcards were usually produced from typical specimens of the top photography studios. Occasionally, the same view was employed in a photograph, a postcard, and an oil painting. For instance, one photograph of a street in Üsküdar taken by the Abdullah Frères in the 1890s was **ill. 268** transposed by Jean-Emile Laurent (1906-?) into an **ill. 269** oil painting, which was published by the shop, Au Bon Marché as a postcard, with the result that it served as a source for an oil painting, a rare work of art, as well as a touristic souvenir.

269 Jean-Emile Laurent. *Marketplace.* Oil on canvas. Collection of Hilal Arslan, İstanbul.

[20] Ahmet Eken, *Kartpostallarda İstanbul* (İstanbul: İstanbul Büyük Şehir Belediyesi Kültür İşleri Daire Başkanlığı Yayınları, 1992), 10–1.

The spread of photography in the Ottoman Empire generated interesting outcomes not only from the standpoint of the Western travelers and painters who visited the city, but also from the perspective of Ottoman painting. At the end of the nineteenth century the offering of painting classes as part of the science curriculum in the military and civilian schools in İstanbul led to the formation of a new and singular group of painters These painters, who are known as "Primitives" made quasi identical enlarged copies of the original photographs. A great proportion of the paintings executed by them during the reign of Abdülhamid II were made after photographs taken from the gardens of Yıldız Palace and other monumental buildings, palaces and kiosks of İstanbul. These paintings occupy an important place in the history of Ottoman and Turkish painting, because they demonstrate the role of photography and are the earliest examples depicting Ottoman palace structures.

ill. 270
ill. 271

270 Vasilaki Kargopoulo. *Ihlamur Summer Palace*. IRCICA, Yıldız Palace Photograph Collection, İstanbul.

XXI The court and photography

271 İbrahim. *Ihlamur Summer Palace*. Oil
on canvas. 62 x 92 cm. Museum of
Painting and Sculpture, Mimar Sinan
University, İstanbul.

XXII An Ottoman Orientalist: Osman Hamdi Bey

In place of a conclusion, it seemed fitting to close this work by the presentation of a profile of Osman Hamdi Bey, who was not only a recognized Orientalist artist of Constantinople, but he also set the Ottoman stamp on this artistic style.

Intimate with the cultures of both the East and the West and accounted as a symbol of Westernization in the Ottoman Empire due to his founding of institutions like the Imperial School of Fine Arts and the Archeological Museum, Osman Hamdi Bey was a man of many talents, among which his artistic talent was the most salient. In 1860, his father, İbrahim Edhem Pasha, sent Osman Hamdi to Paris for the study of law where, after a brief exposure to legal training, he turned to the fine arts and remained until 1869. The fact that his art instruction took place in Paris and that he was a student of Gérôme explains his closeness to the French Orientalists in terms of composition and figural conception. At this time, Jean-Léon Gérôme, who was the strongest representative of Orientalism both in his native land and in Europe and in the United States, represented the greatest influence on Osman Hamdi Bey during his stay in Paris. In terms of the subject matter and composition of Orientalist canvases, the artist's paintings bear a formal resemblance to those of his teacher, Gérôme and the Austrian Orientalists Ludwig Deutsch, and Rudolf Ernst.

Osman Hamdi Bey, who treats the people, their way of life, and the art of the Ottoman Empire in his paintings, carries the distinction of being the only Orientalist artist who was native to the East. The artist put forward his own cultural truths as a response to the ethnic and historical inaccuracies and the biased attitudes portrayed by the European Orientalists. Osman Hamdi Bey, who was also the first Ottoman archeologist, came to maturity during the period when a series of reforms aimed at Westernization were being implemented. Adopting European ways in his personal life, the artist elevated the Ottoman tra-

ill. 272

272 Pascal-Sébah. *Osman Hamdi*, ca. 1882-1885. IRCICA, Yıldız Palace Photograph Collection.

dition and culture in his Orientalist paintings. Osman Hamdi Bey executed both Orientalist paintings as well as a good number of paintings such as portraits of family members and landscapes reflecting nineteenth century naturalism. The difference between the canvases depicting his family circle and his Orientalist works exposes the duality in Osman Hamdi's life between the traditional East and the West, as the champion of innovation and change.

Taken as a whole, examination of his works with Orientalist subjects reveals that Osman Hamdi Bey, the first Ottoman artist to put forward an idea through figural compositions, employed elements that realistically conveyed the life ways, architecture, furnishings, and ornamentation of the Ottoman world. In his paintings, Osman Hamdi Bey portrayed neither the fatalistic, the indolent, the slothful, the cruel, nor the lustful Easterner, but rather the Ottoman intellectual who possessed aspirations and who read and discussed ideas. This position essentially conformed to the motive force behind the Ottoman administration in its efforts to Westernize. In this respect, the image of the book, which appears in numerous of the artist's works, conveys a symbolic value. One interesting work reflecting the artist's attitude is his *Muslim Scholars Disputing at the Mosque Door*. The setting of the subject is the entrance to the cell complex of the *medrese*, or theological college, of Karaman Hatuniye. The photograph of this entrance which was squared for transfer by the artist to be utilized for this painting is preserved in the Museum of Painting and Sculpture in İstanbul. Other identifiable elements incorporated in the painting by the artist are one door leaf of a mosque pulpit from the Alaeddin Mosque in Konya and an oil lamp from the mosque complex of Çoban Mustafa Paşa at Gebze.[1] Left unfinished, this work represents an expression of his questioning religious dogmatism. In contrast to the Eastern characters appearing in most Orientalist paintings, the figures in this painting are men of the cloth who dispute with books in their hand: statuesque figures in possession of self-confidence.

For many of his paintings, the artist relied on photographs for figures, settings, and objects. The male figure in Oriental dress utilized by Osman Hamdi Bey in his works is most often that of the artist himself. He had himself photographed in various of the outfits reflecting the regional diver-

[1] The door leaf and the oil lamp are preserved in the Museum of Turkish and Islamic Works (İstanbul), nos. 246 and 154, respectively. Belgin Demirsar, *Osman Hamdi Tablolarında Gerçekle İlişkiler* (Ankara: Kültür Bakanlığı Yayınları, 1989), 161–2.

273
▼

273 Osman Hamdi. *Muslim Scholars Disputing at the Mosque Door*. Oil on canvas. 140 x 105 cm. Museum of Painting and Sculpture, Mimar Sinan University, İstanbul.

sity of the empire that appeared in the *Les Costumes Populaires de la Turquie*, which was sent to the 1873 Vienna Exhibition and for which he was the Ottoman commissioner. Osman Hamdi Bey, who possessed a rich costume collection, favored to present in his paintings the clothing typical of the southern provinces of the empire. One self-depiction shows the artist at the east entrance to Rüstempaşa Mosque in İstanbul, ill. wearing, as is indicated in *Les Costumes Populaires de la Turquie*, the garments customarily worn by Muslim scholars. As the preacher, he is shown with a *Koran* tucked into the front of his long, inner gown worn beneath a yellow robe, with a green girdle at his waist and a string of prayer beads in his hand. Wound about his skull-cap over a light shawl is a length of white muslin.

The area in which the Orientalist perspective is fully exposed in Western art is undoubtedly the female subject. The inevitable female figure of the harem and the bath, a creation of the Westerner's fantasy, is conceived as an erotic object that is an integral part of the magnificent Eastern setting. Osman Hamdi Bey, however, infuses the female figure in his works with an entirely different significance. His attitude as an advocate of reform becomes self evident by the frequency with which the female and subjects related to the female appear in his Orientalist paintings. The Ottoman female is depicted in the act of playing a musical instrument, reading a book, or arranging flowers in a vase in her home and is always shown fully clothed. In his paintings portraying the Ottoman women in the harem or outside the home, the artist's intention was to show the character of her daily life, her costume, her behavior, the limits set on her freedom, and the structure of her thought. Both the content and the names of his paintings, like *Women at a Tomb*, *A Woman Reading*, *Women at the Mosque Door*, *Turkish Women on an Outing in the Hippodrome*, and *A Woman Picking Lilacs*, clearly illustrate his point of view.

274 Osman Hamdi. *At the Door of Rüstem Paşa Mosque*, 1905. Oil on canvas. 210 x 120 cm. Museum of Painting and Sculpture, Mimar Sinan University, İstanbul.

275 Osman Hamdi. *Turkish Women at Sultan Ahmed Mosque*. Oil on canvas. 112 x 80 cm. Private Collection, İstanbul.

XXII An Ottoman Orientalist: Osman Hamdi Bey

276 Osman Hamdi. *Harem Scene*, 1880.
Oil on canvas. 56 x 116 cm. Private
Collection, İstanbul.

XXII An Ottoman Orientalist: Osman Hamdi Bey

XXII An Ottoman Orientalist: Osman Hamdi Bey

One of Osman Hamdi Bey's works that treats the daily life of the Ottoman woman is *Turkish Women at Sultan Ahmed Mosque*. Generally, the artist depicted women of the upper class. Here, the women whose streetcoats and white veils reflect the vogue and colors of the day are conversing and the two young girls are amusing themselves with the pigeons. The rendering of a figure or a group of figures before a monumental door is a common characteristic of Osman Hamdi Bey's works. The beggar woman in the background holding a child in her arms and the pigeons represent invariable components of İstanbul mosques.

ill. 275

The work by the artist titled *Harem Scene* presents an interpretation that is opposed to the one of Western artists. In this interior setting containing four female figures, the observer may note the glazed, hexagonal revetment tiles and, on the left, a prayer rug of the late Ottoman period and, on the right, a handkerchief and napkins that have been hung up. A fine reed mat is spread over the floor, a common covering used in Ottoman dwellings. The porcelain ewer and copper-gilt basin filled with water recall for the viewer the daily act of ablutions. The women, wearing robes of various patterns and colors with skirts in three panels whose borders are embroidered, have covered their hair with a scarf finished with needlework laces, are probably not waiting for the male to enter the harem but are rather simply displaying a domestic scene. Various creations of Ottoman art and handiwork, including fashion styles, are exposed in Osman Hamdi's harem scene, but erotic images are excluded.

ill. 276

Music was for the upper-class Ottoman woman a constant preoccupation. In the painting of the two female musicians playing the tambur and the tambourine, the setting is, with the exception of the marble screens and the glazed tile border appearing on the right-hand side, the interior of Yeşil Mosque at Bursa.[2] The females, who are dressed in a robe and a dress with three- panelled skirt have tucked their hair under scarves. The leaf of the cupboard with mother-of-pearl inlay, the prayer mats, the glazed revetment tiles, and the marble screens not only enhance the interior setting with Ottoman handicraft products, but the delineation of the young ladies with their musical instruments underscores the importance of art in harem life.

ill. 277

One aspect of Orientalism addressing nine-

[2] Demirsar, 113.

277 Osman Hamdi. *Two Young Female Musicians*, 1880. Oil on canvas. 58 x 39 cm. Collection of Suna and Inan Kıraç, İstanbul.

teenth-century taste, which was typified by a longing for the past and for exoticism and a passion for poetry, ostentation and setting, was the use of ethnographic material. Undoubtedly, relatively more knowledgeable about Eastern culture and life style than the Western artist, Osman Hamdi Bey's sensitive treatment of this subject constitutes one of the primary characteristics of the artist's works. As Adolphe Thalasso indicates in *L'Art Ottoman*

> In my opinion, the Oriental setting spread before the viewer in the works of Hamdi Bey can be found nowhere else. The characteristic of his style resides here....The figural types appearing in his works are not simply Muslim, but he takes pains with the costume, decor, and furnishings to show that they are Turkish. The source of inspiration for everything in Hamdi Bey is the East. The artist does not arrange his subjects in exterior settings that will compel the recollection of Turkey; instead, he renders them in an interior setting directly related to Turkey. All his canvases inspired by this aesthetic are Turkish and clearly impress on the viewer the sense that they have been painted by a Turkish artist.[3]

[3] Thalasso, *L'Art*, 21–2.

[4] Nurhan Atasoy, *Derviş Çeyizi: Türkiyede Tarikat Giyim KuşamTarihi* (İstanbul: T.C.Kültür Bakanlığı Yayınları, 2000), 266.

[5] Demirsar, 147.

ill. 278   In Osman Hamdi Bey's well-known painting of the *Tortoise Trainer* (1906), the artist depicts himself as a wandering dervish, who is holding a reed flute in his hands clasped behind his back and a plectrum attached to a small kettledrum (*nakkare*)[4] carried on his back hangs suspended over one shoulder. The felt cap on his head is wound in a careless fashion with two printed scarves. The thoughtful attitude of the tortoise trainer clearly conveys the impression that he is involved in a very challenging task requiring patience. Because of the futility of employing force to train this creature with a thick shell and sluggish blood, the dervish plans to train the tortoise by blowing on his flute and playing the drum. The only instrument in the hands of the tortoise trainer with whom Osman Hamdi has identified himself is art—symbolized in the painting by musical instruments. The scene, set in one of the upper-story chambers of Yeşil Mosque at Bursa,[5] may be read as a metaphor for the obstacles that he had personally encountered in such enterprises as the founding of the Archeological Museum and the Imperial School of Fine Arts, the issuing of the

278 Osman Hamdi. *Tortoise Trainer*, 1906.
Oil on canvas. 223 x 117 cm. Private
Collection, İstanbul.

XXII An Ottoman Orientalist: Osman Hamdi Bey

Regulation Code Regarding Antiquities, and the general resistance of Ottoman society to change.

The painting executed by Osman Hamdi Bey in 1908 titled *Dervish at the Şehzade Tomb* is another example of the artist employing himself as a model. The dervish garbed in a robe belted at the waist and barefoot has left his staff and dervish slippers (*çedik*)[6] outside the door. The two marble sarcophagi[7] are from the tomb of Damad İbrahim Pasha of Bosnia. With a green turban wound over the light shawl and a large leather pocketbook (*cilbend*)[7] at his waist, the dervish's emotion-laden posture, and the dim lighting of the setting convey a mystical effect in contrast to the inscribed sarcophagus covers, the door leaf, the framed inscriptions, and the oil lamp, which accord precedence to the didactic. These objects, now preserved in the museum he himself founded, today the Museum of Turkish and Islamic Arts, were utilized several times in his paintings.

The artist executed these paintings in the atelier on the upper story of his seaside mansion at Kuruçeşme on the Bosphorus. An article by Ahmed İhsan appearing in *Servet-i Fünun* (H. 1322/1906) reveals that his studio was spacious with windows facing the north, which provided satisfactory lighting, and that it was filled with preliminary studies, a variety of garments, and miscellaneous furnishings. The article also discloses that the canvas *The Arms Merchant* stood to one side in an unfinished state at the time, and that a young man dressed in Eastern costume was being employed as a model for this painting. The

[6] Atasoy, 46.

[7] Atasoy, 256.

[8] Ahmed İhsan, *Servet-i Fünun* (9 Teşrin-i sâni 1322): 101.

[9] Osman Hamdi Bey executed a portrait of Sir Edwin Pears: Edwin Pears, *Forty Years in Constantinople* (London: Herbert Jenkins, 1916), 175.

same article goes on to state that above the desk in one corner of the studio were studies of various parts of İstanbul and other cities in the empire. These were preliminaries for a large-scale painting.[8] Osman Hamdi Bey had another studio in his home in Eskihisar at Gebze.

Osman Hamdi Bey, who in his paintings always remained a faithful adherent of the Paris School, maintained until the end of his life his interest in Orientalist subjects and exhibited such paintings of his as the *Dervish at the Şehzade Tomb, The Fountain of the Water Of Life, Tortoise Trainer*, and *The Arms Merchant* at the Salons des Artistes Français in Paris. Sir Edwin Pears reports that Osman Hamdi Bey showed his paintings for two years in the London Royal Academy. The British diplomat, Pears, who lived from 1873 to 1915 in İstanbul and who was a close friend of Osman Hamdi Bey, states in his memoirs that just prior to his death, the artist was at work on a canvas related to the girding of the dynastic sword by the sultan.[9]

By delineating in his paintings the colorful Eastern garb of ethnic plurality in a detailed architectural decor, Osman Hamdi Bey, who accords a position of pre-eminence to the Ottoman heritage, presented his subjects in a timeless and indefinite setting and most often turned to allegories as his vehicle of expression. While Osman Hamdi Bey —the first and the last "Orientalist" of the Ottoman Empire—was executing his paintings, Orientalism was coming to an end in the West.

279 Osman Hamdi. *Dervish at the Şehzade Tomb*, 1908. Oil on canvas. 122 x 92 cm. Museum of Painting and Sculpture, Mimar Sinan University, İstanbul.

Western artists visiting Istanbul in the 19th century

▲ Date of arrival in Istanbul

■ Date of arrival in the Ottoman Empire

	1. arrival	2. arrival	3. arrival	other arrivals
German				
BERNATZ, Johann Martin (1802–1878)	▲ 1836			
BERNINGER, Edmund (1843–1899)	▲ after 1874			
■ BREDT, Ferdinand–Max (1860 ya da 68–1921)				
DIEMER, Michael Zeno (1867–1939)	▲ after 1906			
FIEDLER, Bernhard (1816–1904)	▲ 1853			
GAYER, Alexius (1816–1883)	▲ 1847			
GENTZ, Karl Wilhelm (1822–1890)	▲ 1851			
GROTEMEYER, Fritz (1864–1947)	▲ 1916			
HAAG, Carl (1820–1915)	▲ 1858			
■ HILDEBRANDT, Eduard (1818–1869)	1851			
KOERNER, Ernst Karl Eugen (1846–1927)	▲ 1873–1874			
KRETZSCHMER, Johann Hermann (1811–1890)	■▲ 1840			
MÜLLER, Léopold Carl (1834–1892)	▲ 1874			
RABES, Max Friedrich (1868–1944)	▲ 1891–92			
REUTER, Wilhelm (1859–?)	▲ reign of Abdülhamid II			
SCHMIDT, Maximillian (1818–1901)	■ 1843–1844	■ 1861	■ 1870	
SCHREYER, Adolphe (1828–1899)	▲ 1856			
SCHLESINGER, Henri Guillaume (1814–1893)	▲ reign of Mahmud II			
WEIDENBACH (1818–1882)	▲ 1845			
WITTMER, Johann Michael (1802–1880)	▲ 1833			
American				
GIFFORD, Sanford Robinson (1823–1880)	▲ 1869			
GOULD, Walter (1829–1893)	▲ 1851			
▲ GUÉRIN, Jules (1866–1946)				
KELLOGG, Miner Kilbourne (1814–1889)	▲ 1844			
SARGENT, John Singer (1856–1925)	▲ 1891			
SMITH, Francis Hopkinson (1838–1915)	▲ 1889			
▲ WEEKS, Edwin Lord (1849 –1903)				
Austrian				
▲ ALT, Franz von (1821–1914)				
ERNST, Rudolf (1854–1932)	▲ end of 1880			
FISCHER, Ludwig Hans (1848–1915)	■ 1875			
▲ HOEFEL Blasius (1790–1871)				
ISRAEL, Daniel (1859–1901)	▲ 1885			
JANESCH, Albert (1889–1973)	▲ I. World War			
KAUFMANN, Adolf (1848 –1916)	reign of Abdülhamid II			
KRAUSZ, Wilhelm Victor (1870–1916)	▲ beginnign of 20th century			
OTTENFELD, Rudolf von (1856–1913)	▲ end of 1870			

■▲ PILNY, Otto (1866–1936)				
SATTLER, Hubert (1817–1904)	▲ 1842–44	▲ after 1875		
SCHÖNN, Alois (1826–1897)	■ beginnign of 1860			
SCHRAM, Alois Hans (1864–1919)	■ 1890s			
STERRER, Franz (1818–1901)	▲ 1848			

Belgian

HUYSMANS, Jan Baptiste (1826–1906)	■ 1856			
JACOBS, Jacob Albrecht Michael (1812–1879)	▲ 1838			
VERVLOET, Frans (1795–1872)	▲ 1844			

Danish

JERICHAU, Harald Adolf Nikolaj (1851–1878)	▲ 1875			
JERICHAU–BAUMANN, Anna Maria Elisabeth (1819–1881)	▲ 1860s			
MELBYE, Daniel Hermann Anton (1818–1875)	▲ 1847–53			
RØRYBE, Martinus Christian Wesseltoft (1803–1848)	▲ 1836			

French

AUBLET, Albert (1851–1938)	▲ 1881			
▲ BACHMANN, Alfred Auguste Félix (1863–1956)				
▲ BÉRARD, Ernest (1829–?)				
BERCHÈRE, Narcisse (1819–1891)	■ 1849–1850			
BERTEAUX, Hippolyte Dominique (1843–1928)	▲ 1870s			
BIDA, Alexandre (1823–1895)	▲ 1843	▲ 1855		
BISTAACGNE, Paul (1850–86)	▲ 1879			
BLANCHARD, Henri Pierre Léon Pharamond (1805–73)	▲ 1852			
BONNAT, Léon Joseph Florentin (1833–1922)	■ 1870			
▲ BONHEUR, Ferdinand (19. yüzyıl)				
▲ BONHEUR, Isidore Jules (1827–1901)				
BRABAZON, Hercules (1821–1906)	▲ 1860			
BREST, Germain Fabius (1823–1900)	▲ 1847	■ 1855–1859		
▲ CATENACCI, Hercule (1816–1884)				
▲ CLUSERET, Gustave Paul (1823–1900)				
CRAPELET, Louis Amable (1822–1867)	▲ 1863			
DEBAT–PONSAN, Édouard Bernard (1874–1913)	▲ 1882			
DECAMPS, Alexandre– Gabriel (1803–1860)	■▲ 1826			
DEFORCADE, Jean Baptiste Étienne,	▲ 1890s			
▲ DELLEPIANE, David (1866–1925)				
DEVÉRIA, Achille Jacques (1800–57)	▲ reign of Mahmud II			
DOUSSAULT, Charles (19.yüzyıl)	▲ 1846			
DUBOIS, François (1790–1871)	▲ reign of Mahmud II			
▲ DUFEU, Édouard Jacques (1840–1900)				
DUPRÉ, Louis (1789–1837)	▲ 1819			
▲ DUVIEUX, Henri (1855–?)				
FLANDIN, Eugène Napoléon (1809–1876)	▲ 1842			
FRÈRE, Charles Thèdore (1814–1888)	▲ 1851			
GÉRÔME, Jean–Léon (1824–1904)	▲ 1854	▲ 1871	▲ 1875	▲ 1879
GIRAUD, Pierre François Eugène (1806–1881)	▲ after 1846			
▲ GODCHAUX, Émile (1860–?)				
GUILLEMET, Pierre Désiré (1827–1878)	▲ 1873–1878			
GUYS, Constantin Ernest Adolphe (1802–1892)	▲ 1848	▲ 1854–55		
HAYETTE, François Claude (1838–?)	▲ 1860–1890			
HUGUET, Victor Pierre (1835–1902)	▲ 1853			

LABBÉ, Charles Emile (1820–1885)	▲ 1856	
▲ LAMBERT, Eugène C. (19.–20. yy)		
LAURENS, Jules Joseph Augustin (1825–1901)	■▲ 1846–48	
LEBLANC, Théodore (1800–1837)	▲ after 1828	
LECOMTE DU NOÜY, Jean Jules Antoine (1842–1923)	■▲ 1875	
LE ROY, Paul Alexandre Alfred (1860–1942)	▲ 1884	
LEVY–DHURMER, Lucien (1865–1953)	▲ 1906	
▲ MALFROY, Henry (1895–1944)		
MELLING, Antoine–Ignace (1763–1831)	▲ 1785–1803	
■ NICOT, François (20.yy)		
PINEL DE GRANDCHAMP, Louis–Emile (1831–1894)	▲ 1849–65	
▲ PRÉVOST, Pierre (1764–1823)		
PRIEUR–BARDIN, François Léon (1870–1939)	▲ 1882–1901	
RAFFET, Auguste (1804–1860),	▲ after 1837	
RAFFORT, Etienne (1802–1895),	▲ after 1844	
ROGIER, Camille (1810–1893)	▲ 1840–43	
SAUX, Jules de Mme (1829–1901) (takma adı Henriette Browne)	▲ 1861	
▲ THÉROND, Emile Theodore (1821–?)		
▲ TOURNEMINE, Charles Émile de (1812–1872),		
VERNET, Horace (1789–1863)	▲ 1840	
YVON, Adolphe (1817–1893)	▲ 1856	
ZIEM, Felix François Georges Philibert (1821 – 1911)	▲ 1847	▲ 1856

Dutch

BAUER, Marius Alexandre Jacques (1867–1932)	■▲ 1885	■ 1896

British

ALLAN, William (1782–1850)	▲ 1830	
ALLOM, Thomas (1804–1872)	■▲ 1836–1838	
BARRETT, Jerry (1814–1906)	▲ 1854–55	
BARKER, Henry Aston (1774–1856)	■▲ 1799–1819	
BARTLETT, William Henry (1809–1854)	▲ 1837	
BRANGYWN, Frank (1867–1956)	▲ 1887	
▲ BURR, A. Margetta (1844–45)		
■ CARELLI, Conrad H. R. (1869–?)		
COOKESLEY, Margaret Murray (?–1927)	▲ 1890s	
DADD, Richard (1817–1886)	■ 1842–43	
ELLIS, Tristam (1844–1922)	▲ after 1885	
▲ GOBLE, Warwick (1862–1943)		
■ HONE, Nathaniel (1831–1917)		
HORSLEY, Walter Charles (1848 ya da 1855–1921)	■▲ 1875	
HUNT, William Holman (1827–1910)	▲ 1855	▲ 1856
■ JOHNSON, Harry (1826–1884)		
JONES, Owen (1809–1874)	■ 1832–33	
LEAR, Edward (1812–1888)	▲ 1848	
LEIGHTON, Frederic (1830–1896)	▲ 1864	
LEWIS, John Frederick (1805–1876)	▲ 1840–41	
MADDOX, Willis (1813–1853)	▲ 1853	
MELVILLE, Arthur (1855–1904),	■ 1881	
MUELLER, William James (1812–45)	■ 1843–44	
PAGE, William (1794–1872)	■▲ 1816–24	■▲ 1830s
PURSER, William (1790–1852)	▲ 1820s	

WALTON, Elijah (1832–1880)	▲ 1860–62		
WILKIE, David (1785–1841)	▲ 1840		

Swiss

GLEYRE, Marc Gabriél Charles (1808–1874)	■ 1834		
■ ▲ PILNY, Otto (1866–1936)			
WEISS, Johann Rudolf (1846–1933)	▲ reign of Abdülaziz		

Italian

ACQUARONE, Luigi (1800–1896)	▲ 1841–96		
BELLO, Pietro (1837–1909)	▲ 1855–66	▲ 1900 –09	
BISEO, Cesare (1843–1909)	▲ 1877–78		
BOSSOLI, Carlo (1815–1884)	▲ 1843	▲ 1847–50	▲ 1854–55
▲ BRANCACCIO, Carlo (1861–1920)			
BRINDESI, Giovanni (Jean)	▲ 1850–77		
CAFFI, Ippolito (1809–1866)	▲ 1843		
■ CARELLI, Gabriele (1820–1900)			
CARELLI, Raffaele (1795–1864)	▲ 1839		
CARELLI, Nicola (1796–1842)	▲ 1830–42		
CORRODI, Hermann David Salomon (1844–1905)	▲ 1884	■ 1887	
DE MANGO, Leonardo (1843–1930)	▲ 1883–1930		
FORMIS BEFANI, Achille (1832–1906)	▲ 1867–70		
FOSSATI, Gaspare (1809–1883)	▲ 1837–1857		
LUCHINI, Pietro (1800–1883)	▲ after 1840		
NETTI, Francesco (1832 ya da 34–1894)	▲ 1884		
PASINI, Alberto (1826–1899)	▲ 1856	■ ▲ 1868–69	
QUERENA, Luigi (1824 ya da 20–1890)	▲ 1870s		
▲ ROSATI, Giulio (1858–1917)			
RUBIO, Luigi (1795–1882)	▲ 1847		
▲ USSI, Stefano (1822 ya da 32–1901)			
VALÉRI, Salvatore (1856–1946)	▲ 1883–1915		
ZONARO, Fausto (1854–1929)	▲ 1891–1911		

Hungarian

■ ▲ SWOBODA, Sandor Alexander (1826–1896)			

Maltese

▲ BROCKTORFF, Luigi			
PREZIOSI, Amadeo (1816–1882)	▲ 1842–1882		
SCHRANZ, Giuseppe (Joseph) (1803–1853 sonrası)	▲ 1832–1853		

Polish

AJDUKIEWICZ, Thaddéus (1852–1916)	▲ 1894		
CHLEBOWSKI, Stanislaw (1835–1884)	▲ 1864–76		
WARNIA–ZARZECKI, Josef (1850–?)	▲ 1883		

Russian

AIVAZOVSKY, Ivan Konstantinovitch (1817– 1900)	▲ 1845	▲ 1857	▲ 1858	▲ 74, 75, 76, 80, 86, 88, 90
BRYULLOV, Karl Pavlovich (1799–1852)	▲ 1835			

Bibliography

Abdülaziz Bey.	*Osmanlı Âdet, Merasim ve Tâbirleri*, 2 vols. İstanbul: Tarih Vakfı Yurt Yayınları, 1995
Acarsoy, Ateş.	"Höchst Porselen Biblolar." *Antik & Dekor Dergisi* 2 (1989): 46–50
Ackerman, Gerald M.	*Les Orientalistes de l'école américaine.* Paris: ACR, 1994.
Ackerman, Gerald M.	*Les Orientalistes de l'école britannique.* Paris: ACR, 1991.
Ackerman, Gerald M.	*Jean-Léon Gérôme.* Paris: ACR, 1986.
Ahmed İhsan.	*Servet-i Fünun* (9 Teşrin-i sâni 1322).
Ahmet Refik (Altınay).	*Kafes ve Ferace Devrinde İstanbul.* İstanbul: Kitabevi, 1998.
Ahmet Refik (Altınay).	*Lale Devri.* Ankara: Başbakanlık Kültür Müsteşarlığı, 1973.
Akın, Nur.	*XIX. Yüzyılın İkinci Yarısında Galata ve Pera.* İstanbul: Literatür Yayınları, 1998.
Akyıldız, Ali.	*Mümin ve Müşrif bir Padişah Kızı: Refia Sultan.* İstanbul: Tarih Vakfı Yurt Yayınları, 1998.
Alus, Sermet Muhtar.	"Göksu ve Alemleri." *Resimli Tarih Mecmuası* (Ekim 1951) : 1032–6.
Alus, Sermet Muhtar.	"II. Abdülhamid'in Cuma Selamlıkları." *Resimli Tarih Mecmuası* (Ağustos 1951):20.
Alus, Sermet Muhtar.	*Masal Olanlar.* İstanbul: İletişim, 1995.

Annuaire: almanach du commerce et de l'industrie. Constantinople: Bureaux de l'Administration, 1880.

Annuaire: almanach de commerce de l'industrie, de l'administration et de la magistrature. Constantinople: Bureaux de l'Administration, 1881.

Annuaire Oriental (ancien indicateur oriental) du commerce. Constantinople: Bureaux de l'administration, 1893–94.

Annuaire Oriental: commerce, industrie, administration, magistrat de l'Empire Ottoman. Constantinople: The Annuaire Oriental, 1912.

Arel, Ayda.	*Onsekizinci Yüzyıl İstanbul Mimarisinde Batılılaşma Süreci.* İstanbul: İstanbul Teknik Universitesi, 1975.
Atasoy, Nurhan.	*Derviş Çeyizi: Türkiyede Tarikat Giyim Kuşam Tarihi.* İstanbul: T.C. Kültür Bakanlığı Yayınları, 2000.
Atıl, Esin.	"The Ottoman World in the Nineteenth Century," 23-53. In *Voyages and Visions: Nineteenth Century European Images of the Middle East from the Victoria and Albert Museum.* Washington: Smithsonian Institution, 1996.
Auldjo, John.	*Journal of a Visit to Constantinople and Some of the Greek Islands in the Spring and Summer of 1833.* London: Longman, 1835.
Ayaşlı, Münevver.	*Dersâadet.* İstanbul: BedirYayınları, 1993.
Balıkhane Nazırı Ali Rıza Bey.	*Bir Zamanlar İstanbul.* İstanbul: Tercüman, n.d.
Baykal, İsmail.	"Abdülmecid Efendi ve Sarayında Cereyan Eden Bazı Olaylar." *Yakın Tarihimiz* (1963), 3: 246–51.
Bénézit, E.	*Dictionnaire critique et documentaire des peintres, sculpteurs, dessinateurs et graveurs* (1999).
Beydilli, Kemal.	"Ignatius Mouradgea D'Ohsson." *Tarih Dergisi: Prof. Dr. M. C. Şehabeddin Tekindağ Hatıra Sayısı* (1984): 247–314.
Beyne, Arthur Baligot de.	"Le bal donné à l'ambassade de France." *L'Illustration* (1 Mars 1856): 147–8.
Blanc, Henri.	*Journal de mon voyage à Constantinople.* Marseille: Marius Olive, 1880.
Blanchard, P.	"Les Fêtes du Ramazan." *L'Illustration* (24 Juillet 1852):53.
Blowitz, de.	*Une course à Constantinople.* Paris: Plon, 1884.

Bohusz, et al.	*Louis-François Cassas, 1756-1827. Im Banne der Sphinx*. Mainz am Rhein: Philipp von Zabern, 1994.
Boppe, Auguste.	*Les peintres du Bosphore au XVIIIe siècle*. Paris: ACR, 1989.
Brassey, Lady.	*Sunshine and Storm in the East*. London: Longmans, 1881.
Bruyn, Cornelis de.	*Reisen van Cornelis de Bruyn*. Delft: Henrik van Krooneveld, 1698.
Caffiero, Gianne and Ivan Samarine.	*Denizler, Şehirler ve Düşler: Ivan Aivazovsky'nin Resimleri*. Londra: Alexandria, 2000.
Cardoso, Vittoria Botteri.	*Alberto Pasini*. Genova: Sagep, 1991.
Casa, Jean-Michel.	*Le palais de France à İstanbul/İstanbul'da Bir Fransız Sarayı*. İstanbul: Yapı Kredi Yayınları, 1995.
Cezar, Mustafa.	"400 Yılın Önemli Eserlerinin Diz Dize Olduğu Semt: Tophane." *Mozaik* (Eylül 1996): 29–38.
Cezar, Mustafa.	*Sanatta Batı'ya Açılış ve Osman Hamdi*, 2 vols. İstanbul: Erol Kerim Aksoy Vakfı, 1995.
Cezar, Mustafa.	*Tipik Yapılarıyla Osmanlı Şehirciliğinde Çarşı ve Klasik Dönem İmar Sistemi*. İstanbul: Mimar Sinan Üniversitesi, 1985.
Clement, Clara Erskine.	*Constantinople: The City of the Sultans*. Boston: Estes and Lauriat, 1895.
Cox, Samuel Sullivan.	*Diversions of a Diplomat in Turkey*. New York: Charles L. Webster, 1887.
Cunningham, Allan.	*The Life of Sir David Wilkie*, 3 vols. London, 1843.
Curatola, Giovanni.	"Drawings by Giovanni Francesco Rossini, Military Attaché of the Venetian Embassy in Constantinople," 225–31. In *Art turc: actes de 10ième congrès international d'art turc*. Genève: Fondation Max van Berchem, 1999.
Çağman, Filiz.	"Women's Clothing," 256-95. *9000 Years of the Anatolian Woman*, Exhibition catalog. İstanbul: Topkapı Sarayı Museum, 1993.
Çelik, Zeynep.	*The Remaking of Istanbul: Portrait of an Ottoman City in the Nineteenth Century*. Seattle: University of Washington Press, 1986.
De Amicis, Edmondo.	*Constantinople*, 2 vols. Philadelphia : Henry T. Coates, 1896.
Demirsar, Belgin V.	*Osman Hamdi Tablolarında Gerçekle İlişkiler*. Ankara: Kültür Bakanlığı Yayınları, 1989.
Desmet-Grégoire, Hélène.	*Büyülü Divan: XVIII. Yüzyıl Fransa'sında Türkler ve Türk Dünyası* [*Le Divan Magique, L'Orient Turc en France au XVIII e Siècle*] . İstanbul: Eren Yayınları, 1991.
Dethier, P.A.	*Boğaziçi ve İstanbul* [*Der Bosphor und Constantinopel*] . İstanbul: Eren Yayınları, 1993.
Dodd, Anna Bowman.	*In the Palaces of the Sultan*. New York: Mead, 1903.
D'Ohsson, Mouradgea.	*Tableau Général de l'Empire Othoman*, 7 vols. Paris: L'Impremerie de Monsieur, 1891.
Doussault, Charles.	"Le portrait du sultan Abdul-Mejid." *L'Illustration* (14 Oct. 1854): 261–2.
Duhani, N. Said.	*Beyoğlu'nun Adı Pera İken* ["Quand Beyoğlu s'appelait Péra," *La Turquie Moderne*] . İstanbul: Çelik Gülersoy Vakfı Yayınları, İstanbul Kütüphanesi, 1990.
Eken, Ahmet.	*Kartpostallarda İstanbul*. İstanbul: İstanbul Büyük Şehir Belediyesi Kültür İşleri Daire Başkanlığı Yayınları, 1992.
Eldem, Edhem.	"Ottoman Period İstanbul," 131–53. *İstanbul-World City*. Exhibition catalog. İstanbul: History Foundation of Turkey, 1996.
Eldem, Sedad Hakkı.	"Boğaziçi Anıları," 39–49. *İstanbul Armağanı 2: Boğaziçi Medeniyeti*. İstanbul: İstanbul Belediyesi Kültür İşleri Yayınları, 1996.
Eldem, Sedad Hakkı.	*İstanbul Anıları*. İstanbul: Aletaş Alarko, 1979.
Eldem, Sedad Hakkı.	*Köşkler ve Kasırlar II*. İstanbul: Devlet Güzel Sanatlar Akademisi, 1974.
Eminoğlu, Münevver, ed.	*1870 Beyoğlu 2000: Bir Efsanenin Monografisi*. İstanbul: Yapı Kredi Yayınları, 2000.
Ernst, Louis.	"Incendie de Galata." *L'Illustration* (25 Mars 1865): 181.
Eudel, Paul.	*Constantinople, Smyrne et Athènes: journal de voyage*. Paris: E. Dentu, 1885.
Europa und der Orient (1800-1900). Sam.kat. Berlin: Martin-Gropius-Bau, 1989.	
Eyice, Semavi.	"Bir Ressamın Gözü ile Kanuni Sultan Süleyman," 129–70. *Kanuni Armağanı*. Ankara: Türk Tarih Kurumu Yayınları, 1970.
Eyice, Semavi.	"İstanbul Halkının ve Padişahların Ünlü Mesiresi: Kağıthane," 75-95. *İstanbul Armağanı 3: Gündelik Hayatın Renkleri*. İstanbul: İstanbul Büyük Şehir Belediyesi Kültür İşleri Yayınları, 1997.

Eyice, Semavi.	"İstanbul'un İlk Turistik Rehberlerinden Timoni'nin Rehberi." *Tarih ve Toplum* (Temmuz 1989).
Eyice, Semavi.	"XVIII. Yüzyılda İstanbul'da İsveçli Cornelius Loos ve İstanbul Resimleri (1710'da İstanbul)," 91-130. *18.Yüzyılda Osmanlı Kültür Ortamı.* İstanbul: Sanat Tarih Derneği, 1998.
Falchi, R., ed.	*Le Tra Stagioni Pittoriche di Fausto Zonaro.* Exhibition catalog. San Remo: Villa Ormondi, 1994–1995.
Farrère, Claude.	"Prenses Seniha'nın Yedi Mektubu." *Hayat Tarih Mecmuası* (Eylül 1971): 52–9.
Ferrard, Christopher.	"The Sublime State." *Visions of the Ottoman Empire.* Exhibition catalog. Edinburgh: Scottish National Portrait Gallery, 1994.
Flaubert, Gustave.	*Lettres de Grèce.* Paris: Editions du Péplos, 1948.
Fontmagne, Durand de.	*Un séjour à l'ambassade de France à Constantinople sous le second empire.* Paris : Librairie Plon, 1902.
Freely, John.	*Inside the Seraglio.* London: Penguin, 1999.
Gardey, L.	*Voyage du sultan Abdülaziz de Stamboul au Caire.* Paris: E. Dentu, 1865.
Gautier, Théophile.	*Constantinople en 1852.* İstanbul: İsis, 1990.
Gautier, Théophile.	"La Collection Khalil Bey." *L'Illustration* (11 Jan.1868).
Germaner, Semra.	"XIX.yüzyıl Sanatından İki Etkileşim Örneği: Oryantalizm ve Türk Resminde Batılılaşma," 116–21. *Hacettepe Üniversitesi, Edebiyat Fakültesi, Sanat Tarihi Bölümü, Uluslararası Sanatta Etkileşim Sempozyumu Bildirileri.* Ankara: Türkiye İş Bankası, 2000.
Germaner, Semra.	"Oryantalist Resimlerde Arap Atları Fantazyalar." *P Dergisi* 11(Güz 1998):.36–51.
Germaner, Semra and Zeynep İnankur.	*Orientalism and Turkey.* İstanbul: Türk Kültürüne Hizmet Vakfı Yayınları, 1989.
Göçek, Fatma Müge.	*East Encounters West: The Ottoman Empire in the Eighteenth Century.* New York: Oxford University Press, 1987.

La grande encyclopédie inventaire raisonné des sciences, des lettres et des arts. Paris: H. Lamirault, n.d.

Gülersoy, Çelik.	*Kayıklar.* İstanbul: Türkiye Turing ve Otomobil Kurumu, 1983.
Gülersoy, Çelik.	"Son 400 Yılda Tophane Semti," 3:1637–50. *VIII.Türk Tarih Kongresi Kongre Bildirileri.* Ankara: Türk Tarih Kurumu Yayınları, 1983.
Gürçağlar, Aykut.	"Fausto Zonaro ve Çağdaşlarının İstanbul'u." Masters thesis, İstanbul Teknik Üniversitesi, Mimarlık Fakültesi, 1991.
Gürçağlar, Aykut.	"Halife Abdülmecid Efendi ve 'Harem'de Beethoven'in Düşündürdükleri," 136-141. *Hacettepe Üniversitesi, Edebiyat Fakültesi, Sanat Tarihi Bölümü, Uluslararası Sanatta Etkileşim Sempozyumu Bildirileri.* Ankara: Türkiye İş Bankası, 2000.
Gürsel, Nedim.	"Pierre Loti'nin Evinde." *P Dergisi* (Yaz 1997): 97–103.
Hafız Hızır İlyas Ağa.	*Tarihi-i Enderun/Letaif-i Enderun (1812-1830).* İstanbul: Güneş Yayınları, 1987.
Haja, Martina and Günther Wimmer.	*Les Orientalistes des écoles allemand et autrichienne.* Paris : ACR, 2000.
Hamsun, Knut and H. C Andersen.	*İstanbul'da İki İskandinav Seyyah* [Hamsun, *Stridende Liv* and Andersen, *En Digters Bazar*]. İstanbul: Yapı Kredi Yayınları, 1993.
Harvey, Mrs.	*Turkish Harems and Circassian Homes.* London: Hurst-Blackett, 1871.
Haskell, Francis.	"A Turk and His Pictures in Nineteenth-century Paris," 175–85. *Past and Present in Art and Taste.* New Haven: Yale University Press, 1987.
Henisch, H. K., and A. B. Henisch.	"James Robertson." *Visions of the Ottoman Empire.* Exhibition catalog. Edinburgh: Scottish National Portrait Gallery, 1994.
Hisar, Abdülhak Şinasi.	*Boğaziçi Yalıları.* İstanbul: Ötüken, 1978.
Hornby, Mrs. Edmund.	*In and Around Istanbul.* Philadelphia: James Challen, 1863.
Höllriegel, Arnold.	"Die Türkische Kunstausstellung in Wien." *Wochen-Ausgabe des Berliner Tageblatts* (5 Juni 1918): 7.
Hürmen, Fatma Rezan, ed.	*Ressam Naciye Neyyal'in Mutlakiyet, Meşrutiyet ve Cumhuriyet Hatıraları.* İstanbul: Pınar Yayınları, 2000.
Işın, Ekrem.	*İstanbul'da Gündelik Hayat.* İstanbul: Yapı Kredi Yayınları, 1999.
İnankur, Zeynep.	"Halil Şerif Paşa." *P Dergisi* (Yaz 1996): 71–80.

İnankur, Zeynep.	"Official Painters of the Ottoman Court," 381–8. *Art turc: actes de 10ième congrès international d'art turc*. Genève: Fondation Max van Berchem, 1999.
İnciciyan, P.	*18. Asırda İstanbul*. İstanbul: Baha Matbaası, 1976.
Jacques, A., Peltre, C., and Yenal, E.	*Jules Laurens'in Türkiye Yolculuğu*. İstanbul: Yapı Kredi Yayınları, 1998.
James Robertson: İstanbul Fotoğrafçısı. Ser.kat. İstanbul, 1991.	
Jean Baptiste Van Mour'un Tablolarıı/Les peintures "turques" de Jean-Baptiste Van Mour 1671–1737. Exhibiton catalog. Ankara and Amsterdam, 1978.	
Jerningham, Hubert E. H.	*To and From Constantinople*. London: Hurst and Blackett, 1873.
Juler, Caroline.	*Les Orientalistes de l'école italienne*. Paris: ACR, 1987.
Kabbani, Rana.	*Europe's Myths of the Orient*. London: Pandora, 1986.
Kafadar, Cemal.	"Eyüp'te Kılıç Kuşanma Törenleri,"50-61. *Eyüp: Dün/Bugün*. İstanbul: Tarih Vakfı Yurt Yayınları, 1994.
Kazgan, Haydar.	"Osmanlı Sanayiinin Dışa Açılması 1893 Şikago Sergisinde Osmanlı Pavyonu." *Ekonomide Diyalog* (Şubat 1984): 63-5.
Koçu, Reşad Ekrem.	"Abdülmecid Efendi." *İstanbul Ansiklopedisi* (1958).
Koçu, Reşad Ekrem.	*Türk Giyim, Kuşam ve Süslenme Sözlüğü*. Ankara: Sümerbank Kültür Yayınları, 1967.
Kuban Doğan.	*İstanbul: Bir Kent Tarihi [Istanbul: An Urban History]*. İstanbul: Tarih Vakfı Yurt Yayınları, 2000.
Kuban Doğan.	*İstanbul Yazıları*. İstanbul: Yapı Endüstri Merkezi Yayınları, 1998.
Lamartine, Alphonse de.	*Voyage en orient*, 2 vols. Paris: Hachette, 1874.
Laprade, Laurence de.	"L'elégance française en Orient." *Figaro Illustré: Constantinople* (1908): 5
Lettres sur le Bosphore, au relation d'un voyage à Constantinople pendant les anneês 1816, 1817, 1818 et 1819. Paris: Locard et Davi, 1822.	
Levey, Michael.	*The World of Ottoman Art*. London: Thames and Hudson, 1975.
Lewis, Bernard.	*The Emergence of Modern Turkey*. London: Oxford UP, 1968.
Lewis, Reina.	*Gendering Orientalism: Race, Femininity and Representation*. London: Routledge, 1996.
Longino, Michèle.	*Imagining the Turk in Seventeenth-Century France: Grelot's Version. http://www.duke.edu/~michèle/projects* (2001 Mayis 1).
Mac Farlane, Charles.	*Constantinople in 1828*, 2 vols. London: Saunders and Otley, 1829.
Majda, Tadeusz.	"European Artistic Tradition and Turkish Taste: Stanislaw von Chlebowski, the Court Painter of Sultan Abdülaziz," 176–85. *Hacettepe Üniversitesi, Edebiyat Fakültesi, Sanat Tarihi Bölümü, Uluslararası Sanatta Etkileşim Sempozyumu Bildirileri*. Ankara: Türkiye İş Bankası Yayınları, 2000.
Mamboury, Ernest.	*Constantinople: guide touristique*. Constantinople: Rizzo, 1925.
Mansel, Philip.	*Constantinople: City of the World's Desire*. London: Penguin, 1997.
McLauchlan, Kathy.	"Nineteenth Century Views of the Orient." *Eastern Art Report* (May 1990): 14–5.
Mehmed Memduh.	*Tanzimattan Meşrutiyete, I: Mir'ât-i Şuûnât*. İstanbul: Nehir Yayınları, 1990.
Melling, Antoine Ignace.	*Voyage pittoresque de Constantinople et des rives du Bosphore*. Paris: Treutel et Wurtz, 1819.
Melman, Billie.	*Women's Orients: English Women and the Middle East, 1718-1918*. Ann Arbor: University of Michigan Press, 1998.
Mintzuri, Hagop.	*İstanbul Anıları: 1897-1940*. İstanbul: Tarih Vakfı Yurt Yayınları, 1993.
Moltke, Helmuth von.	*Moltke'nin Türkiye Mektupları [Unter dem Halbmond, Erlebnisse in der Alten Türkei, 1835-1839]*. İstanbul: Remzi Yayınları, 1969.
Montagu, Mary Wortley (Lady).	*The Turkish Embassy Letters*. London: Virago, 1998.
Mori, Angiolo.	*Gli Italiani a Constantinopoli*. Modena: Soliani, 1906.
Müller, Georgina Max.	*İstanbul'dan Mektuplar [Letters from Constantinople]*. İstanbul: Tercüman, 1978.
Müller-Wiener, Wolfgang.	*Bizans'tan Osmanlı'ya İstanbul Limanı [Die Hafen von Byzantion, Konstantinopolis, Istanbul]*. İstanbul: Tarih Vakfı Yurt Yayınları, 1998.
Müller-Wiener, Wolfgang.	*Bildlexikon zur Topographie İstanbuls*. Tübingen: Ernst Wasmunt, 1977.
Neave, Dorina L.	*Eski İstanbul'da Hayat [Twenty six years on the Bosphorus]*. İstanbul: Tercüman, 1978.

Nerval, Gerard de.	*The Women of Cairo: Scenes of Life in the Orient*, 2 vols. London: Routledge, 1929.
Nerval, Gerard de.	*Voyage en Orient*, 2 vols. Paris: Charpentier, 1862.
Newton, Charles.	"The Artists," 93–123. *Voyages and Visions: Nineteenth Century European Images of the Middle East from the Victoria and Albert Museum*. Washington: Smithsonian Institution, 1995.
Nigar, Salih Keramet.	*Halife İkinci Abdülmecid*. İstanbul: İnkilap ve Aka Yayınları, 1964.
Nochlin, Linda.	*The Politics of Vision: Essays on Nineteenth Century Art and Society*. London: Thames and Hudson, 1991.
O. Hamdy Bey.	"Les cafés de Stamboul." *Figaro Illustré: Constantinople* (Octobre 1908).
Olivier, Guillaume Antoine.	*Türkiye Seyahatnamesi: 1790 Yillarında Türkiye ve İstanbul* [*Voyage dans l'Empire othoman , l'Egypte et la Perse*]. İstanbul: Ayyıldız Yayınları, 1977.
Orgun, Zarif.	"Kubbealtı ve Yapılan Merasim." *Güzel Sanatlar* (Ocak 1949): 91–108.

L' orient des provençaux. Exhibition catalog. Marseille: Musée d'histoire de Marseille, 1982–1983.

Les orientalistes provençaux. Exhibition catalog. Marseille: Musée des beaux arts, 1982–1983.

Ortaylı, İlber.	*İmparatorluğun En Uzun Yüzyılı*. İstanbul: İletişim Yayınları, 1995.
Osmanoğlu, Ayşe.	*Babam Abdülhamid*. İstanbul: Güven Yayınları, 1960.
Öner, Sema.	"Sultan II. Abdülhamid'in Saray Ressamları: Luigi Acquarone ve Fausto Zonaro," 186-191. *Hacettepe Üniversitesi, Edebiyat Fakültesi, Sanat Tarihi Bölümü, Uluslararası Sanatta Etkileşim Sempozyumu Bildirileri*. Ankara: Türkiye İş Bankası, 2000.
Öner, Sema.	"Tanzimat Sonrası Osmanlı Saray Çevresinde Resim Etkinliği (1839-1923)." Ph. D. dissertation. Mimar Sinan Universitesi, Sosyal Bilimler Enstitüsü, 1991.
Önsoy, Rıfat.	"Osmanlı İmparatorluğu'nun Katıldığı İlk Uluslararası Sergiler ve Sergi-i Umumi-i Osmani (1863 İstanbul Sergisi)." *Belleten* (1984): 196–9.
Öymen, Edip Emil.	"İngiliz Malı Fırçadan İki Osmanlı." *Euroclub* (Sonbahar 1987).
Özendes, Engin.	*Abdullah Frères: Osmanlı Sarayının Fotoğrafçıları* [*Abdullah Frères*]. İstanbul: Yapı Kredi Yayınları, 1998.
Özendes, Engin.	*Sébah & Joilliers'den Foto Sabah'a: Fotoğrafta Oryantalizm.* [*From Sébah & Joilliers to Photo Sabah*]. İstanbul: Yapı Kredi Yayınları, 1999.
Öztuncay, Bahattin.	*Vasilaki Kargopoulo: Hazret-i Pâdişâhi'nin Ser Fotografı*. İstanbul: Birleşik Oksijen Yayınları, 2000.
Paget, Pierre.	"Le Salon Exhibition de 1889." *L'Illustration* (27 Avril 1889).
Paget, Pierre.	"Obsèques d'Abdul-Medjid." *L'Illustration* (3 Aout 1861).
Pakalın, Mehmet Zeki.	*Tarih Deyimleri ve Terimleri Sözlüğü*. İstanbul: Milli Eğitim Bakanlığı Yayınları, 1983.
Pamukciyan, Kevork.	"Fausto Zonaro'nun Bilinmeyen Bazı Tabloları." *Tarih ve Toplum* (Ağustos 1987): 24–30.
Pamukciyan, Kevork.	"Manas Ailesi." *İstanbul: Dünden Bugüne İstanbul Ansiklopedisi* (1994).
Pape, Maria Elisabeth.	"Turquerie im 18. Jahrhundert und der 'Recueil Ferriol'," 305–19. *Europa und der Orient (1800-1900)*. Exhibition catalog. Berlin: Martin-Gropius-Bau, 1989.
Pardoe, Julia.	*The City of the Sultans; and Domestic Manners of the Turks, in 1836*, 2 vols. London: Henry Colburn, 1837.
Pardoe, Julia.	*The Beauties of the Bosphorus*. London: George Virtue, 1838.
Patrick, Mary Mills.	*Under Five Sultans*. New York: The Century 1929.
Pears, Edwin.	*Forty Years in Constantinople*. London: Herbert Jenkins, 1916.
Peirce, Leslie.	*Harem-i Hümayun* [*The Imperial Harem , Women and Sovereignty in the Ottoman Empire*]. İstanbul: Tarih Vakfı Yurt Yayınları, 1993.
Penzer, N.	*The Sultans' Harem*. İstanbul: Elya, 1998.
Perot, Jacques,	Frederic Hitzel, and Robert Anhegger. *Hatice Sultan ile Melling Kalfa*. İstanbul: Tarih Vakfı Yurt Yayınları, 2001.

"Pierre Loti'nin Abdülmecid Efendi'ye Mektupları." *Hayat Tarih Mecmuası* (1 Kasim 1965): 12–3

"Pierre Loti ve Claude Farrère'in Abdülmecid Efendi'ye Mektupları." *Hayat Tarih Mecmuası* (1 Aralik 1965): 44-53.

Raby, Julian.	*Venice, Dürer and the Oriental Mode*. London: Islamic Art, 1982.
Rautmann, Peter.	*Delacroix*. Paris, 1997

Renan, Ary.	"La Peinture Orientaliste." *Gazette des Beaux Arts*, Tome 11 (1894): 43–53.
Renda, Günsel.	"Portrenin Son Yüzyılı," 442-542. *Padişahın Portresi: Tesavir-i Âl-i Osman* [*The Sultan's Portrait: Picturing the House of Osman*]. İstanbul: Türkiye İş Bankası Kültür Yayınları, 2000.
Renda, Günsel.	"Resimlerde İstanbul." *Yüzyıllar Boyunca Venedik ve İstanbul Görünümleri / Vedute di ed Istanbul attraverso i Secoli*. Exhibition catalog. İstanbul: Topkapı Sarayı Müzesi, 1995.
Renda, Günsel.	"Ressam Kostantin Kapıdağlı Hakkında Yeni Görüşler," 139-62. *19. Yüzyıl İstanbul'unda Sanat Ortamı*. İstanbul: Sanat Tarihi Derneği, 1996.
Renda, Günsel.	"Selim III's Portraits and the European Connection," 567-79. *Art turc: actes de 10ième congrès international d'art turc*. Genève: Fondation Max van Berchem, 1999.
Rewald, John.	*Histoire de l'Impressionnisme, I (1855-1873)*. Paris: Albin Michel, 1965.
Rouillard, Clarence Dana.	*The Turk in French History, Thought, and Literature (1520–1660)*. Paris: Boivin, 1938.
Sabuncuzâde Luis Alberi.	*Sultan II. Abdülhamid'in Hal Tercümesi*. İstanbul, 1997.
Sakaoğlu, Necdet.	*Bu Mülkün Sultanları*. İstanbul: Oğlak Yayınları, 1999.
Sakaoğlu, Necdet.	"Osmanlı Sarayında Bayram." *Skylife* (Ocak 2000): 24–35.
Sakaoğlu, Necdet and Nuri Akbayar.	*Osmanlı'da Zenaatten Sanata*, vol. 2. İstanbul, Körfezbank, 2000.
Sakaoğlu, Necdet.	"İstanbul Sularına Şehrengiz." *İstanbul* (Ocak 1994): 26–44.
Salaheddin Bey.	*La Turquie à l'exposition universelle de 1867*. Paris: Hachette, 1867
Sandys, George.	*Relation of a journey begun An. Dom. 1610. foure bookes containing a description of t the Turkish Empire, of Aegypt, of the Holy Land, of the remote parts of Italy, and islands adioyning*. London, 1621.
Saz, Leyla.	*The Imperal Harem of the Sultans*. İstanbul: Peva Yayınları, 1994.
Schurr, Gérald and Pierre Cabanne.	*Dictionnaire des Petits Maitres de la peinture. 1820-1920*. 2 vols. Paris: Les Editions de l'Amateur, 1996.
Sevinç, Gülsen.	"Ressam Şehzade Abdülmecid Efendi'nin 'Sultan II. Abdülhamid'in Tahttan İndirilişi' Adlı Tablosuna Dair Çözümlemeler." *Türkiye'de Sanat* (Eylül–Ekim 2000): 16–21.
Soustiel, Jean and Lynne Thorntorn.	*Mahmal et Attatichs: peintres et voyageurs en Turquie, en Egypte et en Afrique du Nord*. Exhibition catalog. Paris: Galerie Soustiel, 1975.
Sperco, Willy.	*Istanbul: paysage littéraire*. Paris: La nef de Paris, 1955.
Sullivan James.	*Diary of a Tour: In the Autumn of 1856 to Gibraltar, Malta, Smyrna, Dardanelles, Marmora, Constantinople*. London, 1857.
Sweetman John.	*The Oriental Obsession: Islamic Inspiration in British and American Art and Architecture 1500-1920*. Cambridge: Cambridge University Press, 1991.
Şair Nigar.	*Hayatımın Hikayesi*. İstanbul: Ekin Yayınları, 1959.
Şehsuvaroğlu, Haluk, Y.	"Osmanlı Padişahlarının Kılıç Kuşanma Merasimi." *Resimli Tarih Mecmuası* (Temmuz 1950): 270–2.
Şehsuvaroğlu, Haluk, Y.	"Sultan İkinci Abdülhamid." *Resimli Tarih Mecmuası* (Ocak 1955): 3628–33.
Talû, Ercüment Ekrem,	"Eski İstanbul'da Kadın Hamamları." *Resimli Tarih Mecmuası* (2 Şubat 1950): 65–7.
Tanman, Baha M.	"Rıfaî Âsitanesi." *İstanbul: Dünden Bugüne İstanbul Ansiklopedisi* (1994).
Tanyeli, Gülsün and Yegan Kahya.	"Galata Köprüsü." *İstanbul: Dünden Bugüne İstanbul Ansiklopedisi* (1994).
Tavernier, Jean Baptiste.	*Topkapı Sarayında Yaşam* [*Nouvelle Relation de l'Intérieur du Serrail du Grand Seigneur*]. İstanbul: Çağdaş Yayınları, 1984.
Tekeli, İlhan.	"Haritalar." *İstanbul: Dünden Bugüne İstanbul Ansiklopedisi*. 1994.
Tekeli, İlhan.	"19. yüzyılda İstanbul Metropol Alanının Dönüşümü," 19-30. *Modernleşme Sürecinde Osmanlı Kentleri*. İstanbul: Tarih Vakfı Yurt Yayınları, 1999.
Tezcan, Hülya.	"16.–17. Yüzyıl Osmanlı Sarayında Kadın Modası." *P Dergisi* 12 (Kış 1998–99): 56–69.
Tezcan, Hülya.	"On Sekizinci Yüzyılda Osmanlı Kumaş Sanatı." *P Dergisi* 8 (Kış 1997): 72–85.
Tezcan, Hülya.	"Osmanlı İmparatorluğu'nun Son Yüzyılında Kadın Kıyafetlerinde Batılılaşma." *Sanat Dünyamız* 37 (1988): 45–51.
Thalasso, Adolphe.	*L'art Ottoman: les peintres de Turquie*. Paris: Librairie Artistique Internationale,1910
Thalasso, Adolphe.	"Fausto Zonaro: peintre de S. M. I. le Sultan." *Figaro Illustré* (1907).
Thalasso, Adolphe.	"Les origines de la peinture Turque." *L'Art et les Artistes* (Octobre 1907).

Thalasso, Adolphe.	"Les premiers salons de Constantinople: le premier salon de Stamboul." *L'Art et les artistes* (1906): 3–14.
Theolin, Sture.	*The Swedish Palace in Istanbul/İstanbul'da Bir İsveç Sarayı.* İstanbul: Yapı Kredi Yayınları, 2000.
Thévenot, Jean.	*1655–56'da Türkiye* [*Voyage du Levant*]. İstanbul: Tercüman, 1978.
Thieme-Becker: Allgemeines Lexikon der Bildenden Künstler, 1999 ed.	
Thornton, Lynne.	*Women as Portrayed in Orientalist Painting.* Paris: ACR, 1985.
Timur, Taner.	"Sultan Abdülaziz'in Avrupa Seyahatı, II." *Tarih ve Toplum* (Aralık 1984): 16–25.
Tinayre, Marcelle.	*Notes d'une voyageuse en Turquie.* Paris: Calmann Levy, n.d.
Toros, Taha.	"Halil Paşa." *Antik–Dekor* 45: 70–8.
Toros, Taha. "	İstanbul Varşova Köprüsünde Koskoca Bir Tarih Var." *Milliyet Gazetesi* (14 Ocak 1982).
Toros, Taha.	"Mecid Efendi Köşkü." *Sanat Dünyamız* 31 (1984): 2–9.
Tunaya, Tarık Zafer.	*Batılılaşma Hareketleri,* vol. 1. İstanbul: Cumhuriyet Yayınları, 1999.
Ubucini, Jean Henri Abdolonyme.	*1855'de Türkiye* [*La Turquie actuelle*], 2 vols. İstanbul: Tercüman, 1977.
Ubucini, Jean Henri Abdolonyme.	"Les Petits Metiers a Constantinople," *L'Illustration* (10 Juin 1854): 362.
Uluçay, Çağatay.	*Harem,* II. Ankara: Türk Tarih Kurumu Yayınları, 1992.
Ulunay, Refi' Cevad.	*Sayılı Fırtınalar.* İstanbul: Bolayır, 1958.
Unat, Faik Reşit.	*Osmanlı Sefirleri ve Sefaretnameleri.* Ankara: Türk Tarih Kurumu Yayınları, 1992.
Uzunçarşılı, İsmail Hakkı.	*Osmanlı Devletinin Merkez ve Bahriye Teşkilatı.* Ankara: Türk Tarih Kurumu Yayınları, 1988.
Ünver, Süheyl.	*Türkiye'de Kahve ve Kahvehaneler.* Ankara: Türk Tarih Kurumu Yayınları, 1963.
Üsdiken, Behzat.	"Beyoğlu'nun Eski ve Ünlü Otelleri." *Tarih ve Toplum* (Eylül 1991): 34–8; (Kasım 1991): 27–32; (Mart 1992): 28–35.
Vane, C. W. (Marquess of Londonderry).	*A Steam Voyage to Constantinople by the Rhine and the Danube in 1840-41,* vol. 1. London: Henry Colburn, 1842.
Van Luttervelt, R.	*De "Turkse" Schilderijen van J.B: Van Mour en zijn school.* İstanbul: 1958.
Van Mour, Jean-Baptiste.	*Recueil de cent estampes représentant différentes nations du Levant tirées sur les tableaux peints d'après nature en 1707 et 1708 par l'ordre de M.de Ferriol Ambassadeur du Roi à la Porte,* Paris, 1714. Edited by Şevket Rado. İstanbul: Apa Ofset, 1979.
Verhaeghe, Léon.	*Voyage en Orient 1862-1863.* Paris: Librairie Internationale, 1865.
Vigier, René.	*Un Parisien à Constantinople.* Paris: G. Rougier, 1886.
Vigne, Henri.	"Les pompiers de Constantinople." *L'Illustration* (2 Juillet 1870): 11.
Walker, Mrs. [Marie Adelaide].	*Sketches of Eastern Life and Scenery.* London: Chapman and Hall, 1886.
Walsh, Robert and Thomas Allom.	*Constantinople and the Scenery of the Seven Churches of Asia Minor/Drawing from Nature by Thomas Allom,* 2 vols. London: Fisher, 1838.
Wheatcroft, Andrew.	*The Ottomans: Dissolving Images.* London: Penguin, 1995.
White, Charles.	*Three Years in Constantinople,* vol. 2. London: Henry Colburn, 1845.
Xeazell, Ruth Bernard.	*Harems of the Mind.* New Haven: Yale University Press, 2000.
Ziem, Félix.	*Journal (1854-1898).* Arles: Actes Sud, 1994.
Ziya Şakir.	"Saray Harem Musikisi ve Harem Bandosu." *Resimli Tarih Mecmuası* (Aralık 1953): 2759-61.

Index